Wish

I will wait for you a hundred years until we can meet again.

4

TOKYOPOP®

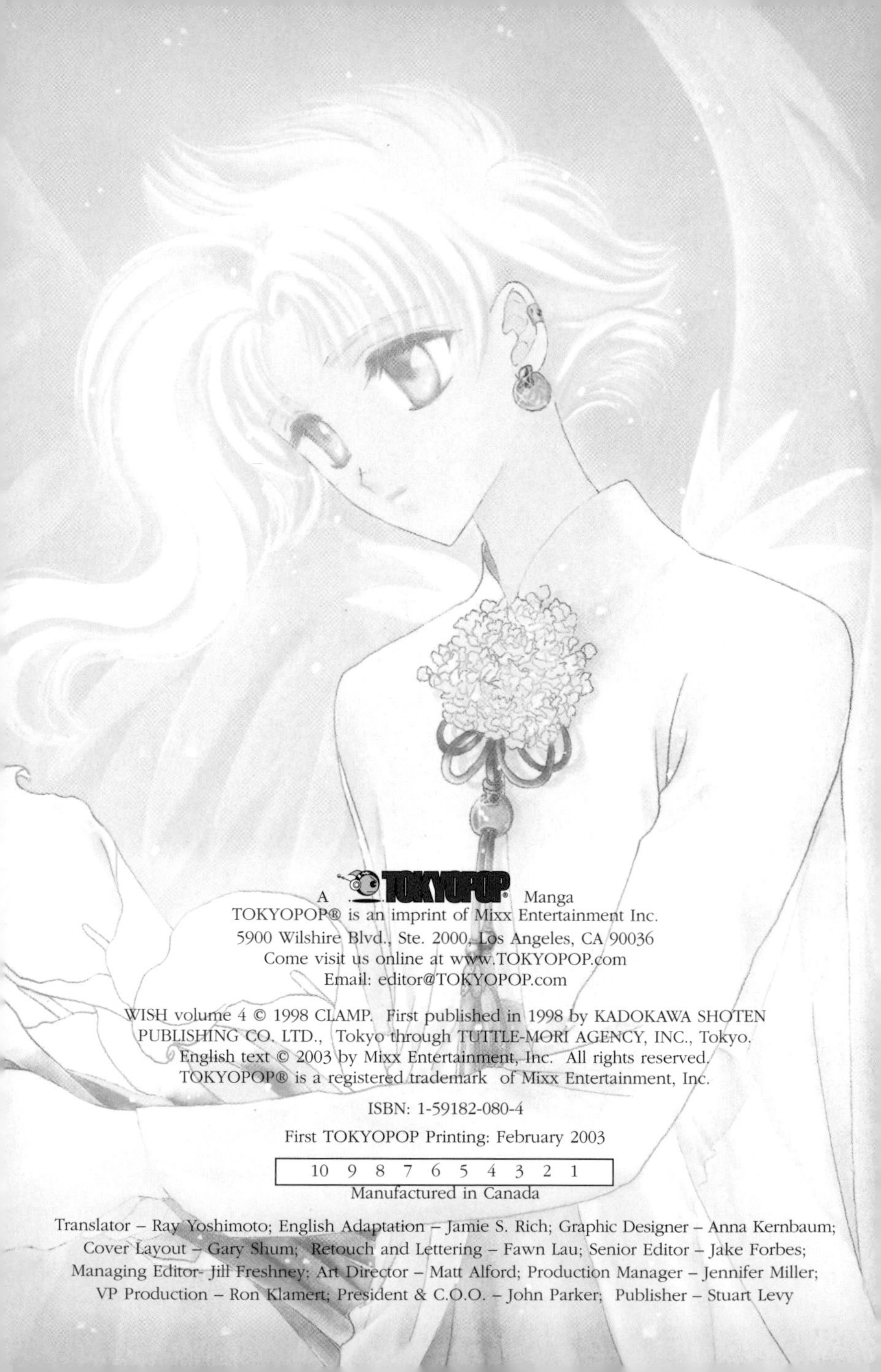

A TOKYOPOP Manga
TOKYOPOP® is an imprint of Mixx Entertainment Inc.
5900 Wilshire Blvd., Ste. 2000, Los Angeles, CA 90036
Come visit us online at www.TOKYOPOP.com
Email: editor@TOKYOPOP.com

ISBN: 1-59182-080-4

First TOKYOPOP Printing: February 2003

10 9 8 7 6 5 4 3 2 1

Manufactured in Canada

Translator – Ray Yoshimoto; English Adaptation – Jamie S. Rich; Graphic Designer – Anna Kernbaum; Cover Layout – Gary Shum; Retouch and Lettering – Fawn Lau; Senior Editor – Jake Forbes; Managing Editor- Jill Freshney; Art Director – Matt Alford; Production Manager – Jennifer Miller; VP Production – Ron Klamert; President & C.O.O. – John Parker; Publisher – Stuart Levy

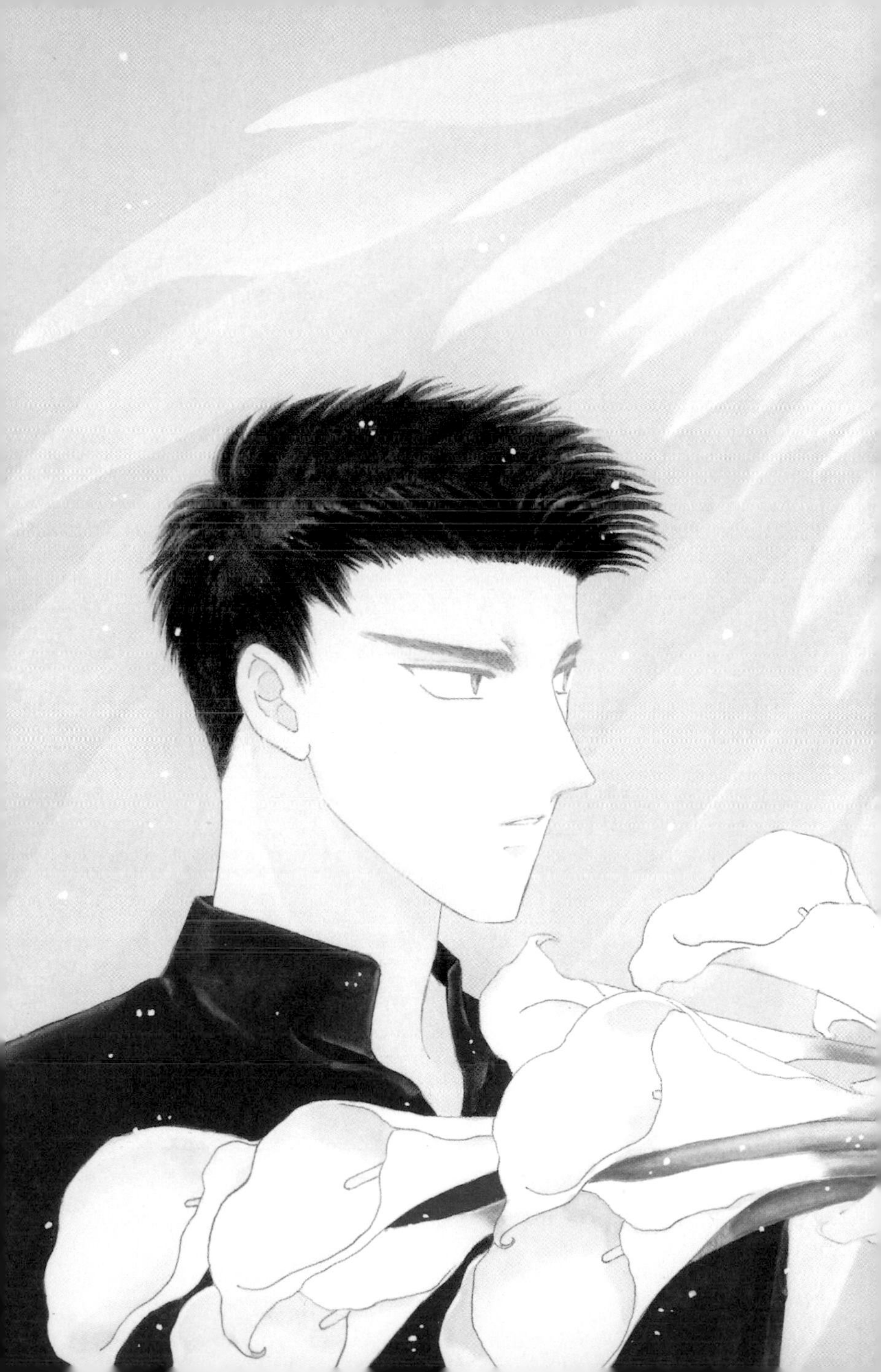

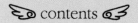 contents

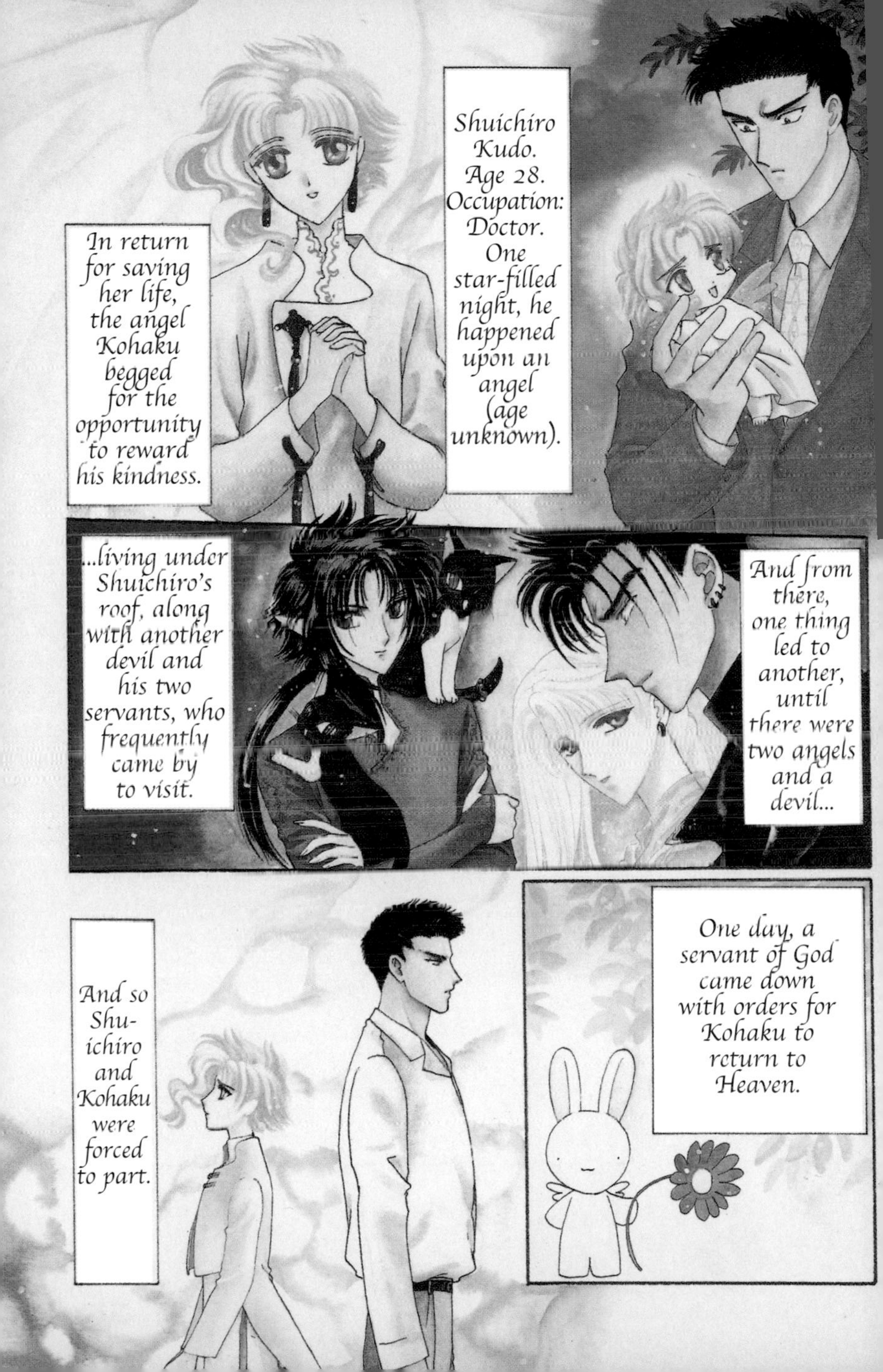
Shuichiro Kudo. Age 28. Occupation: Doctor. One star-filled night, he happened upon an angel (age unknown).
In return for saving her life, the angel Kohaku begged for the opportunity to reward his kindness.
And from there, one thing led to another, until there were two angels and a devil...
...living under Shuichiro's roof, along with another devil and his two servants, who frequently came by to visit.
One day, a servant of God came down with orders for Kohaku to return to Heaven.
And so Shuichiro and Kohaku were forced to part.

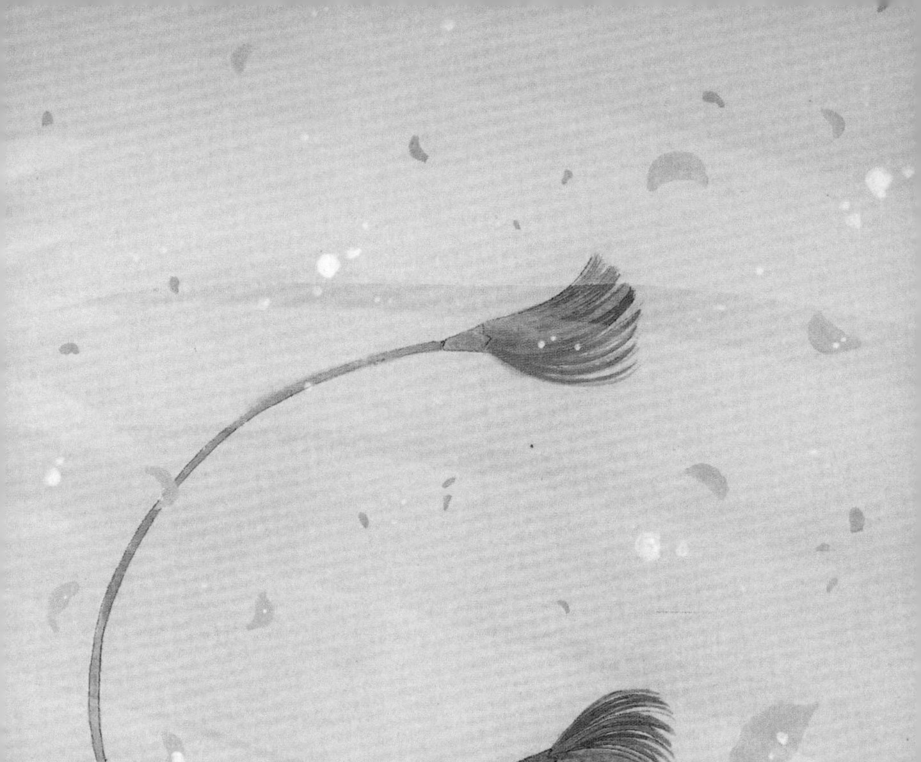

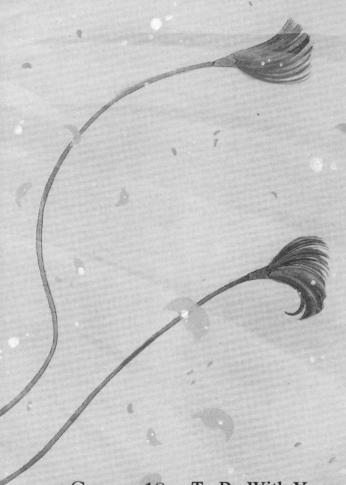

Contact.18 To Be With You

あいたい

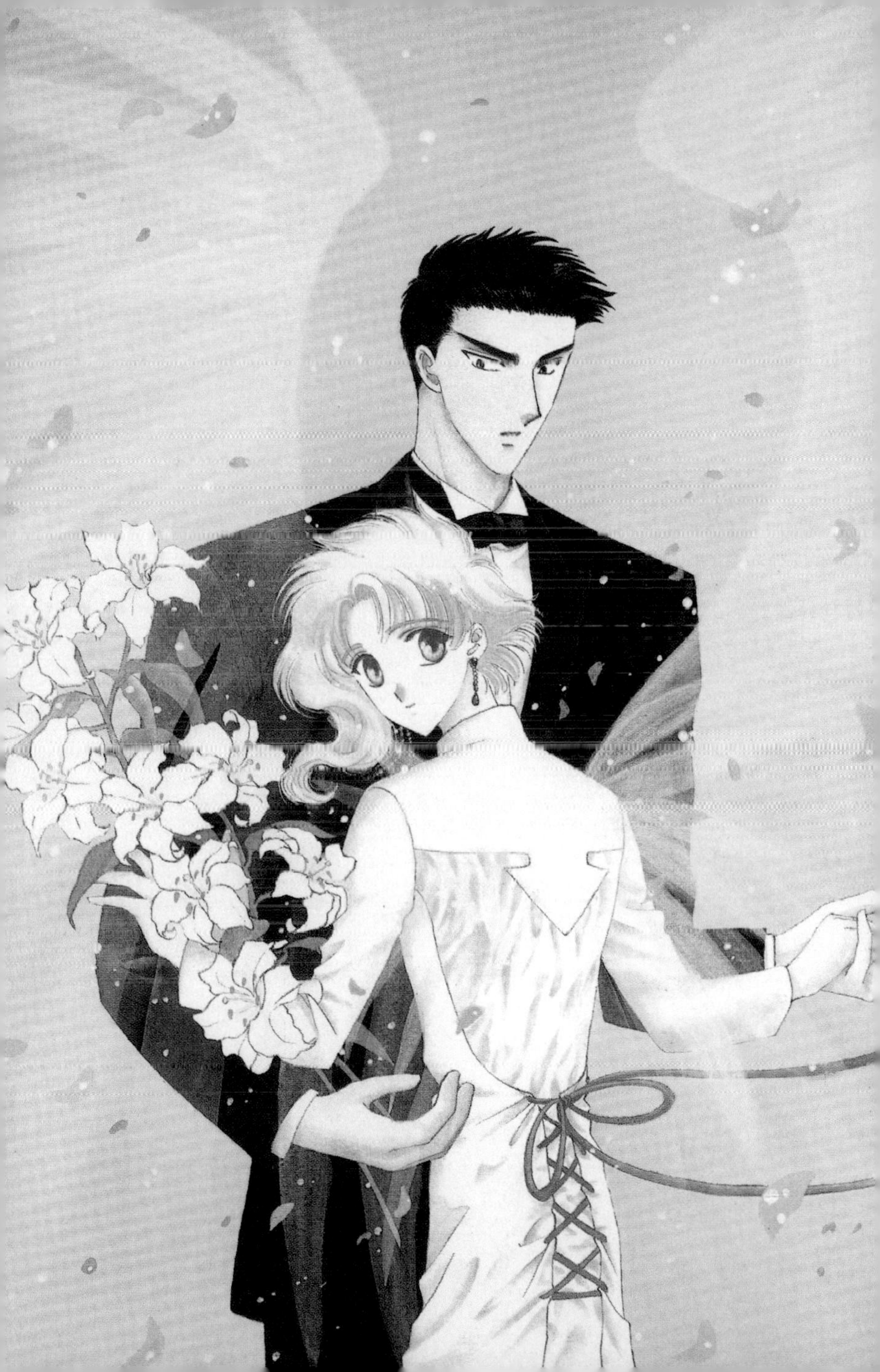

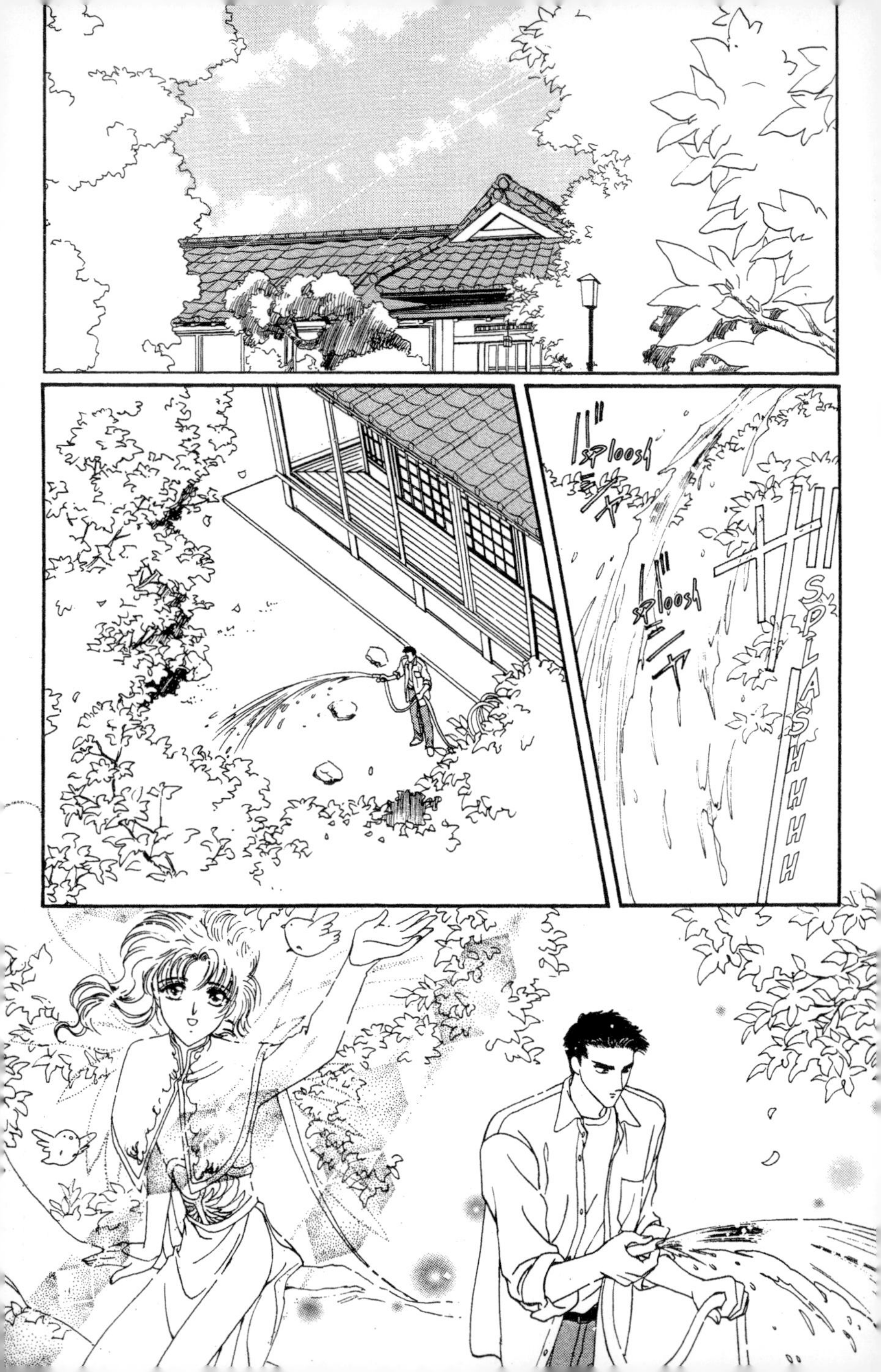
SPLASHHHHH
sploosh
sploosh

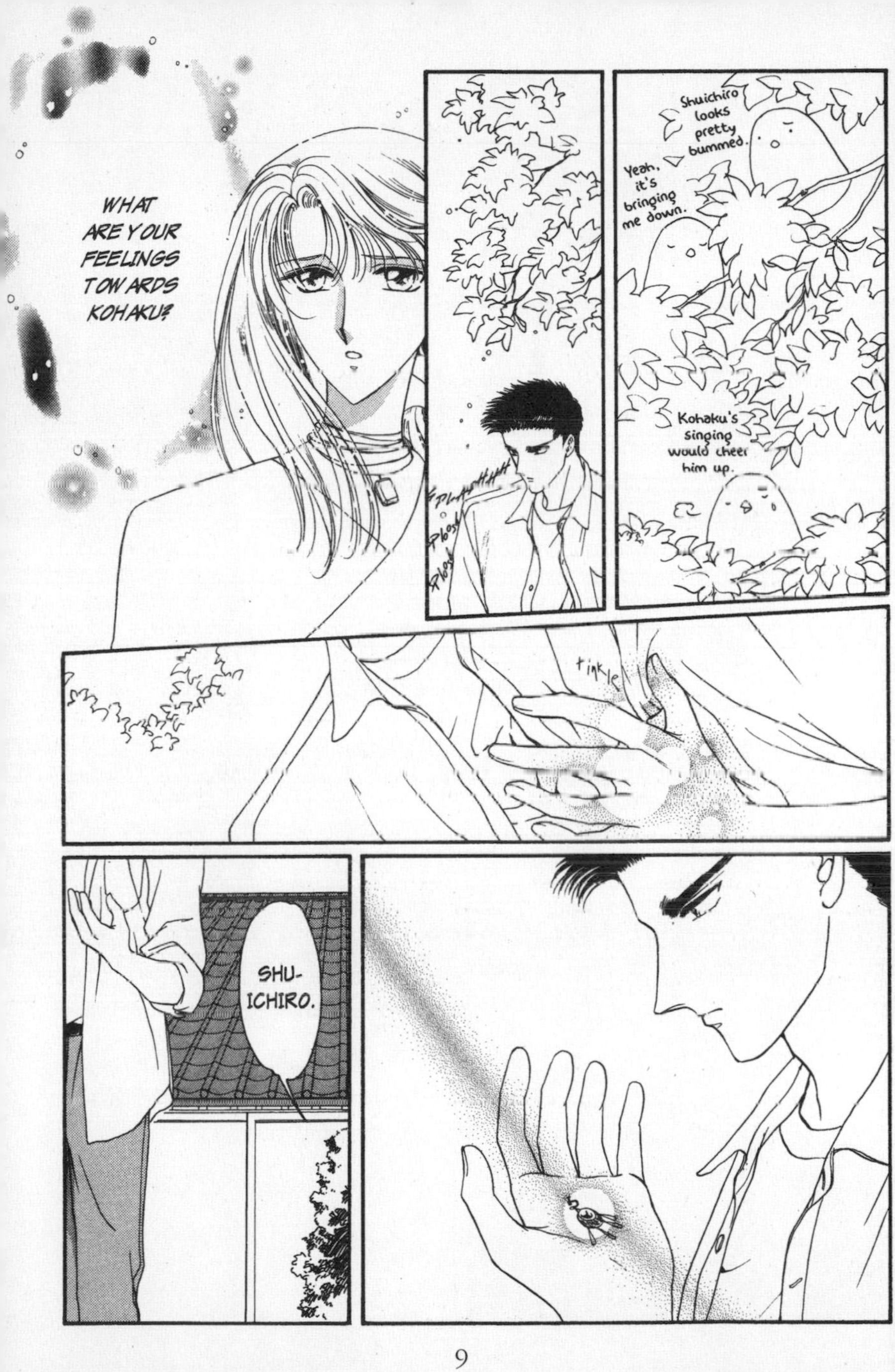
Shuichiro looks pretty bummed.
Yeah, it's bringing me down.
Kohaku's singing would cheer him up.
PLASHHHH
Plosh
Plosh
WHAT ARE YOUR FEELINGS TOWARDS KOHAKU?
tinkle
SHU-ICHIRO.

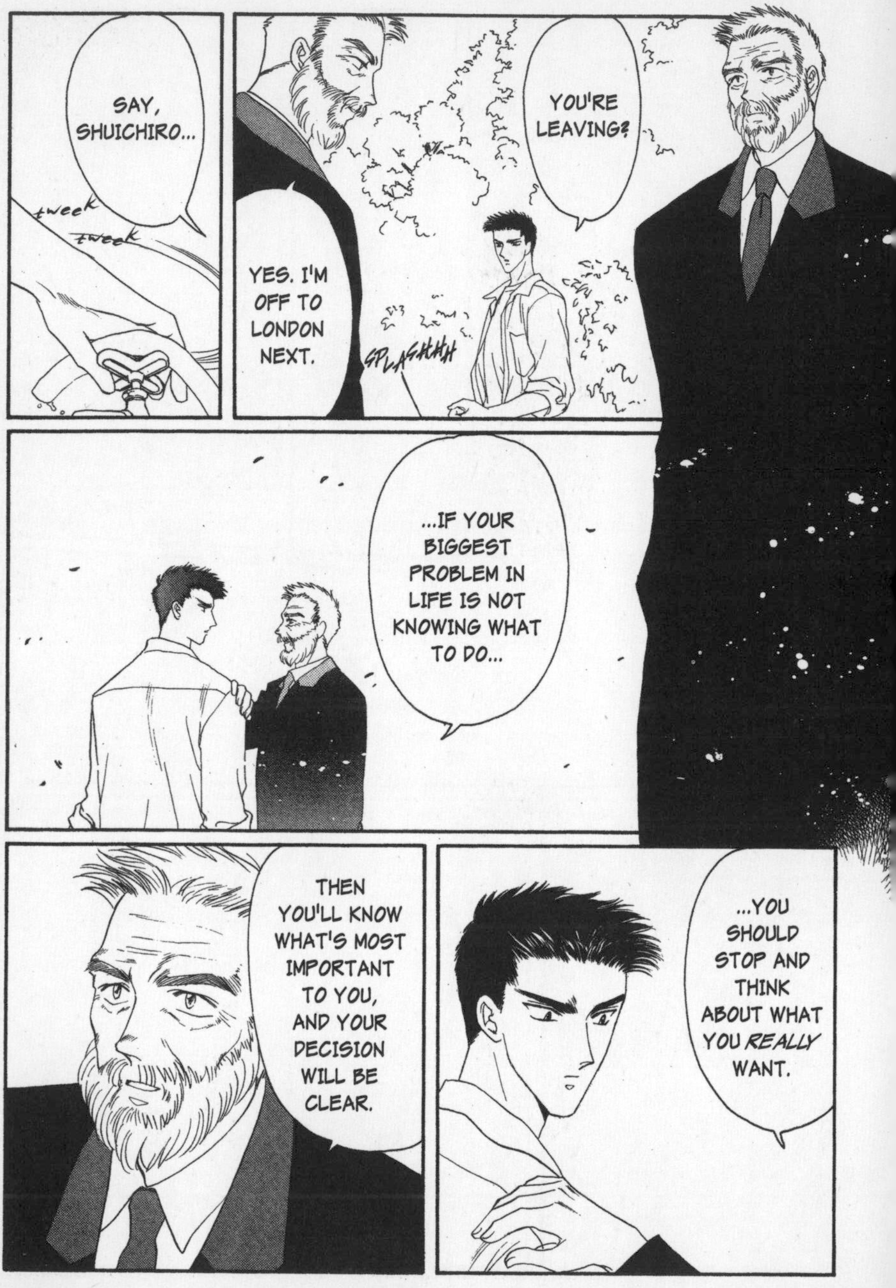
YOU'RE LEAVING?
YES. I'M OFF TO LONDON NEXT.
SPLASHHH
SAY, SHUICHIRO...
tweek tweek
...IF YOUR BIGGEST PROBLEM IN LIFE IS NOT KNOWING WHAT TO DO...
...YOU SHOULD STOP AND THINK ABOUT WHAT YOU *REALLY* WANT.
THEN YOU'LL KNOW WHAT'S MOST IMPORTANT TO YOU, AND YOUR DECISION WILL BE CLEAR.

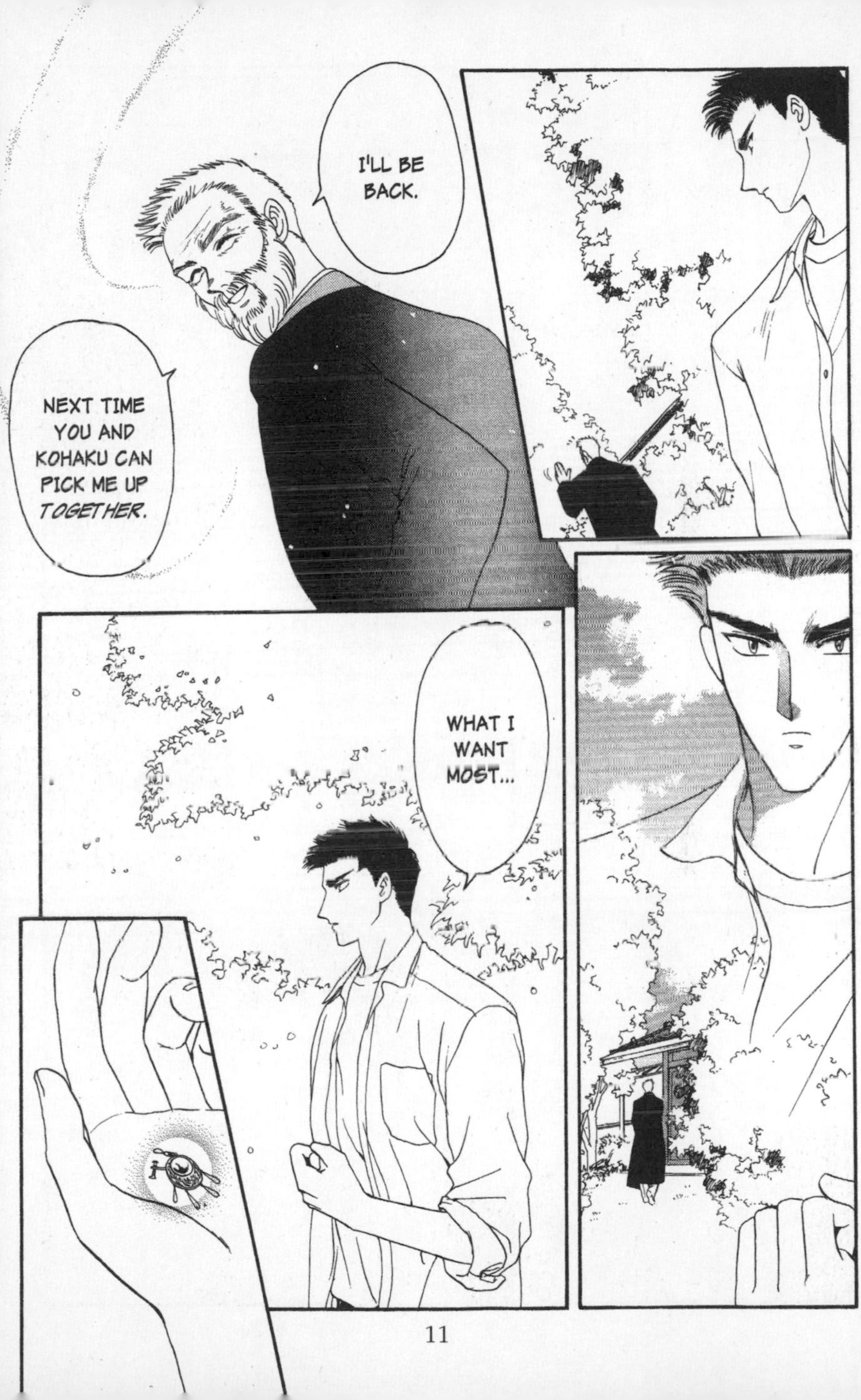

I'LL BE BACK.
NEXT TIME YOU AND KOHAKU CAN PICK ME UP *TOGETHER*.
WHAT I WANT MOST...

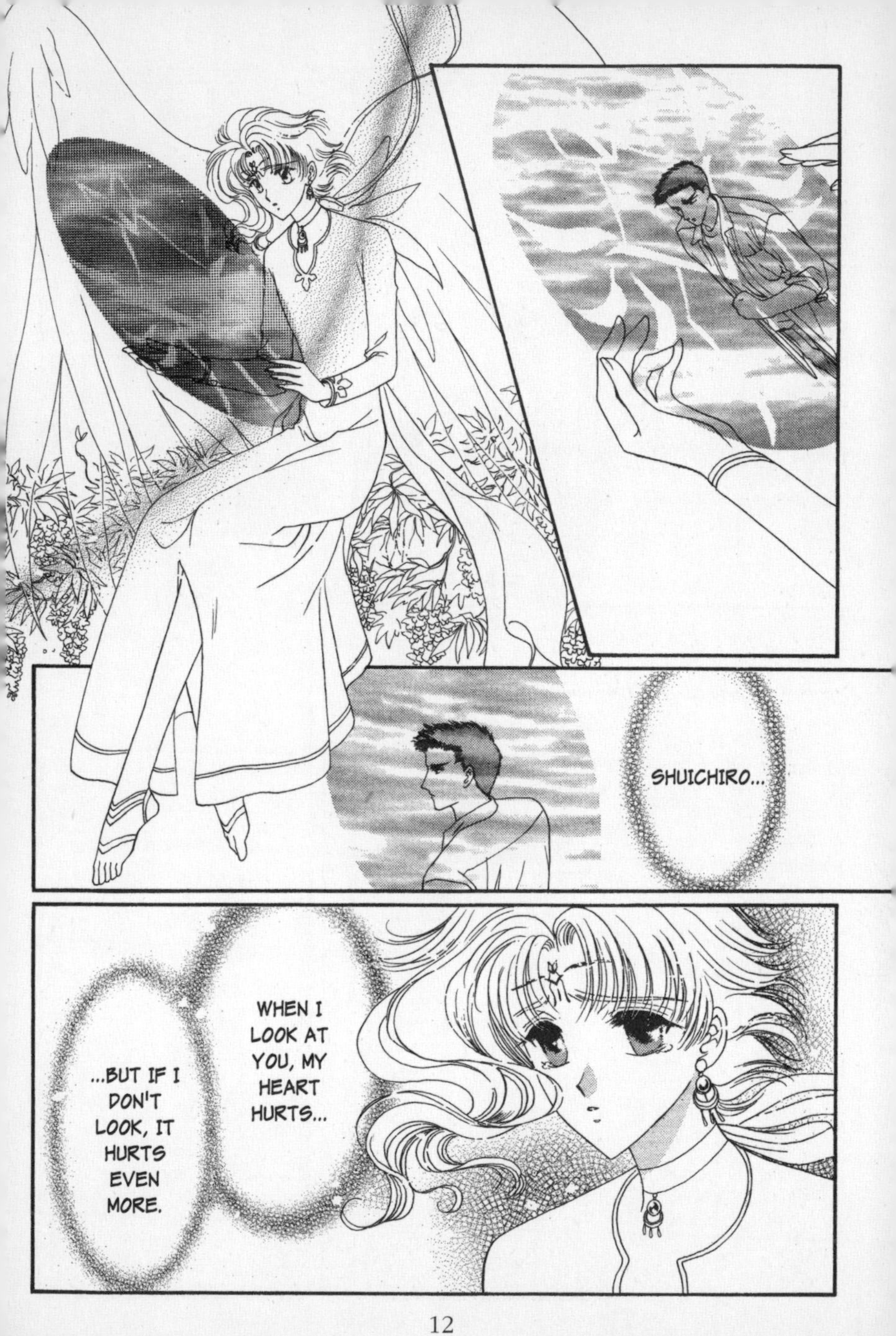
SHUICHIRO...
WHEN I LOOK AT YOU, MY HEART HURTS...
...BUT IF I DON'T LOOK, IT HURTS EVEN MORE.

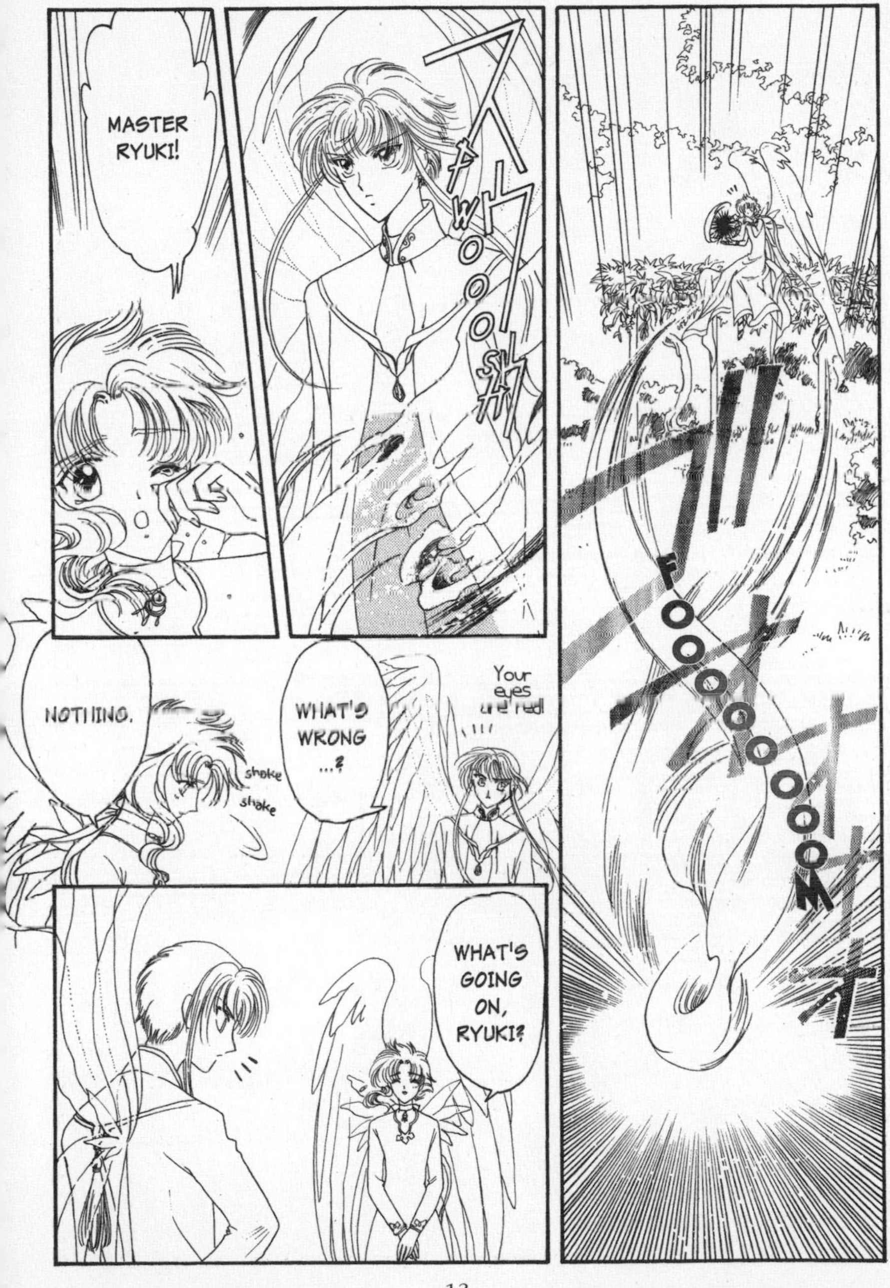
FOOOOOOOOOM
WHOOOOSH
MASTER RYUKI!
Your eyes are red!
WHAT'S WRONG ...?
NOTHING.
shake
shake
WHAT'S GOING ON, RYUKI?

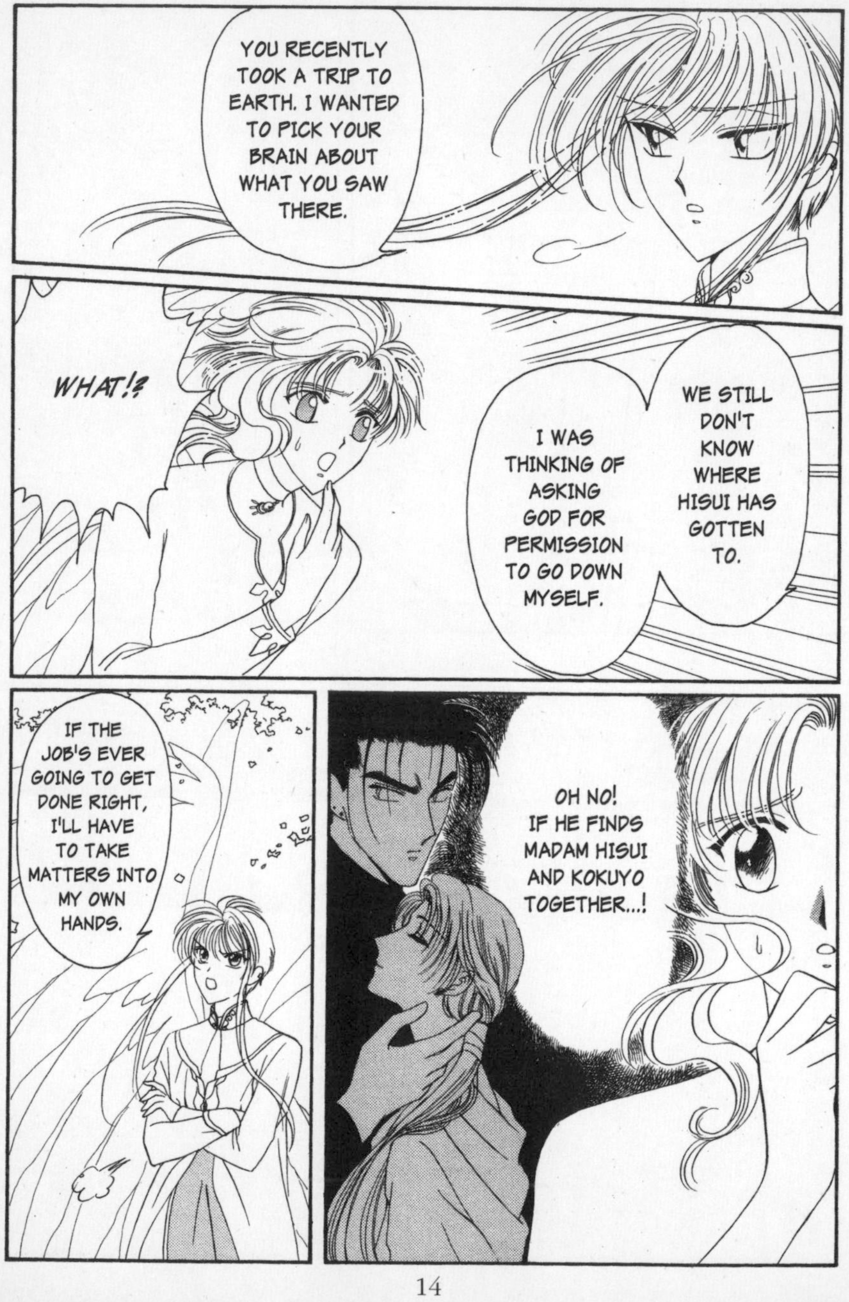
YOU RECENTLY TOOK A TRIP TO EARTH. I WANTED TO PICK YOUR BRAIN ABOUT WHAT YOU SAW THERE.
WE STILL DON'T KNOW WHERE HISUI HAS GOTTEN TO.
I WAS THINKING OF ASKING GOD FOR PERMISSION TO GO DOWN MYSELF.
WHAT!?
OH NO! IF HE FINDS MADAM HISUI AND KOKUYO TOGETHER...!
IF THE JOB'S EVER GOING TO GET DONE RIGHT, I'LL HAVE TO TAKE MATTERS INTO MY OWN HANDS.

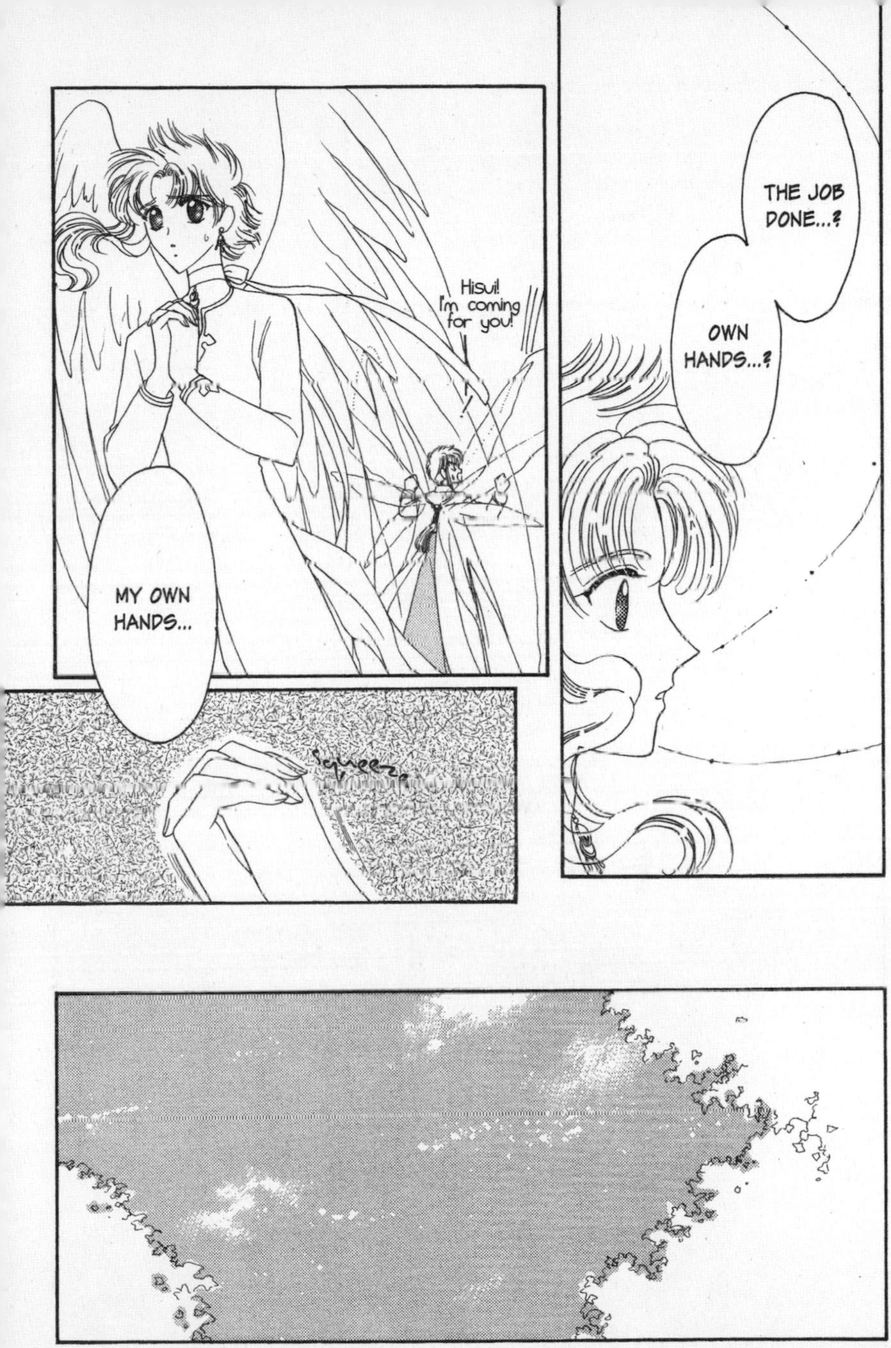
THE JOB DONE...?
OWN HANDS...?
Hisui! I'm coming for you!
MY OWN HANDS...
squeeze

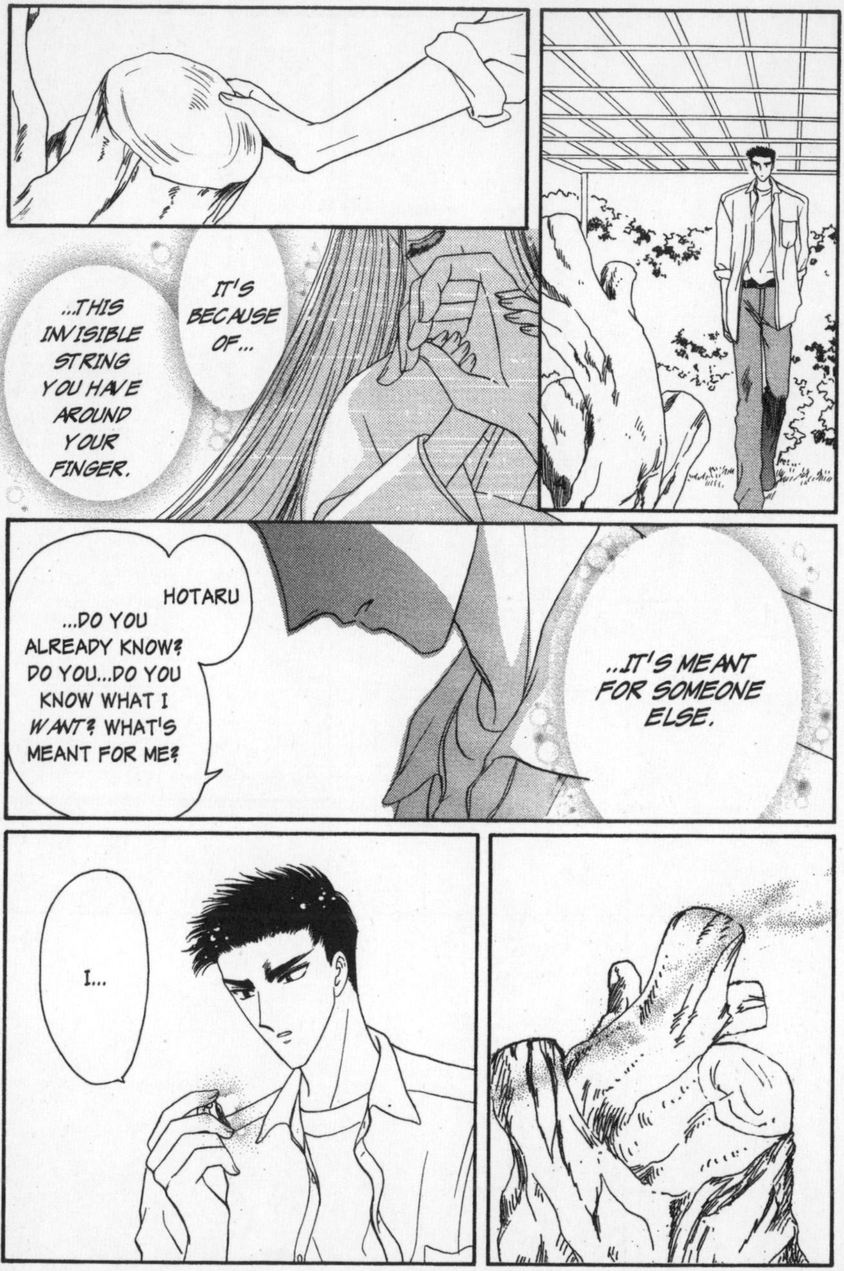
IT'S BECAUSE OF...
...THIS INVISIBLE STRING YOU HAVE AROUND YOUR FINGER.
...IT'S MEANT FOR SOMEONE ELSE.
HOTARU ...DO YOU ALREADY KNOW? DO YOU...DO YOU KNOW WHAT I *WANT*? WHAT'S MEANT FOR ME?
I...

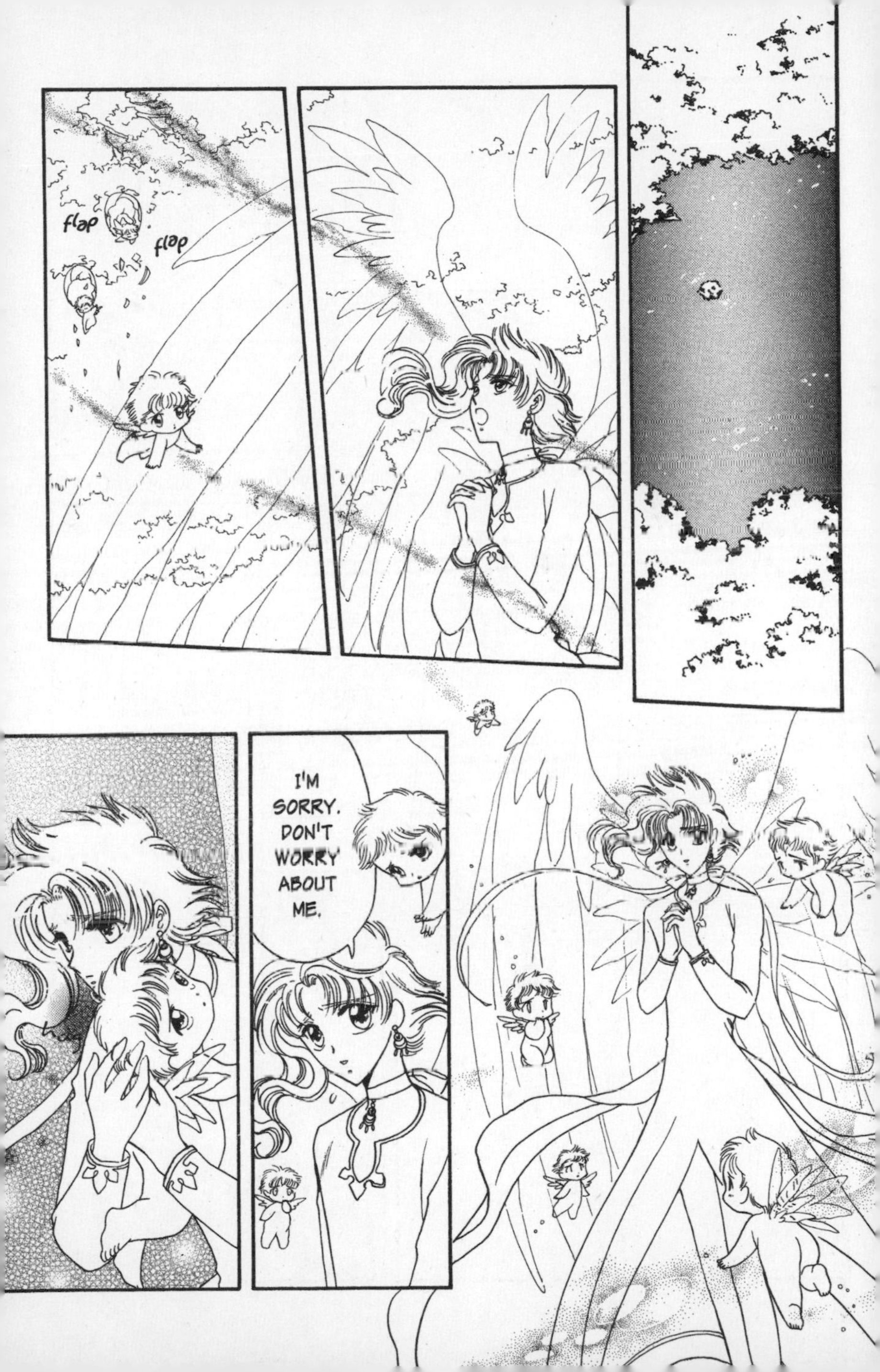
flap
flap
I'M SORRY. DON'T WORRY ABOUT ME.

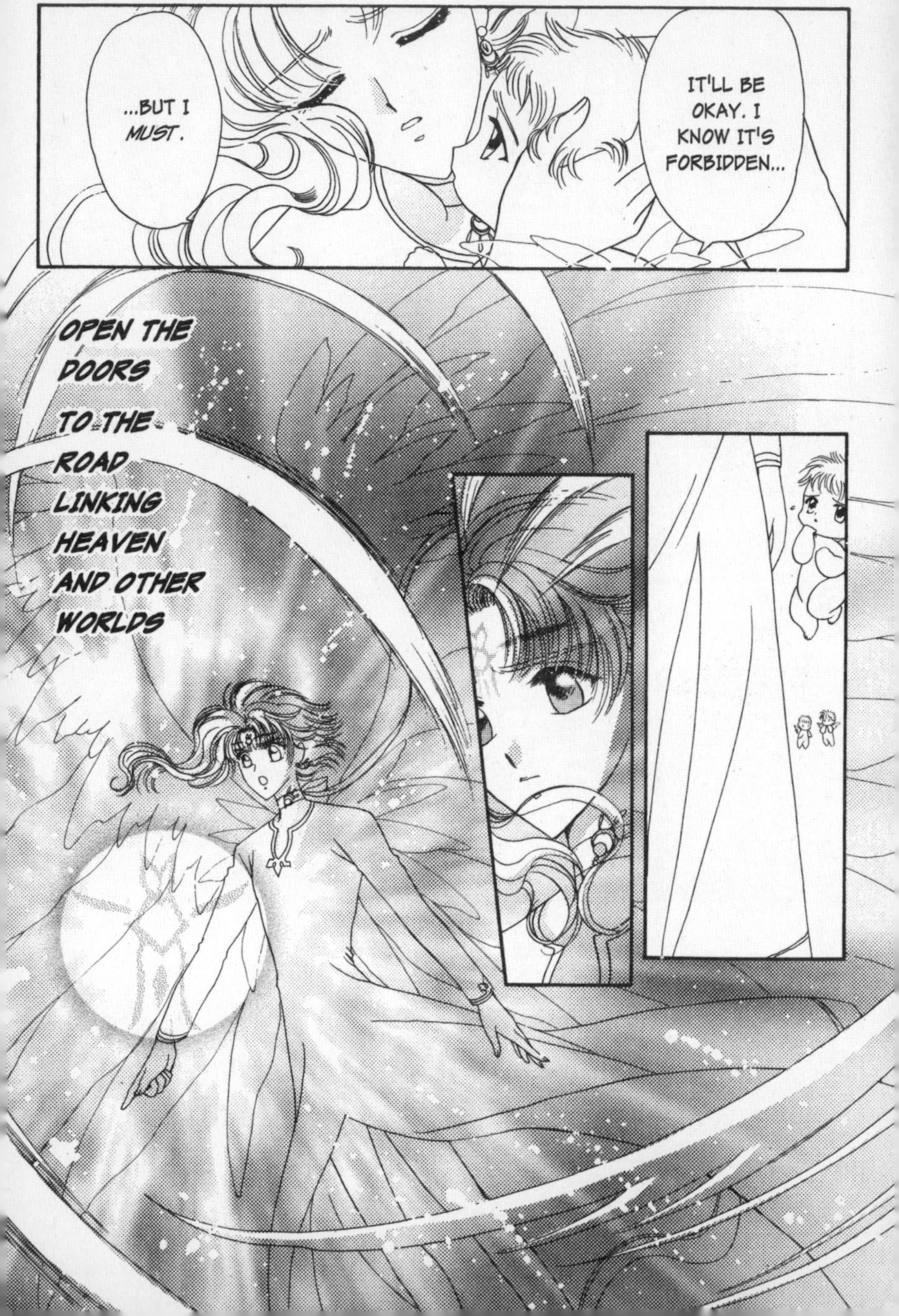
IT'LL BE OKAY. I KNOW IT'S FORBIDDEN...
...BUT I MUST.
OPEN THE DOORS TO THE ROAD LINKING HEAVEN AND OTHER WORLDS

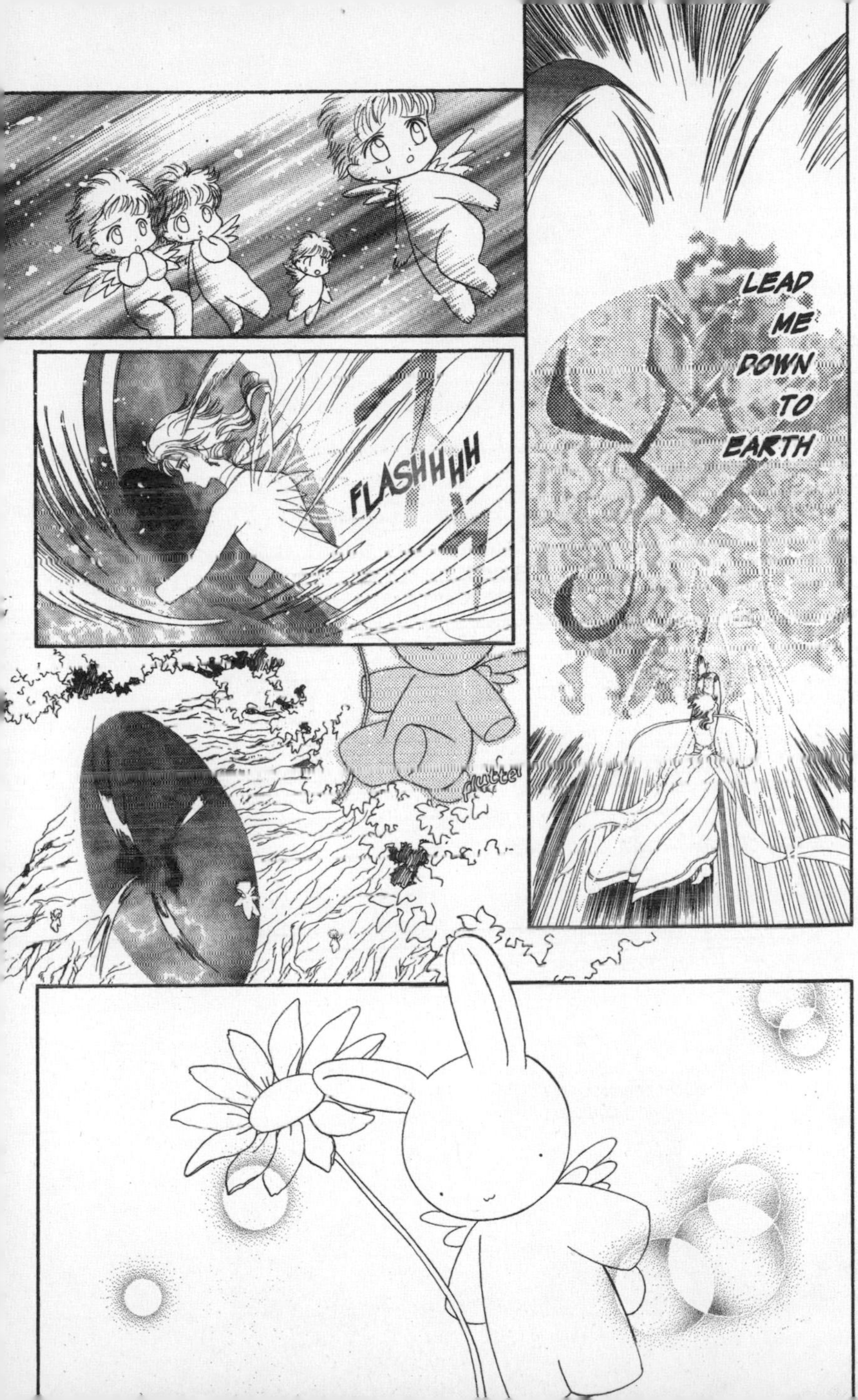
LEAD ME DOWN TO EARTH
FLASHHHH
flutter

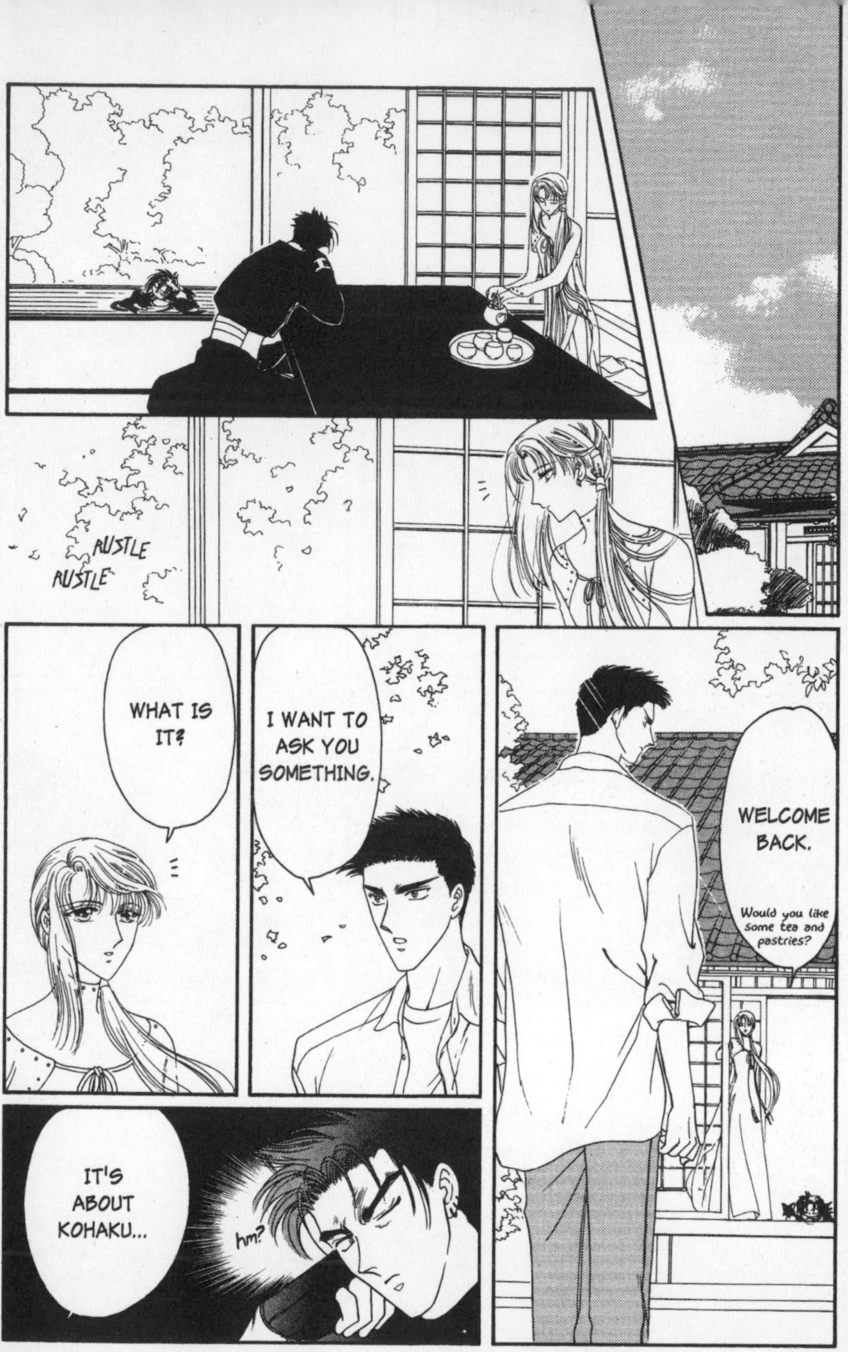
RUSTLE
RUSTLE
WELCOME BACK.
Would you like some tea and pastries?
I WANT TO ASK YOU SOMETHING.
WHAT IS IT?
IT'S ABOUT KOHAKU...
hm?

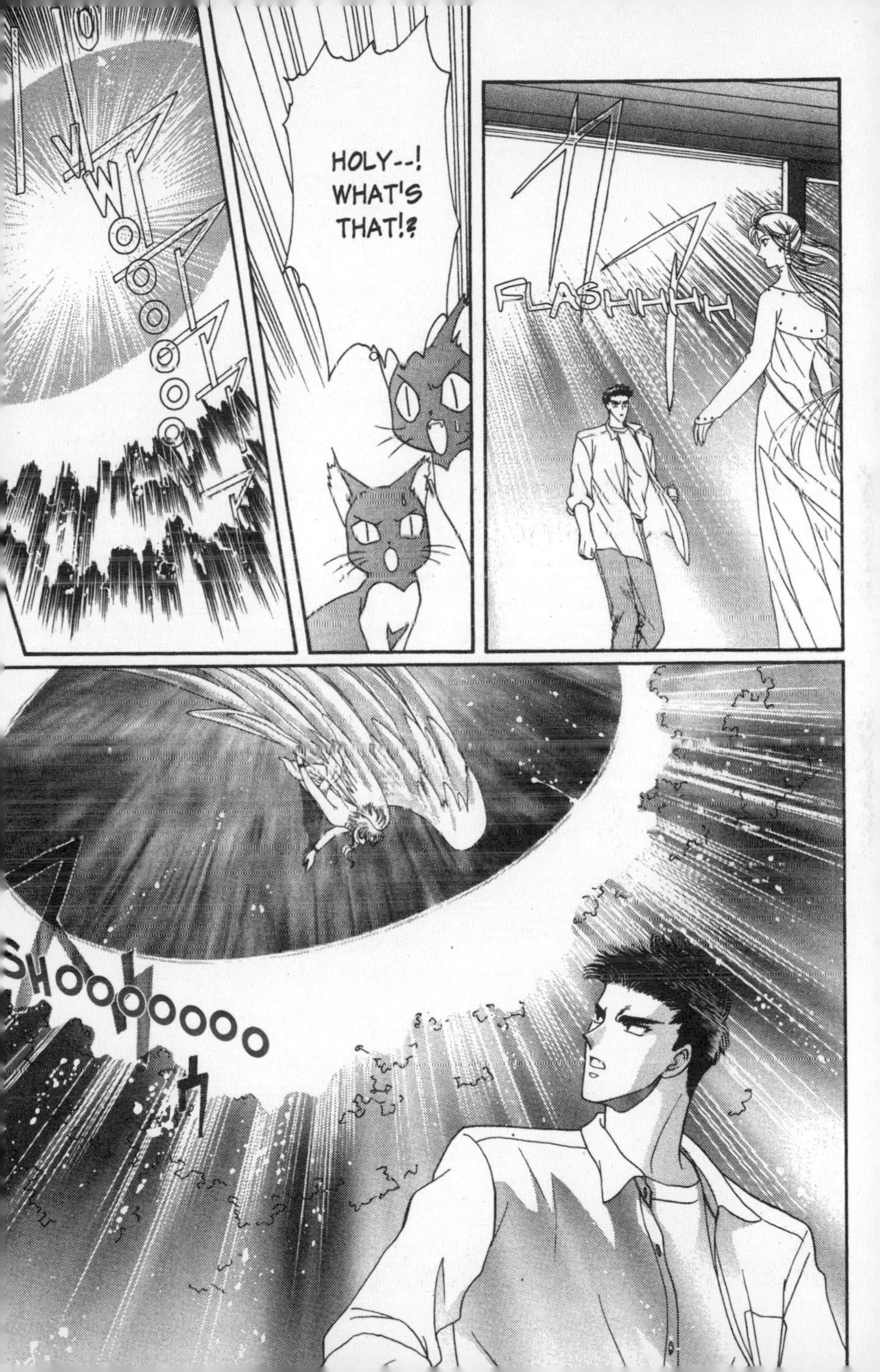
FLASHHHHH
HOLY--! WHAT'S THAT!?
VWOOOOOOM
SHOOOOOOOH

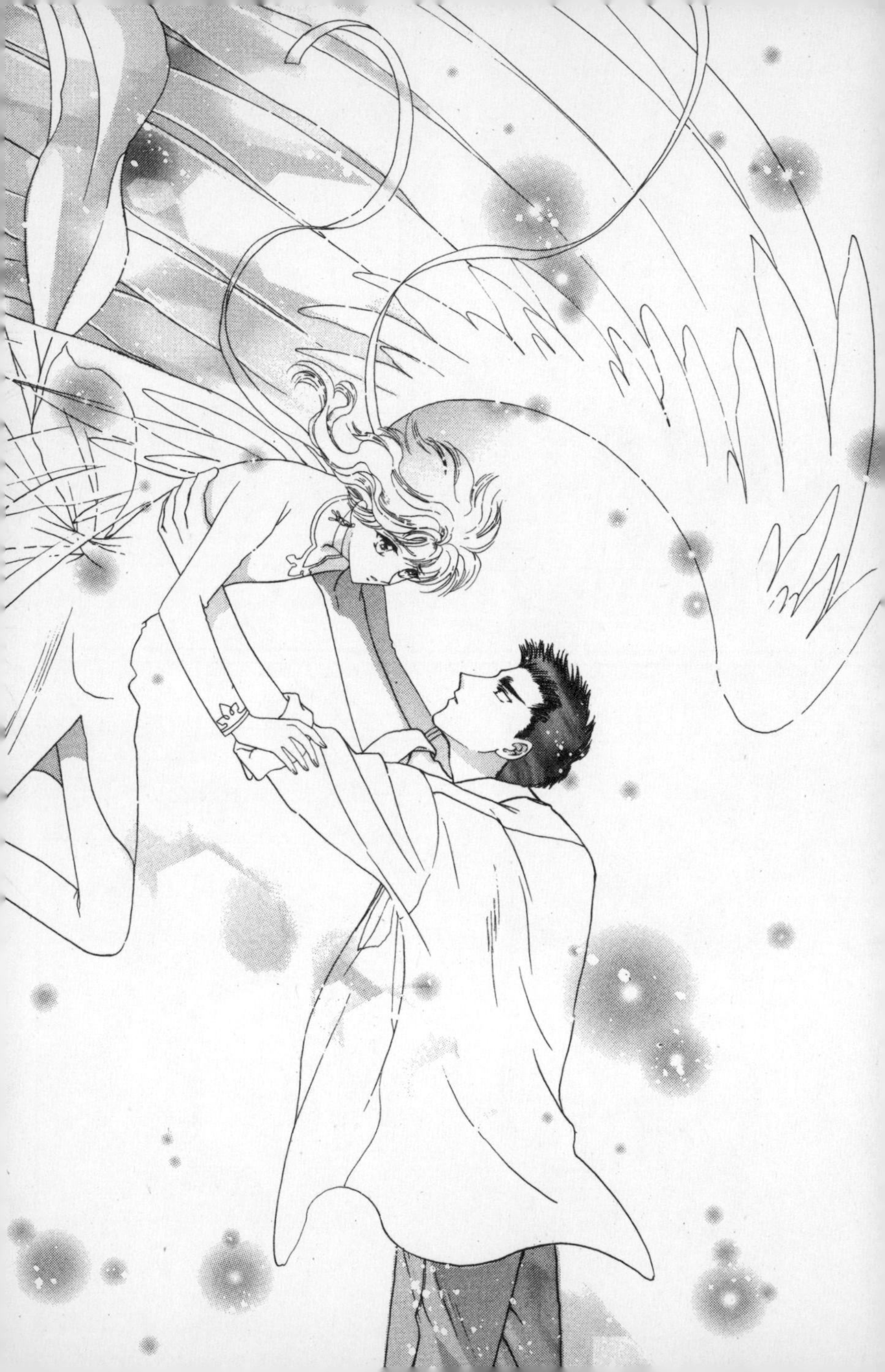

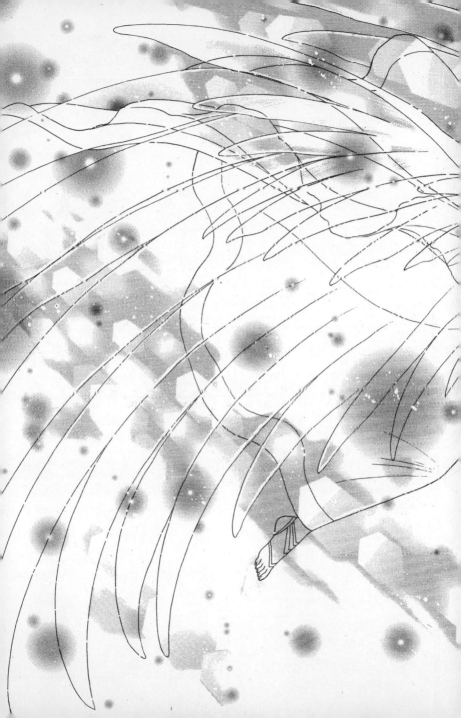

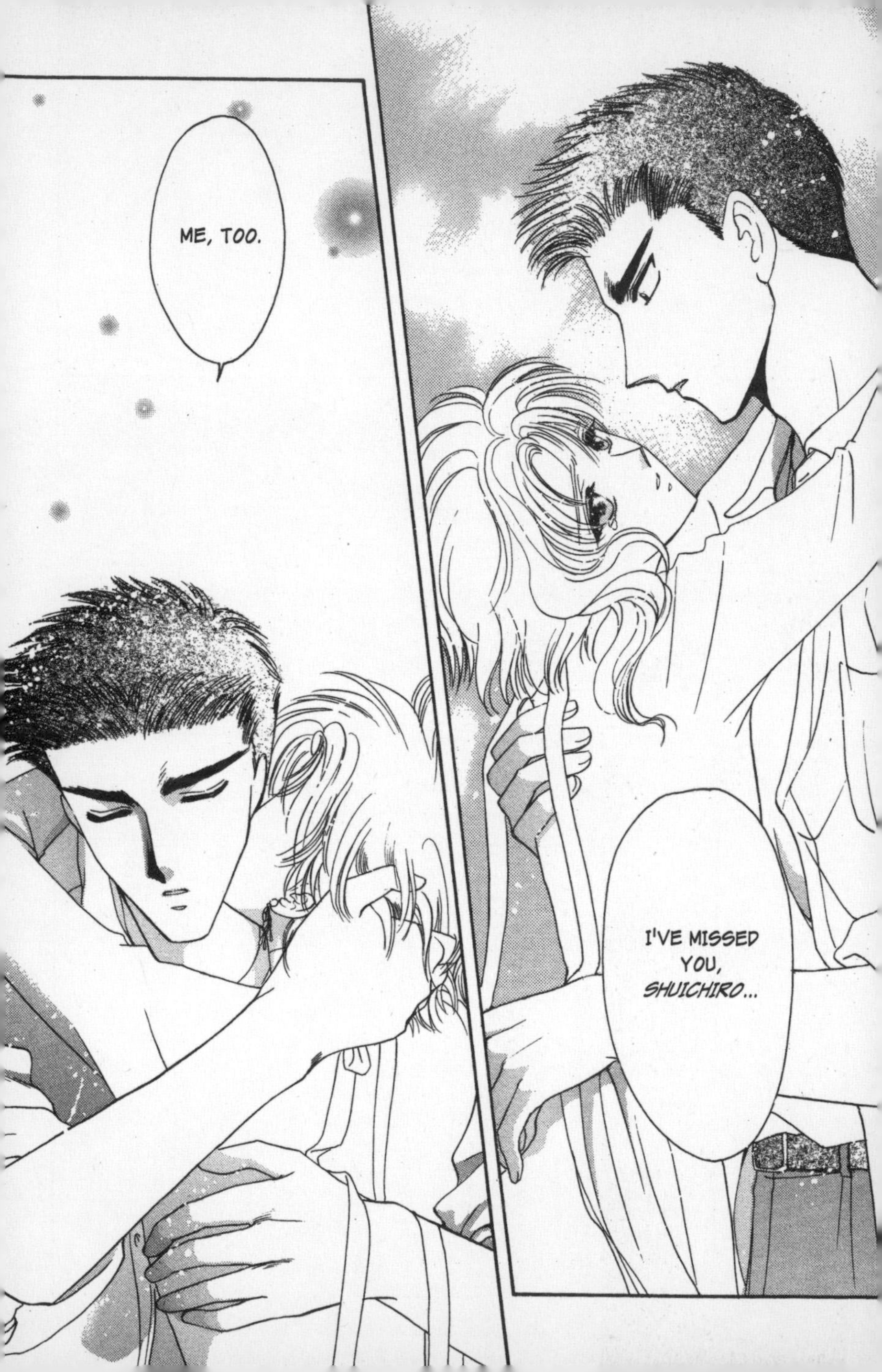
I'VE MISSED YOU, SHUICHIRO...
ME, TOO.

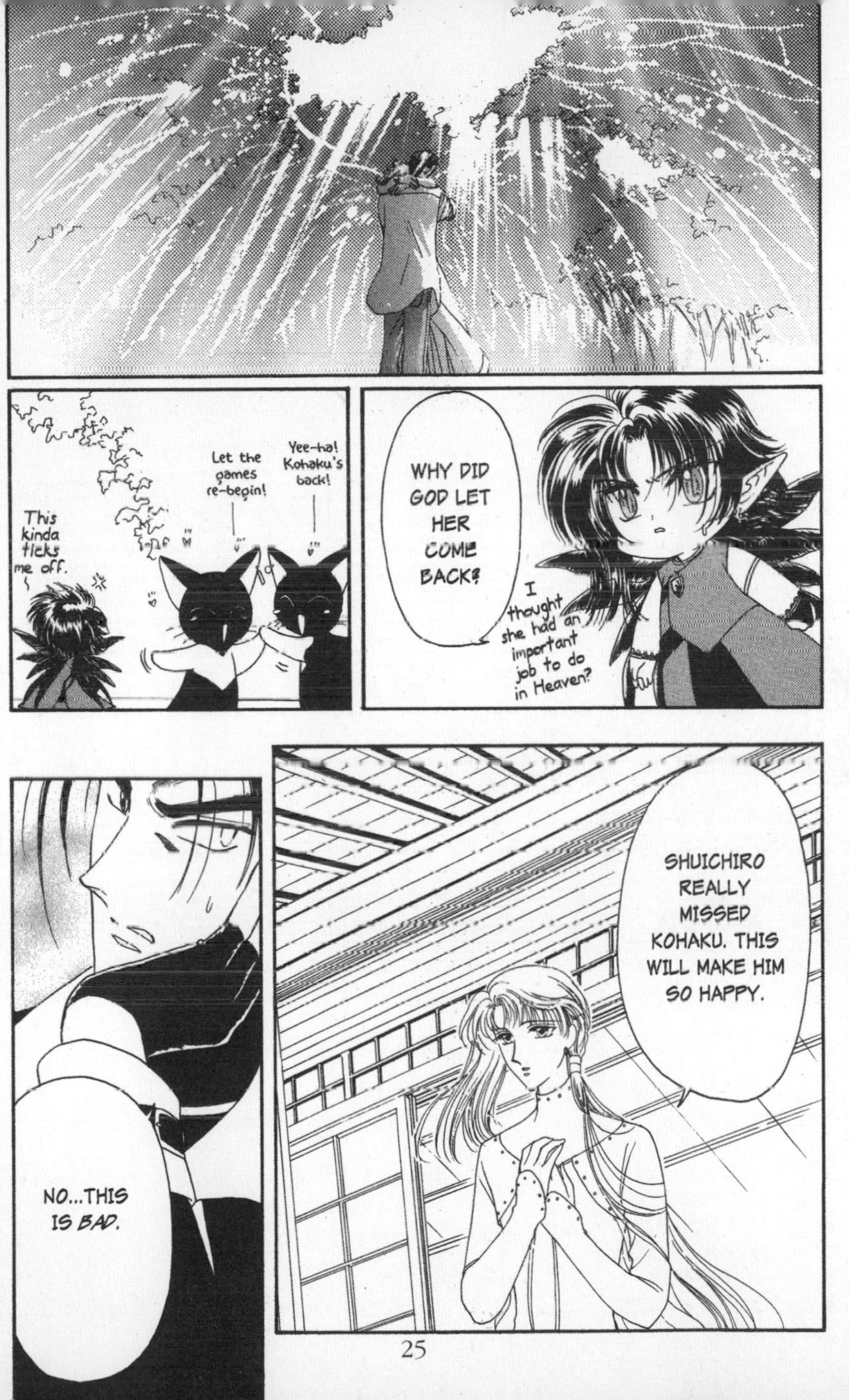
WHY DID GOD LET HER COME BACK?
I thought she had an important job to do in Heaven?
Yee-ha! Kohaku's back!
Let the games re-begin!
This kinda ticks me off.
SHUICHIRO REALLY MISSED KOHAKU. THIS WILL MAKE HIM SO HAPPY.
NO...THIS IS *BAD*.

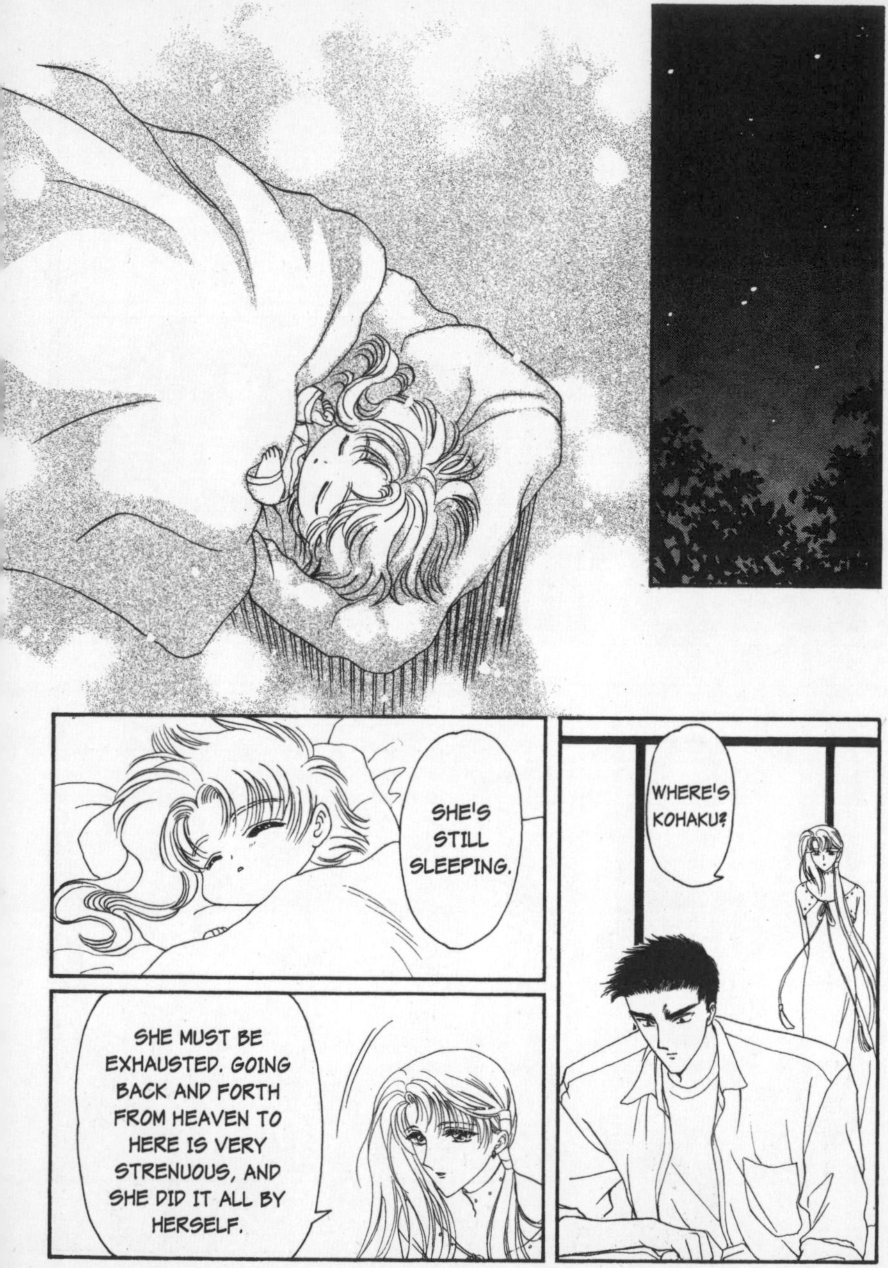
WHERE'S KOHAKU?
SHE'S STILL SLEEPING.
SHE MUST BE EXHAUSTED. GOING BACK AND FORTH FROM HEAVEN TO HERE IS VERY STRENUOUS, AND SHE DID IT ALL BY HERSELF.

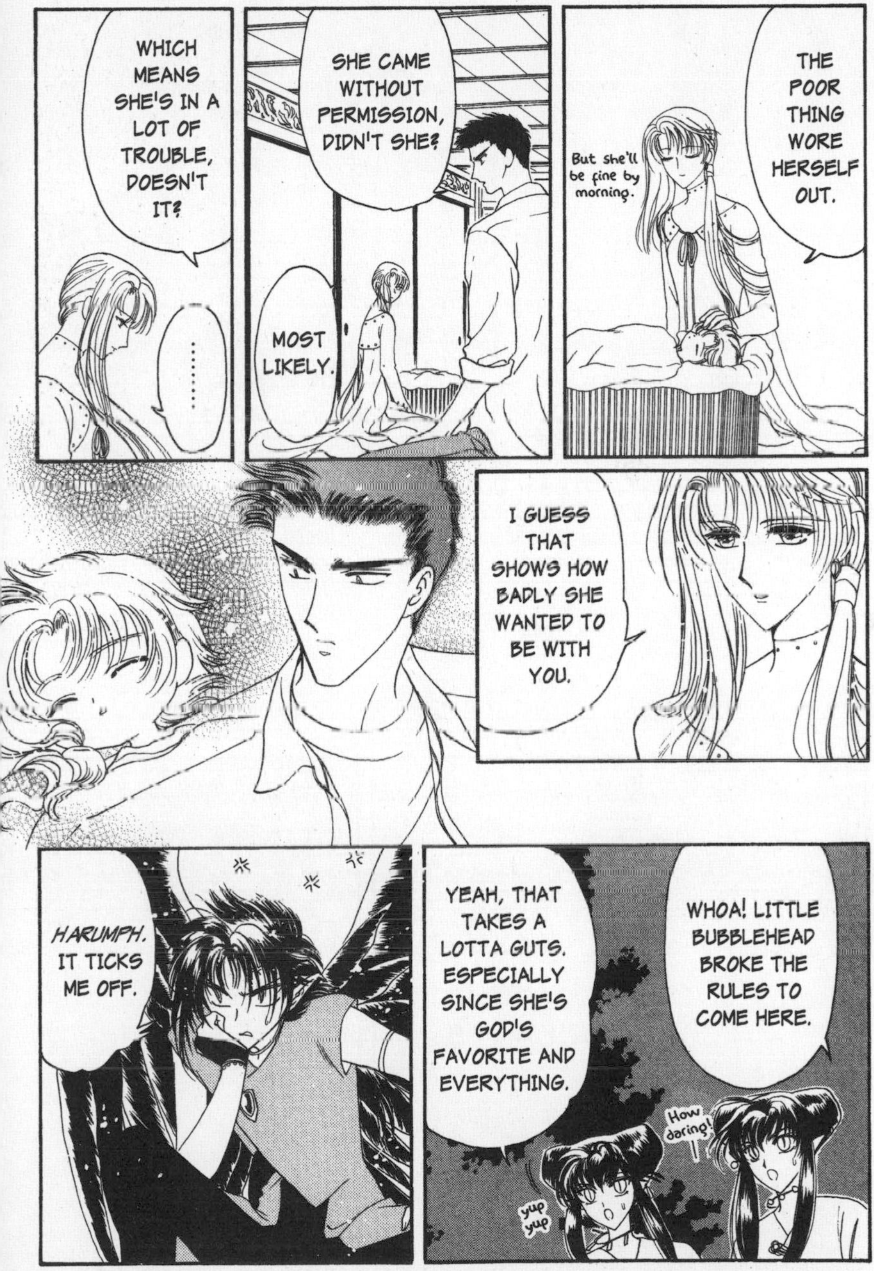
THE POOR THING WORE HERSELF OUT.
But she'll be fine by morning.
SHE CAME WITHOUT PERMISSION, DIDN'T SHE?
MOST LIKELY.
WHICH MEANS SHE'S IN A LOT OF TROUBLE, DOESN'T IT?
......
I GUESS THAT SHOWS HOW BADLY SHE WANTED TO BE WITH YOU.
WHOA! LITTLE BUBBLEHEAD BROKE THE RULES TO COME HERE.
How daring!
YEAH, THAT TAKES A LOTTA GUTS. ESPECIALLY SINCE SHE'S GOD'S FAVORITE AND EVERYTHING.
yup yup
HARUMPH. IT TICKS ME OFF.

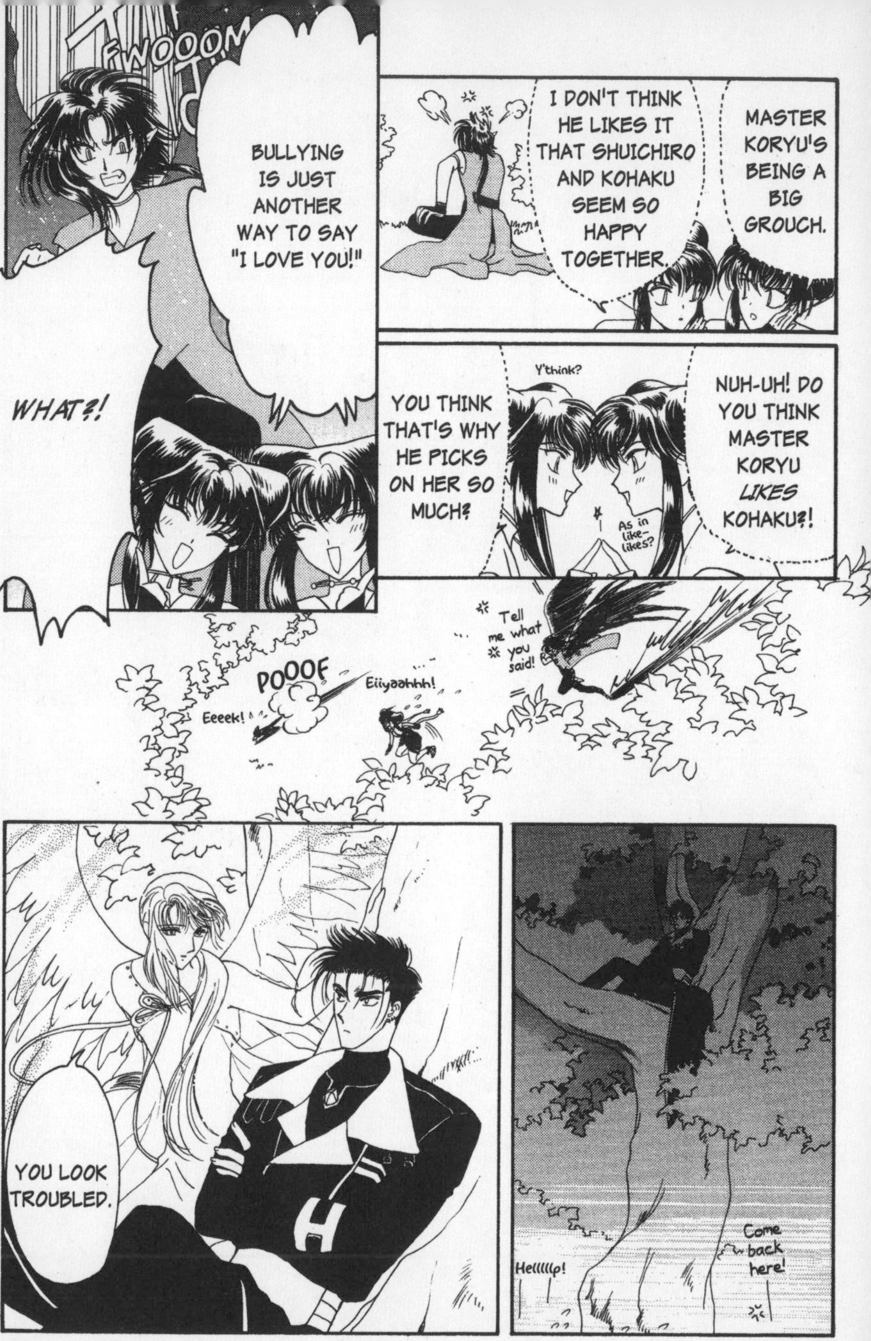
MASTER KORYU'S BEING A BIG GROUCH.
I DON'T THINK HE LIKES IT THAT SHUICHIRO AND KOHAKU SEEM SO HAPPY TOGETHER.
NUH-UH! DO YOU THINK MASTER KORYU *LIKES* KOHAKU?!
As in like-likes?
Y'think?
YOU THINK THAT'S WHY HE PICKS ON HER SO MUCH?
FWOOOM
BULLYING IS JUST ANOTHER WAY TO SAY "I LOVE YOU!"
WHAT?!
Tell me what you said!
Eiiyaahhh!
POOOF
Eeeek!
Come back here!
Hellllp!
YOU LOOK TROUBLED.

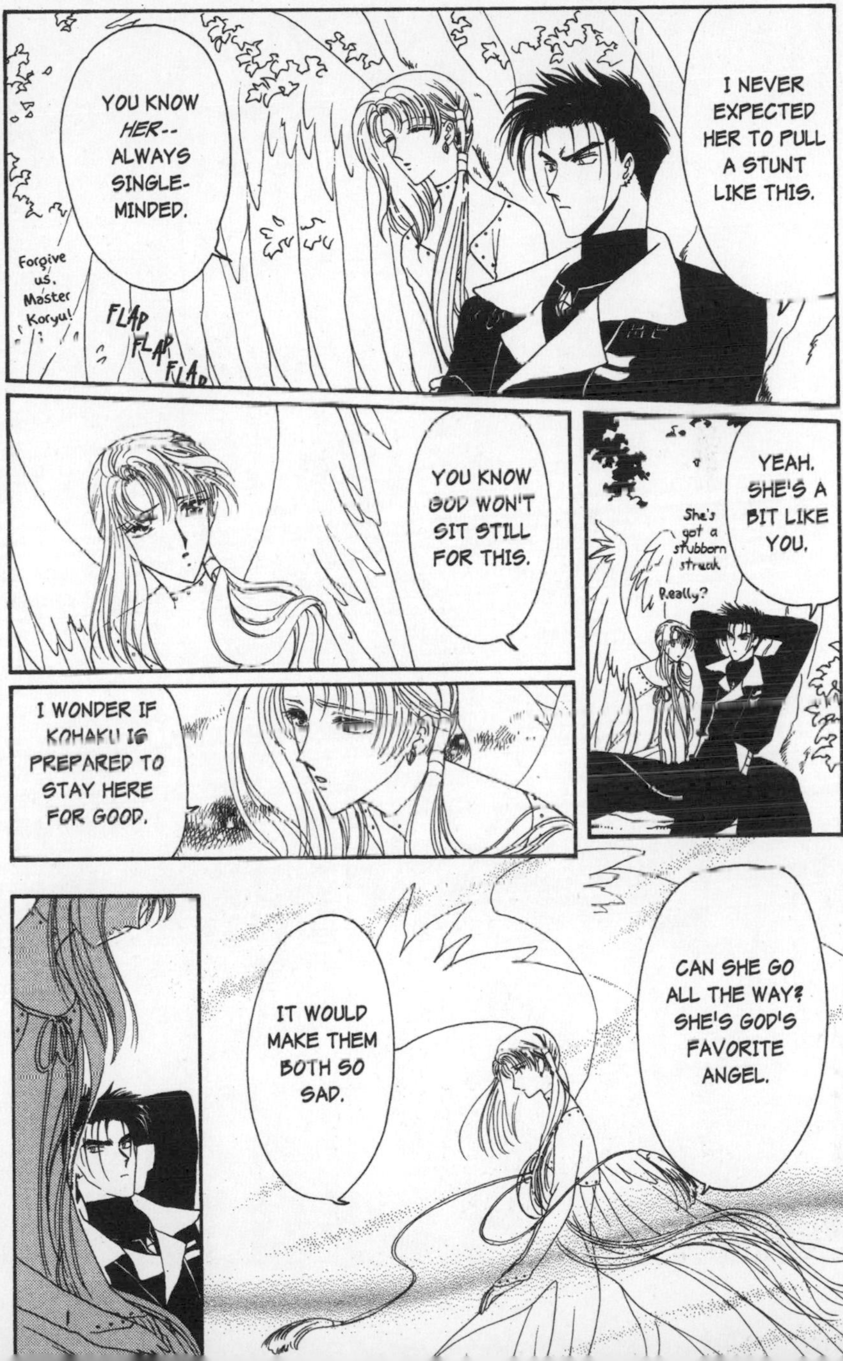
I NEVER EXPECTED HER TO PULL A STUNT LIKE THIS.
YOU KNOW HER-- ALWAYS SINGLE-MINDED.
Forgive us, Master Koryu!
FLAP FLAP FLAP
YEAH. SHE'S A BIT LIKE YOU.
She's got a stubborn streak
Really?
YOU KNOW GOD WON'T SIT STILL FOR THIS.
I WONDER IF KOHAKU IS PREPARED TO STAY HERE FOR GOOD.
CAN SHE GO ALL THE WAY? SHE'S GOD'S FAVORITE ANGEL.
IT WOULD MAKE THEM BOTH SO SAD.

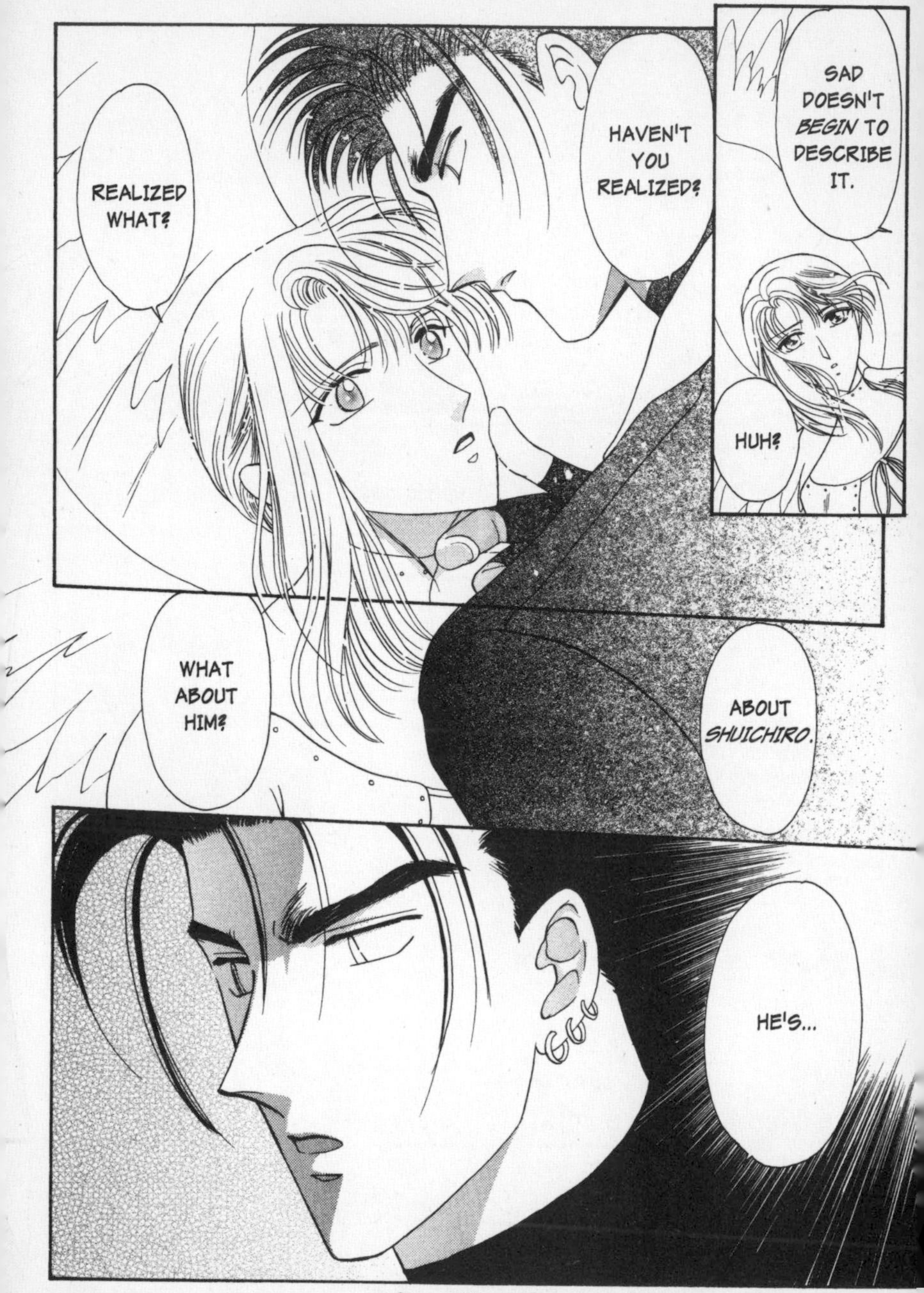
SAD DOESN'T *BEGIN* TO DESCRIBE IT.
HUH?
HAVEN'T YOU REALIZED?
REALIZED WHAT?
ABOUT *SHUICHIRO*.
WHAT ABOUT HIM?
HE'S...

END

Contact.19　Time Together

ふたりの時間

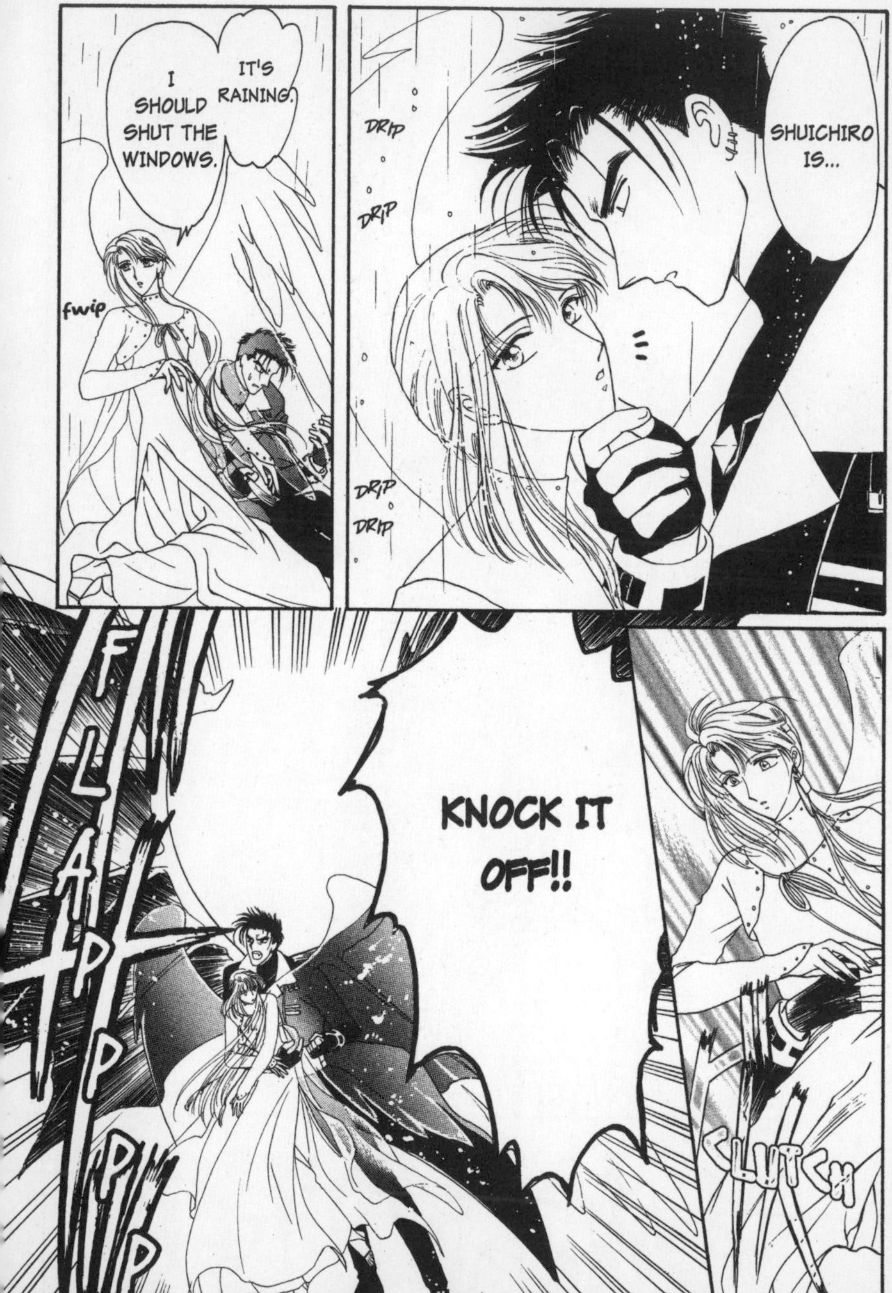
SHUICHIRO IS...
DRIP
DRIP
DRIP
DRIP
IT'S RAINING.
I SHOULD SHUT THE WINDOWS.
fwip
CLUTCH
KNOCK IT OFF!!
FLAPPPP

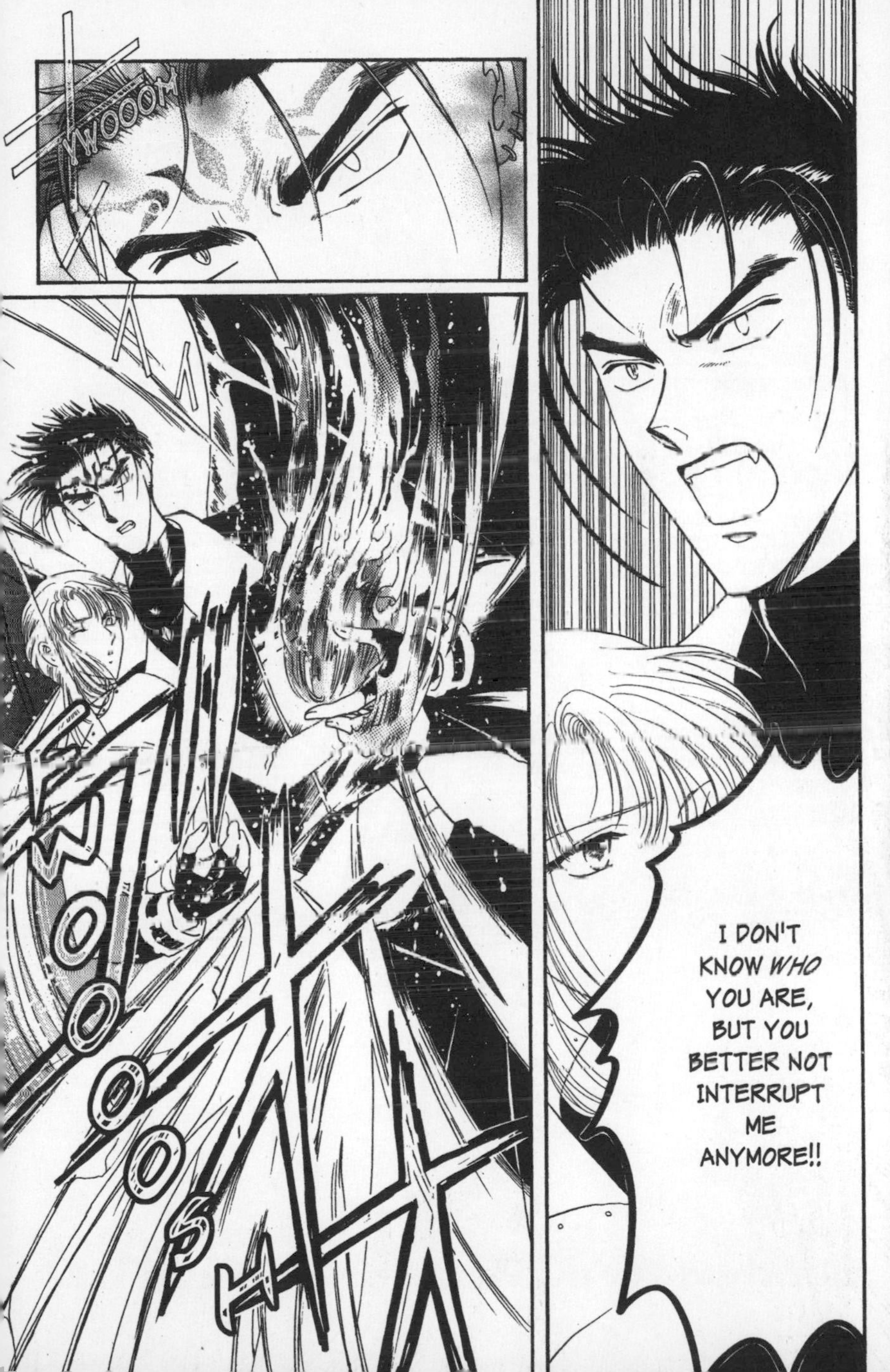
I DON'T KNOW *WHO* YOU ARE, BUT YOU BETTER NOT INTERRUPT ME ANYMORE!!
VWOOOM
WOOOOSH

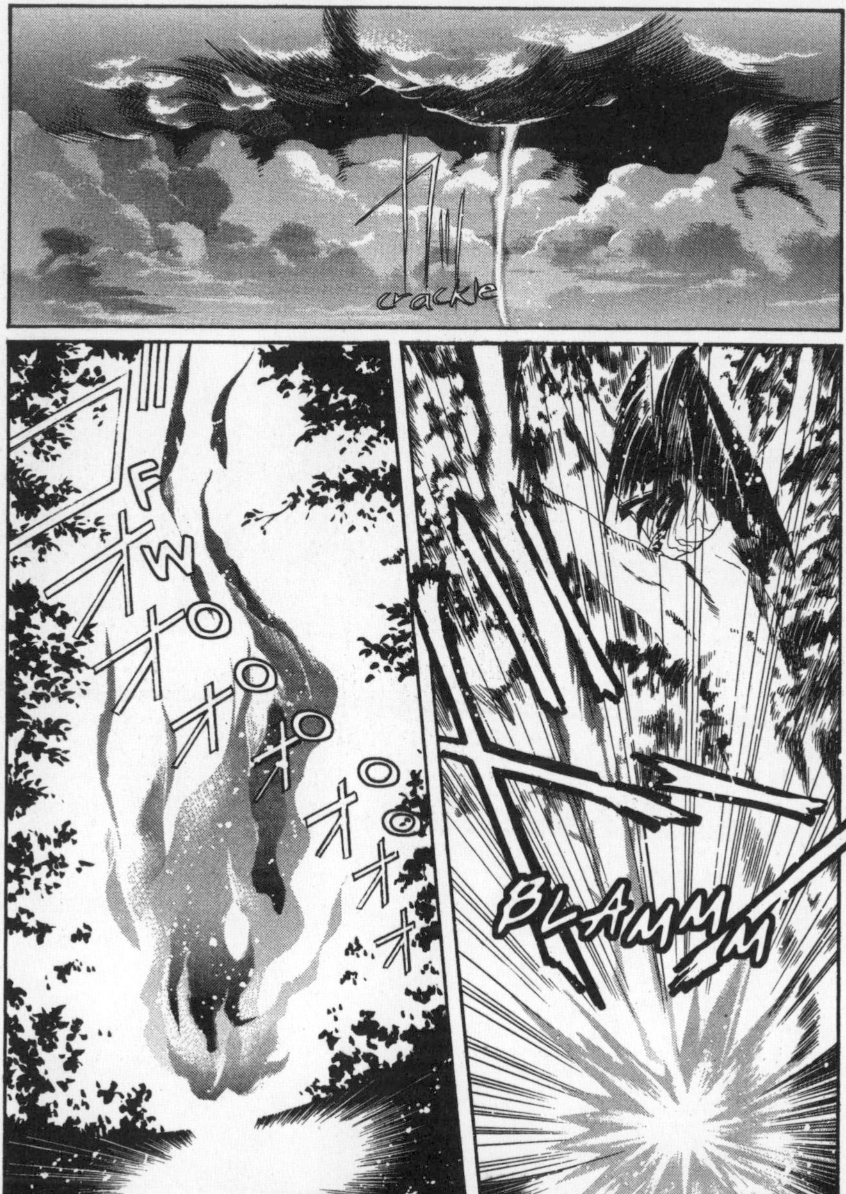
crackle
BLAMMM
FWOOOOO

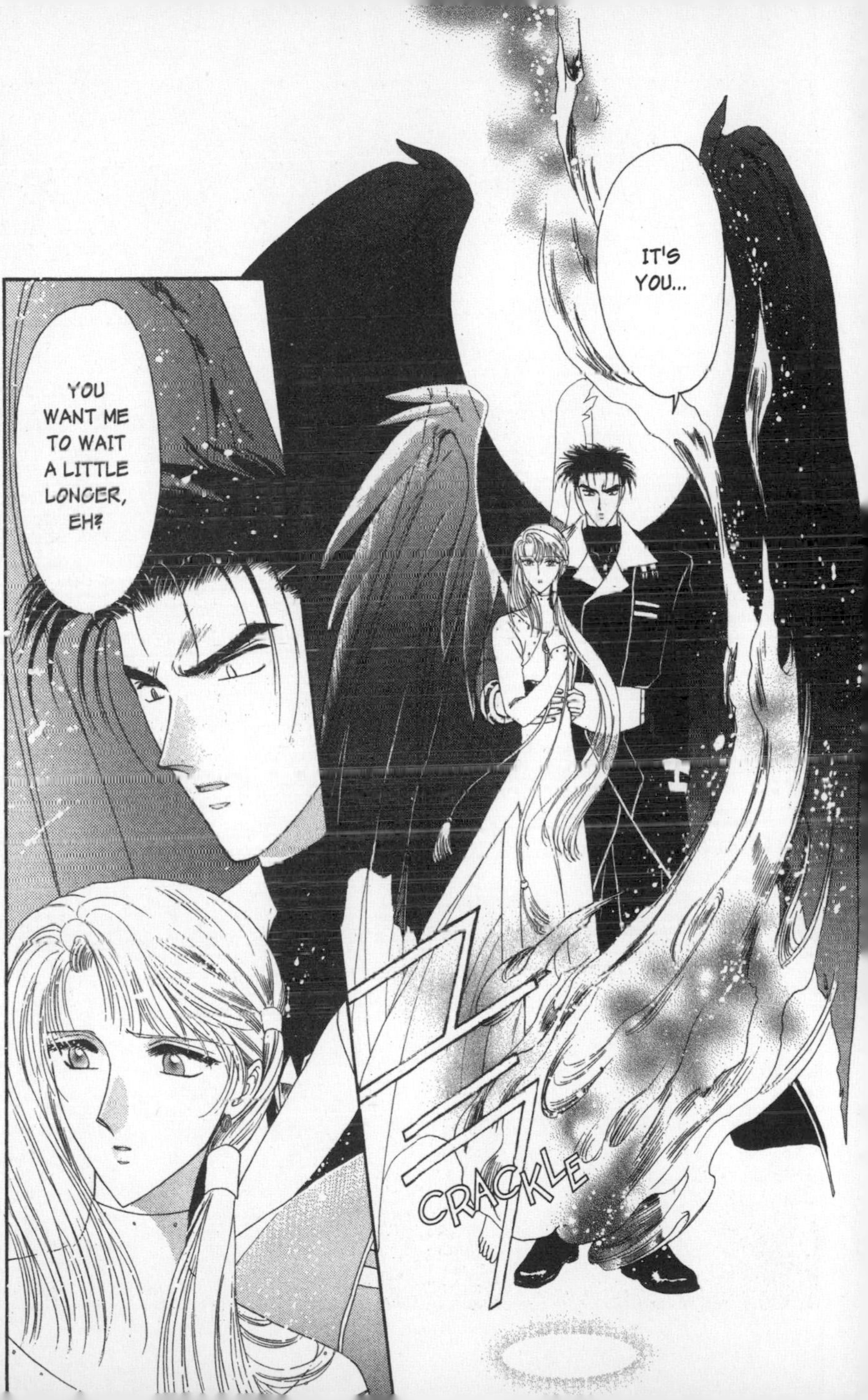
IT'S YOU...
YOU WANT ME TO WAIT A LITTLE LONGER, EH?
CRACKLE

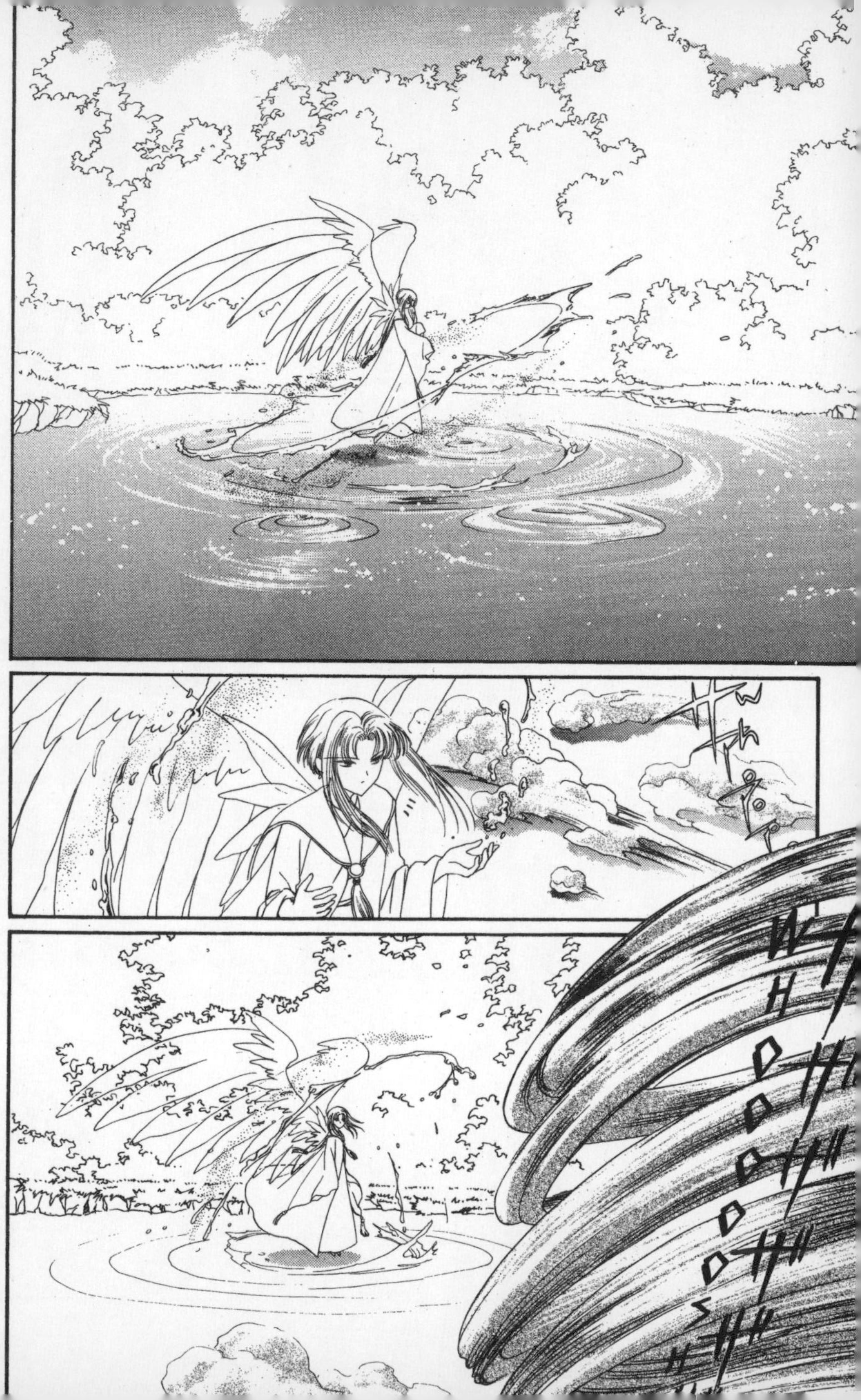
whoop
WHOOOOOSH

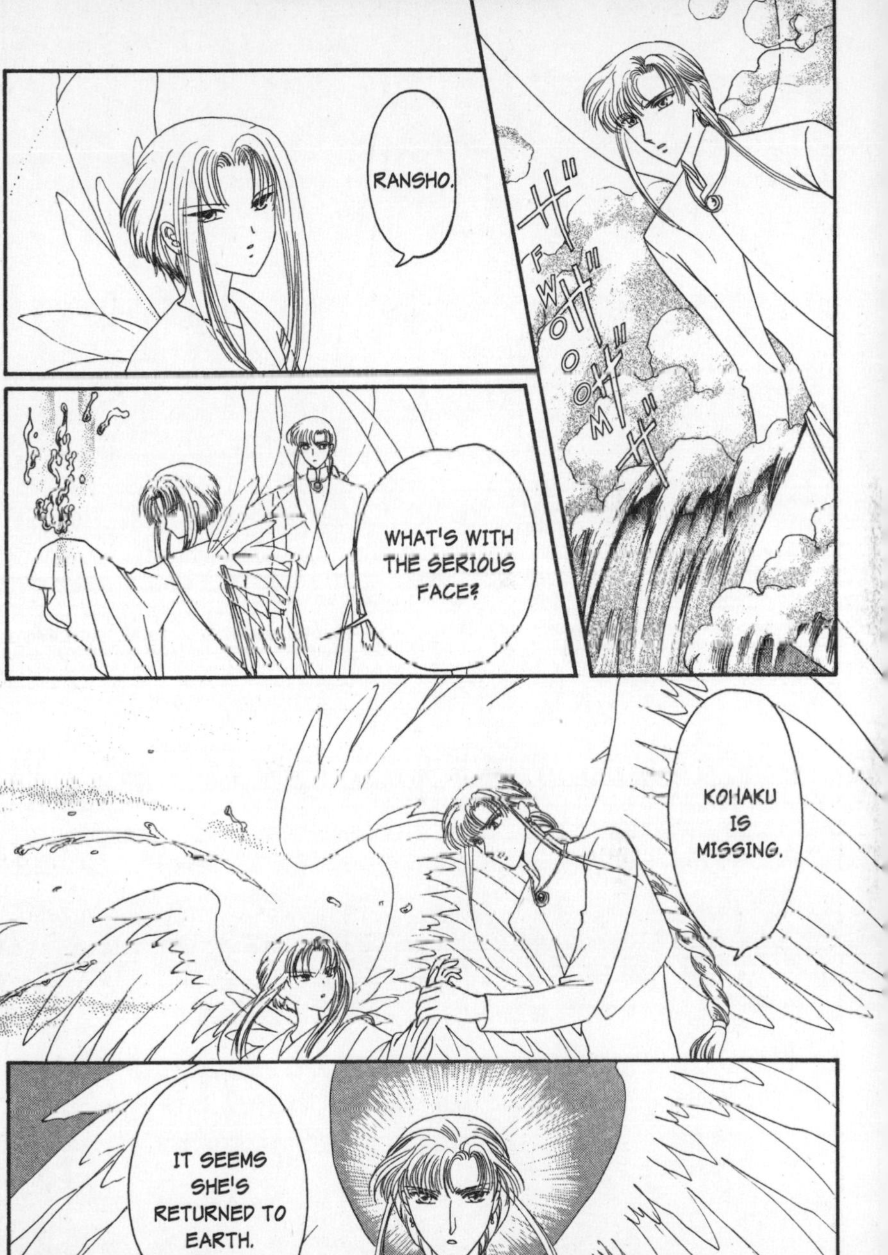
FWOOOM
RANSHO.
WHAT'S WITH THE SERIOUS FACE?
KOHAKU IS MISSING.
IT SEEMS SHE'S RETURNED TO EARTH.

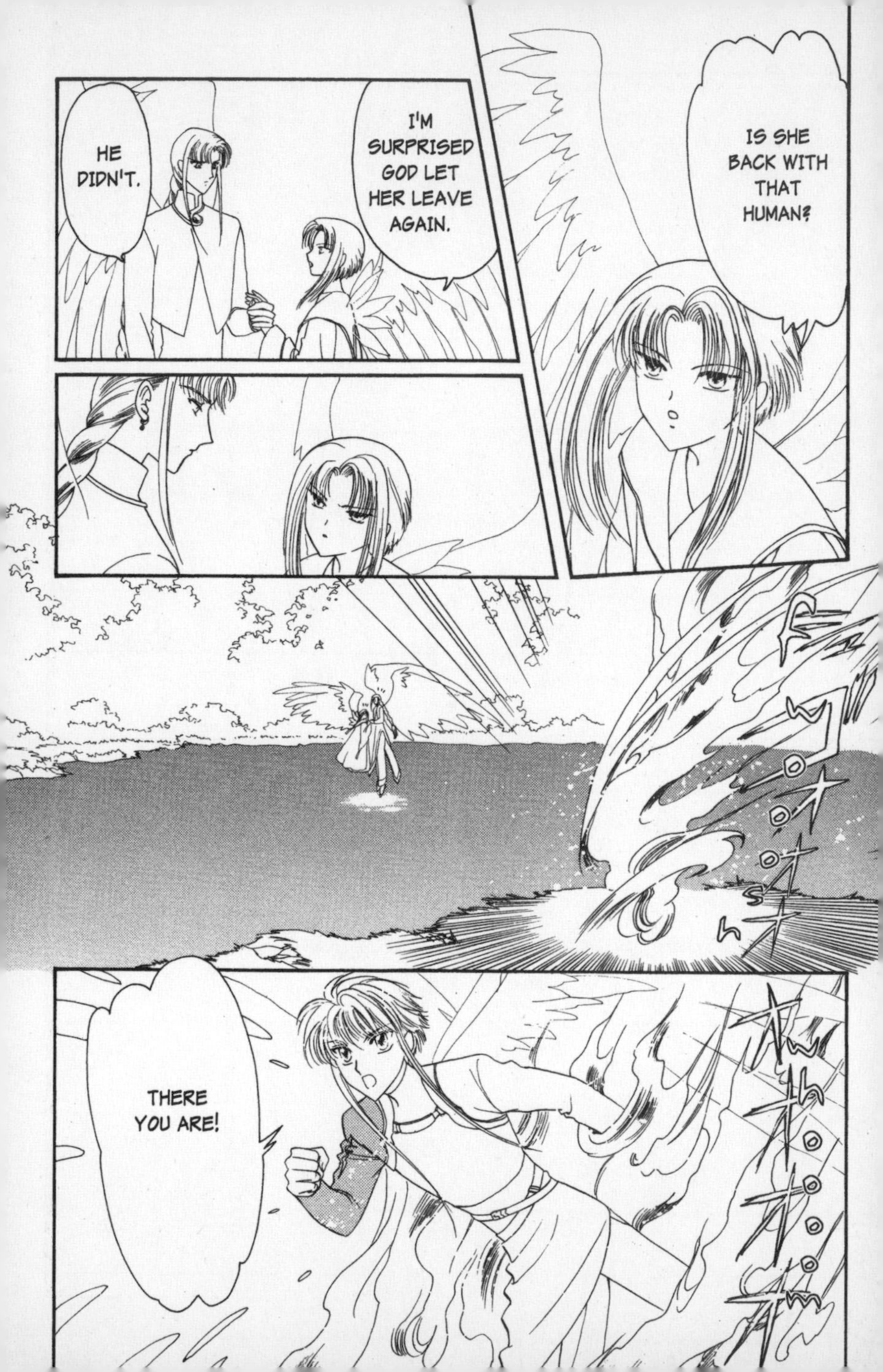

IS SHE BACK WITH THAT HUMAN?
I'M SURPRISED GOD LET HER LEAVE AGAIN.
HE DIDN'T.
Fwooosh
Whoooooom
THERE YOU ARE!

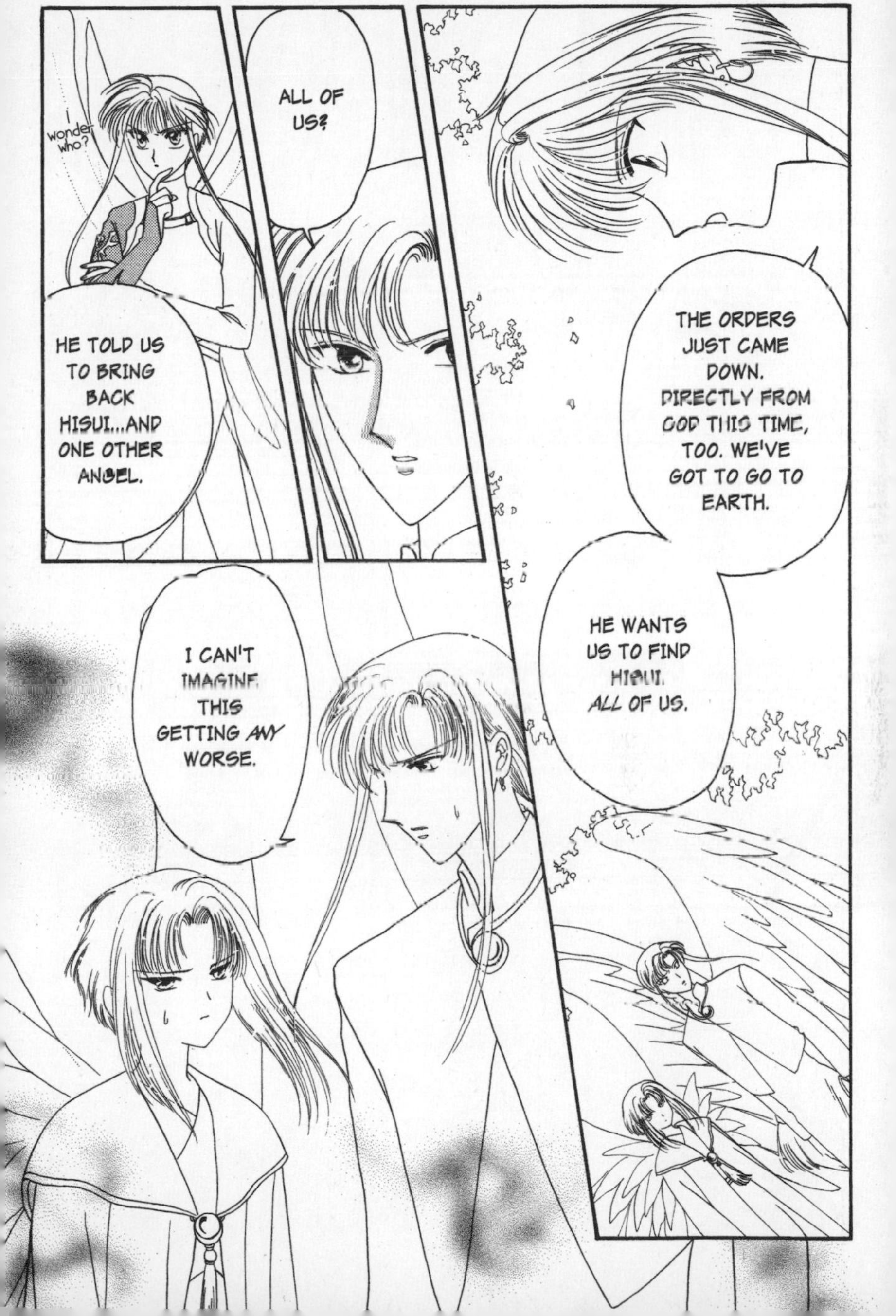
THE ORDERS JUST CAME DOWN. DIRECTLY FROM GOD THIS TIME, TOO. WE'VE GOT TO GO TO EARTH.
HE WANTS US TO FIND HISUI. *ALL* OF US.
ALL OF US?
HE TOLD US TO BRING BACK HISUI...AND ONE OTHER ANGEL.
I wonder who?
I CAN'T IMAGINE THIS GETTING *ANY* WORSE.

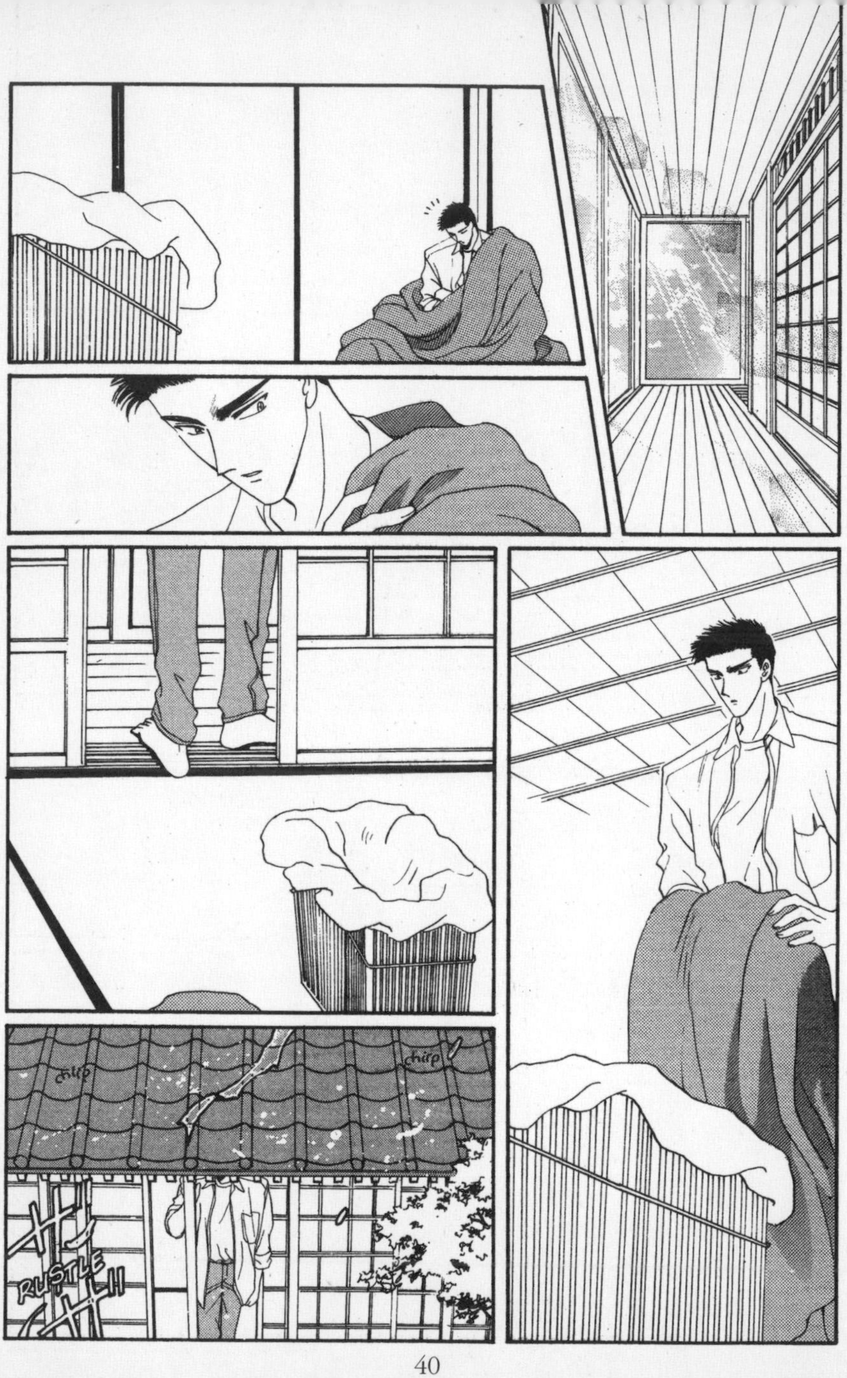
chirp
chirp
RUSTLE

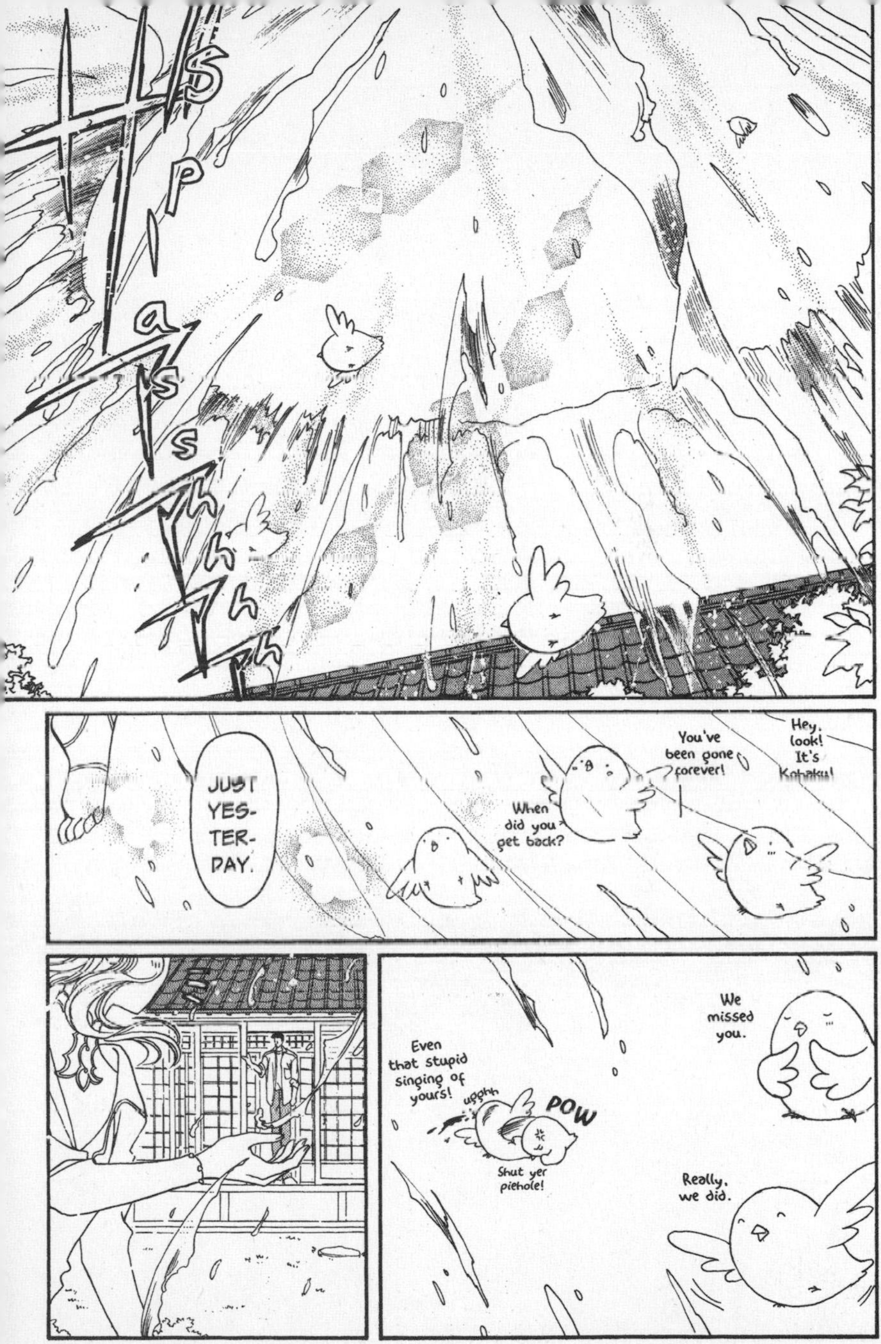
Splasshhhh
Hey, look! It's Kohaku!
You've been gone forever!
When did you get back?
JUST YESTERDAY.
We missed you.
Even that stupid singing of yours!
ugghh
POW
Shut yer piehole!
Really, we did.

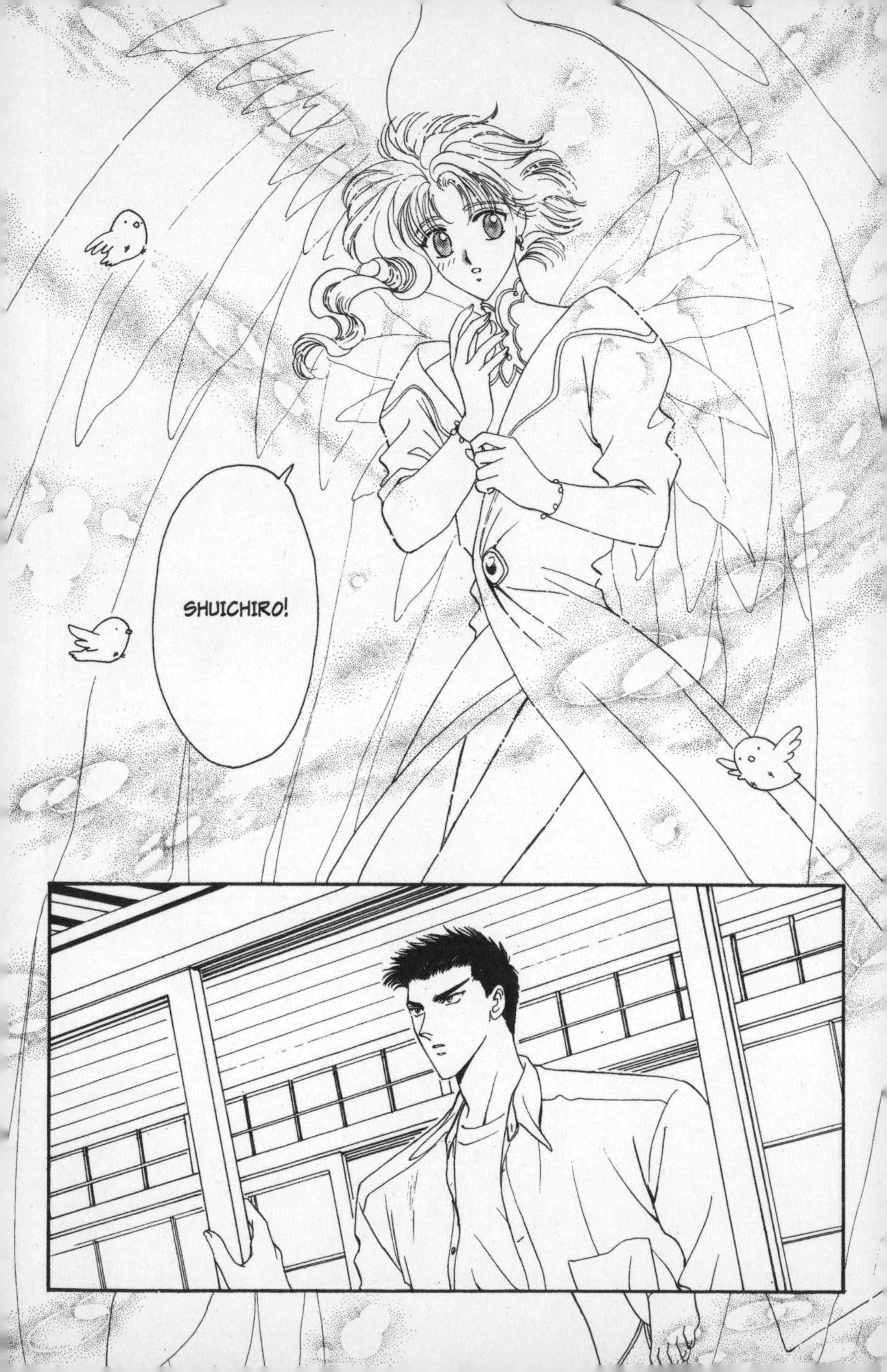
SHUICHIRO!

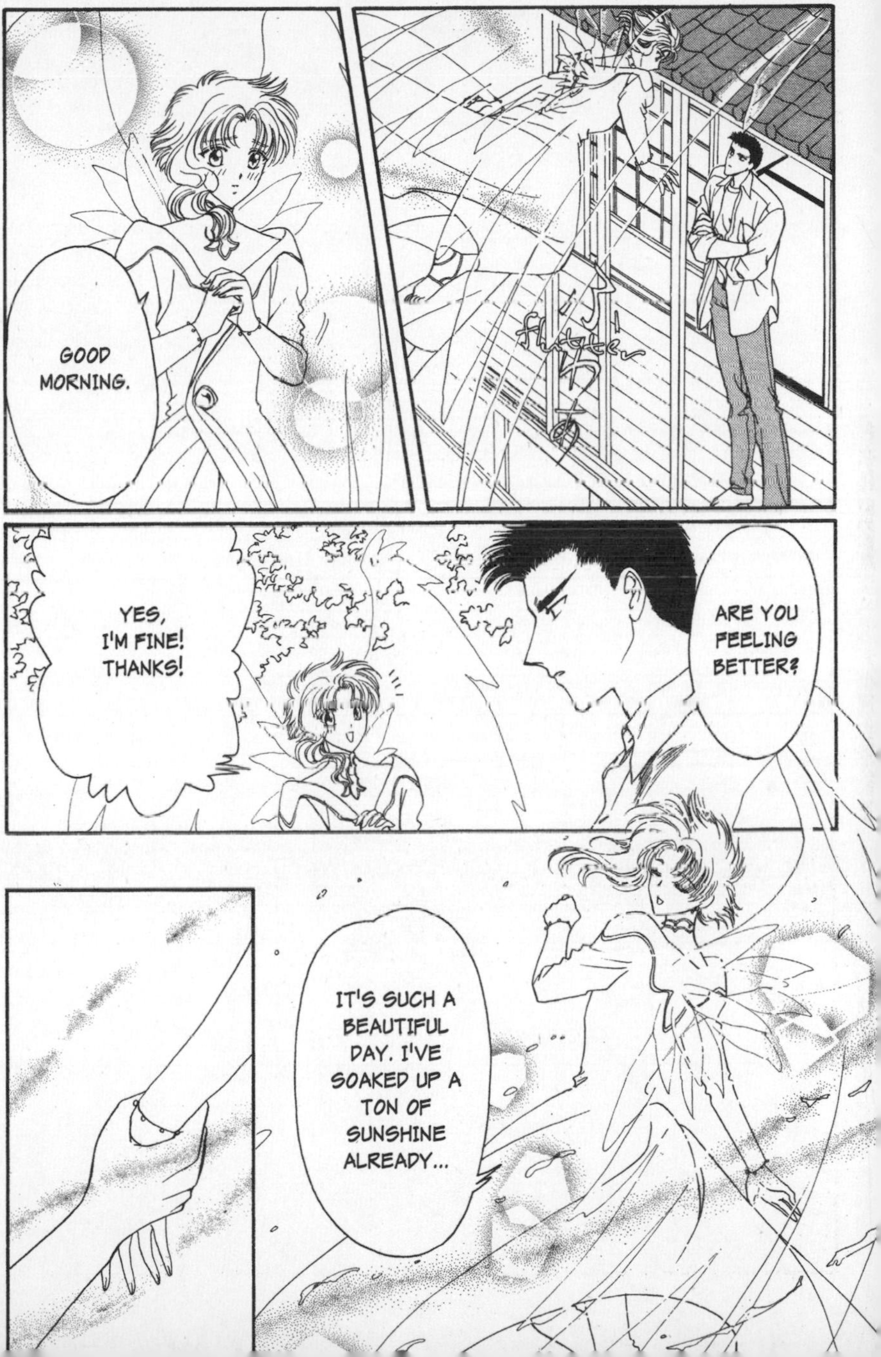
flutter
GOOD MORNING.
ARE YOU FEELING BETTER?
YES, I'M FINE! THANKS!
IT'S SUCH A BEAUTIFUL DAY. I'VE SOAKED UP A TON OF SUNSHINE ALREADY...

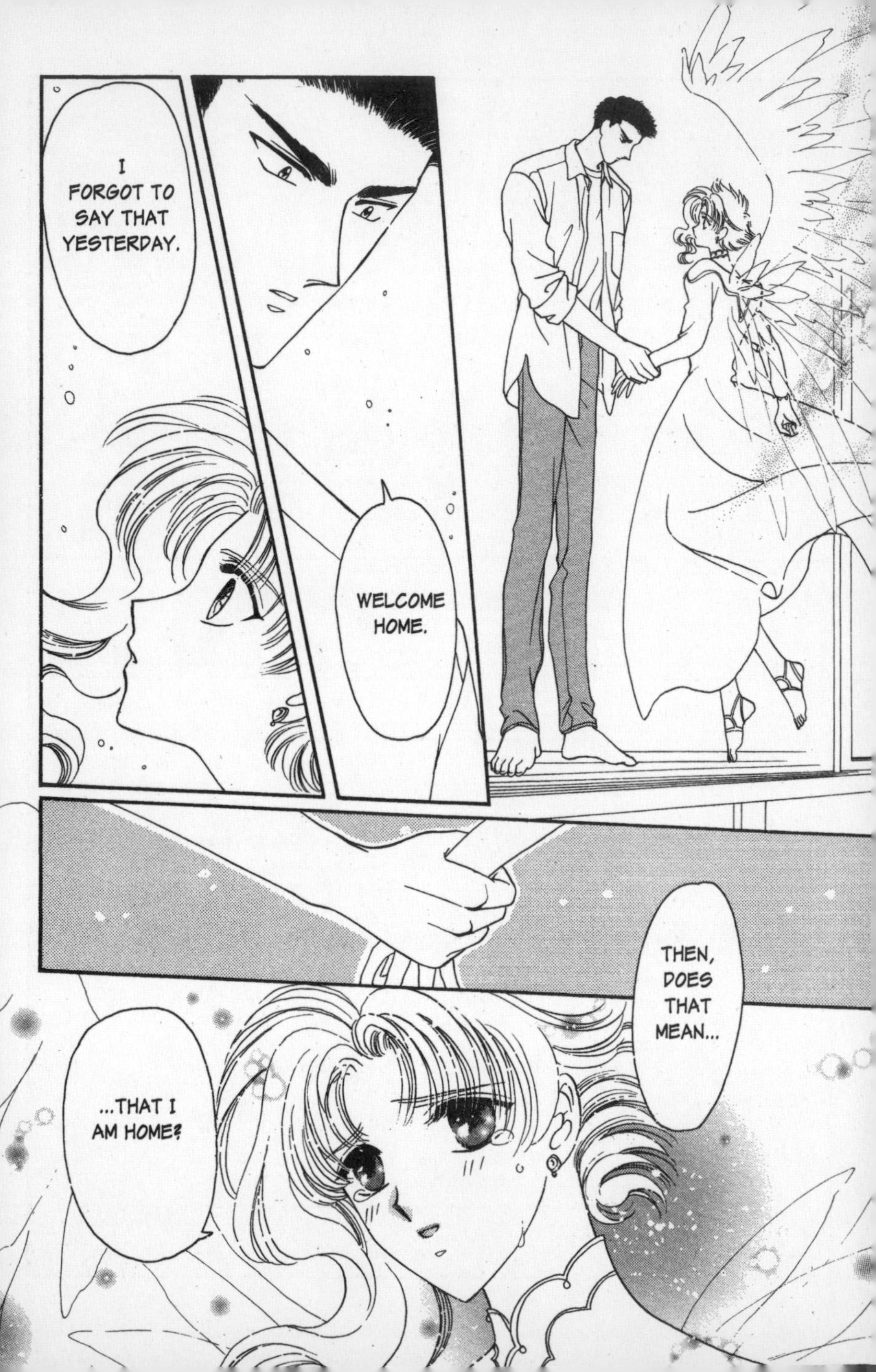
WELCOME HOME.
I FORGOT TO SAY THAT YESTERDAY.
THEN, DOES THAT MEAN...
...THAT I AM HOME?

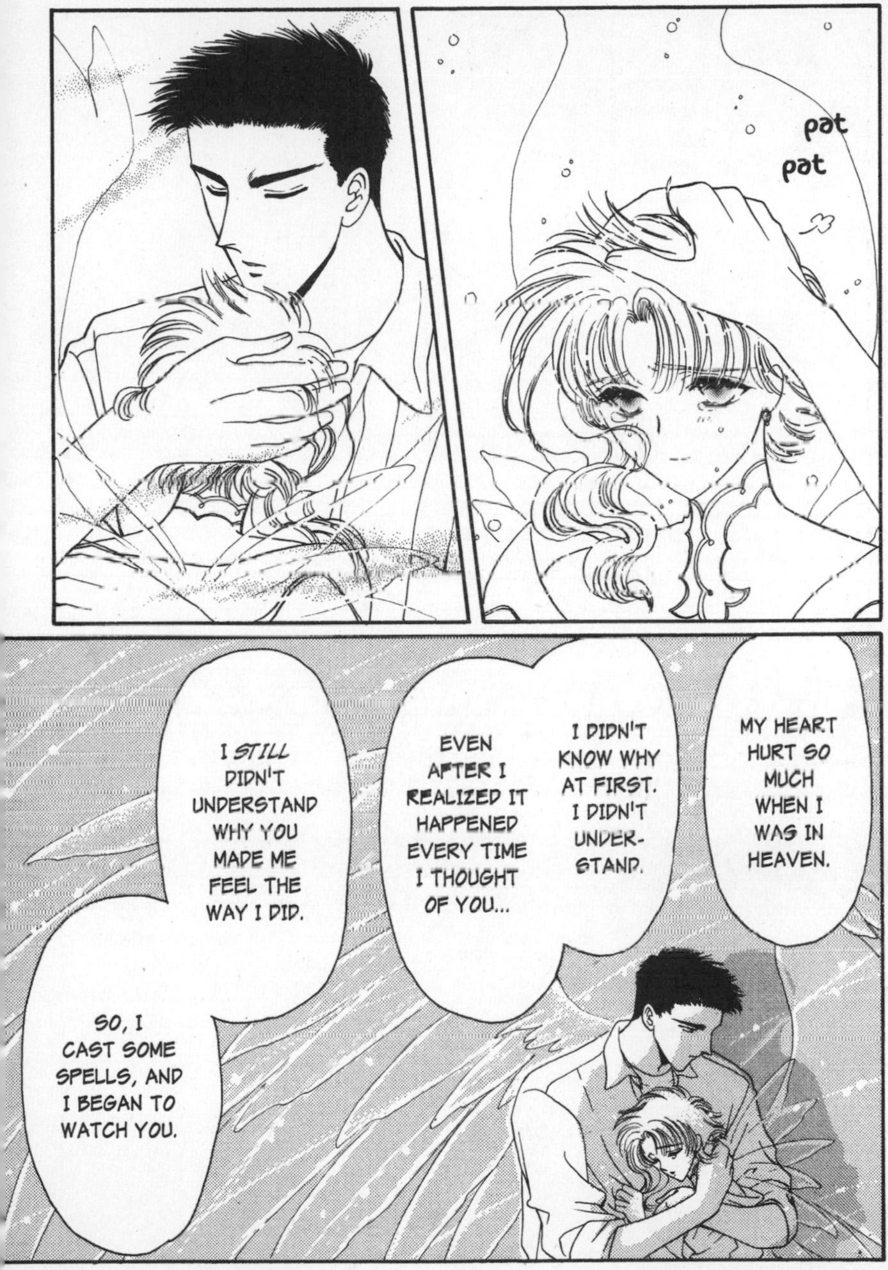
pat
pat
MY HEART HURT SO MUCH WHEN I WAS IN HEAVEN.
I DIDN'T KNOW WHY AT FIRST. I DIDN'T UNDER-STAND.
EVEN AFTER I REALIZED IT HAPPENED EVERY TIME I THOUGHT OF YOU...
I *STILL* DIDN'T UNDERSTAND WHY YOU MADE ME FEEL THE WAY I DID.
SO, I CAST SOME SPELLS, AND I BEGAN TO WATCH YOU.

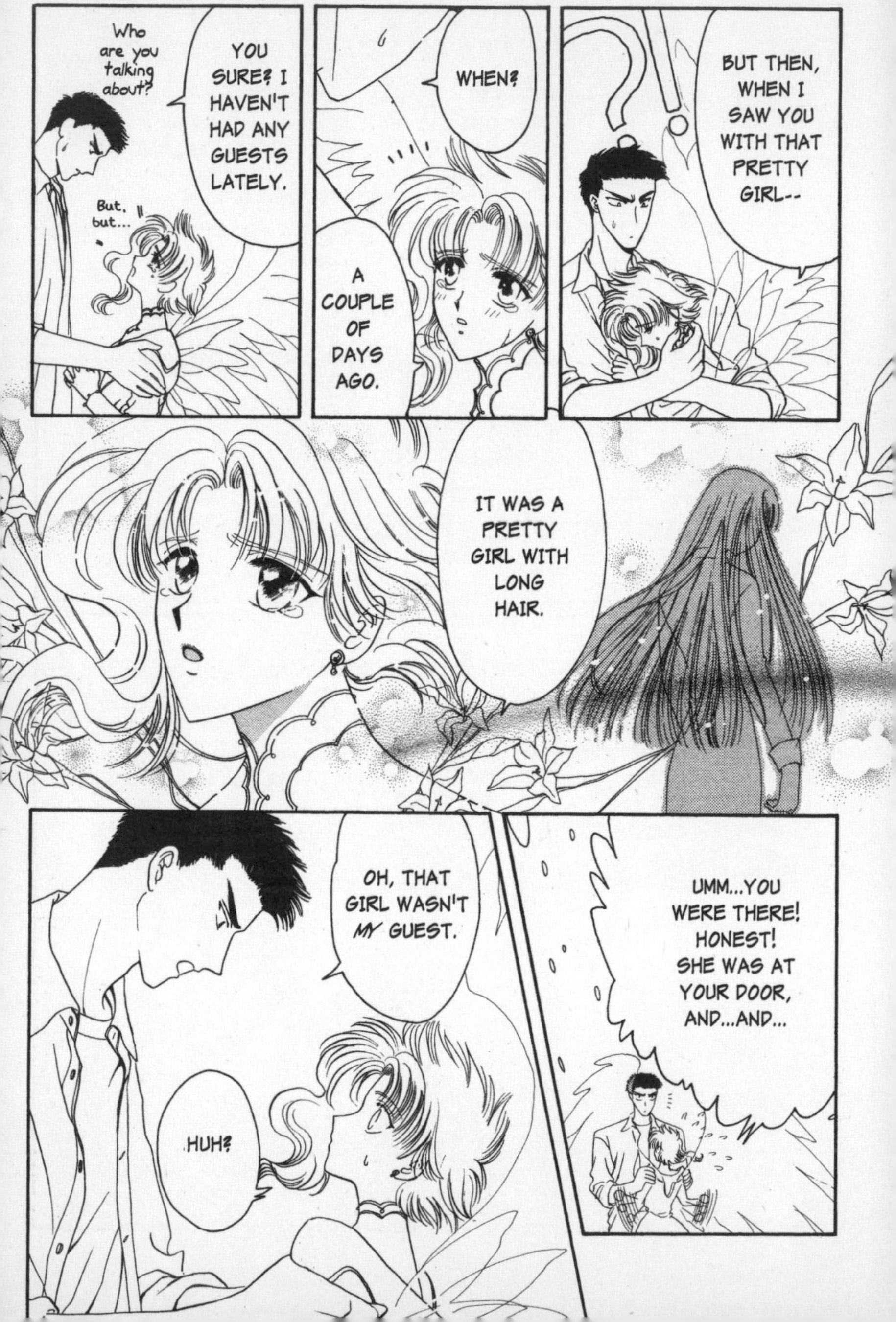
BUT THEN, WHEN I SAW YOU WITH THAT PRETTY GIRL--
WHEN?
A COUPLE OF DAYS AGO.
YOU SURE? I HAVEN'T HAD ANY GUESTS LATELY.
Who are you talking about?
But, but...
IT WAS A PRETTY GIRL WITH LONG HAIR.
UMM...YOU WERE THERE! HONEST! SHE WAS AT YOUR DOOR, AND...AND...
OH, THAT GIRL WASN'T *MY* GUEST.
HUH?

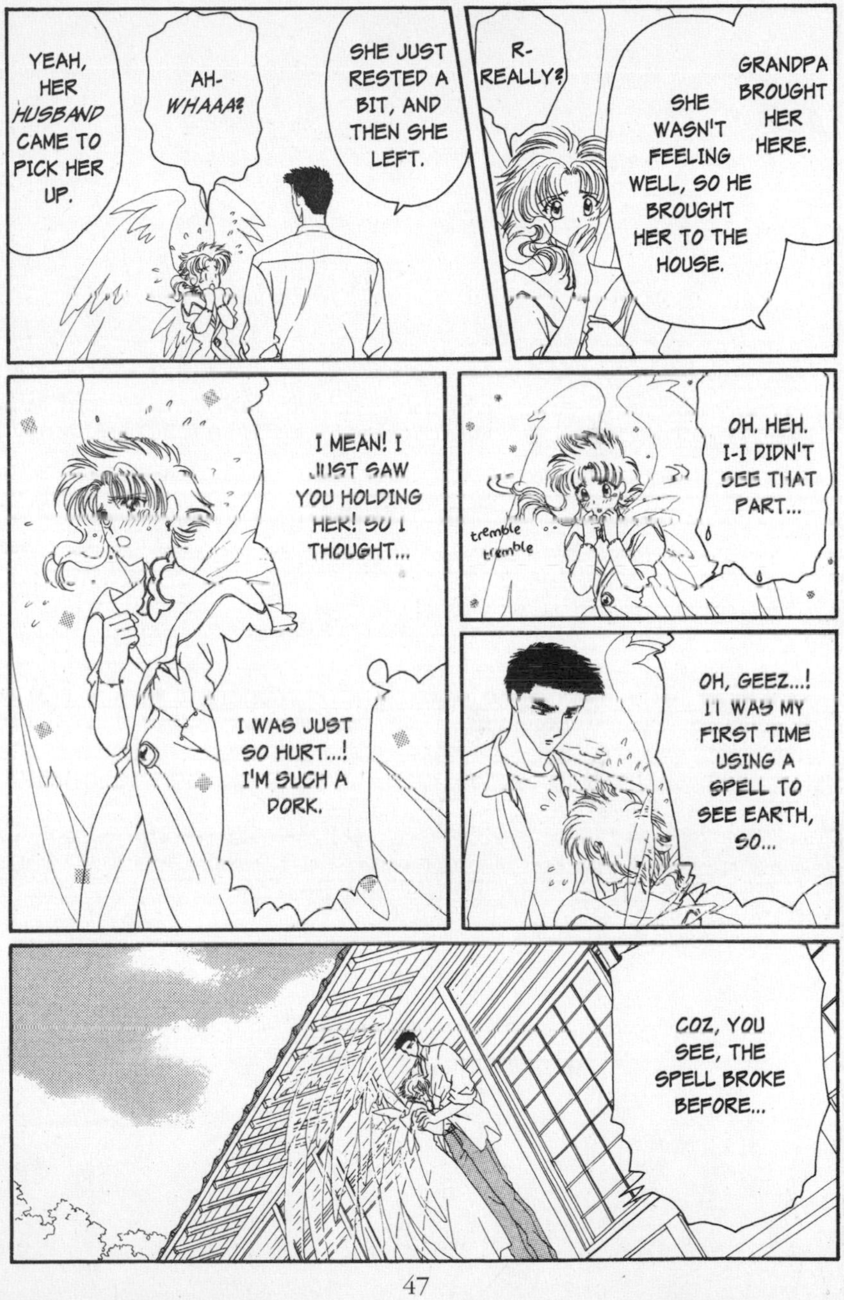
GRANDPA BROUGHT HER HERE.
SHE WASN'T FEELING WELL, SO HE BROUGHT HER TO THE HOUSE.
R-REALLY?
SHE JUST RESTED A BIT, AND THEN SHE LEFT.
AH- *WHAAA?*
YEAH, HER *HUSBAND* CAME TO PICK HER UP.
OH. HEH. I-I DIDN'T SEE THAT PART...
tremble tremble
OH, GEEZ...! IT WAS MY FIRST TIME USING A SPELL TO SEE EARTH, SO...
I MEAN! I JUST SAW YOU HOLDING HER! SO I THOUGHT...
I WAS JUST SO HURT...! I'M SUCH A DORK.
COZ, YOU SEE, THE SPELL BROKE BEFORE...

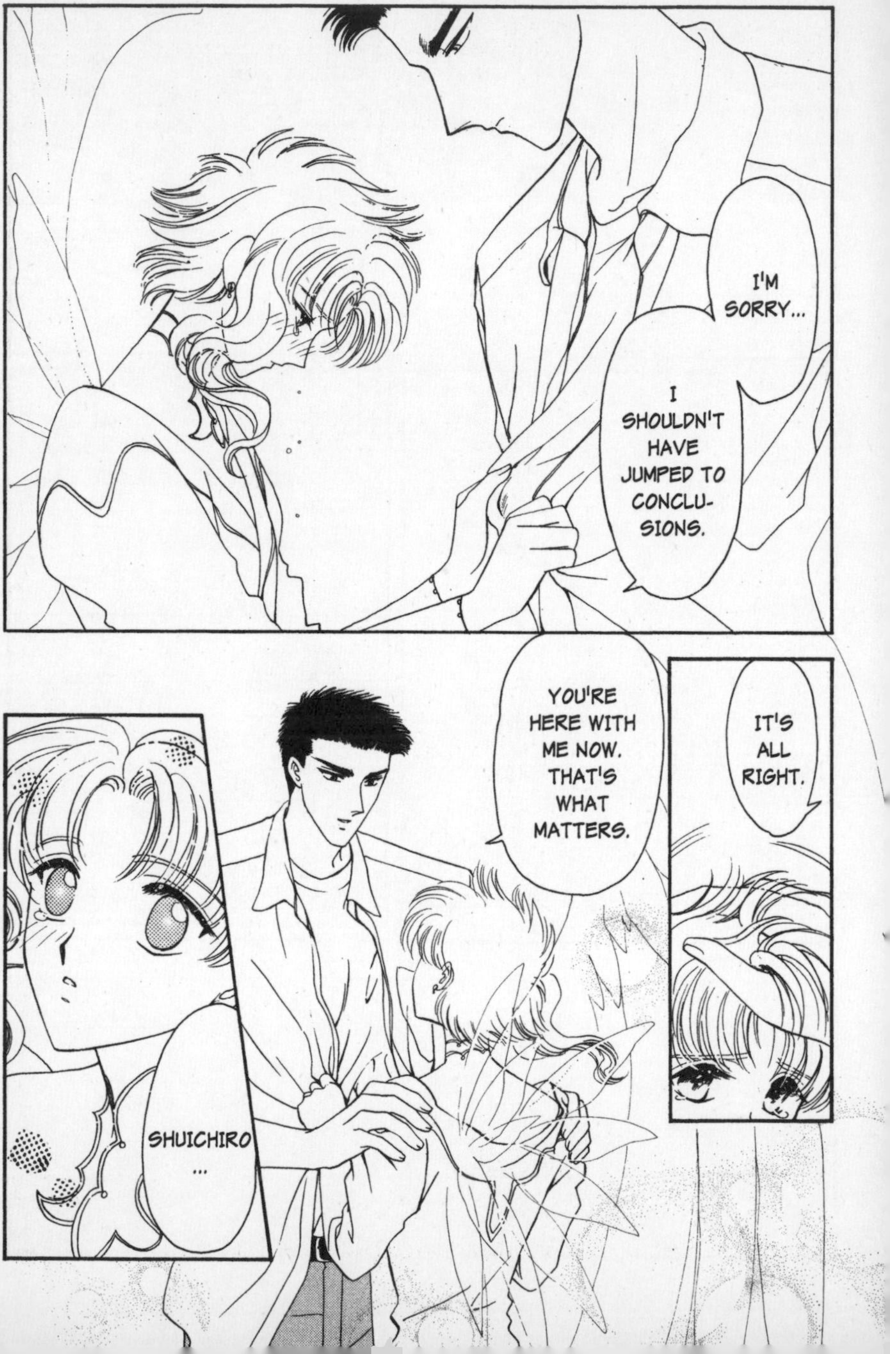
I'M SORRY...
I SHOULDN'T HAVE JUMPED TO CONCLUSIONS.
IT'S ALL RIGHT.
YOU'RE HERE WITH ME NOW. THAT'S WHAT MATTERS.
SHUICHIRO ...

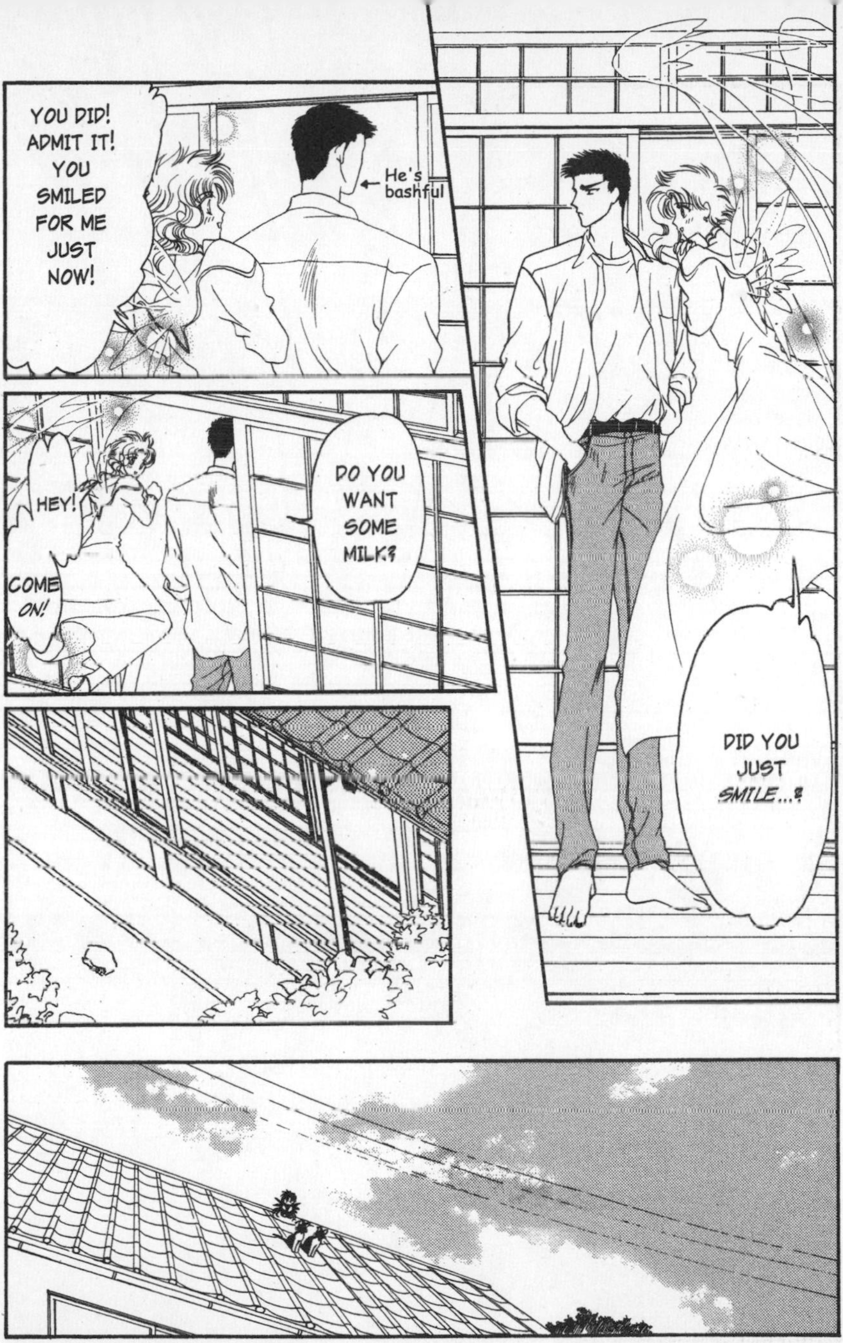
DID YOU JUST SMILE...?
YOU DID! ADMIT IT! YOU SMILED FOR ME JUST NOW!
He's bashful
DO YOU WANT SOME MILK?
HEY!
COME ON!

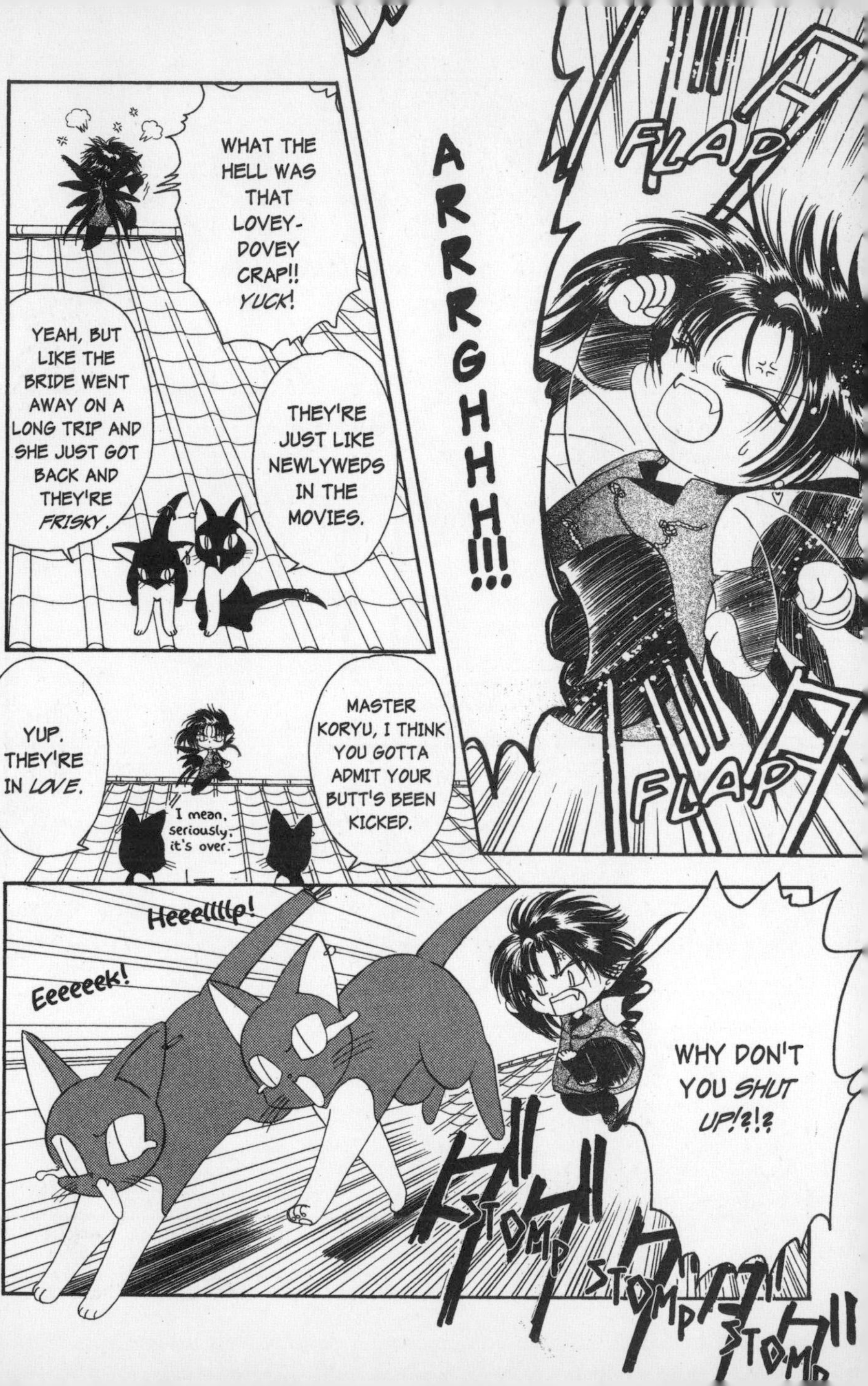
FLAP
ARRRGHHH!!!
FLAP
WHAT THE HELL WAS THAT LOVEY-DOVEY CRAP!! *YUCK*!
THEY'RE JUST LIKE NEWLYWEDS IN THE MOVIES.
YEAH, BUT LIKE THE BRIDE WENT AWAY ON A LONG TRIP AND SHE JUST GOT BACK AND THEY'RE *FRISKY*.
MASTER KORYU, I THINK YOU GOTTA ADMIT YOUR BUTT'S BEEN KICKED.
I mean, seriously, it's over.
YUP. THEY'RE IN *LOVE*.
WHY DON'T YOU *SHUT UP*!?!?
Heeellllp!
Eeeeeek!
STOMP STOMP STOMP

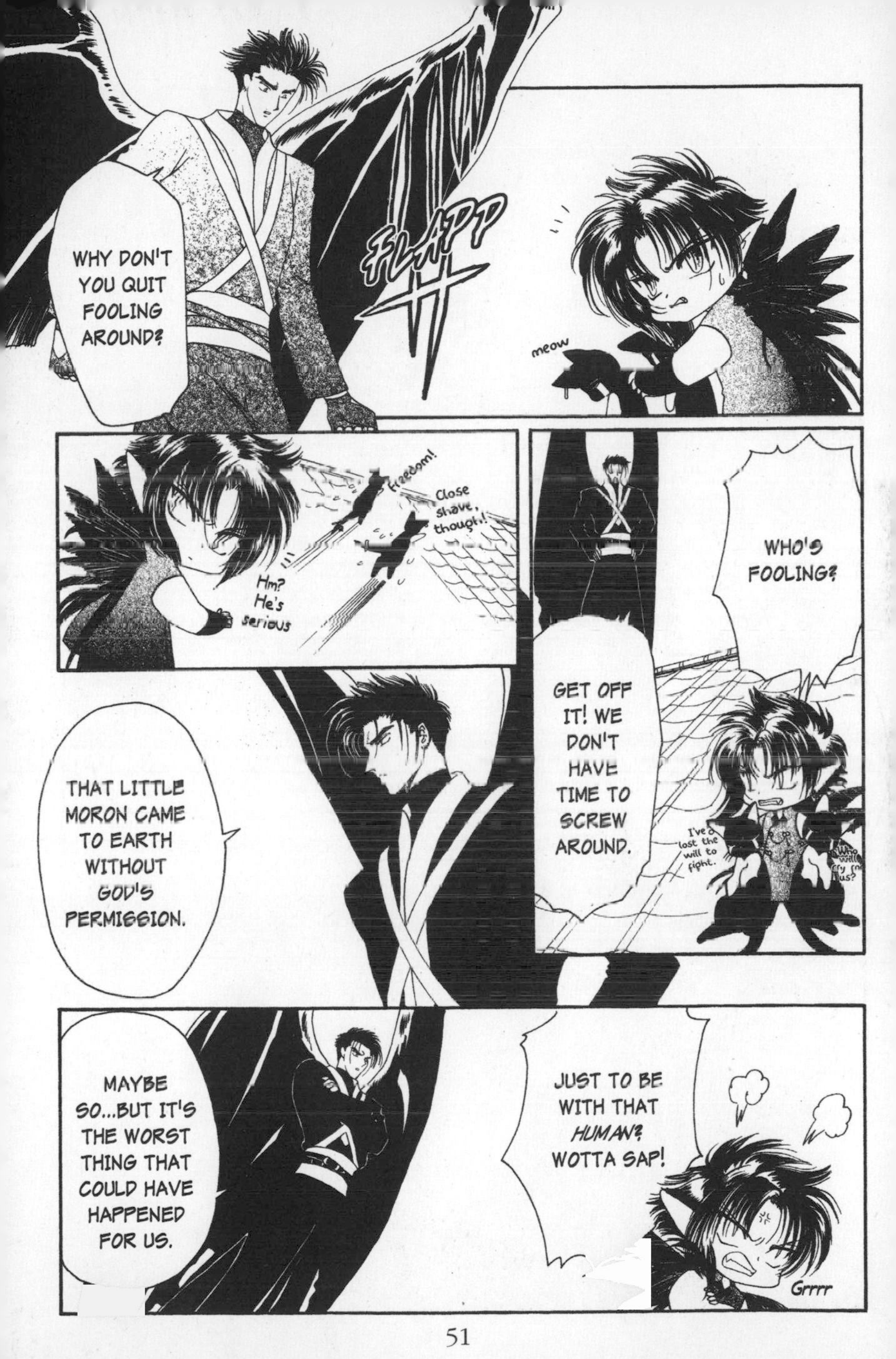
meow
FLAPP
WHY DON'T YOU QUIT FOOLING AROUND?
WHO'S FOOLING?
GET OFF IT! WE DON'T HAVE TIME TO SCREW AROUND.
I've lost the will to fight.
Freedom!
Close shave, though!
Hm? He's serious
THAT LITTLE MORON CAME TO EARTH WITHOUT GOD'S PERMISSION.
JUST TO BE WITH THAT *HUMAN*? WOTTA SAP!
Grrrr
MAYBE SO...BUT IT'S THE WORST THING THAT COULD HAVE HAPPENED FOR US.

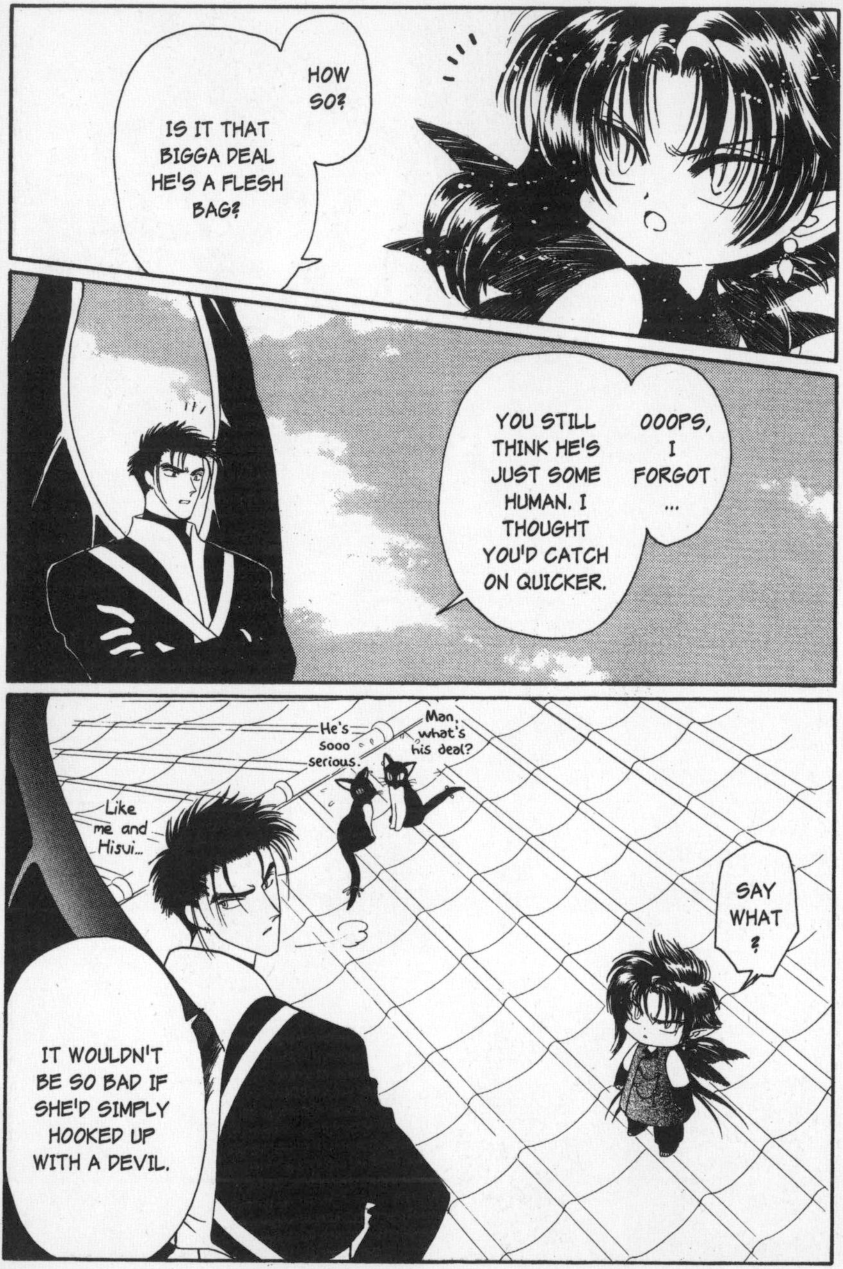
HOW SO?
IS IT THAT BIGGA DEAL HE'S A FLESH BAG?
OOOPS, I FORGOT ...
YOU STILL THINK HE'S JUST SOME HUMAN. I THOUGHT YOU'D CATCH ON QUICKER.
SAY WHAT?
Man, what's his deal?
He's sooo serious.
Like me and Hisui...
IT WOULDN'T BE SO BAD IF SHE'D SIMPLY HOOKED UP WITH A DEVIL.

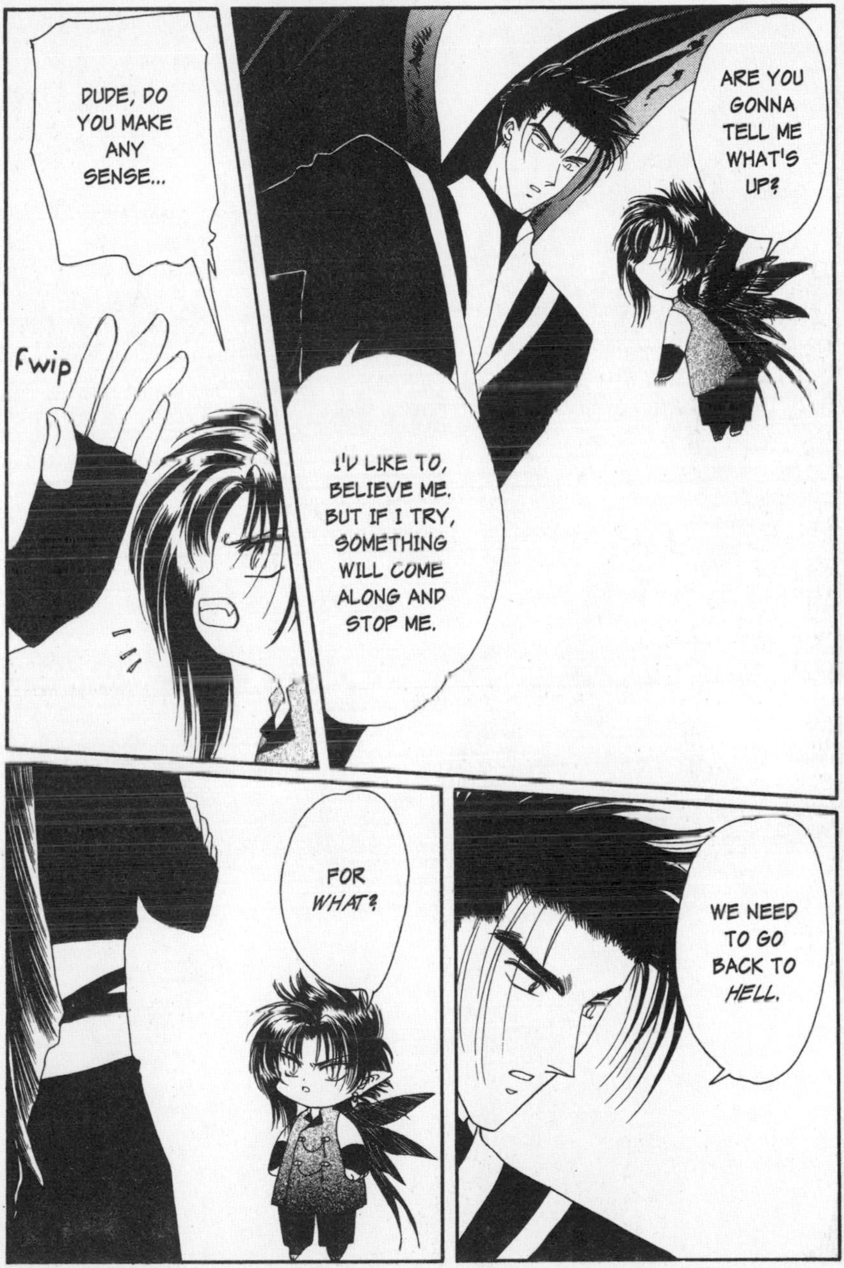
ARE YOU GONNA TELL ME WHAT'S UP?
I'D LIKE TO, BELIEVE ME. BUT IF I TRY, SOMETHING WILL COME ALONG AND STOP ME.
DUDE, DO YOU MAKE ANY SENSE...
fwip
WE NEED TO GO BACK TO *HELL*.
FOR *WHAT?*

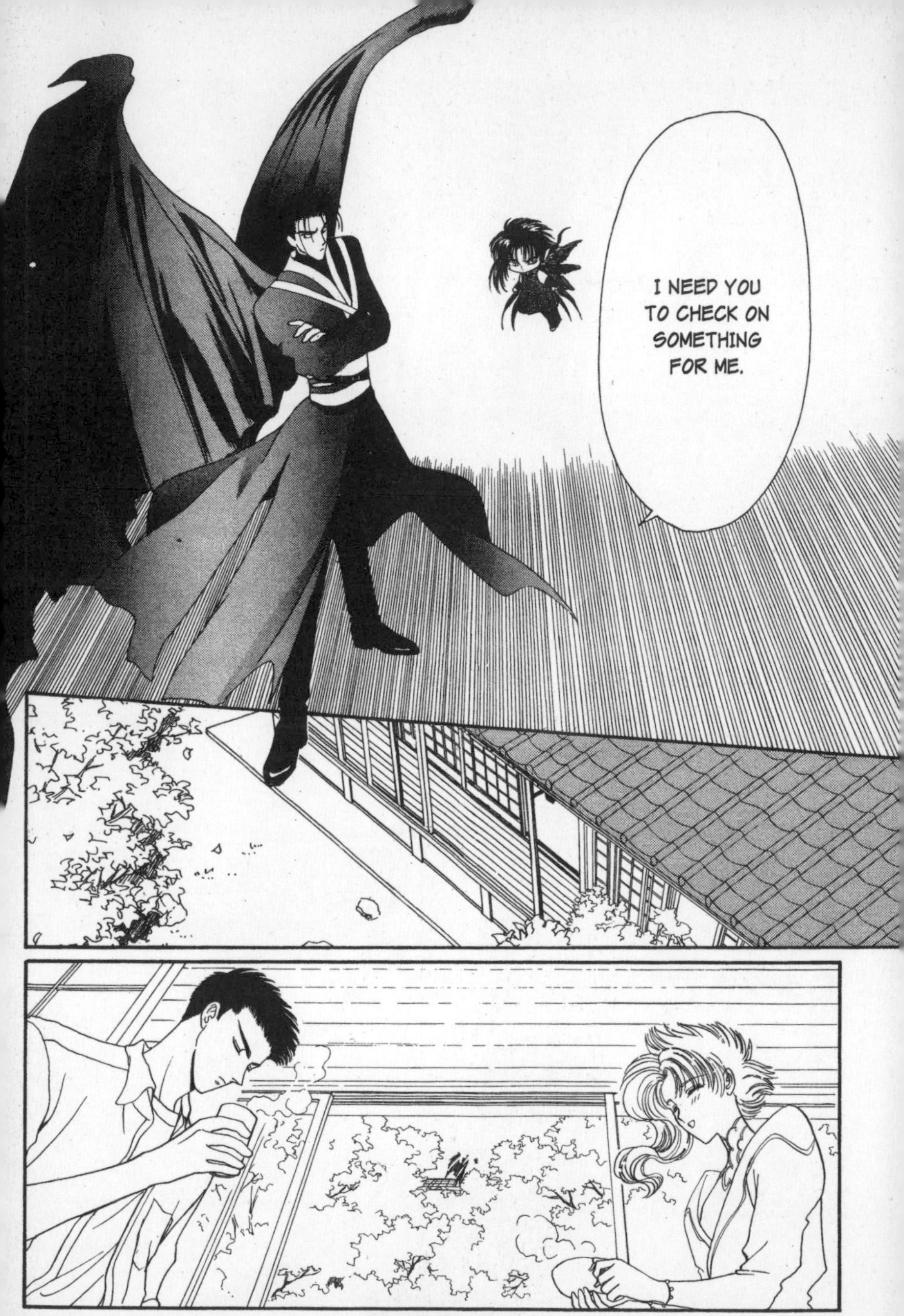
I NEED YOU TO CHECK ON SOMETHING FOR ME.

END

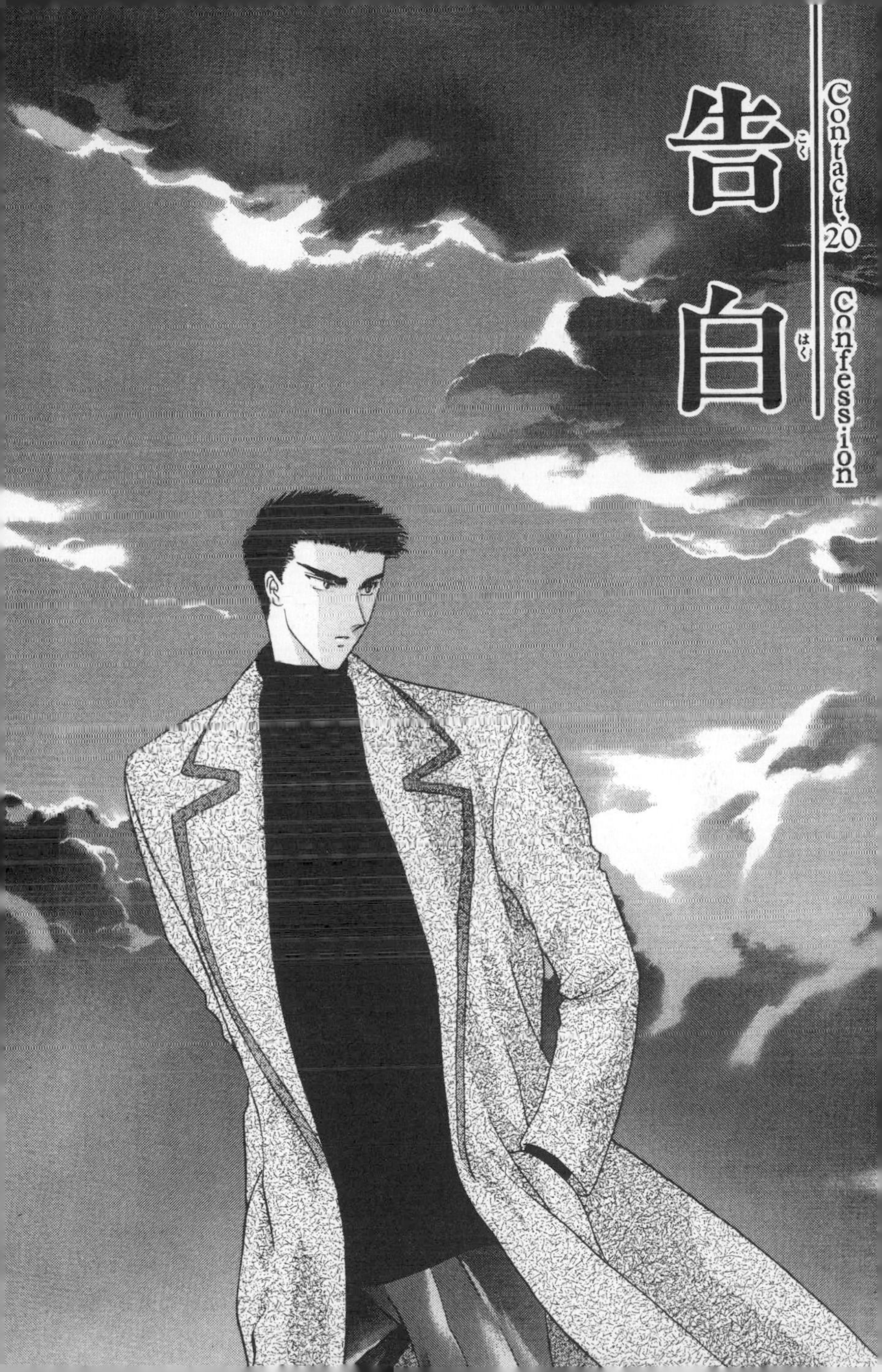
告白
こく
はく
Contact.20 Confession

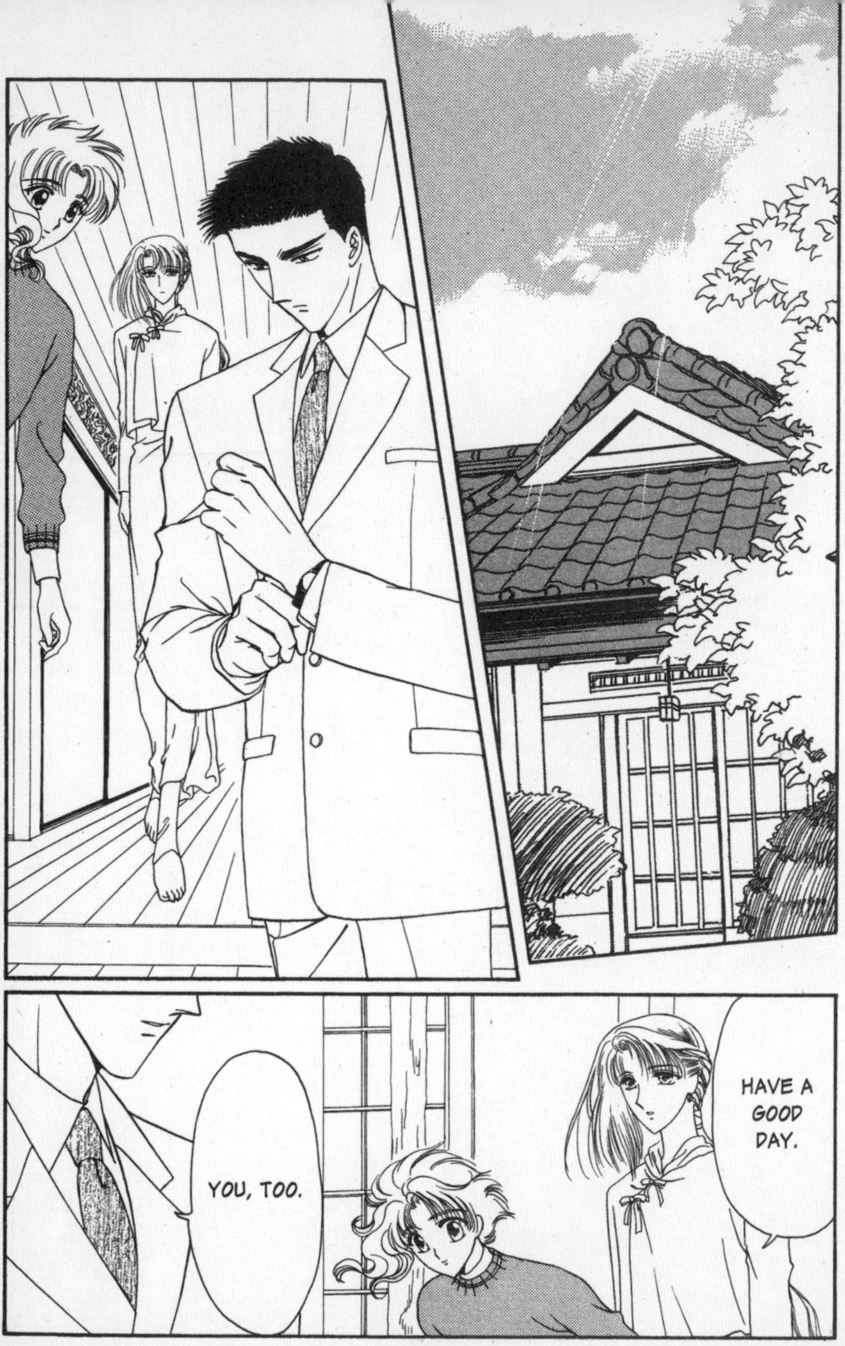
HAVE A GOOD DAY.
YOU, TOO.

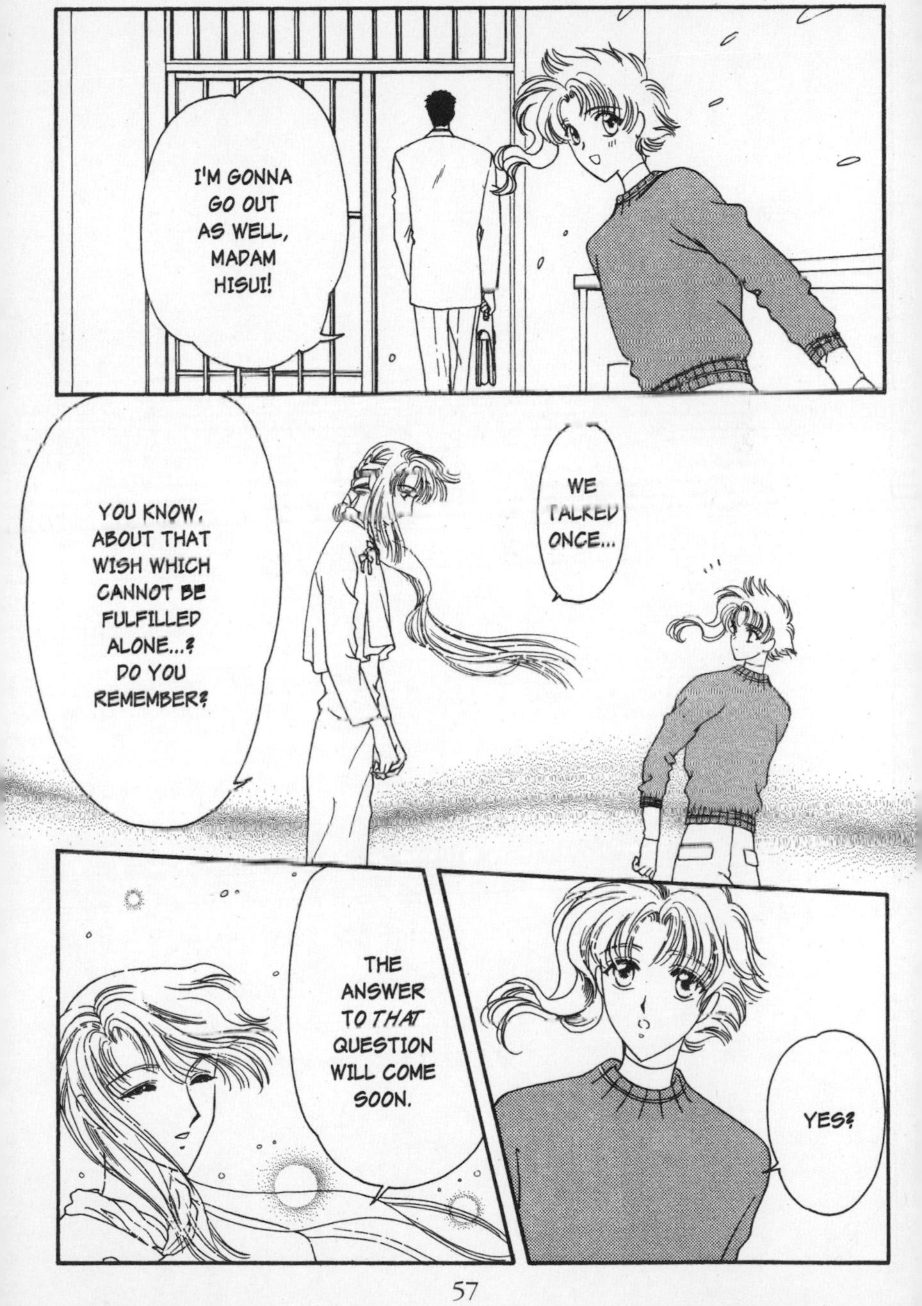
I'M GONNA GO OUT AS WELL, MADAM HISUI!
WE TALKED ONCE...
YOU KNOW, ABOUT THAT WISH WHICH CANNOT BE FULFILLED ALONE...? DO YOU REMEMBER?
YES?
THE ANSWER TO *THAT* QUESTION WILL COME SOON.

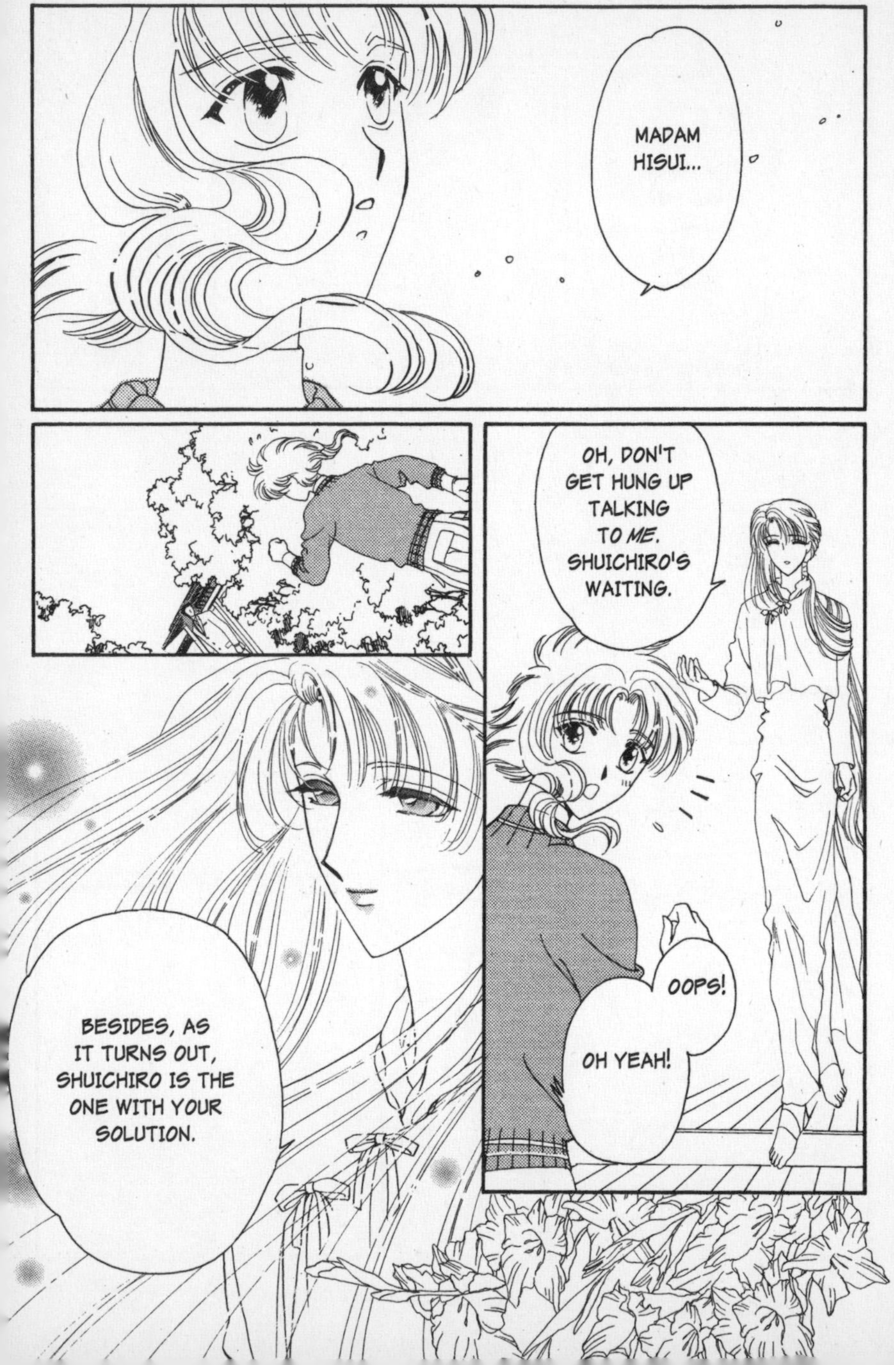
MADAM HISUI...
OH, DON'T GET HUNG UP TALKING TO *ME*. SHUICHIRO'S WAITING.
OOPS!
OH YEAH!
BESIDES, AS IT TURNS OUT, SHUICHIRO IS THE ONE WITH YOUR SOLUTION.

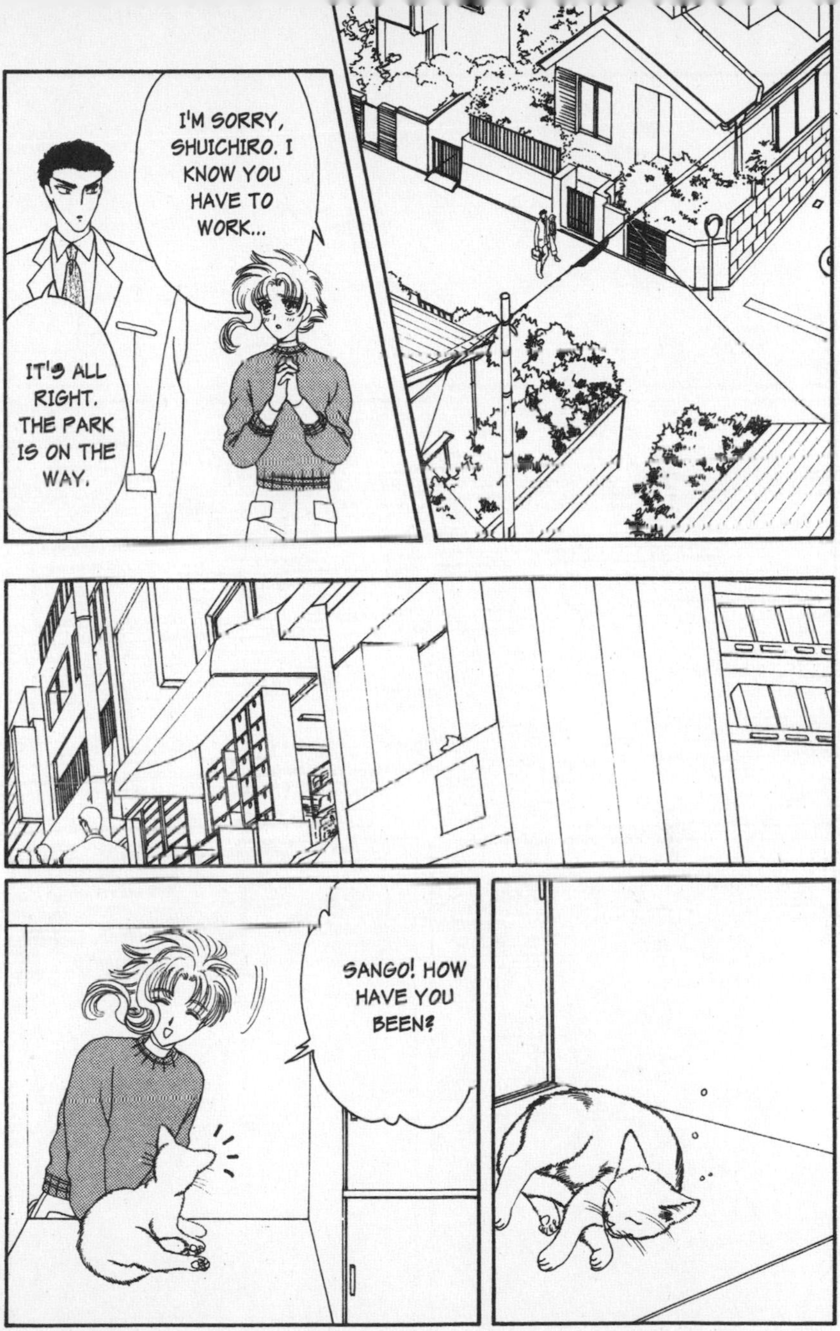
I'M SORRY, SHUICHIRO. I KNOW YOU HAVE TO WORK...
IT'S ALL RIGHT. THE PARK IS ON THE WAY.
SANGO! HOW HAVE YOU BEEN?

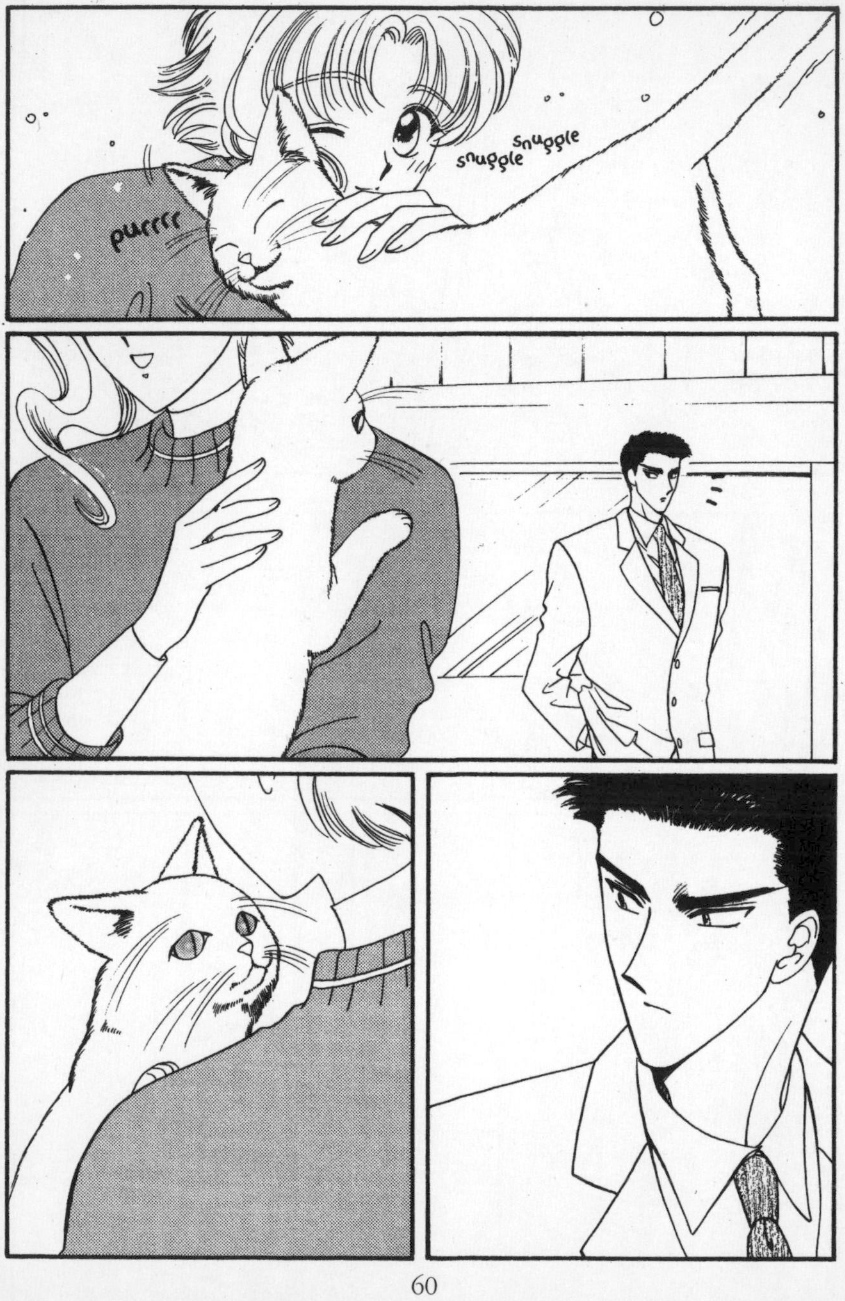
snuggle snuggle
purrrr

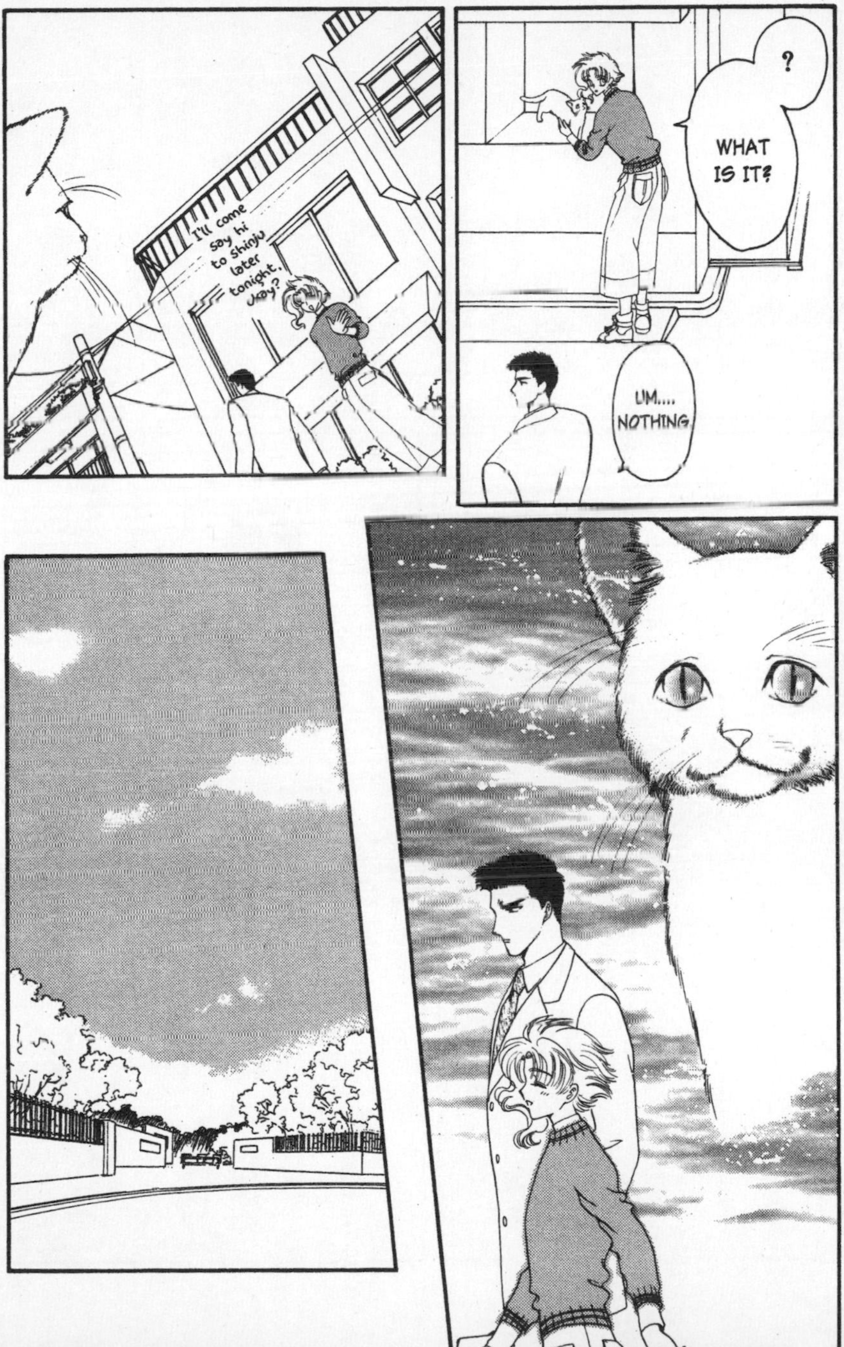
?
WHAT IS IT?
UM.... NOTHING.
I'll come say hi to Shinju later tonight, okay?

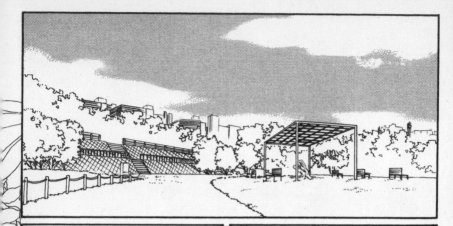

I BET YOU HE'S THINKING OF HOTARU.

62

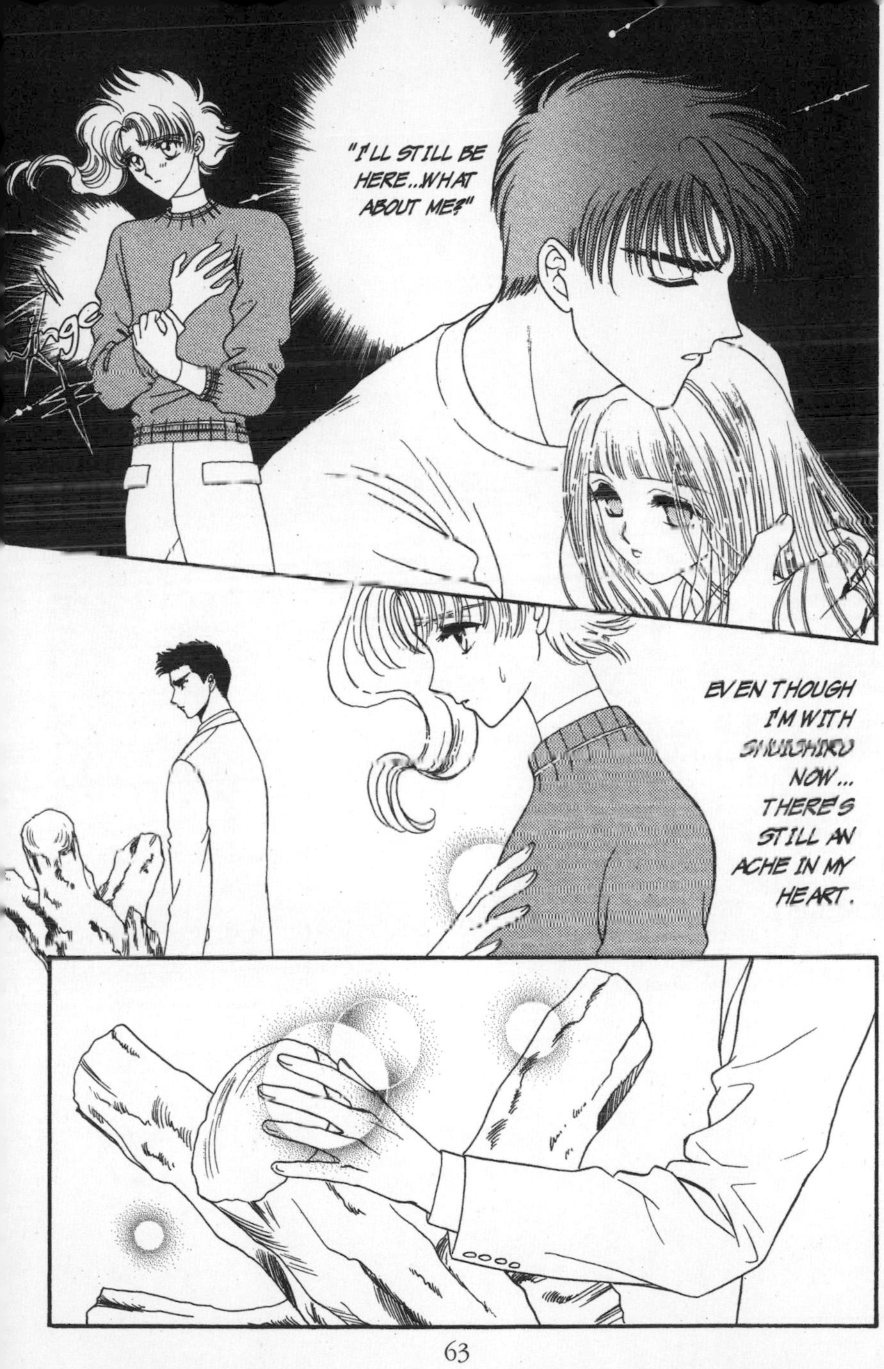
"I'LL STILL BE HERE...WHAT ABOUT ME?"
winge
EVEN THOUGH I'M WITH SHUICHIRO NOW... THERE'S STILL AN ACHE IN MY HEART.

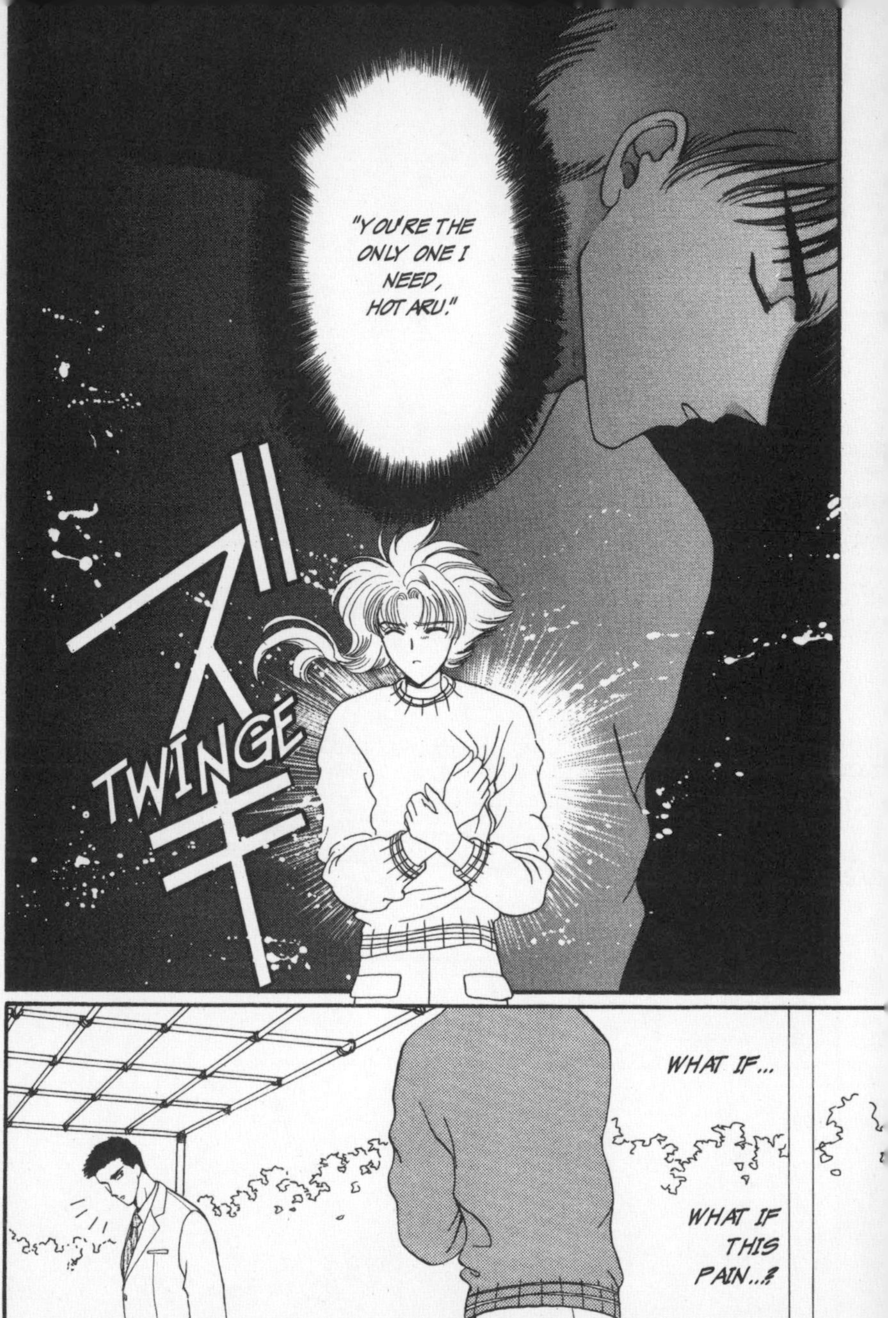
"YOU'RE THE ONLY ONE I NEED, HOTARU."
TWINGE
WHAT IF...
WHAT IF THIS PAIN...?

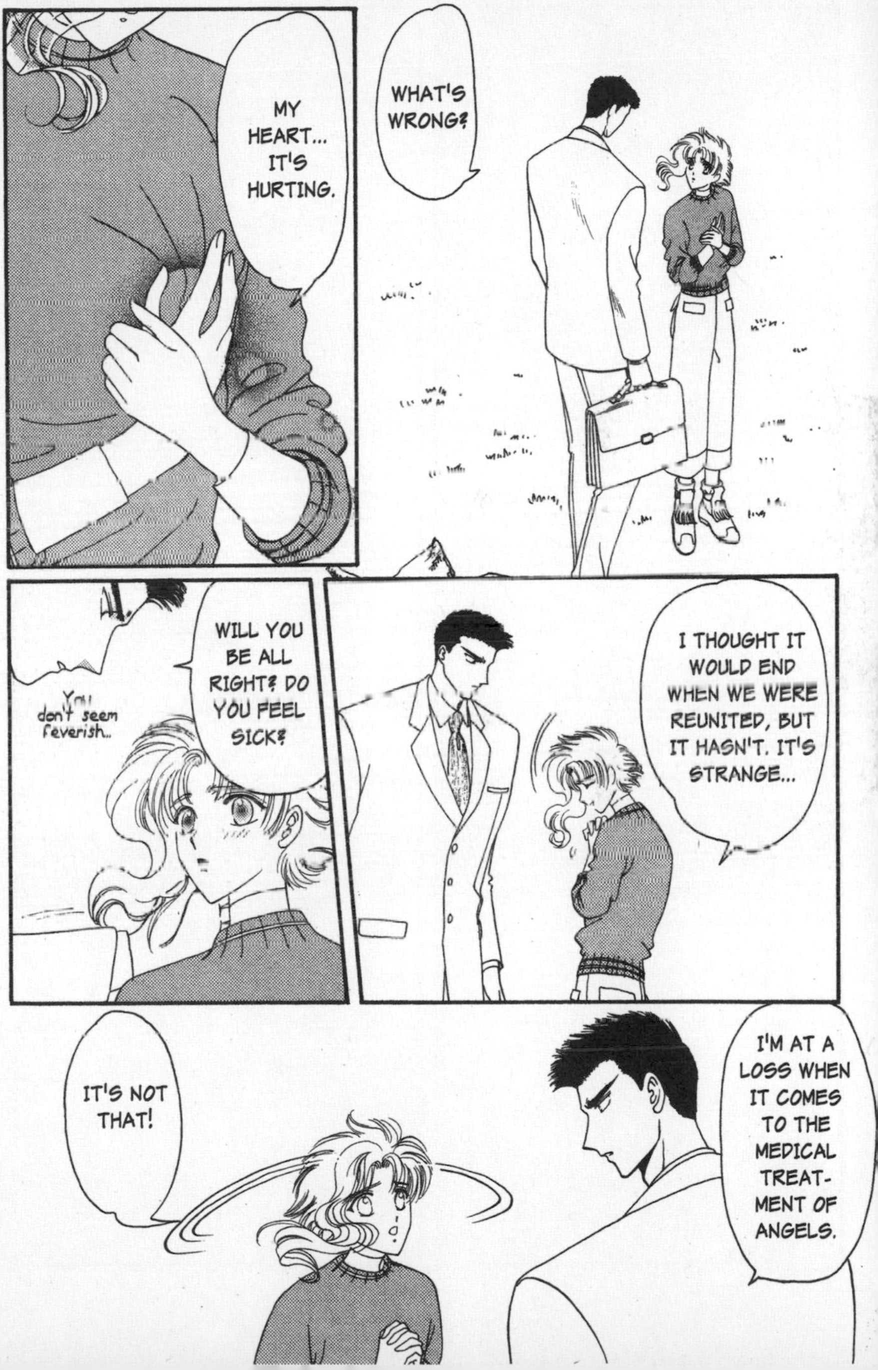
WHAT'S WRONG?
MY HEART... IT'S HURTING.
I THOUGHT IT WOULD END WHEN WE WERE REUNITED, BUT IT HASN'T. IT'S STRANGE...
WILL YOU BE ALL RIGHT? DO YOU FEEL SICK?
You don't seem feverish...
I'M AT A LOSS WHEN IT COMES TO THE MEDICAL TREAT-MENT OF ANGELS.
IT'S NOT THAT!

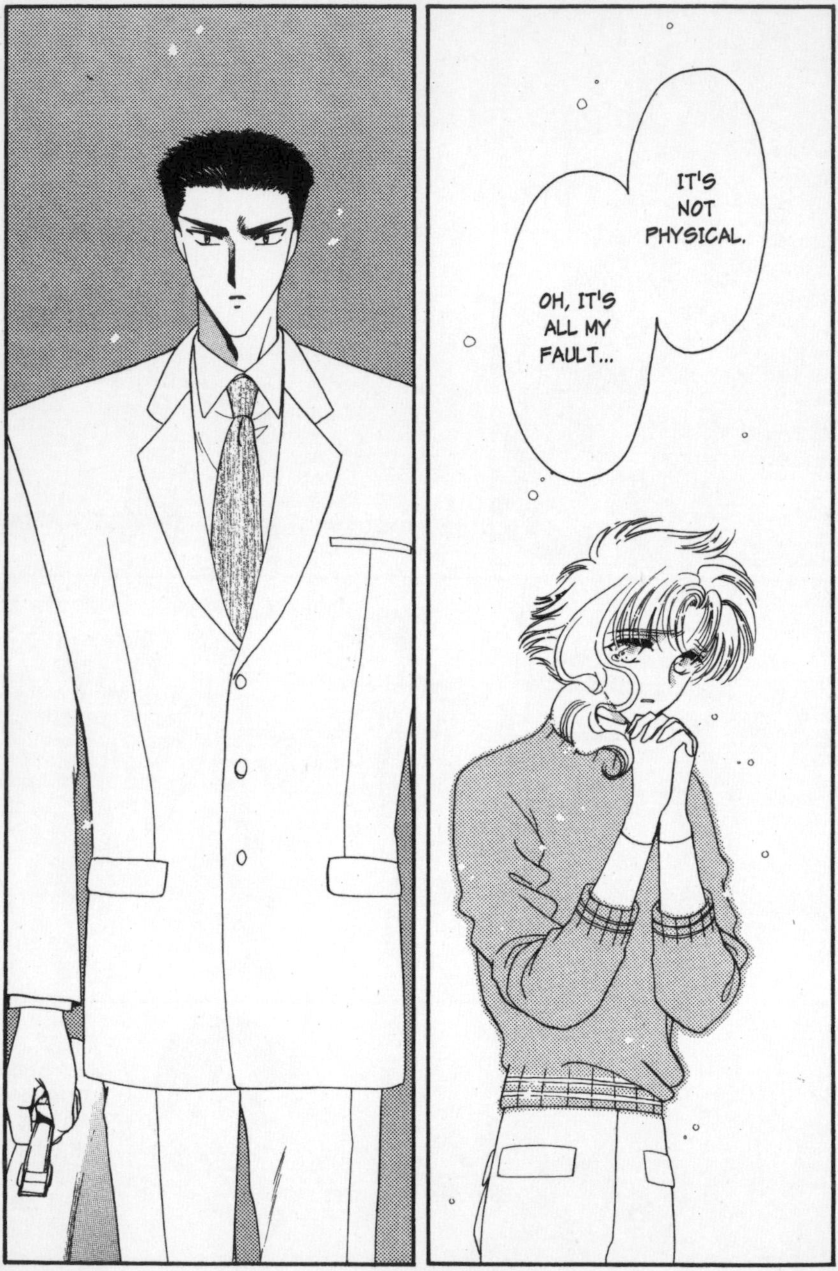
IT'S NOT PHYSICAL.
OH, IT'S ALL MY FAULT...

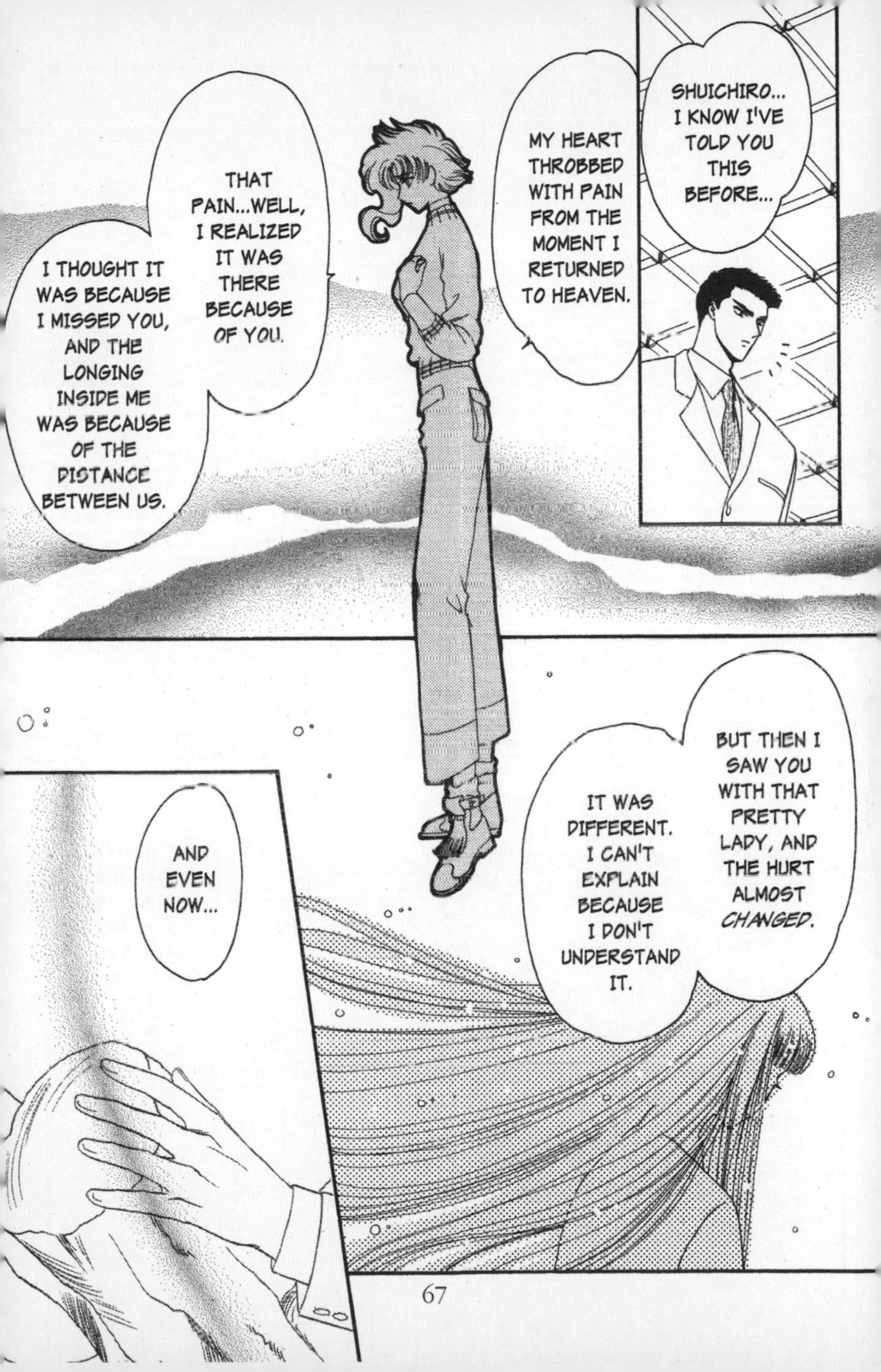
SHUICHIRO... I KNOW I'VE TOLD YOU THIS BEFORE...
MY HEART THROBBED WITH PAIN FROM THE MOMENT I RETURNED TO HEAVEN.
THAT PAIN...WELL, I REALIZED IT WAS THERE BECAUSE OF YOU.
I THOUGHT IT WAS BECAUSE I MISSED YOU, AND THE LONGING INSIDE ME WAS BECAUSE OF THE DISTANCE BETWEEN US.
BUT THEN I SAW YOU WITH THAT PRETTY LADY, AND THE HURT ALMOST *CHANGED*.
IT WAS DIFFERENT. I CAN'T EXPLAIN BECAUSE I DON'T UNDERSTAND IT.
AND EVEN NOW...

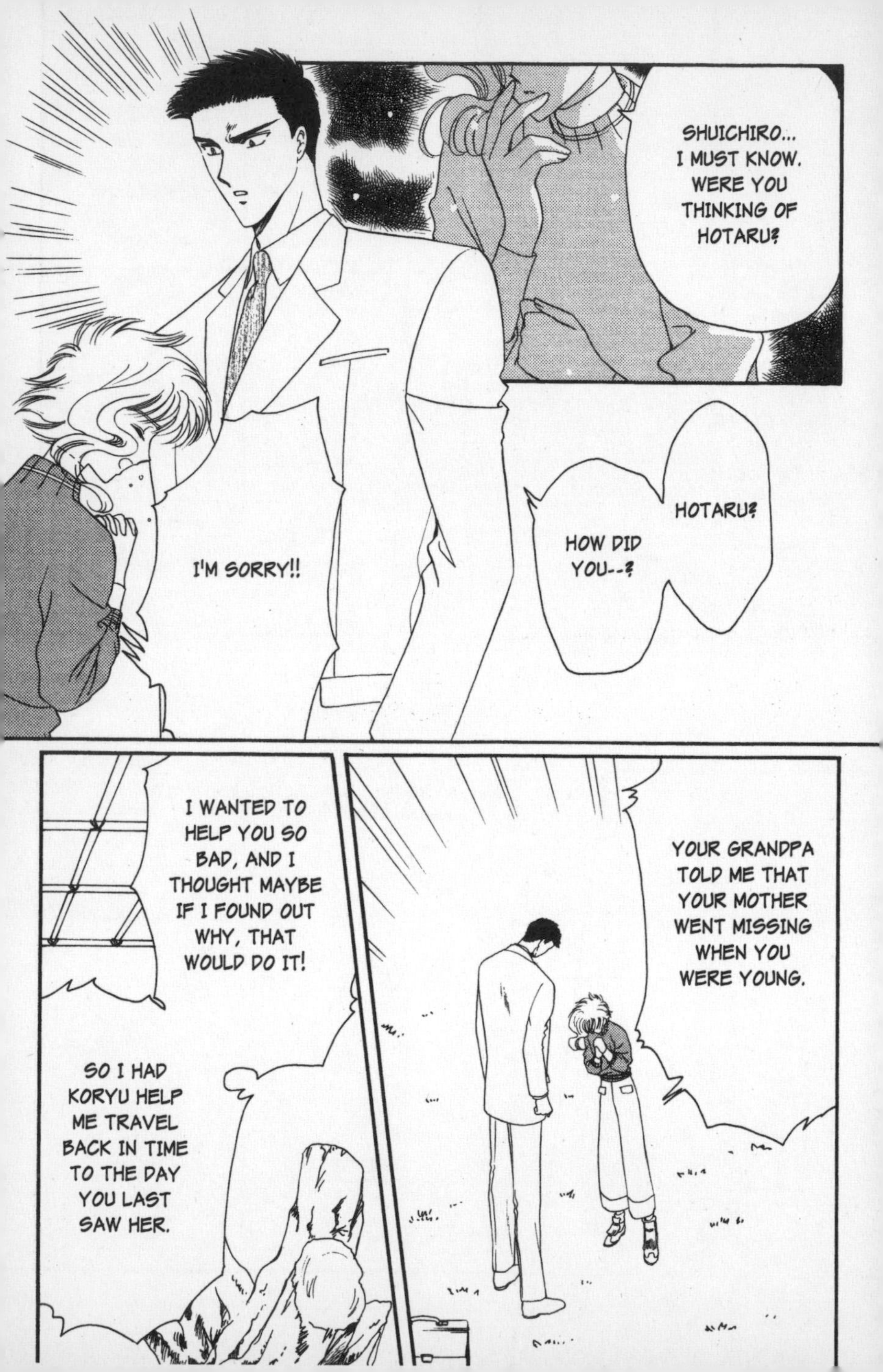
SHUICHIRO... I MUST KNOW. WERE YOU THINKING OF HOTARU?
HOTARU? HOW DID YOU--?
I'M SORRY!!
YOUR GRANDPA TOLD ME THAT YOUR MOTHER WENT MISSING WHEN YOU WERE YOUNG.
I WANTED TO HELP YOU SO BAD, AND I THOUGHT MAYBE IF I FOUND OUT WHY, THAT WOULD DO IT!
SO I HAD KORYU HELP ME TRAVEL BACK IN TIME TO THE DAY YOU LAST SAW HER.

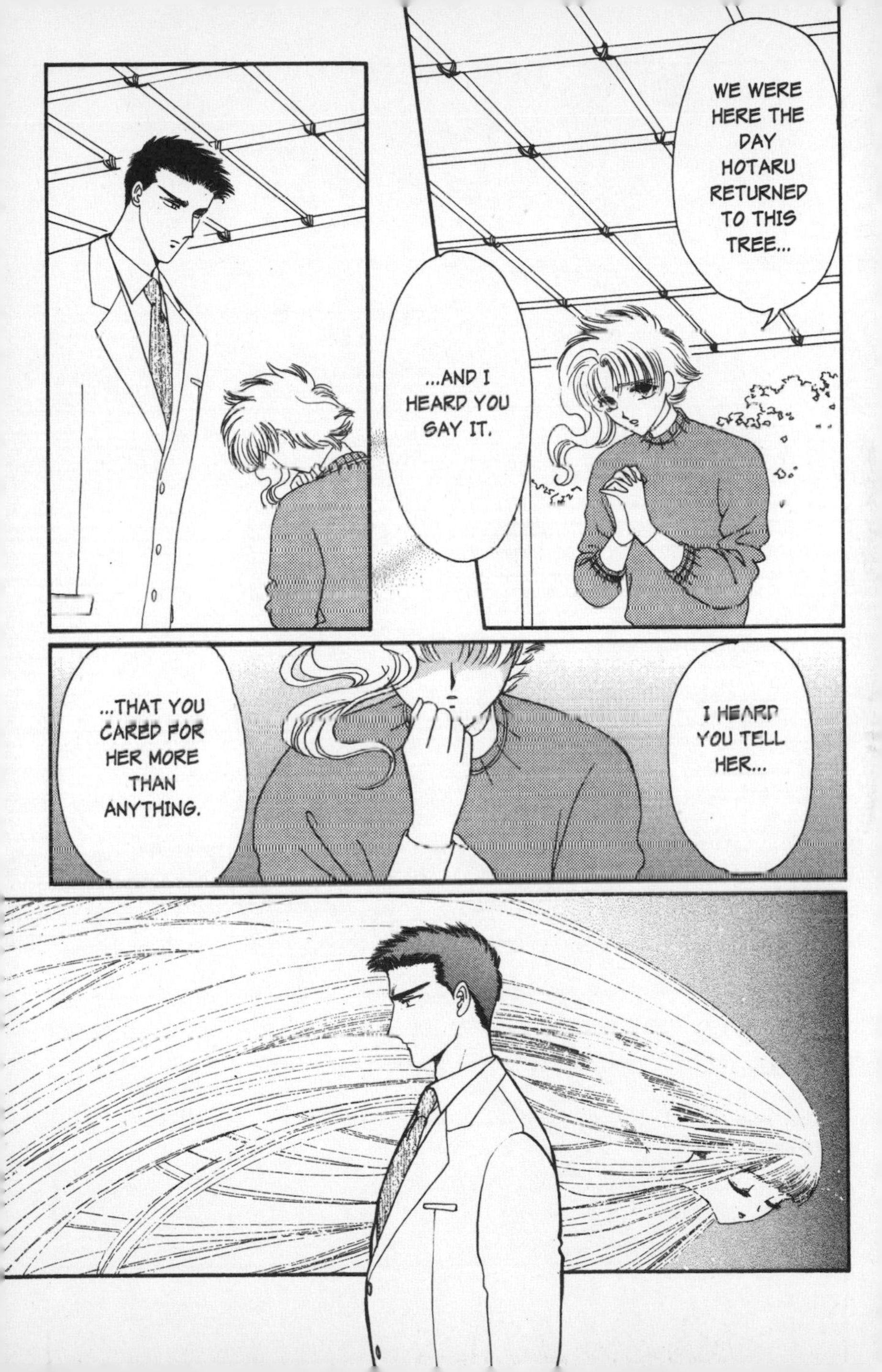
WE WERE HERE THE DAY HOTARU RETURNED TO THIS TREE...
...AND I HEARD YOU SAY IT.
I HEARD YOU TELL HER...
...THAT YOU CARED FOR HER MORE THAN ANYTHING.

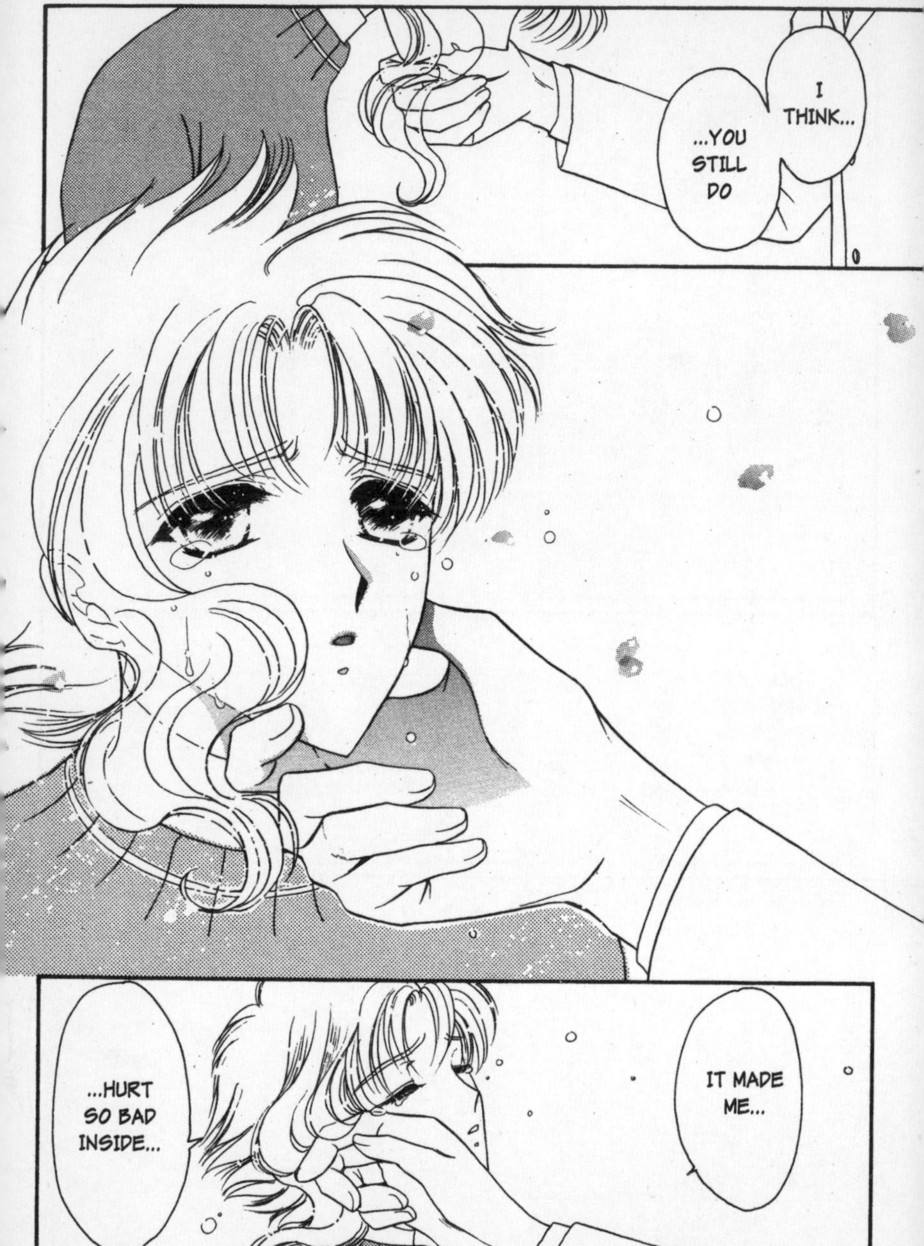
I THINK...
...YOU STILL DO
IT MADE ME...
...HURT SO BAD INSIDE...

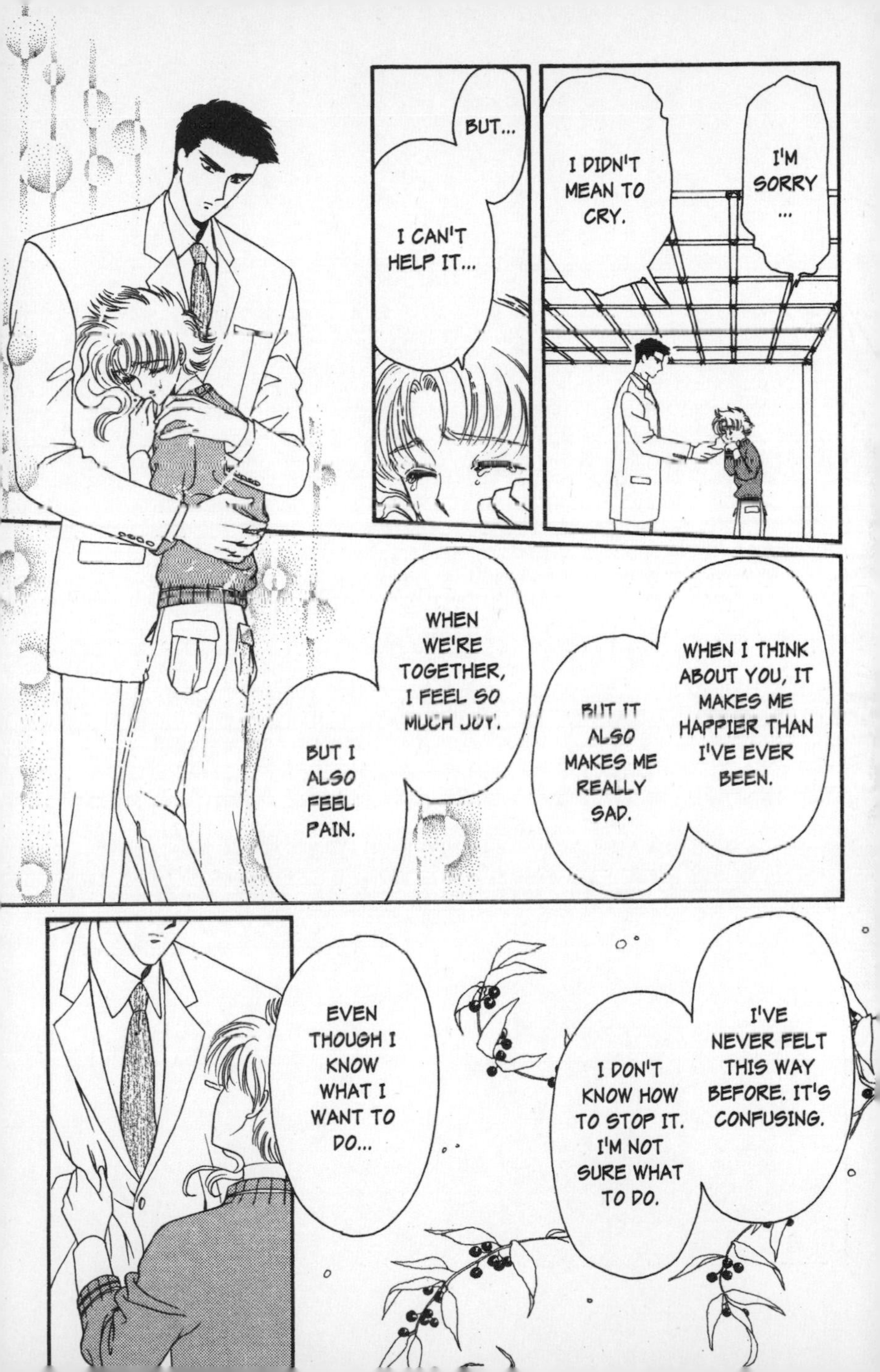
I'M SORRY ...
I DIDN'T MEAN TO CRY.
BUT...
I CAN'T HELP IT...
WHEN I THINK ABOUT YOU, IT MAKES ME HAPPIER THAN I'VE EVER BEEN.
BUT IT ALSO MAKES ME REALLY SAD.
WHEN WE'RE TOGETHER, I FEEL SO MUCH JOY.
BUT I ALSO FEEL PAIN.
I'VE NEVER FELT THIS WAY BEFORE. IT'S CONFUSING.
I DON'T KNOW HOW TO STOP IT. I'M NOT SURE WHAT TO DO.
EVEN THOUGH I KNOW WHAT I WANT TO DO...

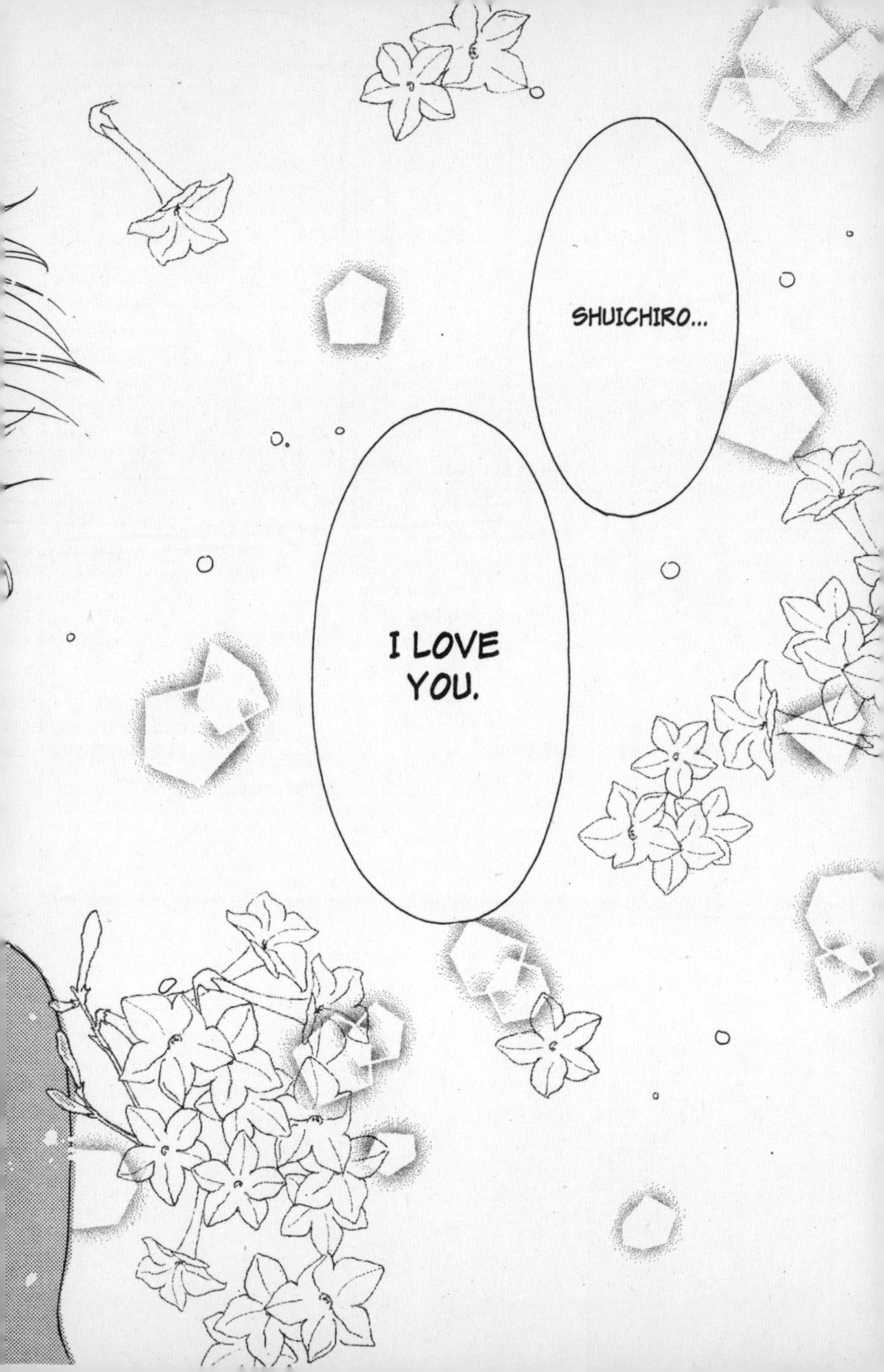
SHUICHIRO...
I LOVE YOU.

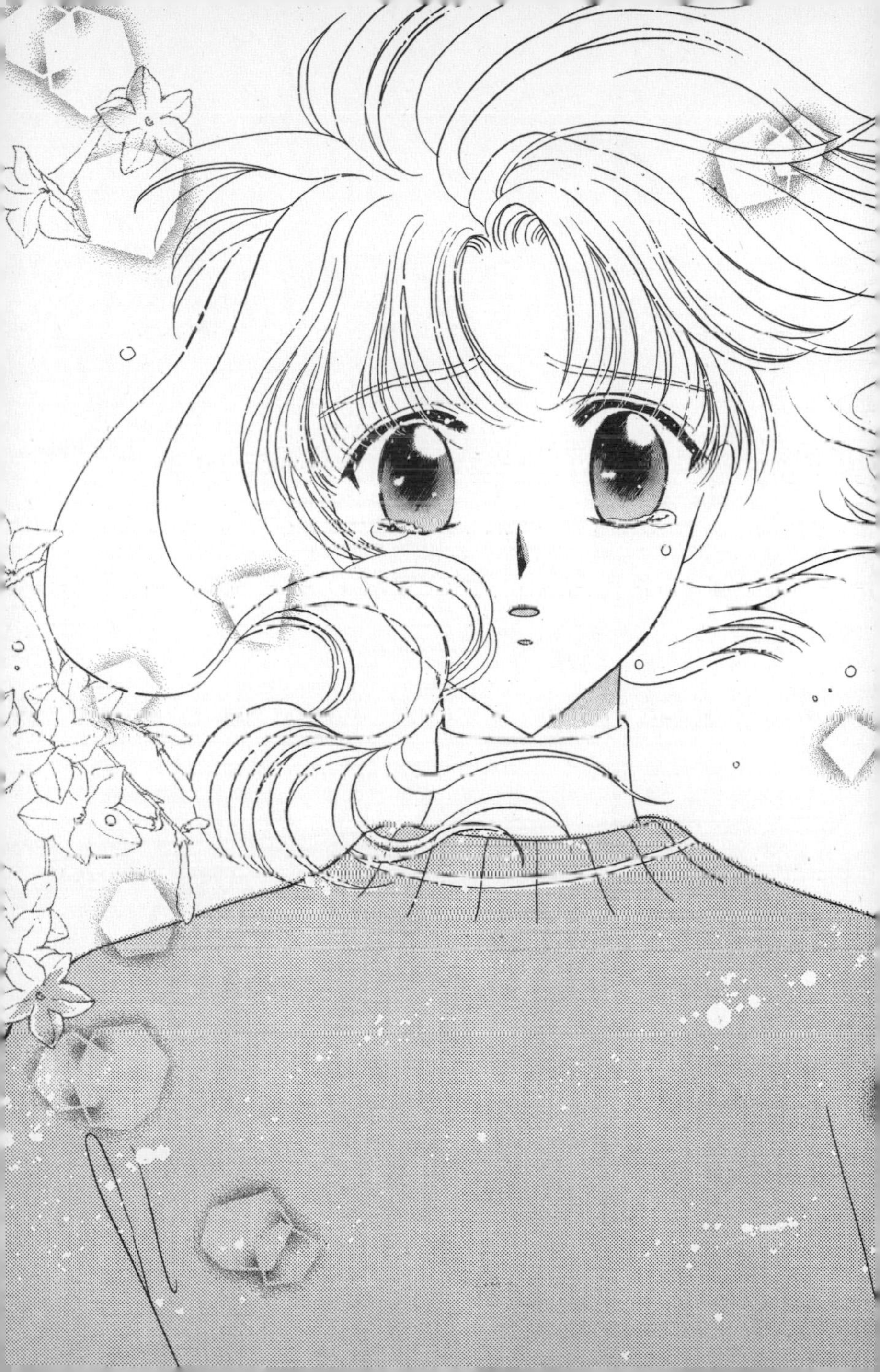

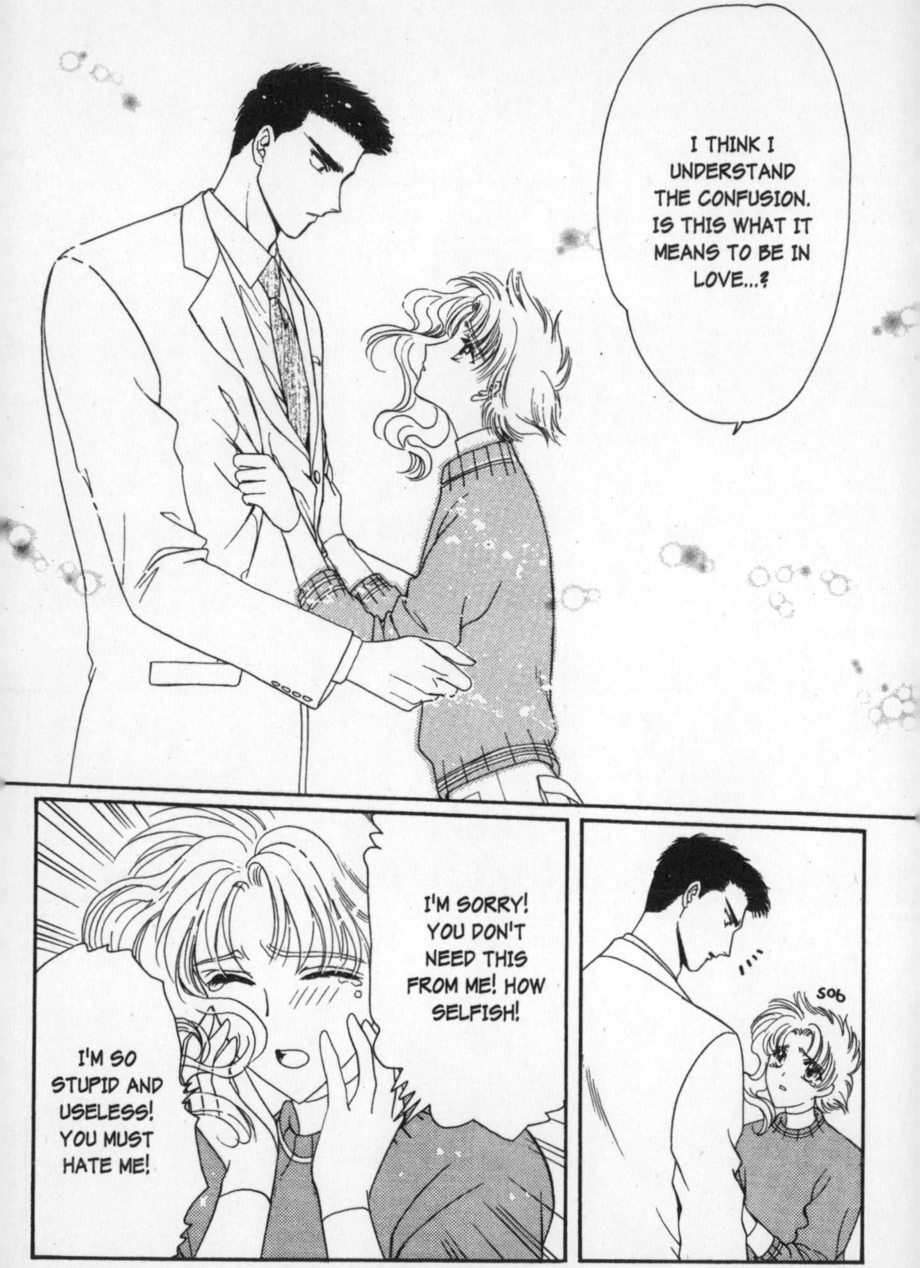
I THINK I UNDERSTAND THE CONFUSION. IS THIS WHAT IT MEANS TO BE IN LOVE...?
SOB
I'M SORRY! YOU DON'T NEED THIS FROM ME! HOW SELFISH!
I'M SO STUPID AND USELESS! YOU MUST HATE ME!

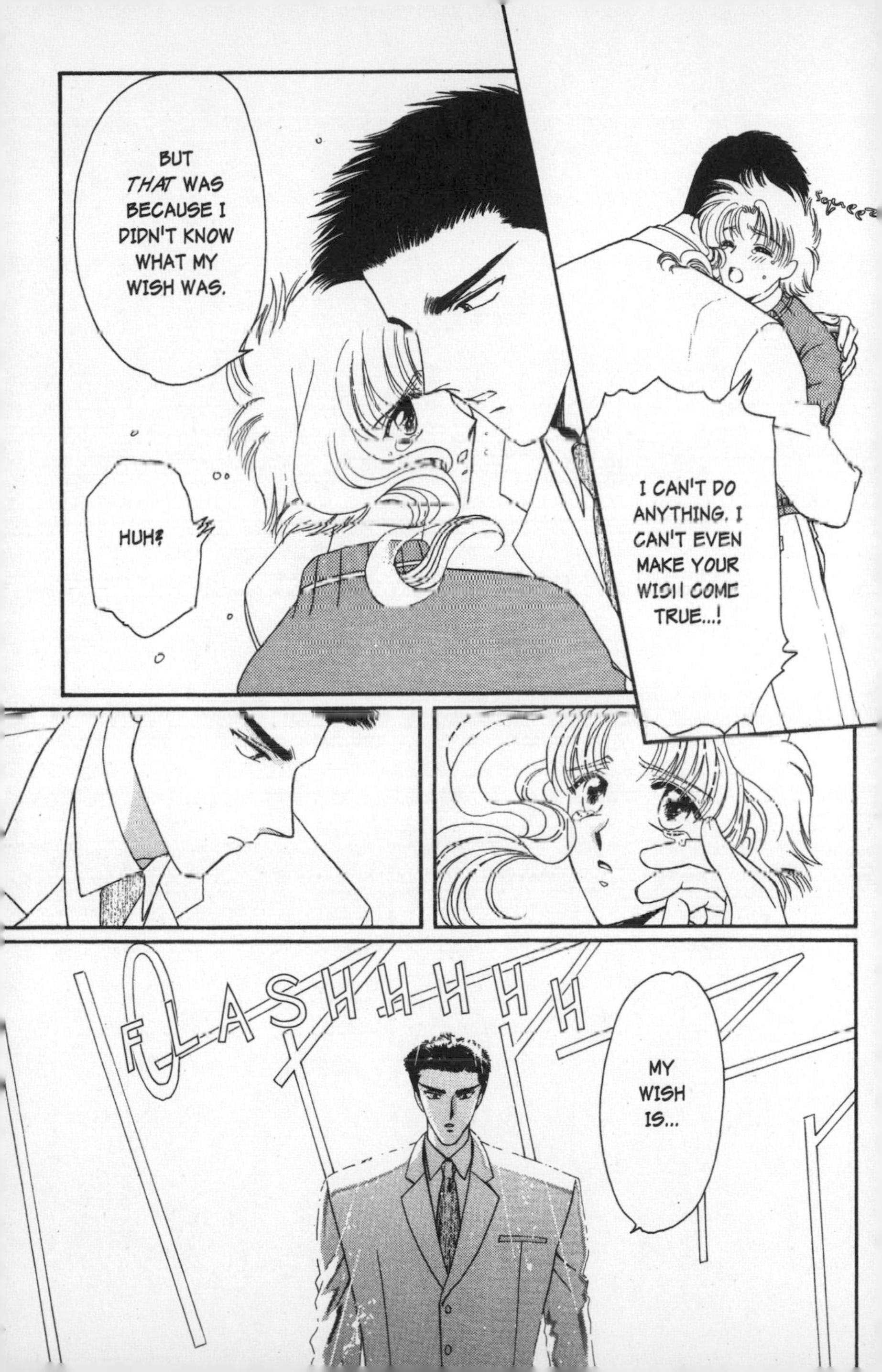
Squeeze
I CAN'T DO ANYTHING. I CAN'T EVEN MAKE YOUR WISH COME TRUE...!
BUT *THAT* WAS BECAUSE I DIDN'T KNOW WHAT MY WISH WAS.
HUH?
FLASHHHHHH
MY WISH IS...

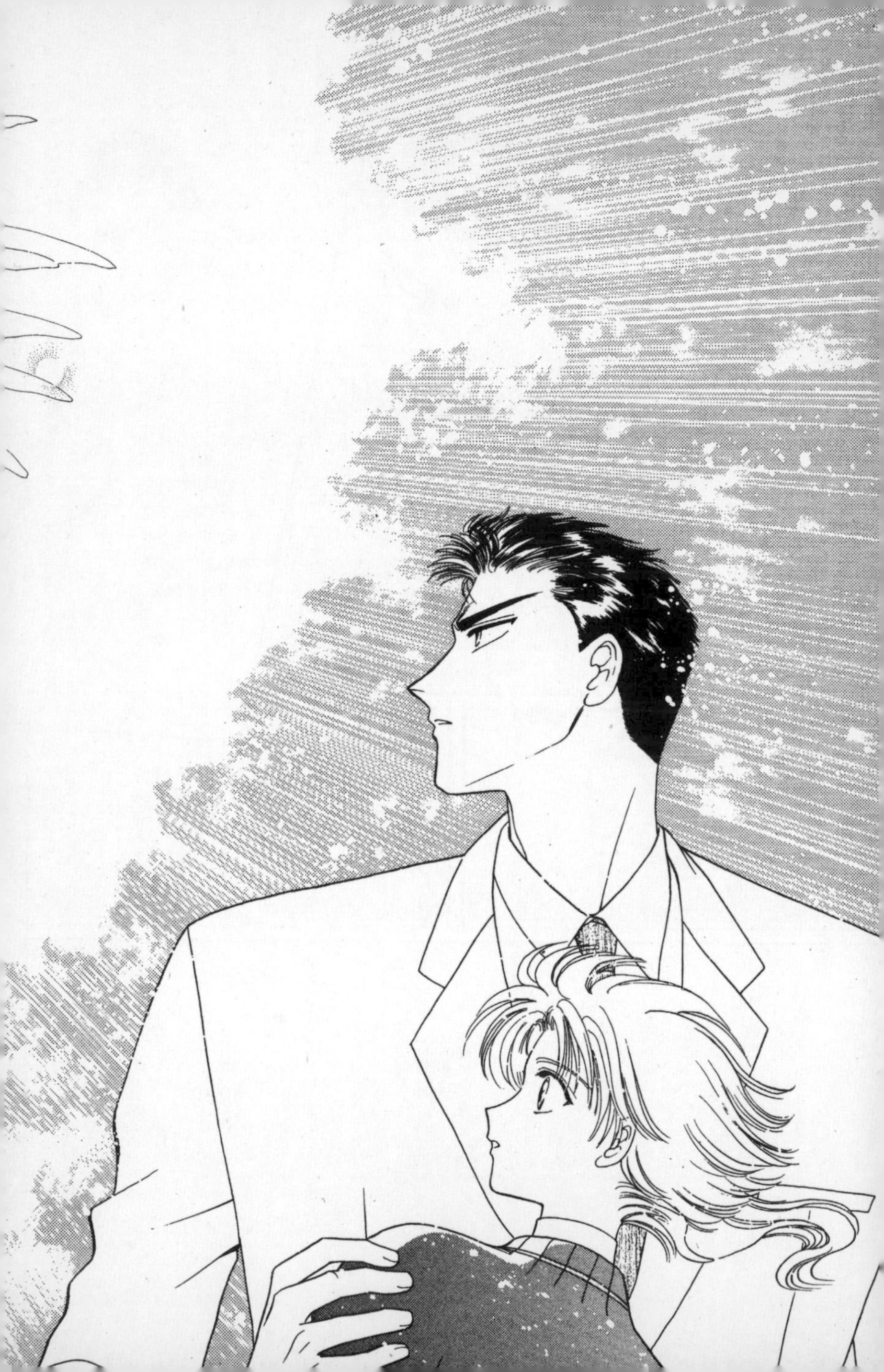

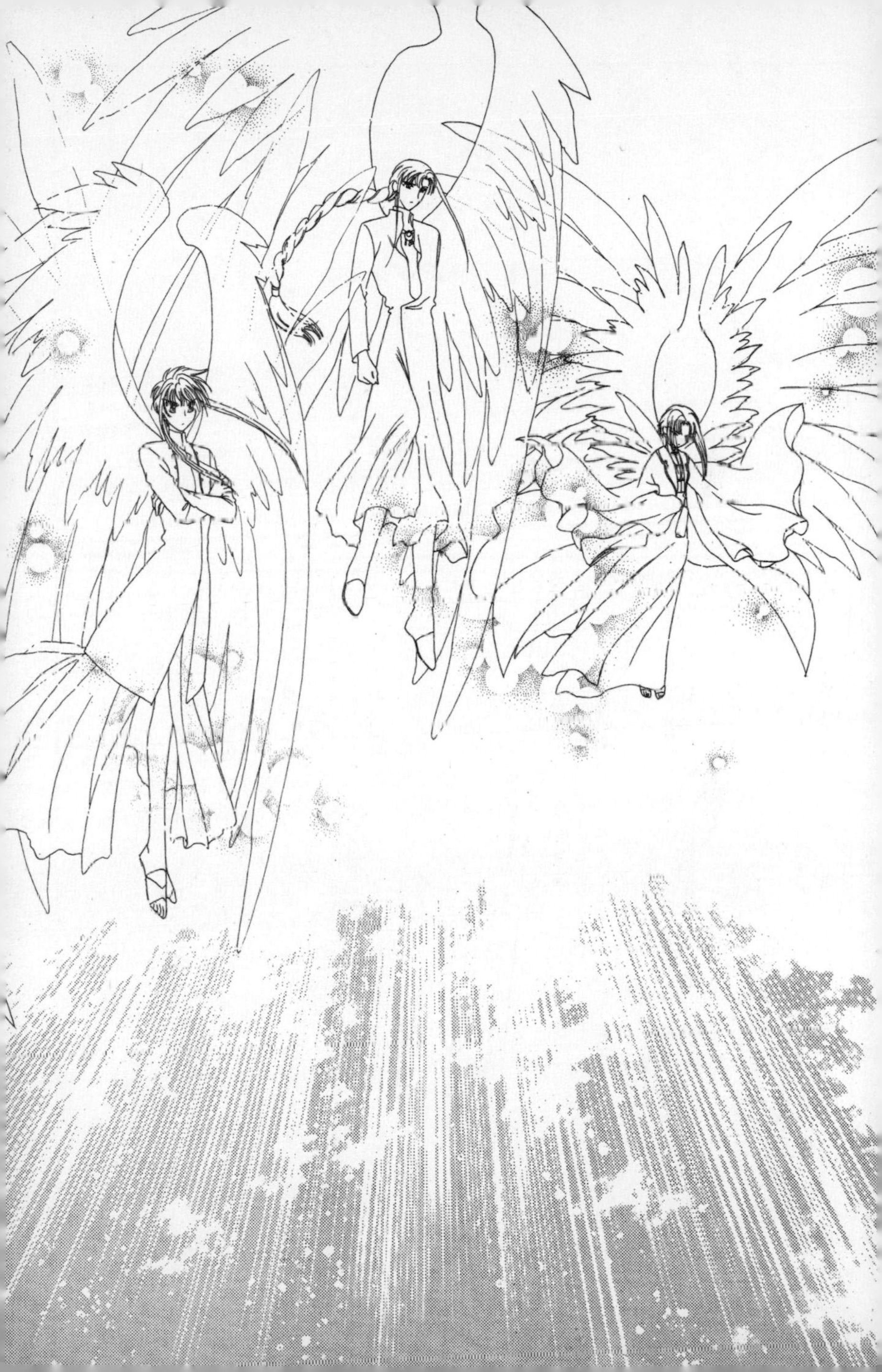

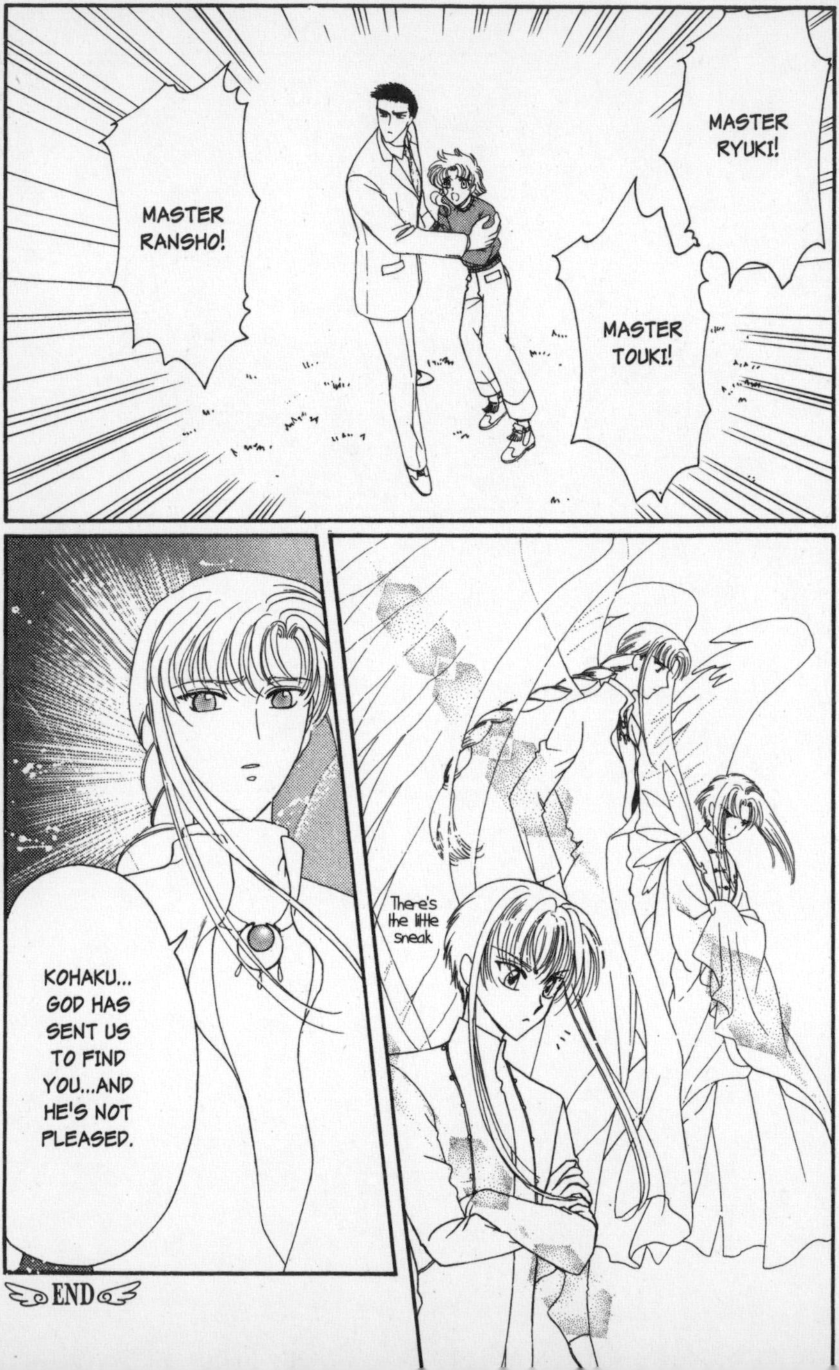
MASTER RYUKI!
MASTER TOUKI!
MASTER RANSHO!
There's the little sneak
KOHAKU... GOD HAS SENT US TO FIND YOU...AND HE'S NOT PLEASED.
END

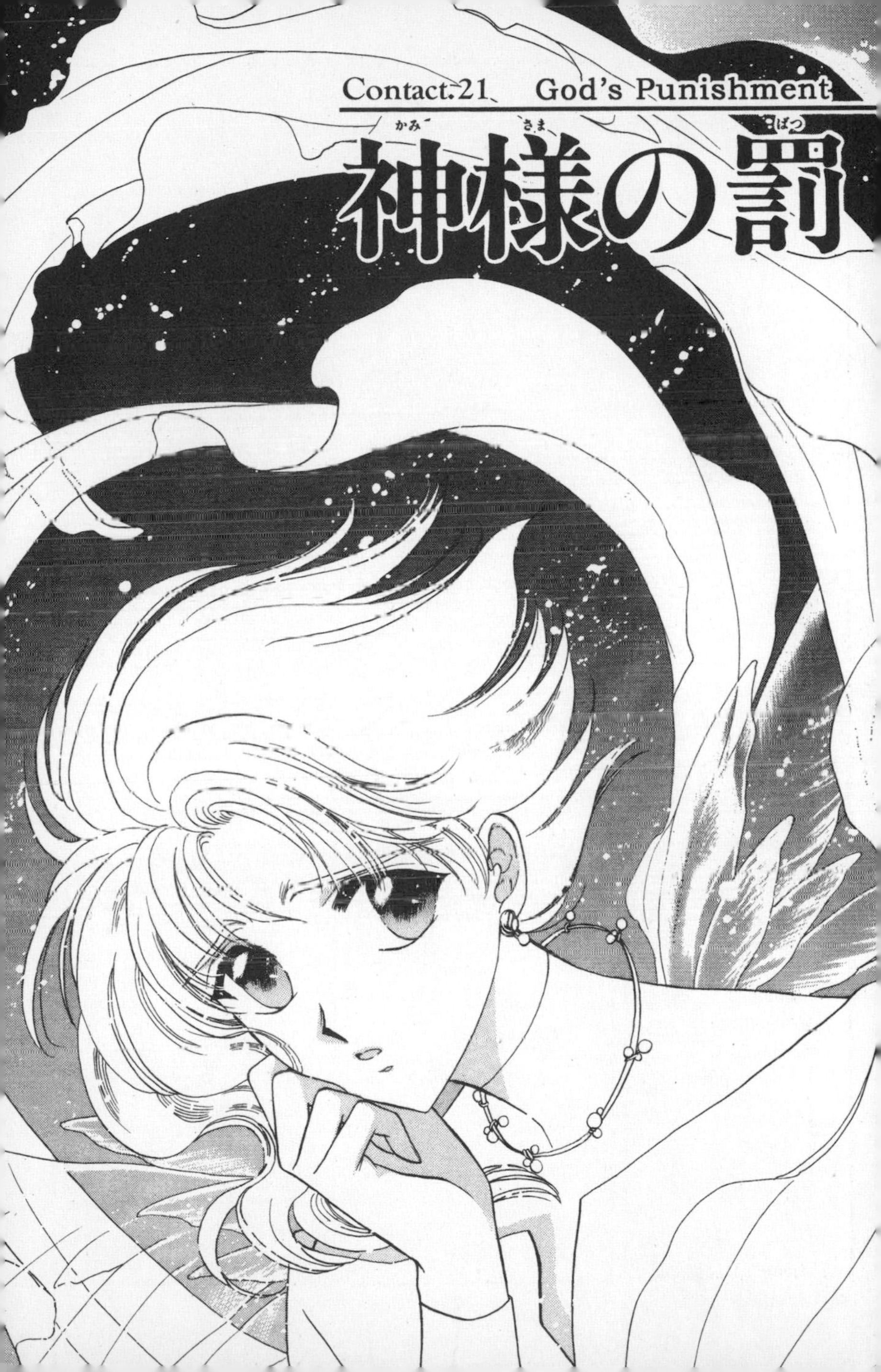
Contact.21 God's Punishment
神様の罰

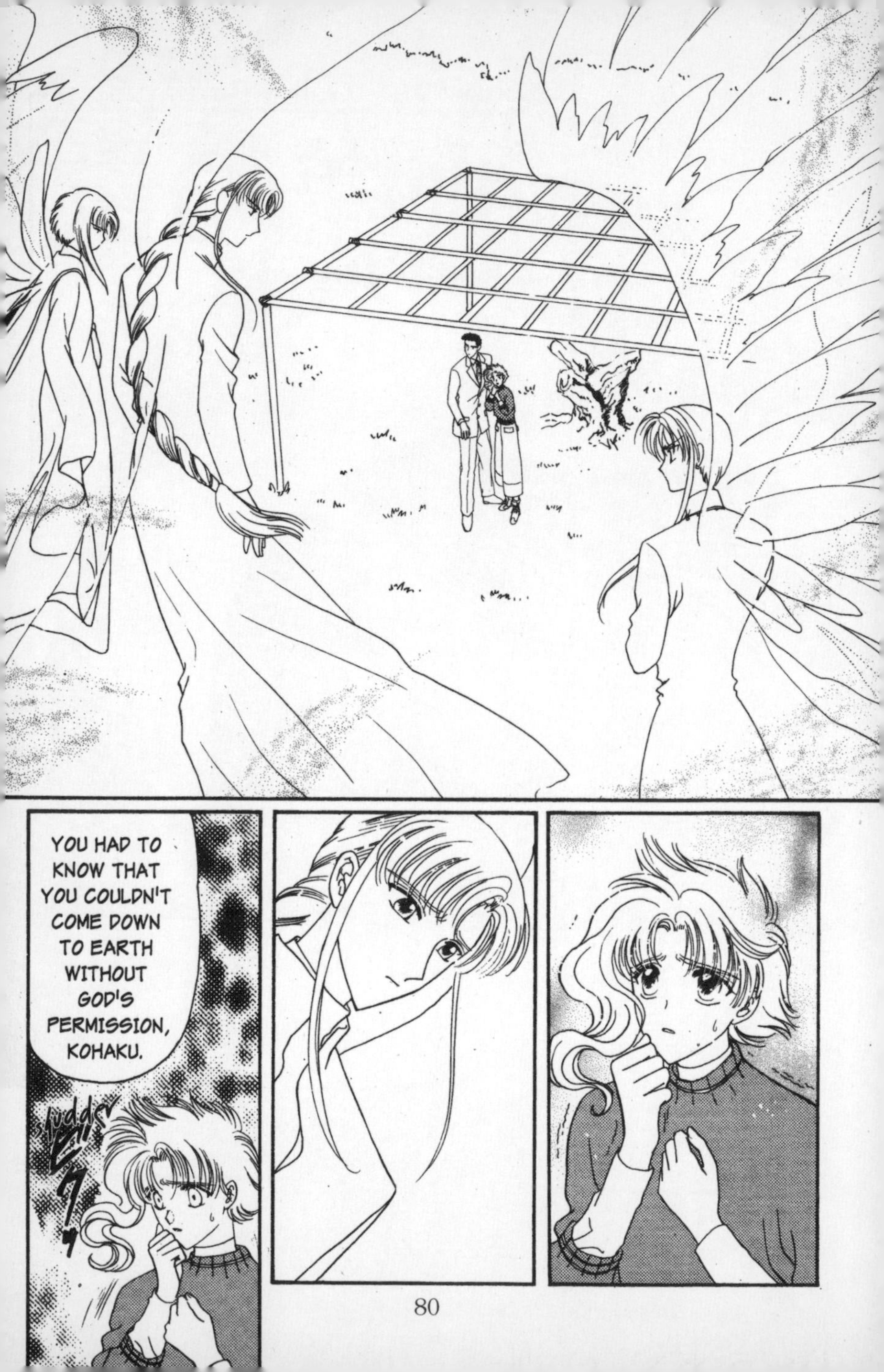
YOU HAD TO KNOW THAT YOU COULDN'T COME DOWN TO EARTH WITHOUT GOD'S PERMISSION, KOHAKU.

YOU'VE BROKEN DIVINE LAW. YOU KNOW HOW SERIOUS THAT IS, RIGHT?

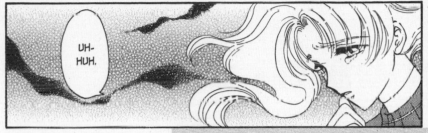

UH-HUH.

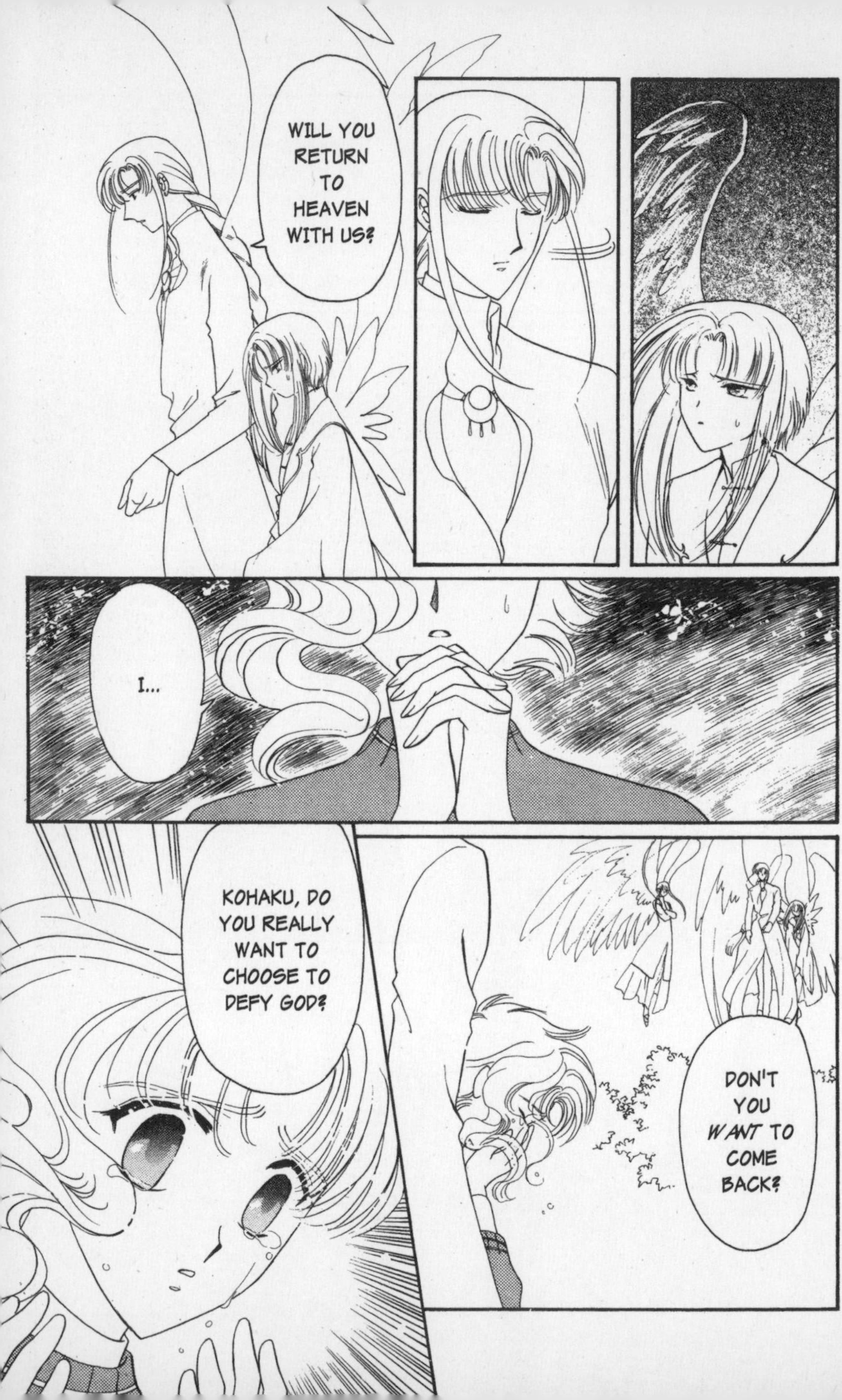
WILL YOU RETURN TO HEAVEN WITH US?
I...
DON'T YOU *WANT* TO COME BACK?
KOHAKU, DO YOU REALLY WANT TO CHOOSE TO DEFY GOD?

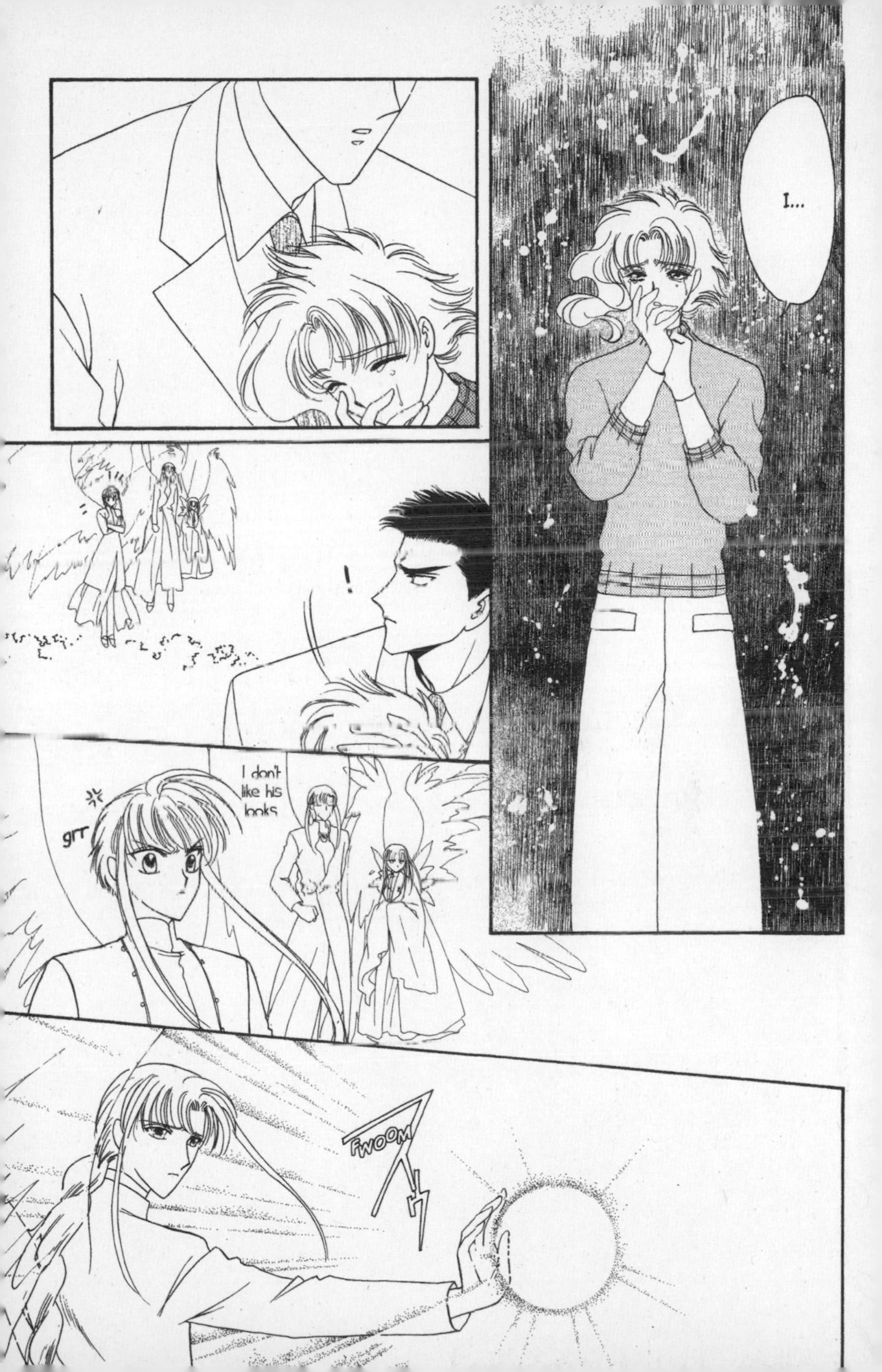
I...
!
I don't like his looks
grr
FWOOM

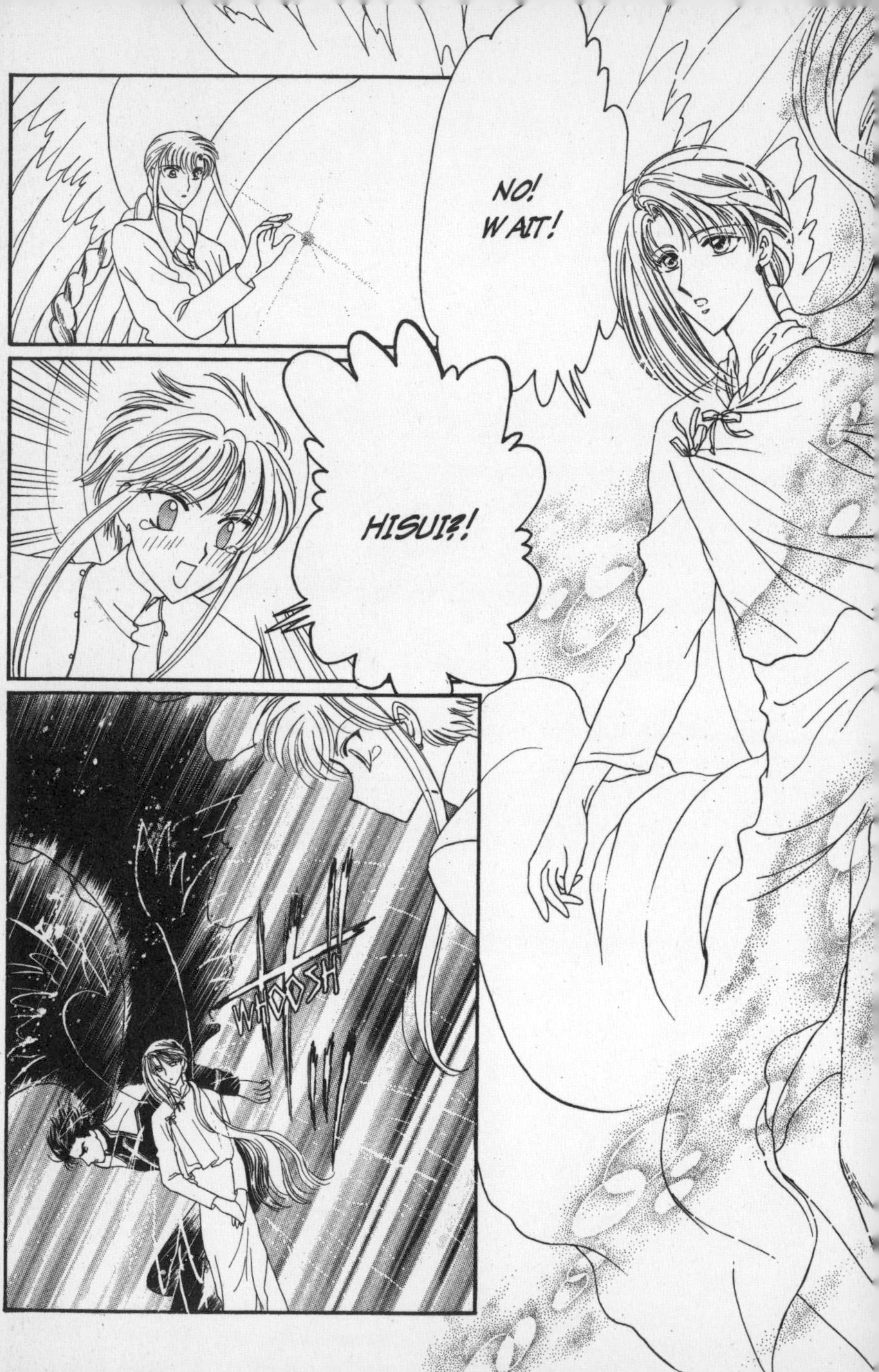
NO! WAIT!
HISUI?!
WHOOSH

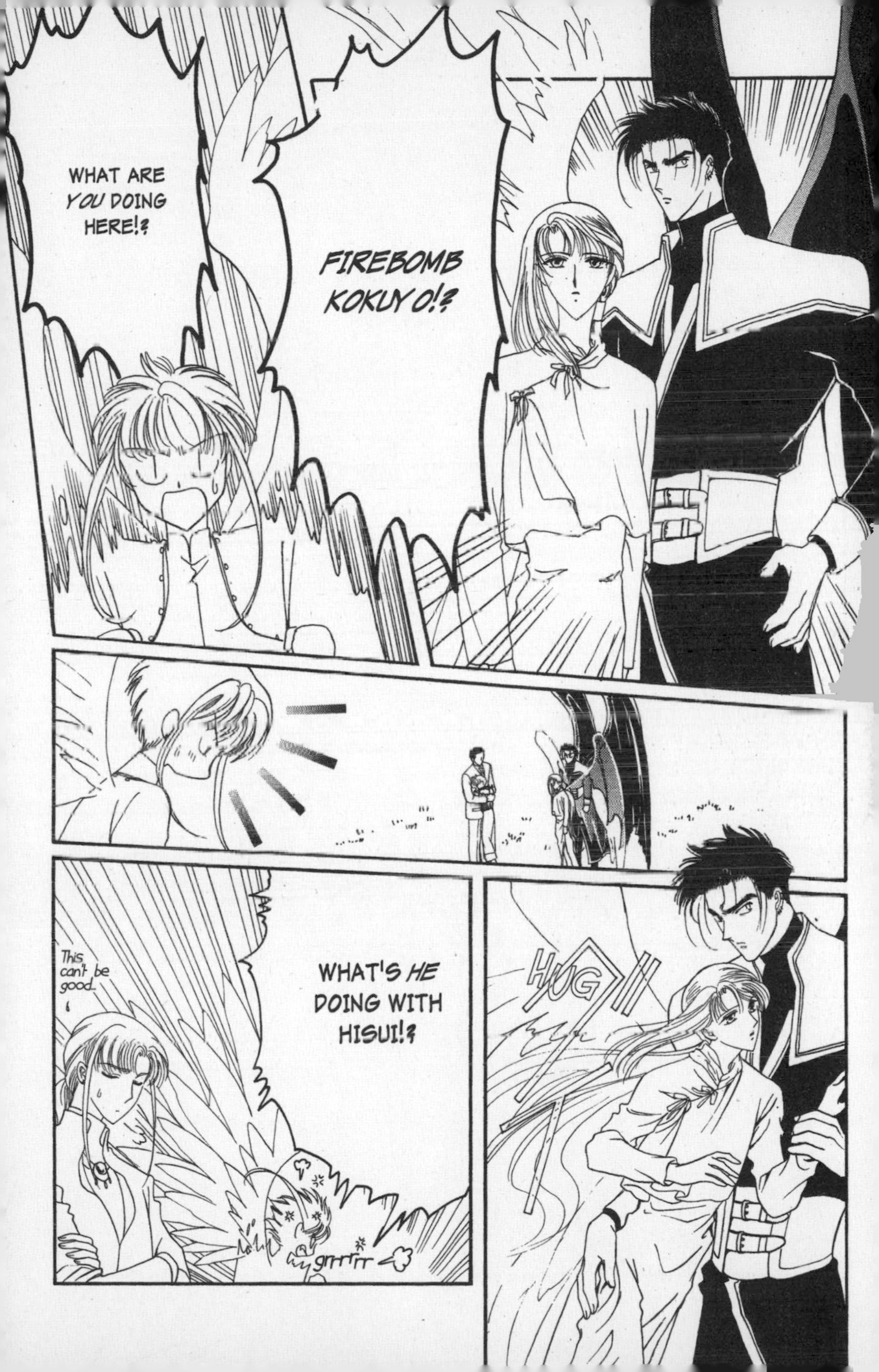
FIREBOMB KOKUYO!?
WHAT ARE YOU DOING HERE!?
HUG
WHAT'S HE DOING WITH HISUI!?
This can't be good..
grrrrr

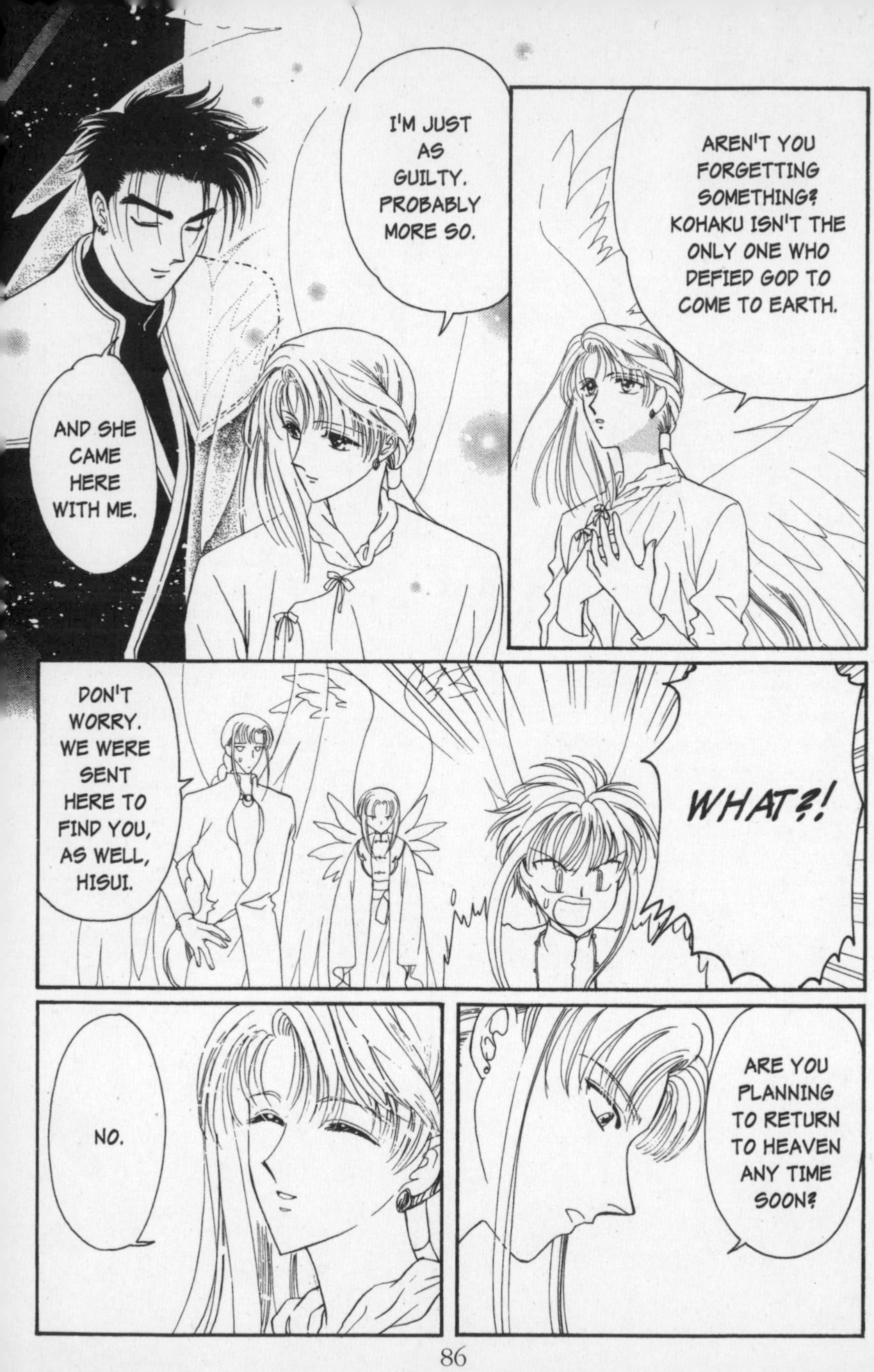
AREN'T YOU FORGETTING SOMETHING? KOHAKU ISN'T THE ONLY ONE WHO DEFIED GOD TO COME TO EARTH.
I'M JUST AS GUILTY. PROBABLY MORE SO.
AND SHE CAME HERE WITH ME.
WHAT?!
DON'T WORRY. WE WERE SENT HERE TO FIND YOU, AS WELL, HISUI.
ARE YOU PLANNING TO RETURN TO HEAVEN ANY TIME SOON?
NO.

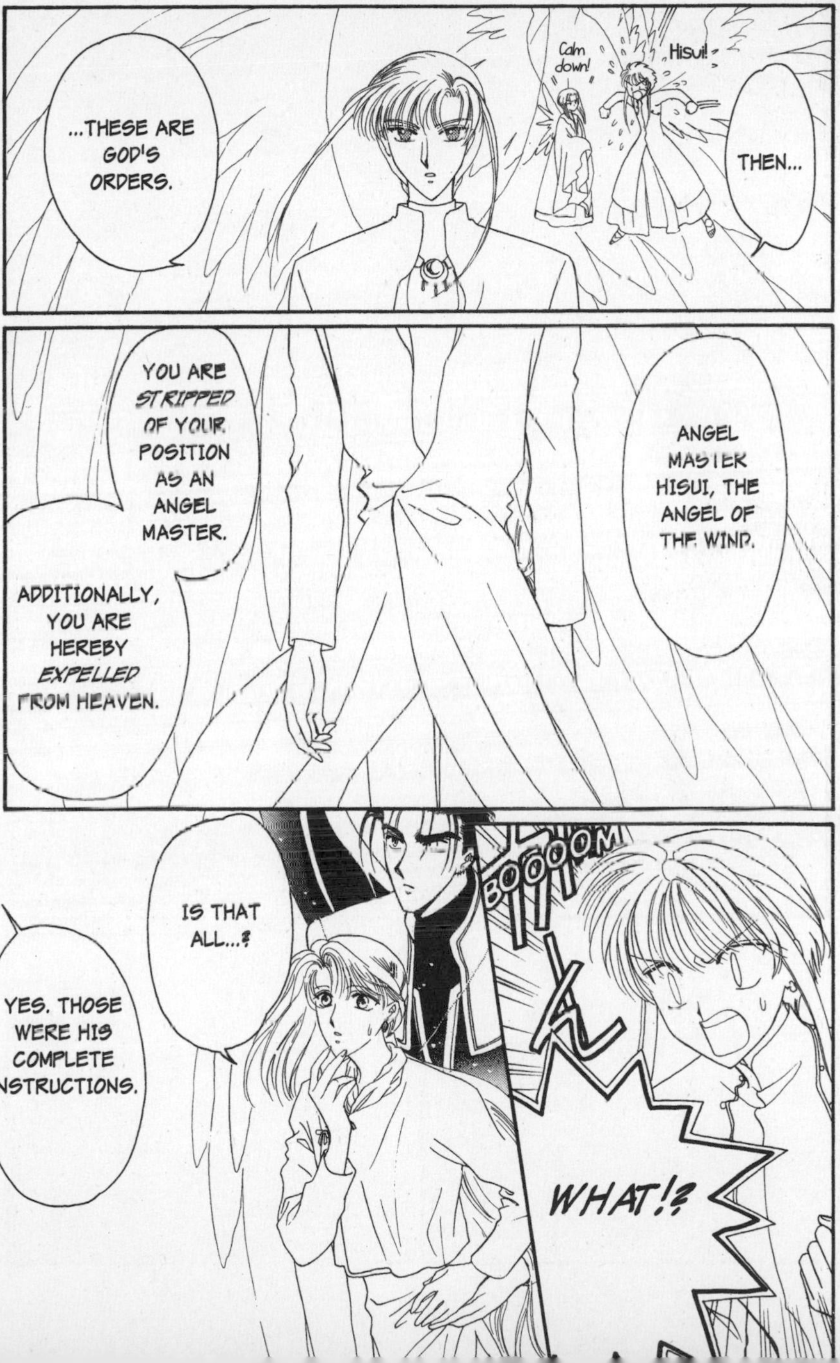
THEN...
Hisui!
Calm down!
...THESE ARE GOD'S ORDERS.
ANGEL MASTER HISUI, THE ANGEL OF THE WIND.
YOU ARE STRIPPED OF YOUR POSITION AS AN ANGEL MASTER.
ADDITIONALLY, YOU ARE HEREBY EXPELLED FROM HEAVEN.
BOOOOOM
WHAT!?
IS THAT ALL...?
YES. THOSE WERE HIS COMPLETE INSTRUCTIONS.

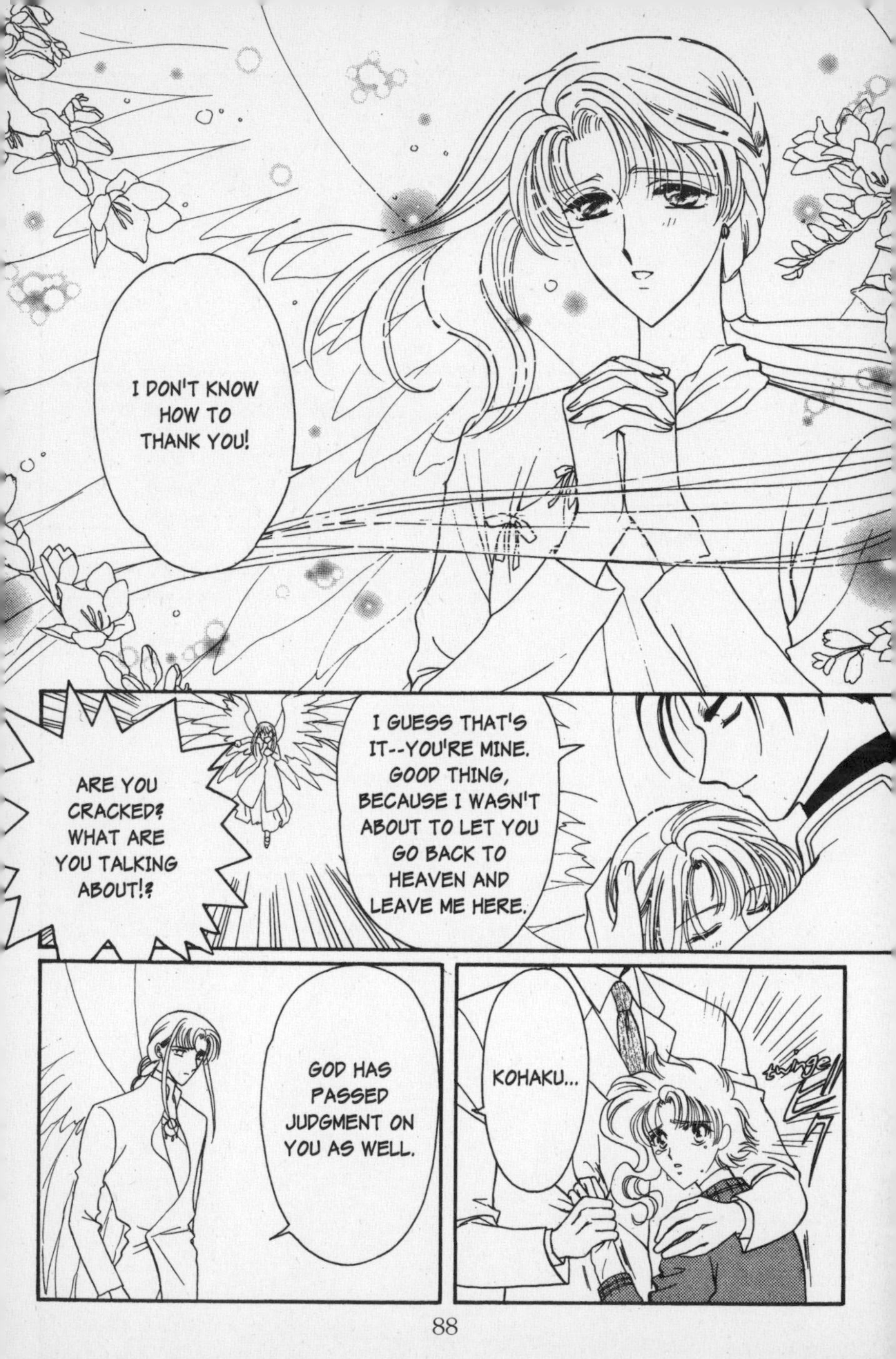
I DON'T KNOW HOW TO THANK YOU!
I GUESS THAT'S IT--YOU'RE MINE. GOOD THING, BECAUSE I WASN'T ABOUT TO LET YOU GO BACK TO HEAVEN AND LEAVE ME HERE.
ARE YOU CRACKED? WHAT ARE YOU TALKING ABOUT!?
KOHAKU...
twinge
GOD HAS PASSED JUDGMENT ON YOU AS WELL.

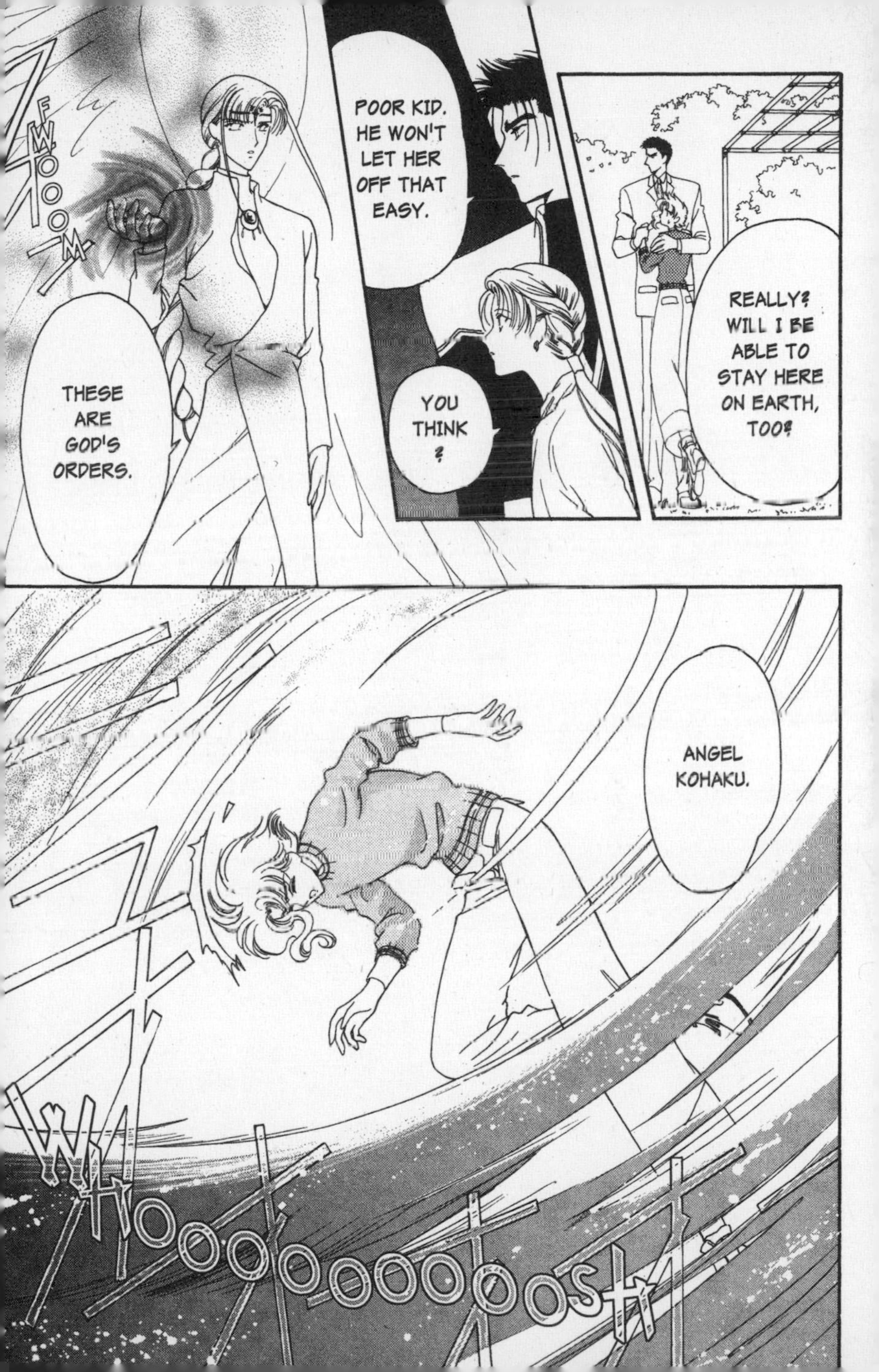
REALLY? WILL I BE ABLE TO STAY HERE ON EARTH, TOO?
POOR KID. HE WON'T LET HER OFF THAT EASY.
YOU THINK?
FWOOOM
THESE ARE GOD'S ORDERS.
ANGEL KOHAKU.
WHOOOOOOOOOSH

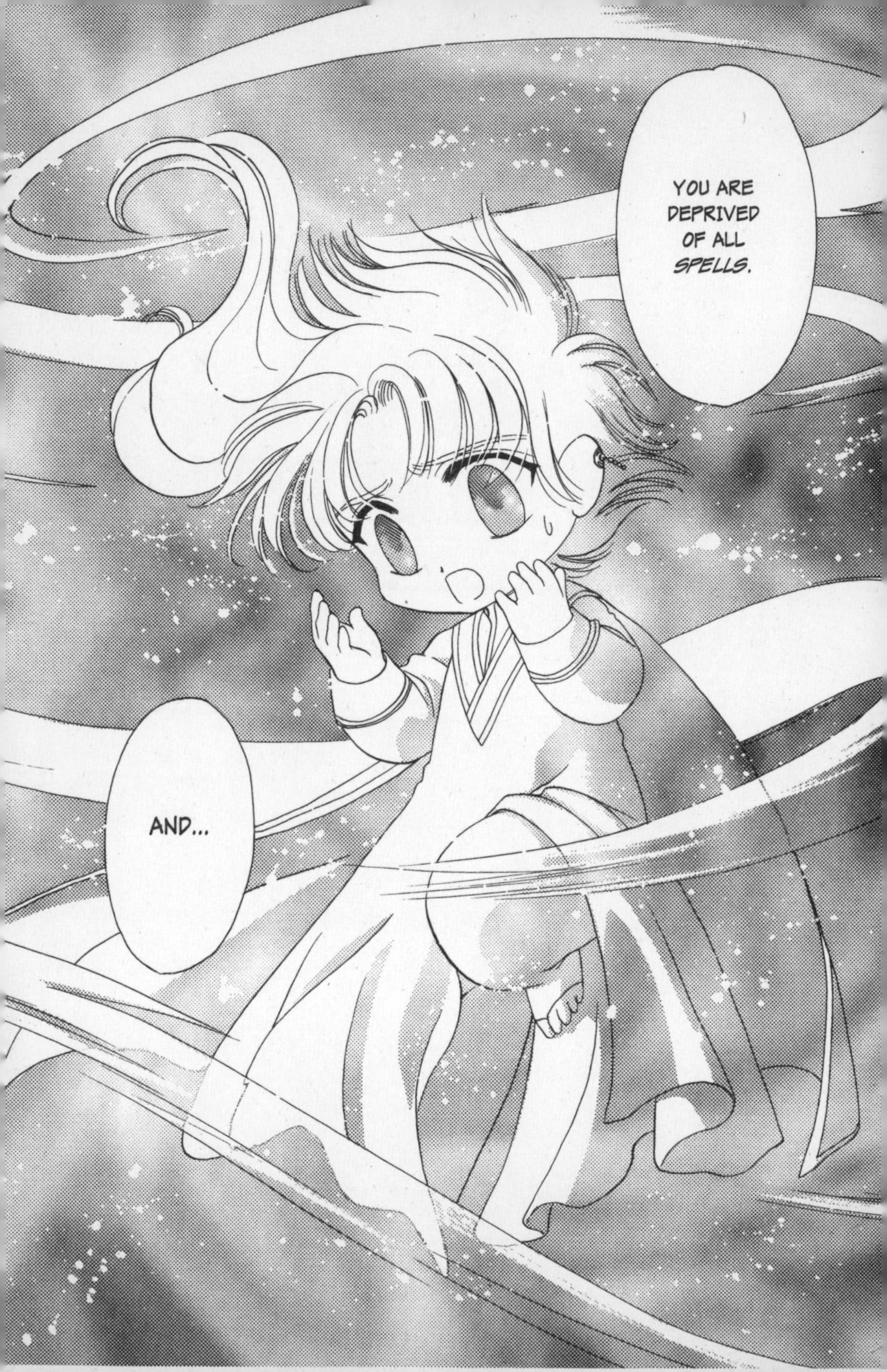
YOU ARE DEPRIVED OF ALL *SPELLS*.
AND...

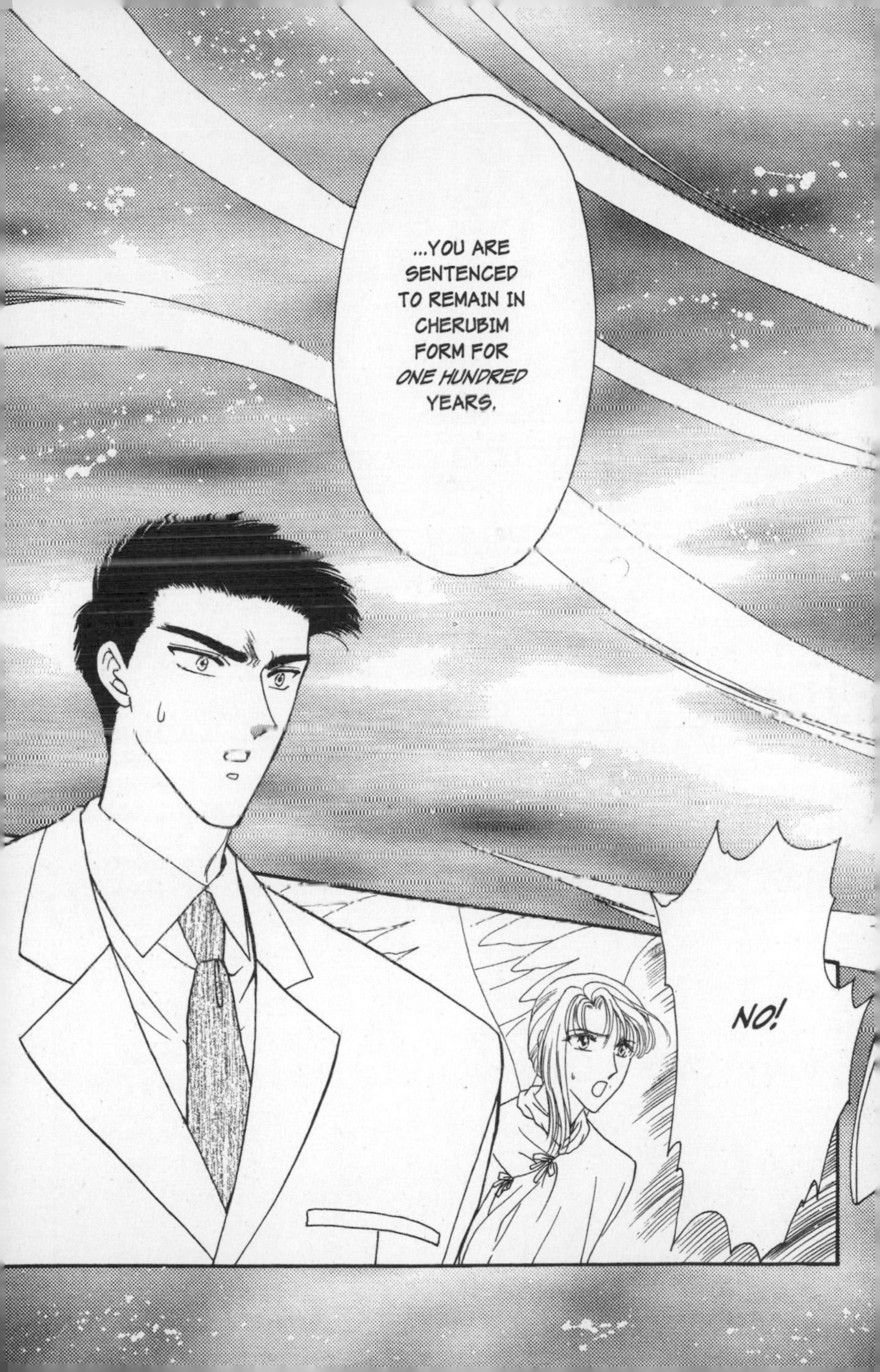
...YOU ARE SENTENCED TO REMAIN IN CHERUBIM FORM FOR *ONE HUNDRED* YEARS.
NO!

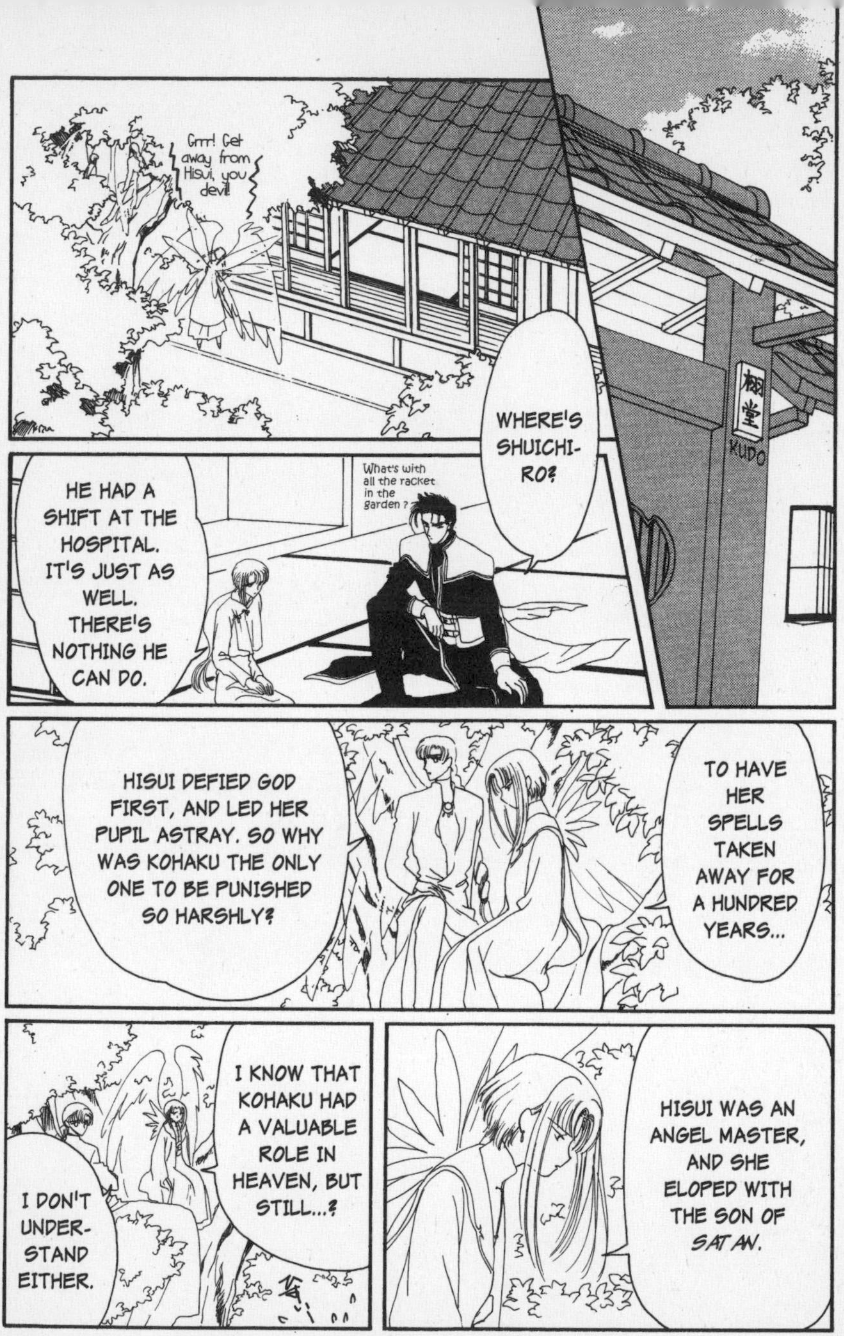
KUDO
WHERE'S SHUICHIRO?
Grrr! Get away from Hisui, you devil!
What's with all the racket in the garden?
HE HAD A SHIFT AT THE HOSPITAL. IT'S JUST AS WELL. THERE'S NOTHING HE CAN DO.
TO HAVE HER SPELLS TAKEN AWAY FOR A HUNDRED YEARS...
HISUI DEFIED GOD FIRST, AND LED HER PUPIL ASTRAY. SO WHY WAS KOHAKU THE ONLY ONE TO BE PUNISHED SO HARSHLY?
HISUI WAS AN ANGEL MASTER, AND SHE ELOPED WITH THE SON OF *SATAN*.
I KNOW THAT KOHAKU HAD A VALUABLE ROLE IN HEAVEN, BUT STILL...?
I DON'T UNDERSTAND EITHER.

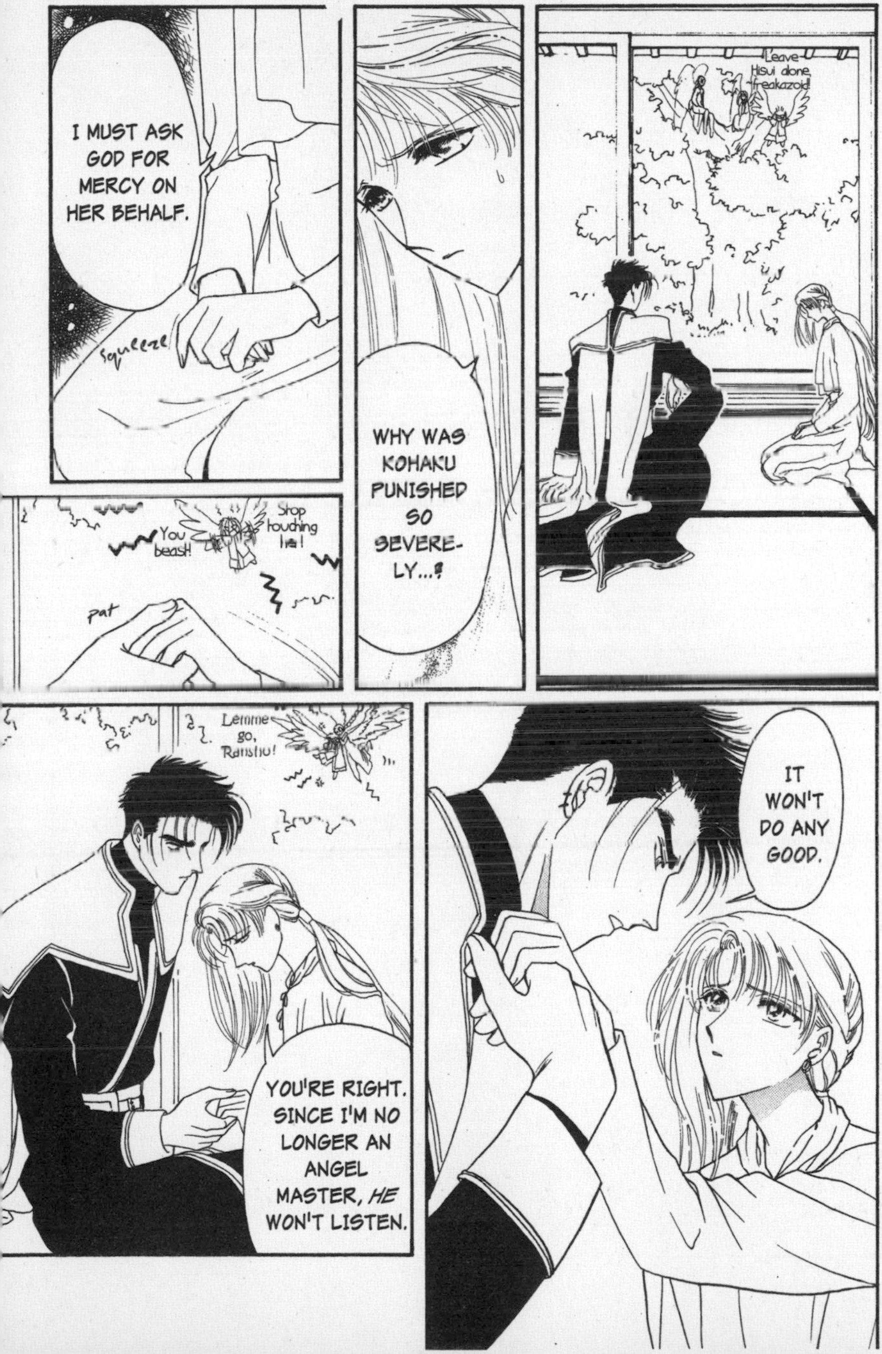

Leave Hisui alone, freakazoid!
WHY WAS KOHAKU PUNISHED SO SEVERE-LY...?!
I MUST ASK GOD FOR MERCY ON HER BEHALF.
squeeze
Stop touching her!
You beast!
pat
IT WON'T DO ANY GOOD.
Lemme go, Ranshu!
YOU'RE RIGHT. SINCE I'M NO LONGER AN ANGEL MASTER, *HE* WON'T LISTEN.

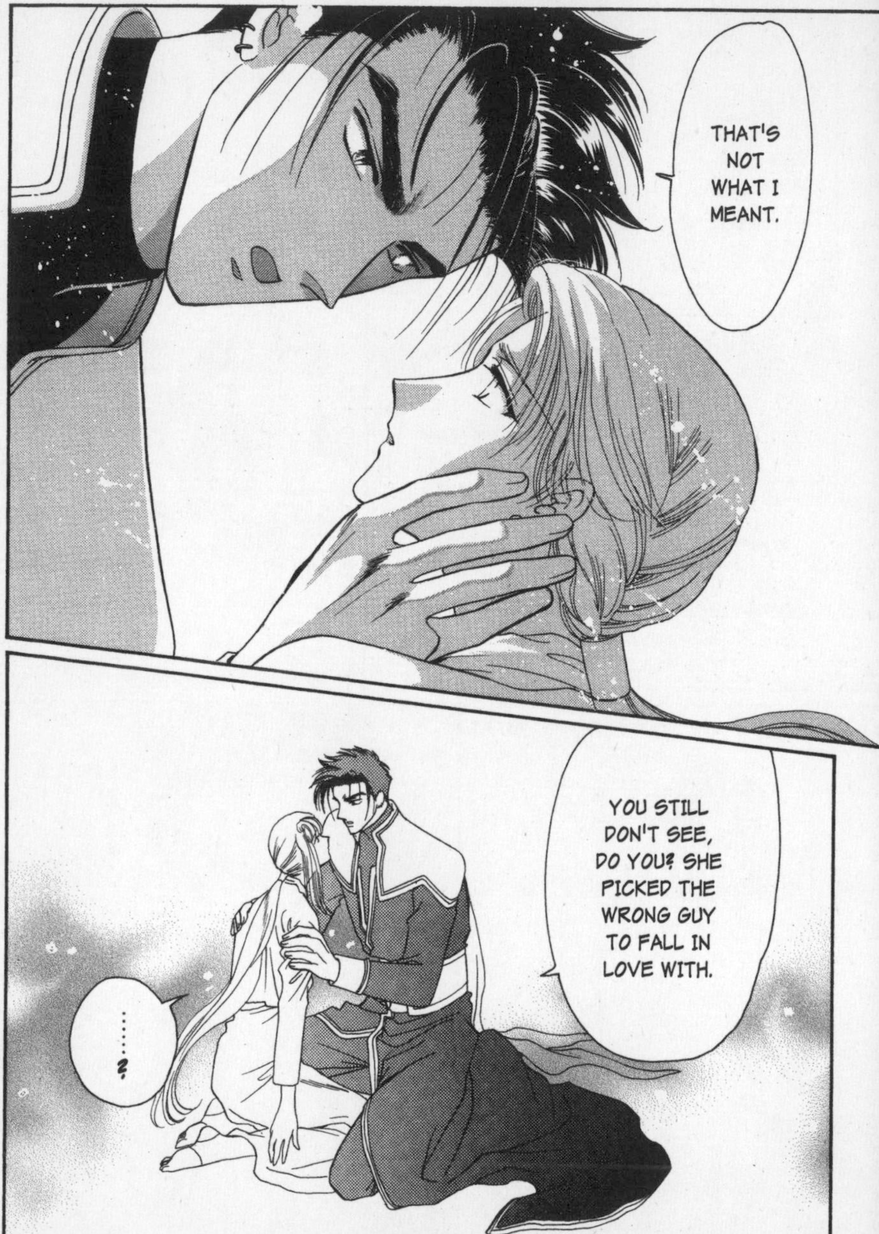
THAT'S NOT WHAT I MEANT.
YOU STILL DON'T SEE, DO YOU? SHE PICKED THE WRONG GUY TO FALL IN LOVE WITH.
......?

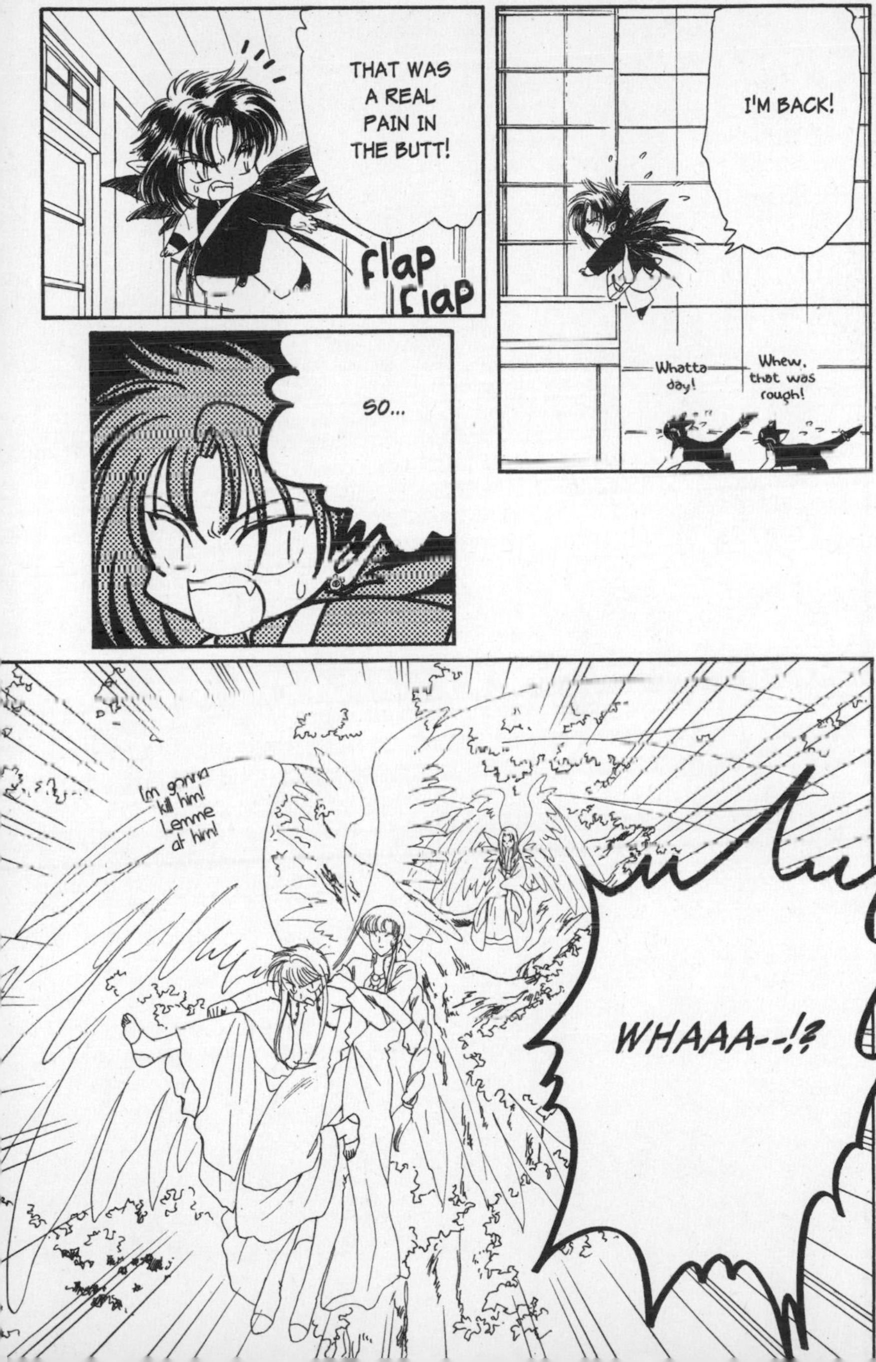
I'M BACK!
Whew, that was rough!
Whatta day!
THAT WAS A REAL PAIN IN THE BUTT!
flap flap
SO...
WHAAA--!?
I'm gonna kill him! Lemme at him!

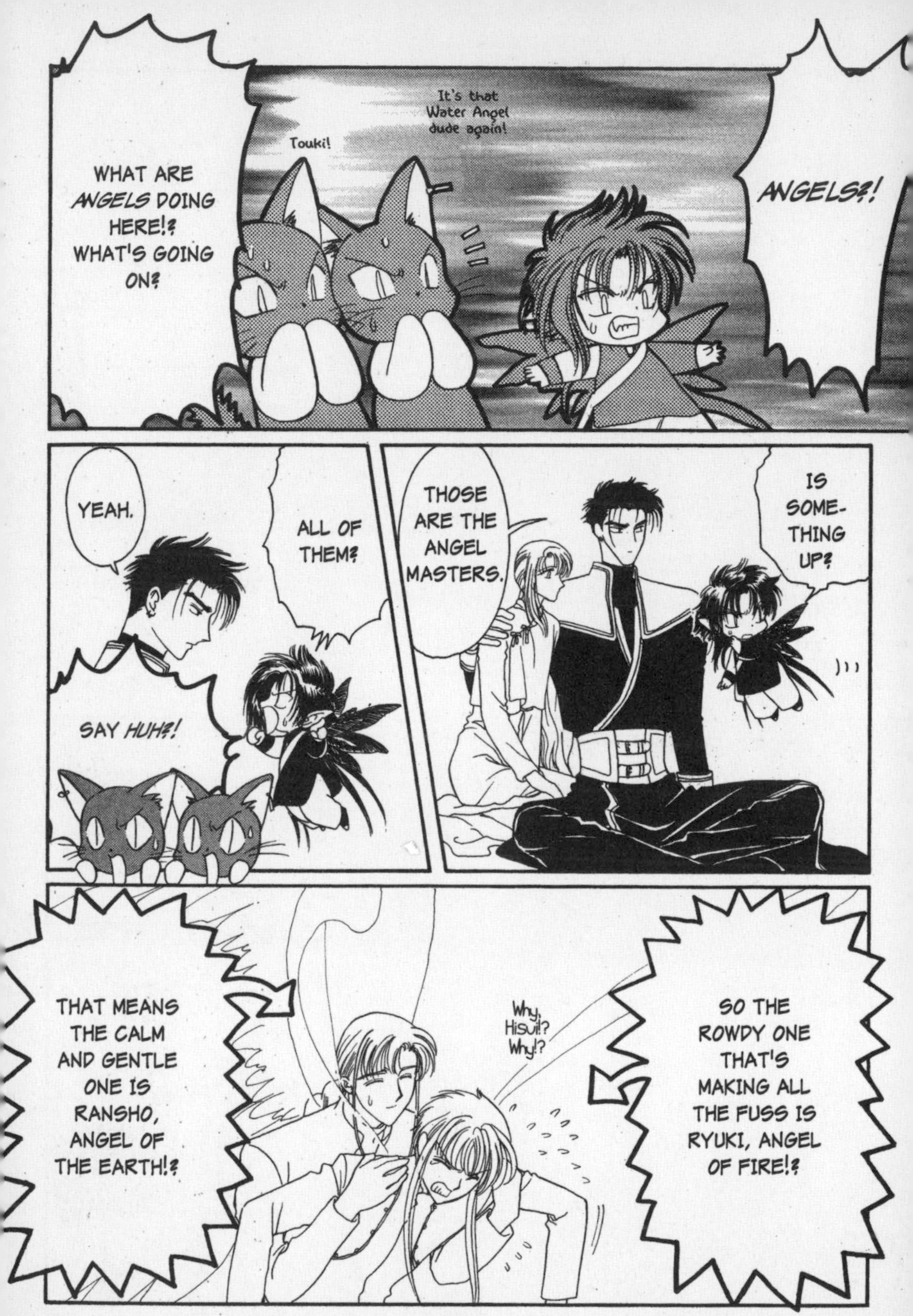
ANGELS?!
It's that Water Angel dude again!
Touki!
WHAT ARE ANGELS DOING HERE!? WHAT'S GOING ON?
IS SOME-THING UP?
THOSE ARE THE ANGEL MASTERS.
ALL OF THEM?
YEAH.
SAY HUH?!
SO THE ROWDY ONE THAT'S MAKING ALL THE FUSS IS RYUKI, ANGEL OF FIRE!?
Why, Hisui!? Why!?
THAT MEANS THE CALM AND GENTLE ONE IS RANSHO, ANGEL OF THE EARTH!?

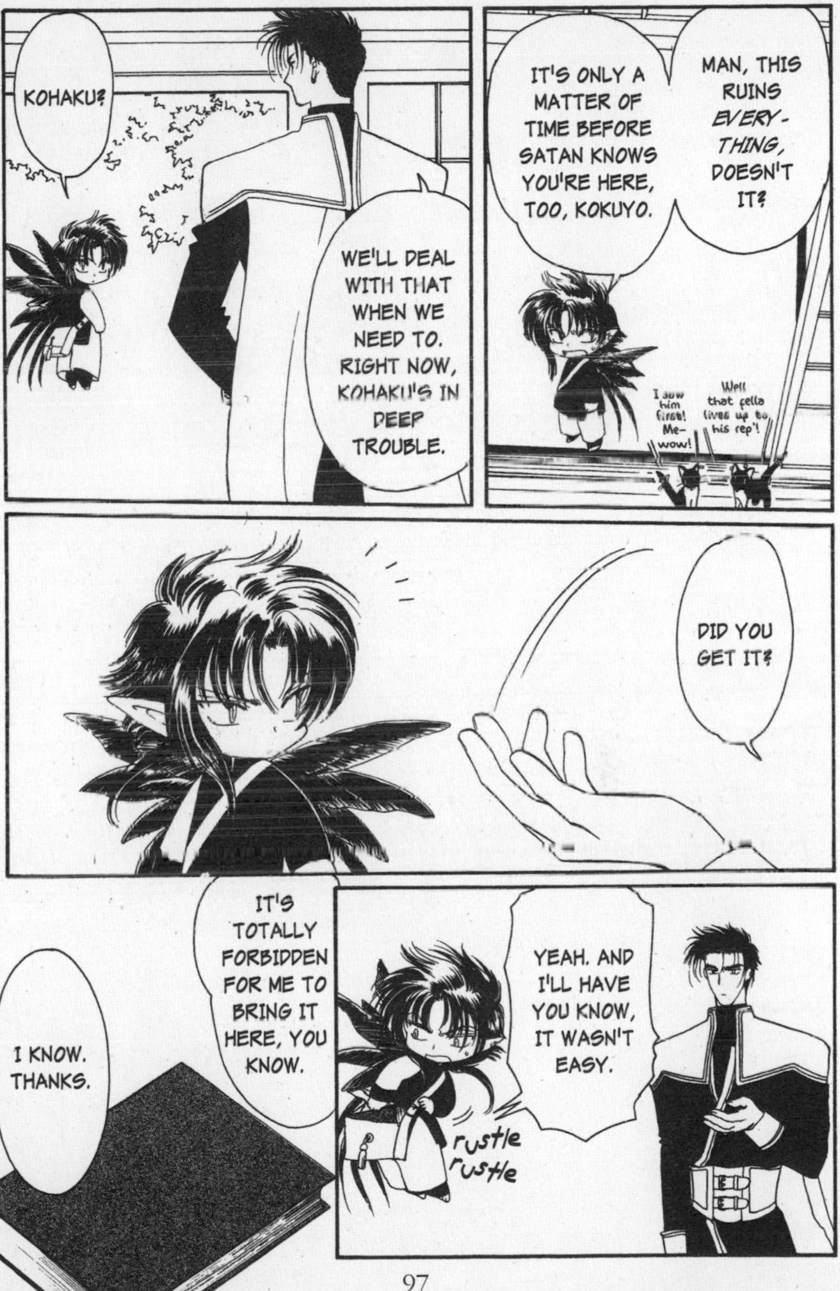
MAN, THIS RUINS EVERY-THING, DOESN'T IT?
IT'S ONLY A MATTER OF TIME BEFORE SATAN KNOWS YOU'RE HERE, TOO, KOKUYO.
Well that fella lives up to his rep'!
I saw him first! Me-wow!
WE'LL DEAL WITH THAT WHEN WE NEED TO. RIGHT NOW, KOHAKU'S IN DEEP TROUBLE.
KOHAKU?
DID YOU GET IT?
YEAH. AND I'LL HAVE YOU KNOW, IT WASN'T EASY.
rustle rustle
IT'S TOTALLY FORBIDDEN FOR ME TO BRING IT HERE, YOU KNOW.
I KNOW. THANKS.

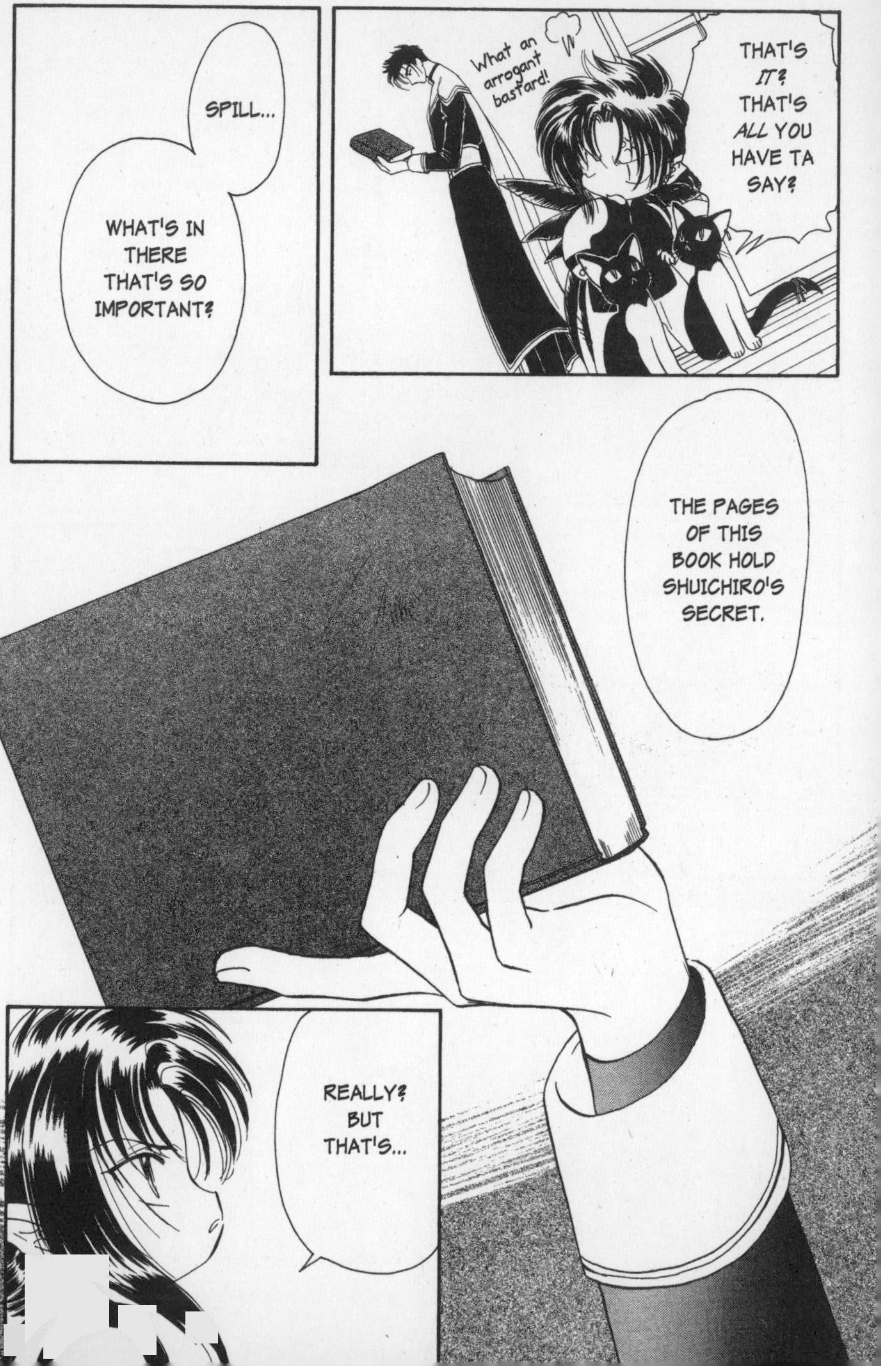
THAT'S IT? THAT'S ALL YOU HAVE TA SAY?
What an arrogant bastard!
SPILL...
WHAT'S IN THERE THAT'S SO IMPORTANT?
THE PAGES OF THIS BOOK HOLD SHUICHIRO'S SECRET.
REALLY? BUT THAT'S...

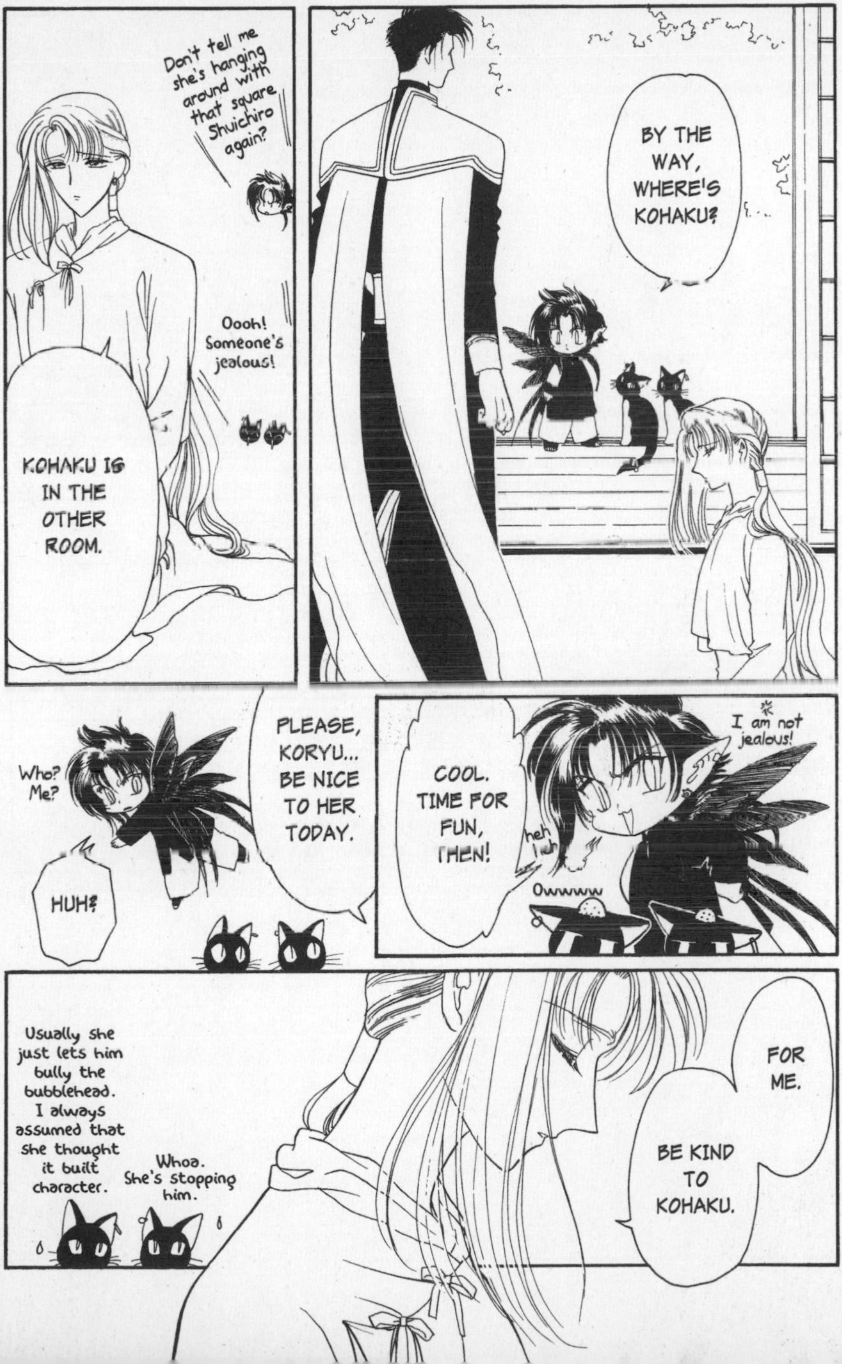
BY THE WAY, WHERE'S KOHAKU?
Don't tell me she's hanging around with that square Shuichiro again?
Oooh! Someone's jealous!
KOHAKU IS IN THE OTHER ROOM.
I am not jealous!
COOL. TIME FOR FUN, THEN!
heh heh
Owwww
PLEASE, KORYU... BE NICE TO HER TODAY.
Who? Me?
HUH?
FOR ME.
BE KIND TO KOHAKU.
Whoa. She's stopping him.
Usually she just lets him bully the bubblehead. I always assumed that she thought it built character.

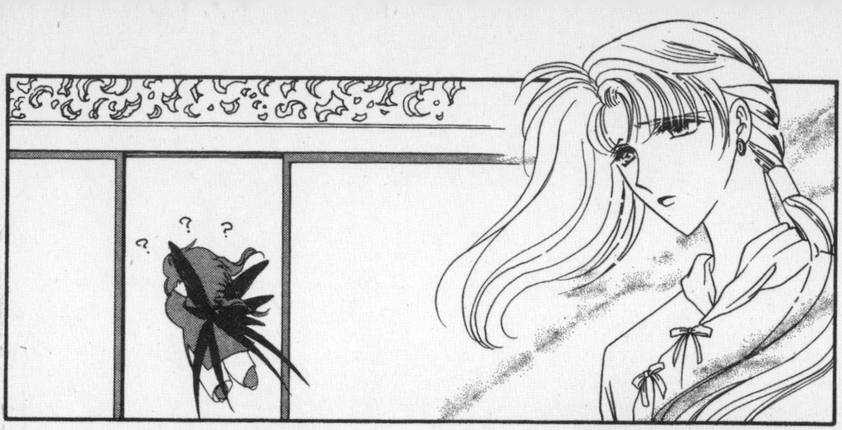
? ? ?

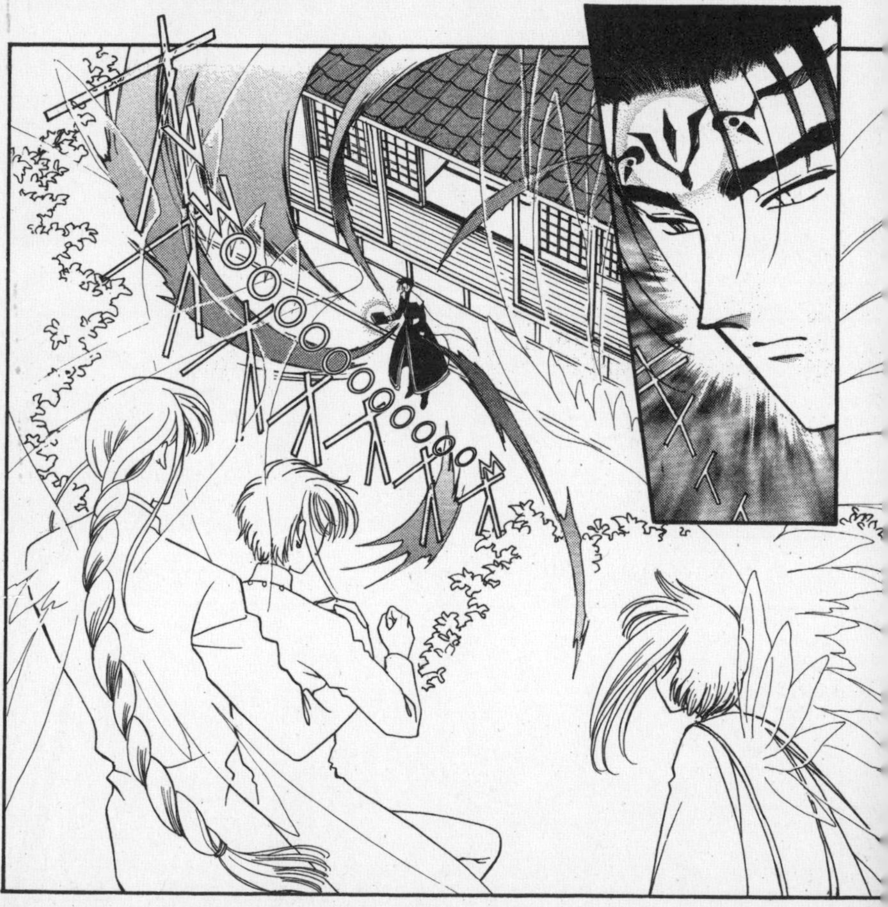
WOOOOOOOOOOOM

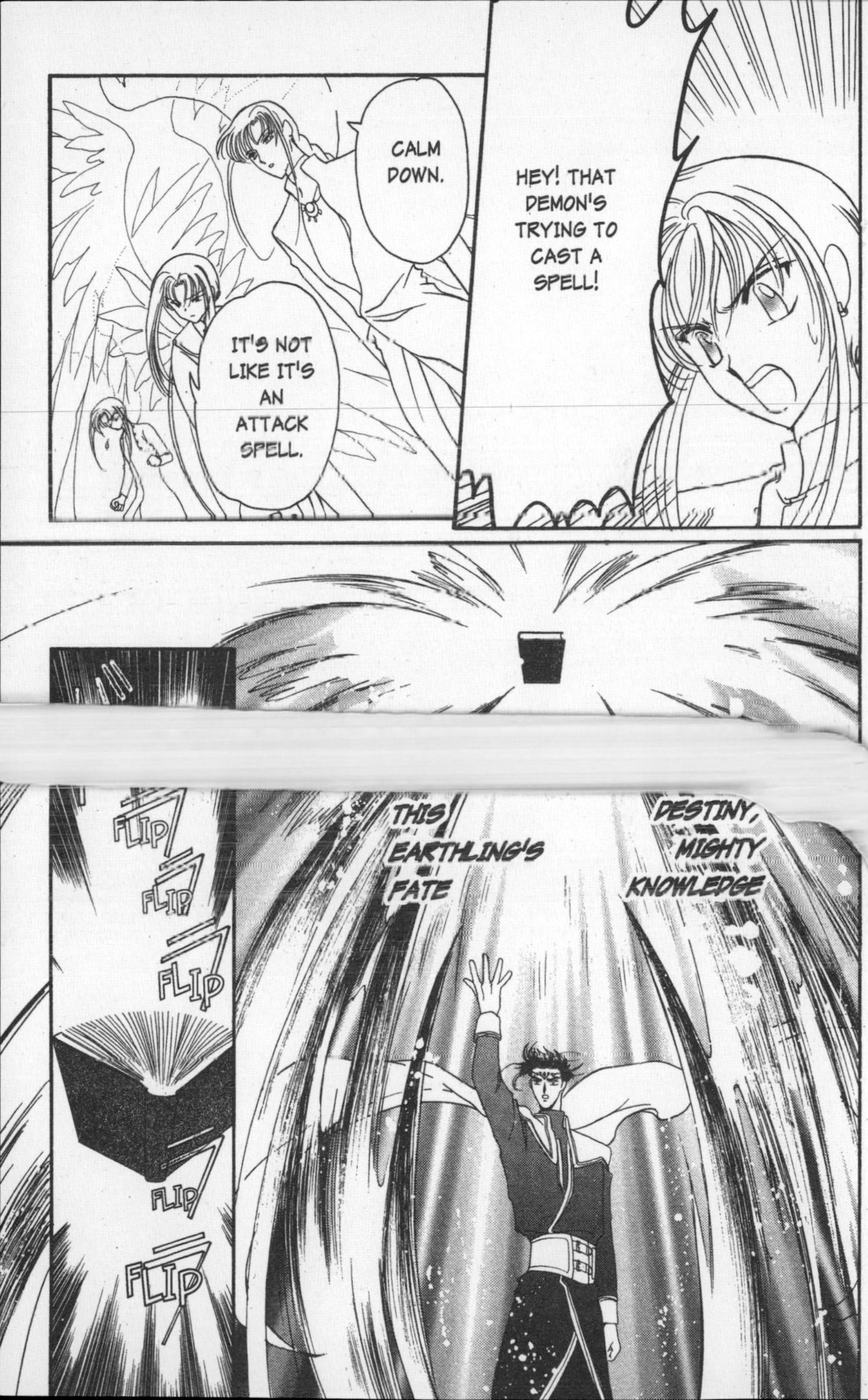
HEY! THAT DEMON'S TRYING TO CAST A SPELL!
CALM DOWN.
IT'S NOT LIKE IT'S AN ATTACK SPELL.
DESTINY, MIGHTY KNOWLEDGE
THIS EARTHLING'S FATE
FLIP
FLIP
FLIP
FLIP
FLIP

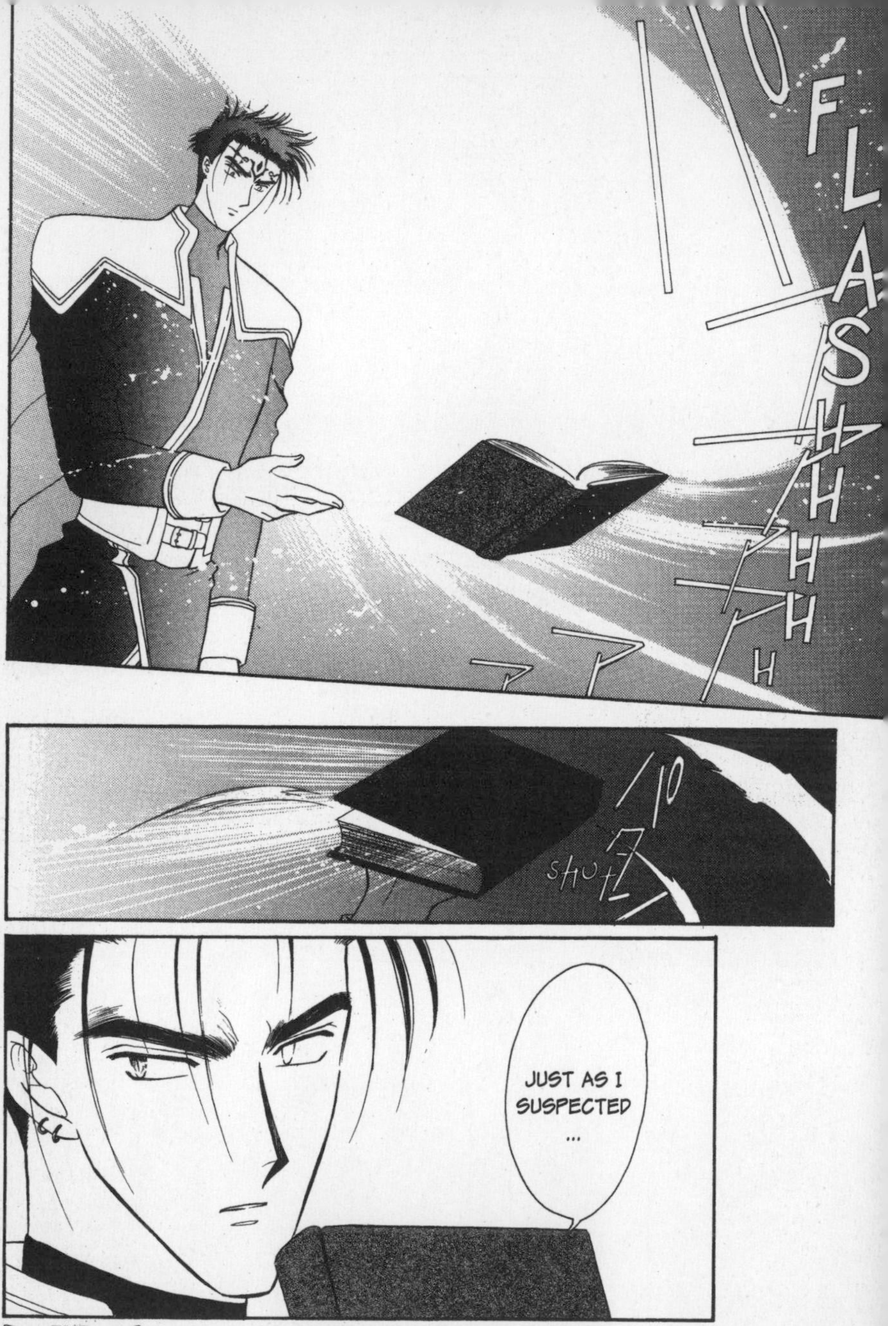
FLASHHHHH
SHUT
JUST AS I SUSPECTED ...

END

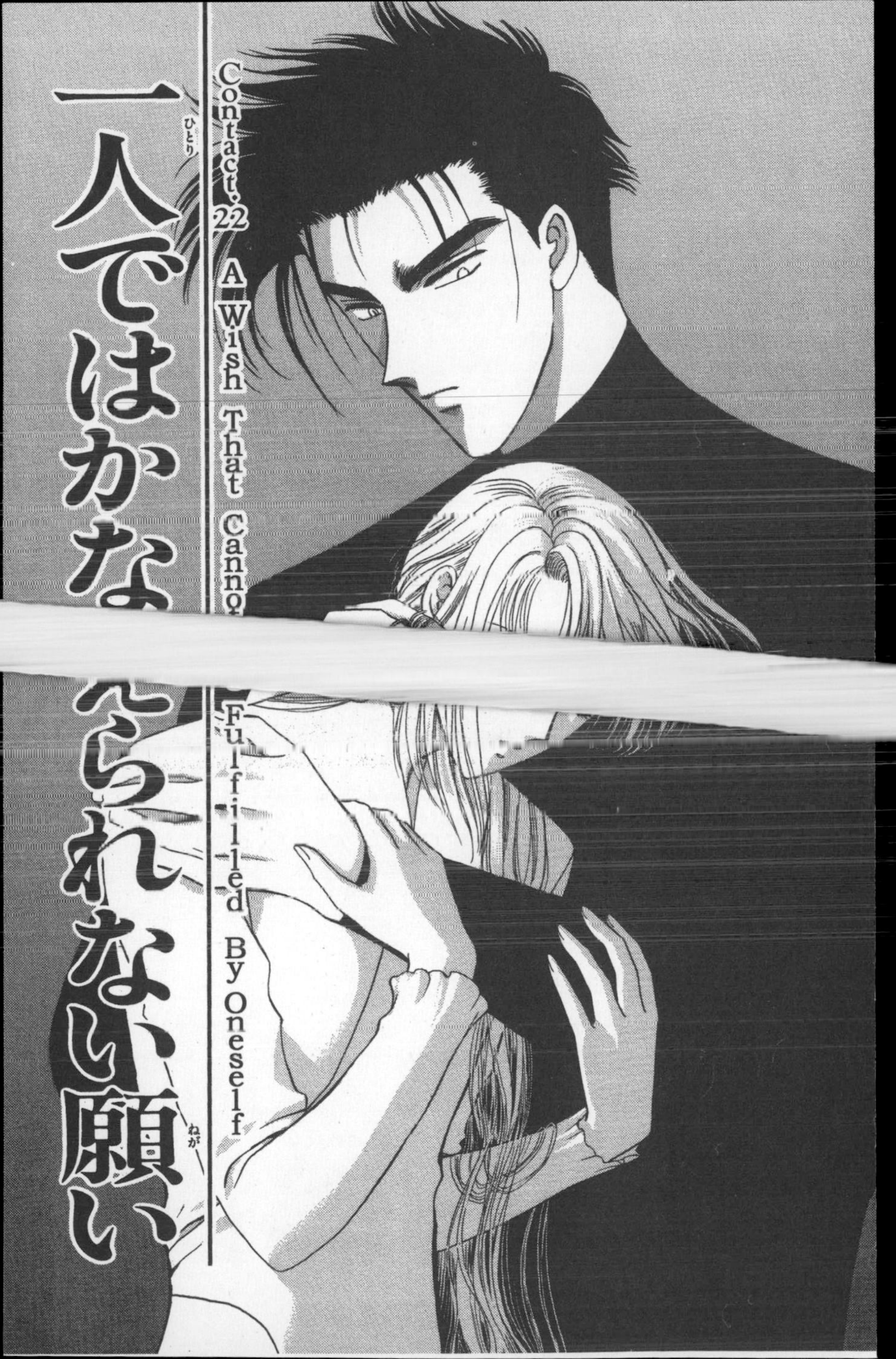

一人ではかな
られない願い
Contact.22
A Wish That Canno
Fulfilled By Oneself

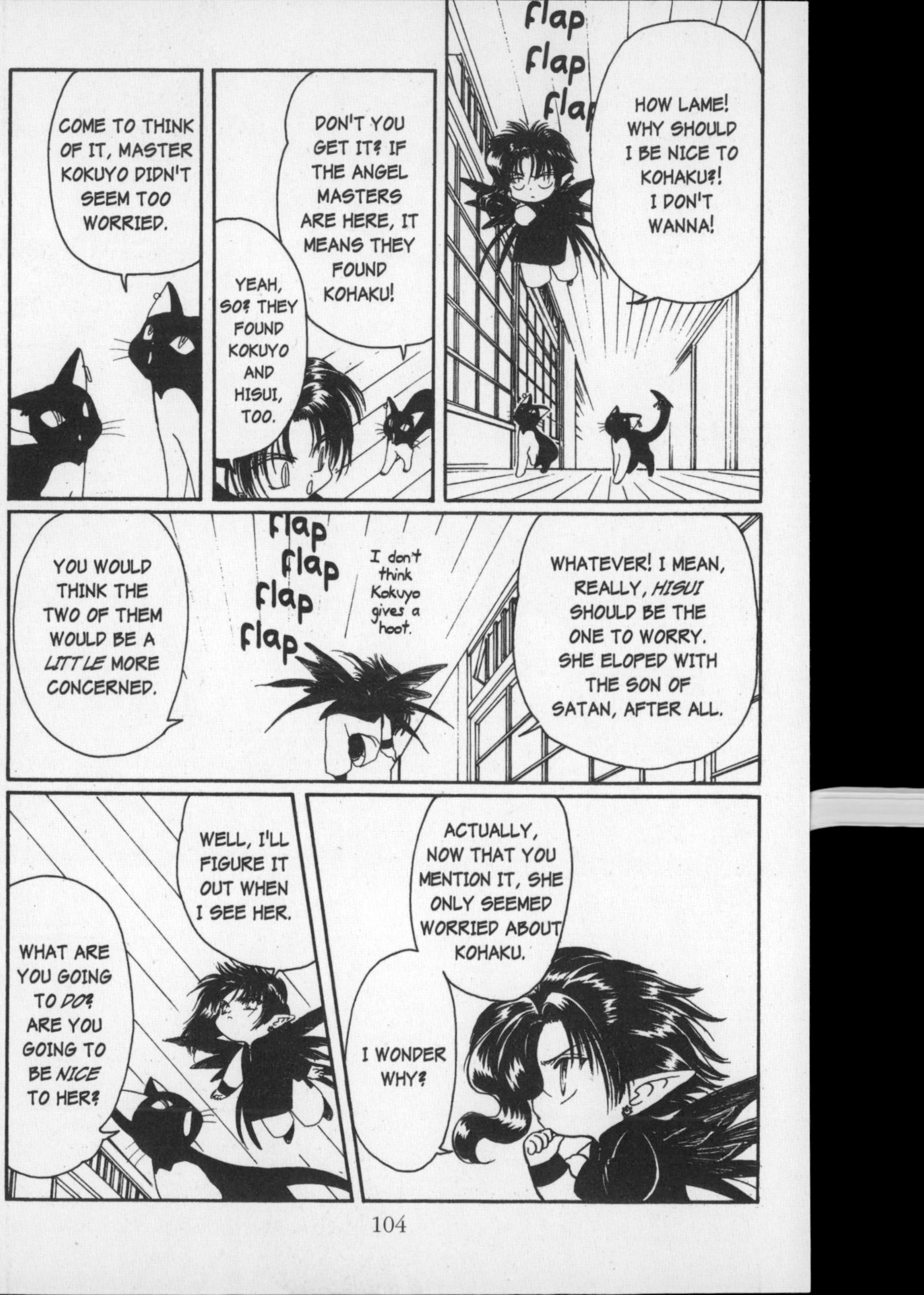
flap
flap
flap
HOW LAME! WHY SHOULD I BE NICE TO KOHAKU?! I DON'T WANNA!
DON'T YOU GET IT? IF THE ANGEL MASTERS ARE HERE, IT MEANS THEY FOUND KOHAKU!
YEAH, SO? THEY FOUND KOKUYO AND HISUI, TOO.
COME TO THINK OF IT, MASTER KOKUYO DIDN'T SEEM TOO WORRIED.
WHATEVER! I MEAN, REALLY, *HISUI* SHOULD BE THE ONE TO WORRY. SHE ELOPED WITH THE SON OF SATAN, AFTER ALL.
flap
flap
flap
flap
I don't think Kokuyo gives a hoot.
YOU WOULD THINK THE TWO OF THEM WOULD BE A *LITTLE* MORE CONCERNED.
ACTUALLY, NOW THAT YOU MENTION IT, SHE ONLY SEEMED WORRIED ABOUT KOHAKU.
I WONDER WHY?
WELL, I'LL FIGURE IT OUT WHEN I SEE HER.
WHAT ARE YOU GOING TO *DO*? ARE YOU GOING TO BE *NICE* TO HER?

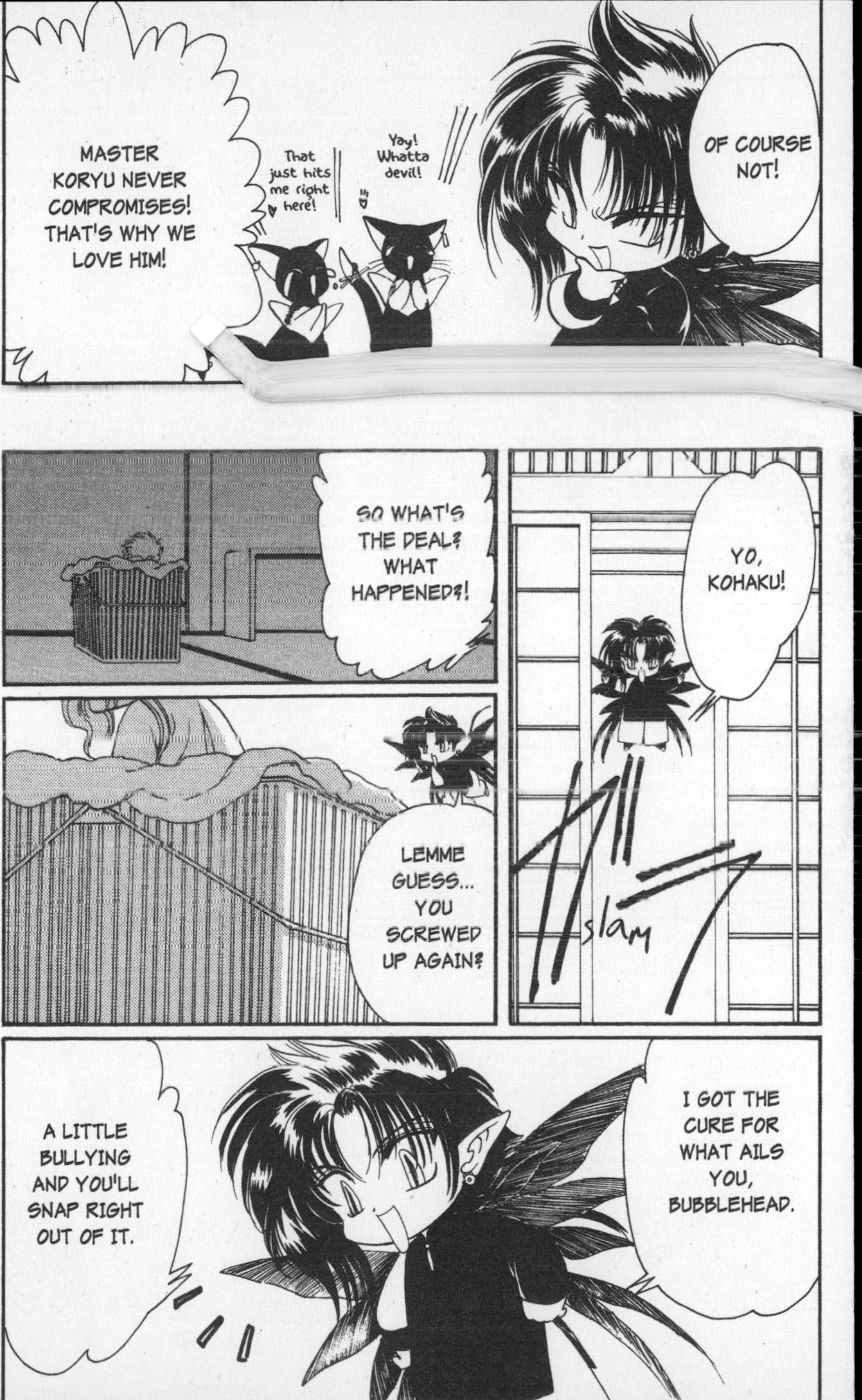
OF COURSE NOT!
Yay! Whatta devil!
That just hits me right here!
MASTER KORYU NEVER COMPROMISES! THAT'S WHY WE LOVE HIM!
YO, KOHAKU!
slam
SO WHAT'S THE DEAL? WHAT HAPPENED?!
LEMME GUESS... YOU SCREWED UP AGAIN?
I GOT THE CURE FOR WHAT AILS YOU, BUBBLEHEAD.
A LITTLE BULLYING AND YOU'LL SNAP RIGHT OUT OF IT.

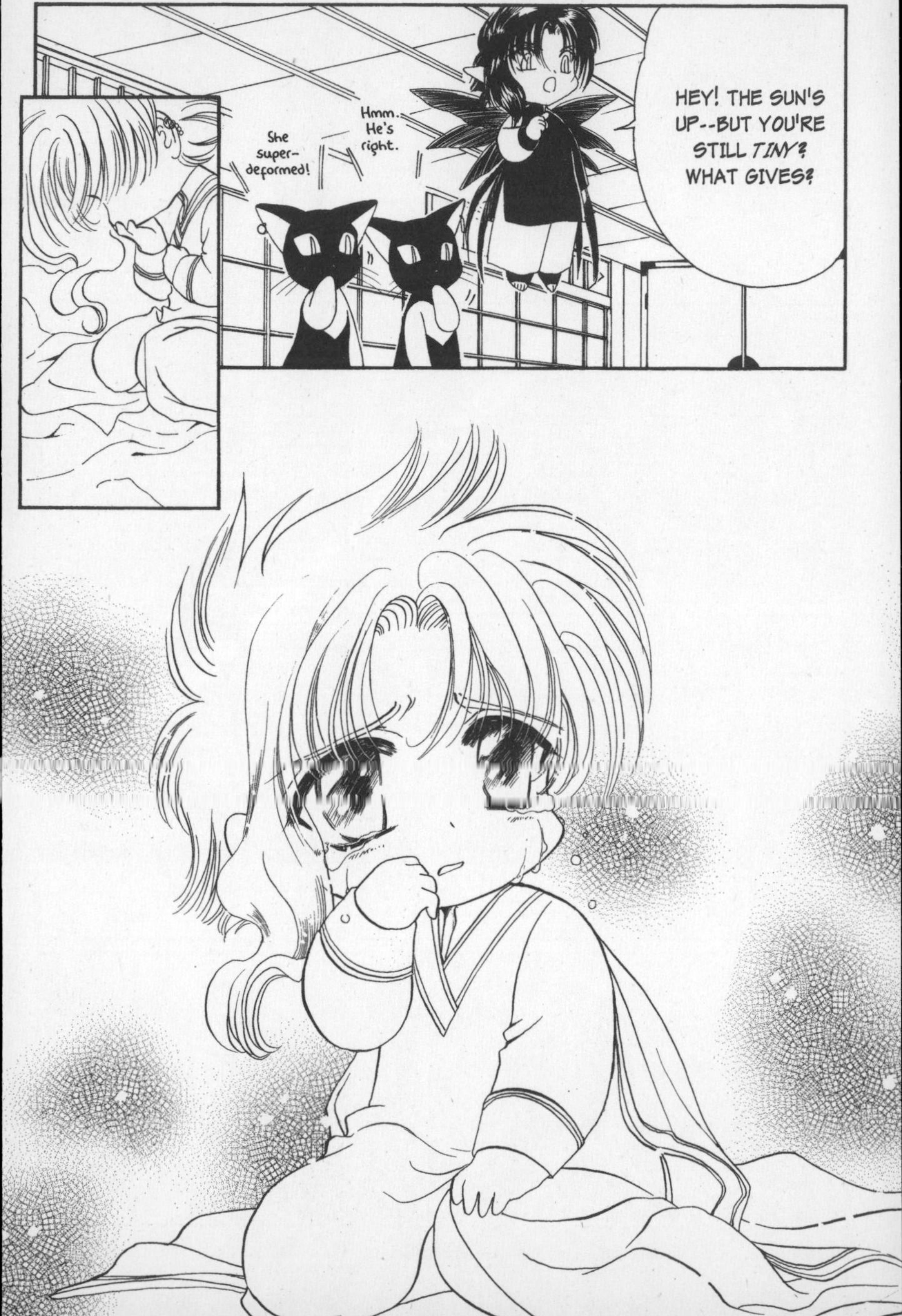
HEY! THE SUN'S UP--BUT YOU'RE STILL TINY? WHAT GIVES?
Hmm. He's right.
She super-deformed!

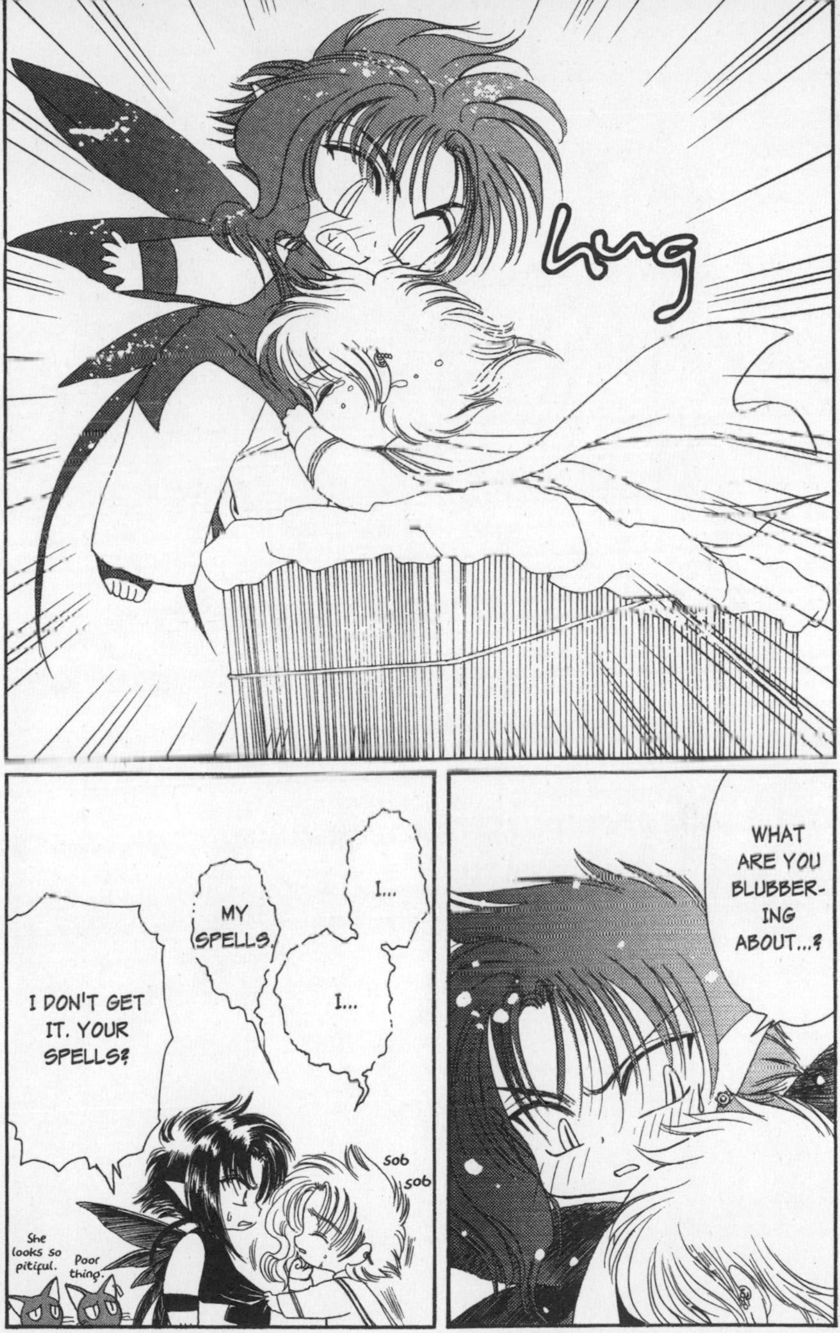
HUG
WHAT ARE YOU BLUBBER-ING ABOUT...?
I...
MY SPELLS.
I...
I DON'T GET IT. YOUR SPELLS?
sob sob
Poor thing.
She looks so pitiful.

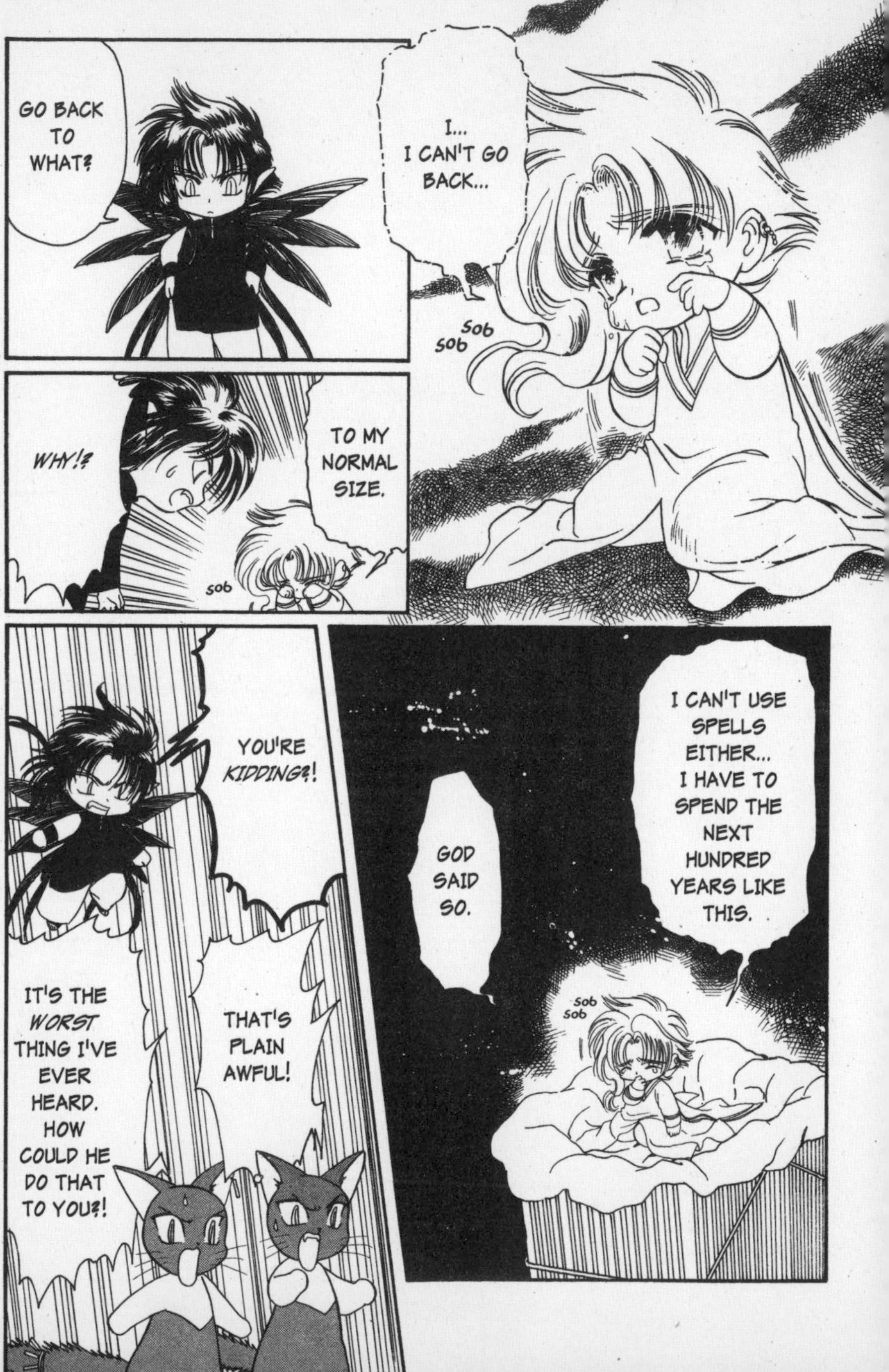
I... I CAN'T GO BACK...
Sob sob
GO BACK TO WHAT?
TO MY NORMAL SIZE.
WHY!?
sob
I CAN'T USE SPELLS EITHER... I HAVE TO SPEND THE NEXT HUNDRED YEARS LIKE THIS.
GOD SAID SO.
Sob Sob
YOU'RE *KIDDING*?!
THAT'S PLAIN AWFUL!
IT'S THE *WORST* THING I'VE EVER HEARD. HOW COULD HE DO THAT TO YOU?!

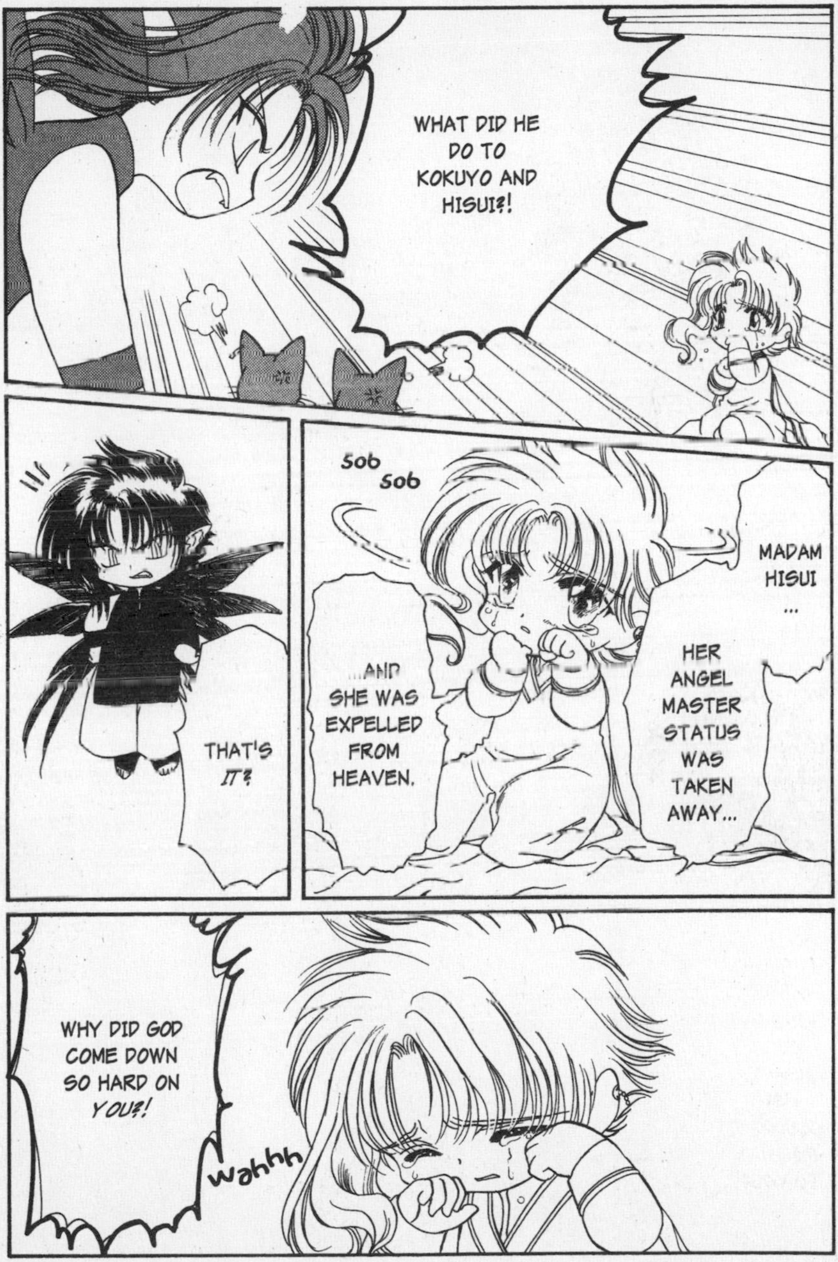

WHAT DID HE DO TO KOKUYO AND HISUI?!
MADAM HISUI ...
Sob sob
HER ANGEL MASTER STATUS WAS TAKEN AWAY...
...AND SHE WAS EXPELLED FROM HEAVEN.
THAT'S *IT*?
WHY DID GOD COME DOWN SO HARD ON *YOU*?!
wahhh

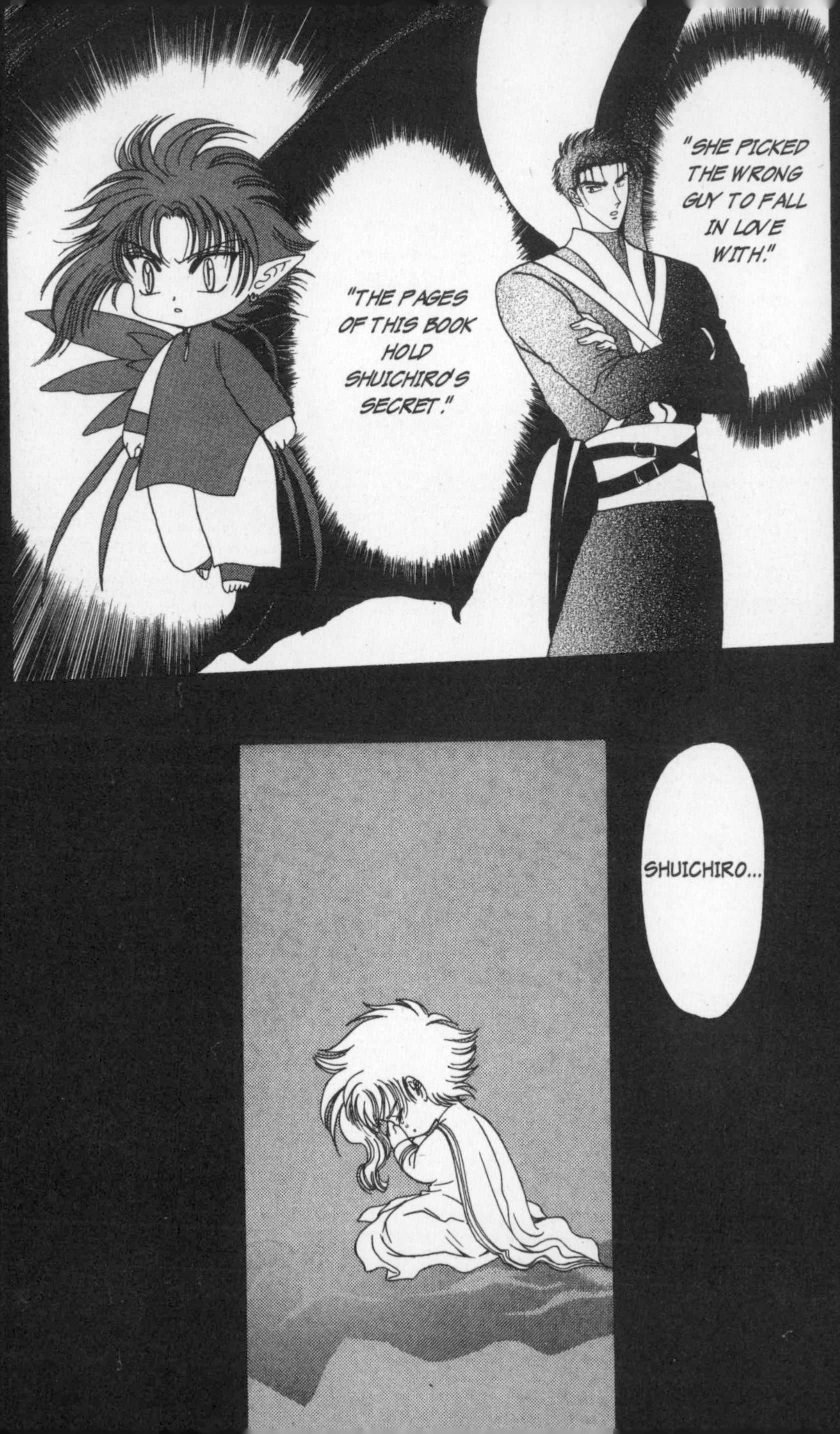
"SHE PICKED THE WRONG GUY TO FALL IN LOVE WITH."
"THE PAGES OF THIS BOOK HOLD SHUICHIRO'S SECRET."
SHUICHIRO...

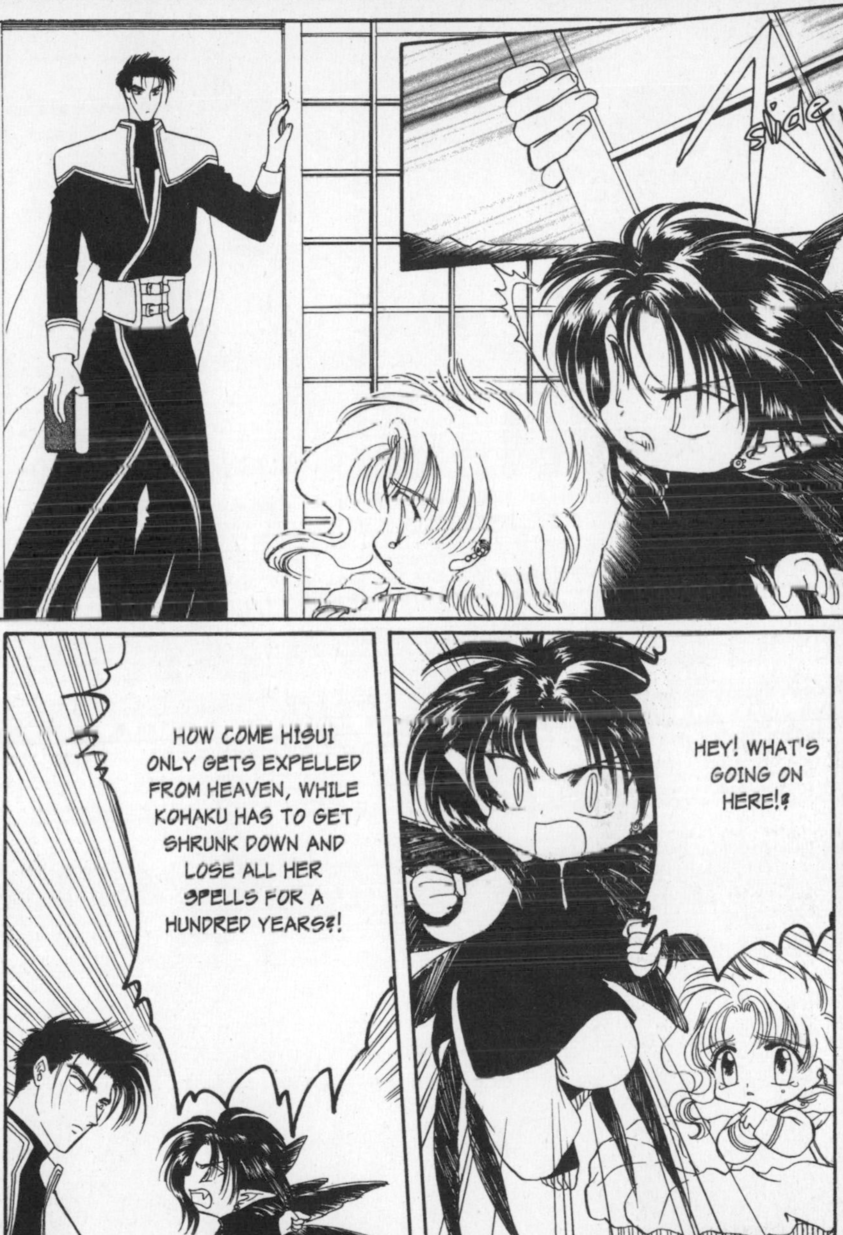
slide
HEY! WHAT'S GOING ON HERE!?
HOW COME HISUI ONLY GETS EXPELLED FROM HEAVEN, WHILE KOHAKU HAS TO GET SHRUNK DOWN AND LOSE ALL HER SPELLS FOR A HUNDRED YEARS?!

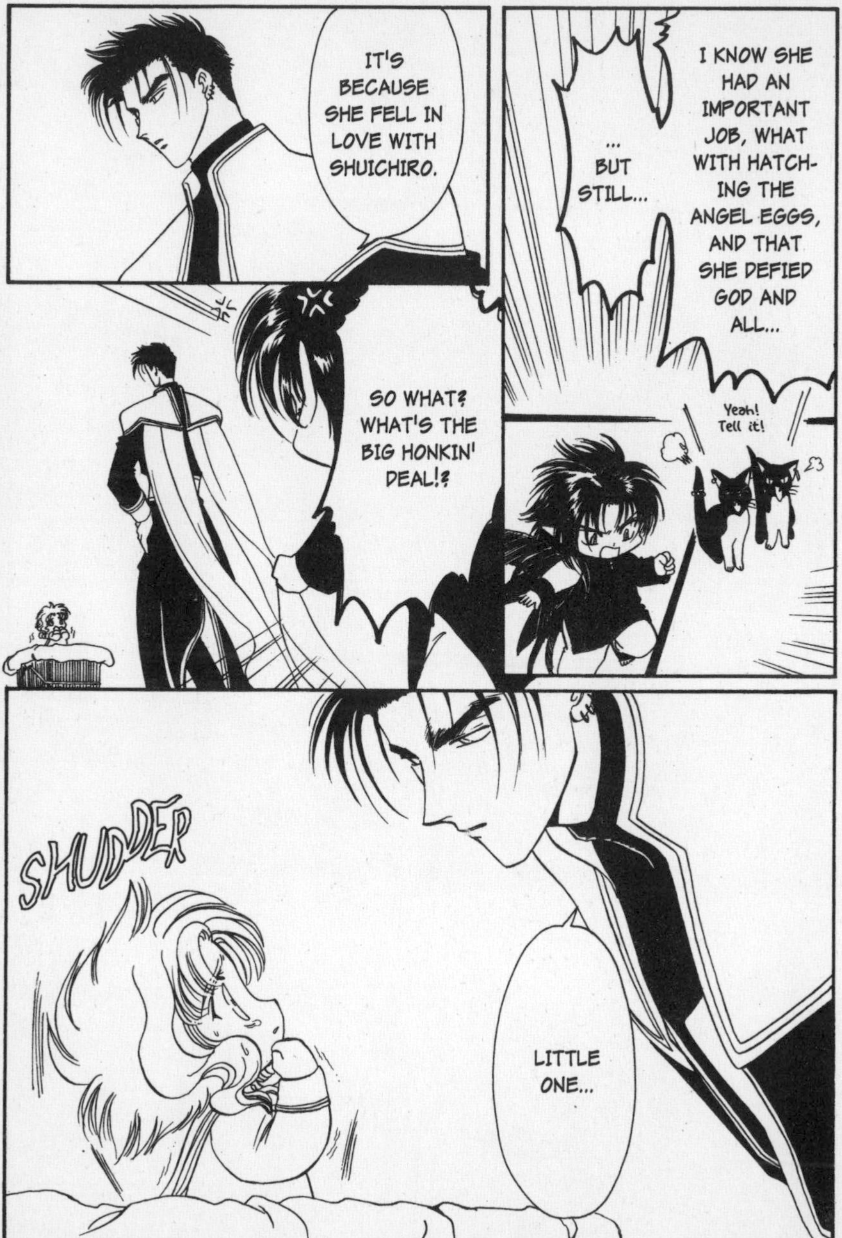
I KNOW SHE HAD AN IMPORTANT JOB, WHAT WITH HATCH-ING THE ANGEL EGGS, AND THAT SHE DEFIED GOD AND ALL...
... BUT STILL...
IT'S BECAUSE SHE FELL IN LOVE WITH SHUICHIRO.
Yeah! Tell it!
SO WHAT? WHAT'S THE BIG HONKIN' DEAL!?
SHUDDER
LITTLE ONE...

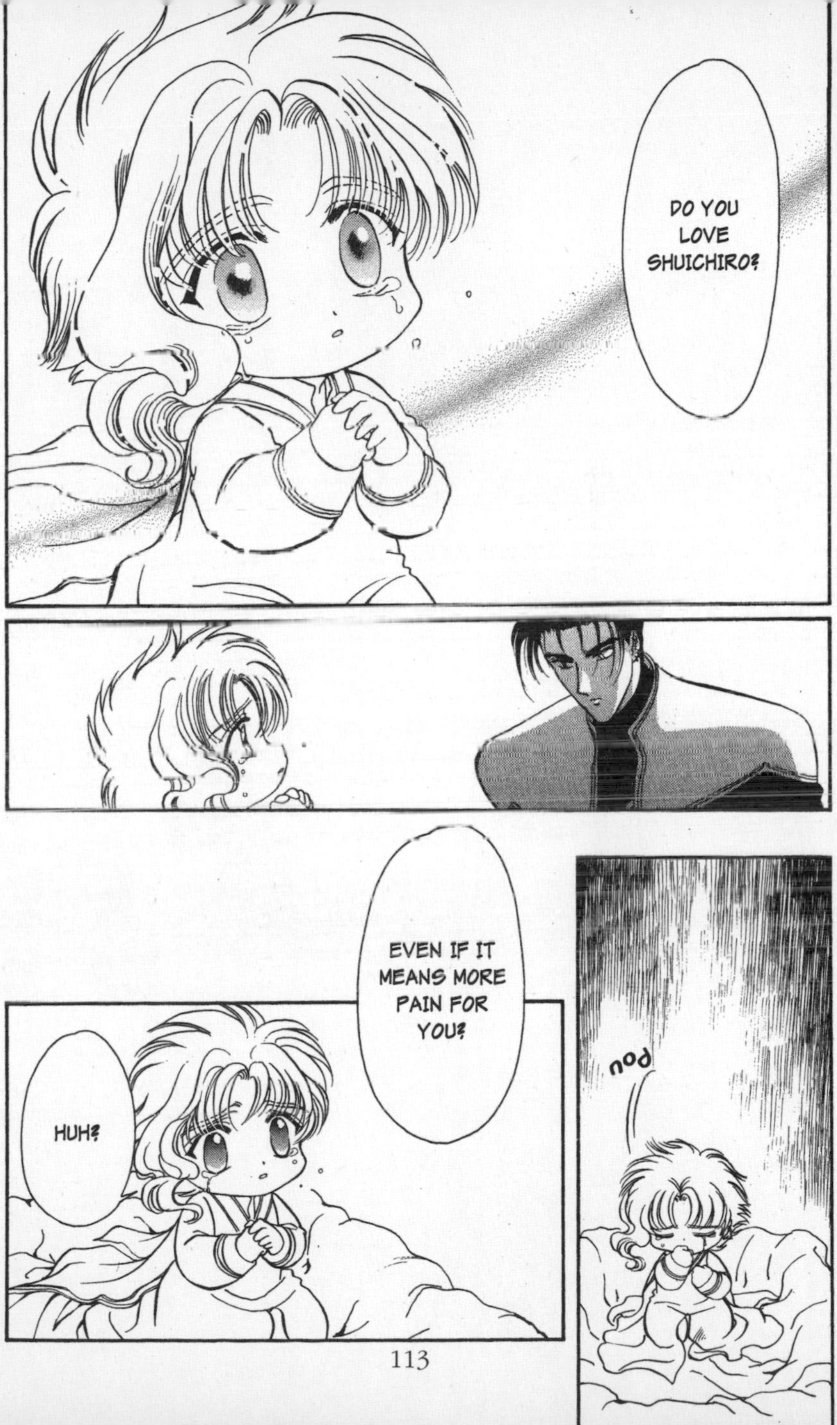
DO YOU LOVE SHUICHIRO?
EVEN IF IT MEANS MORE PAIN FOR YOU?
HUH?
nod

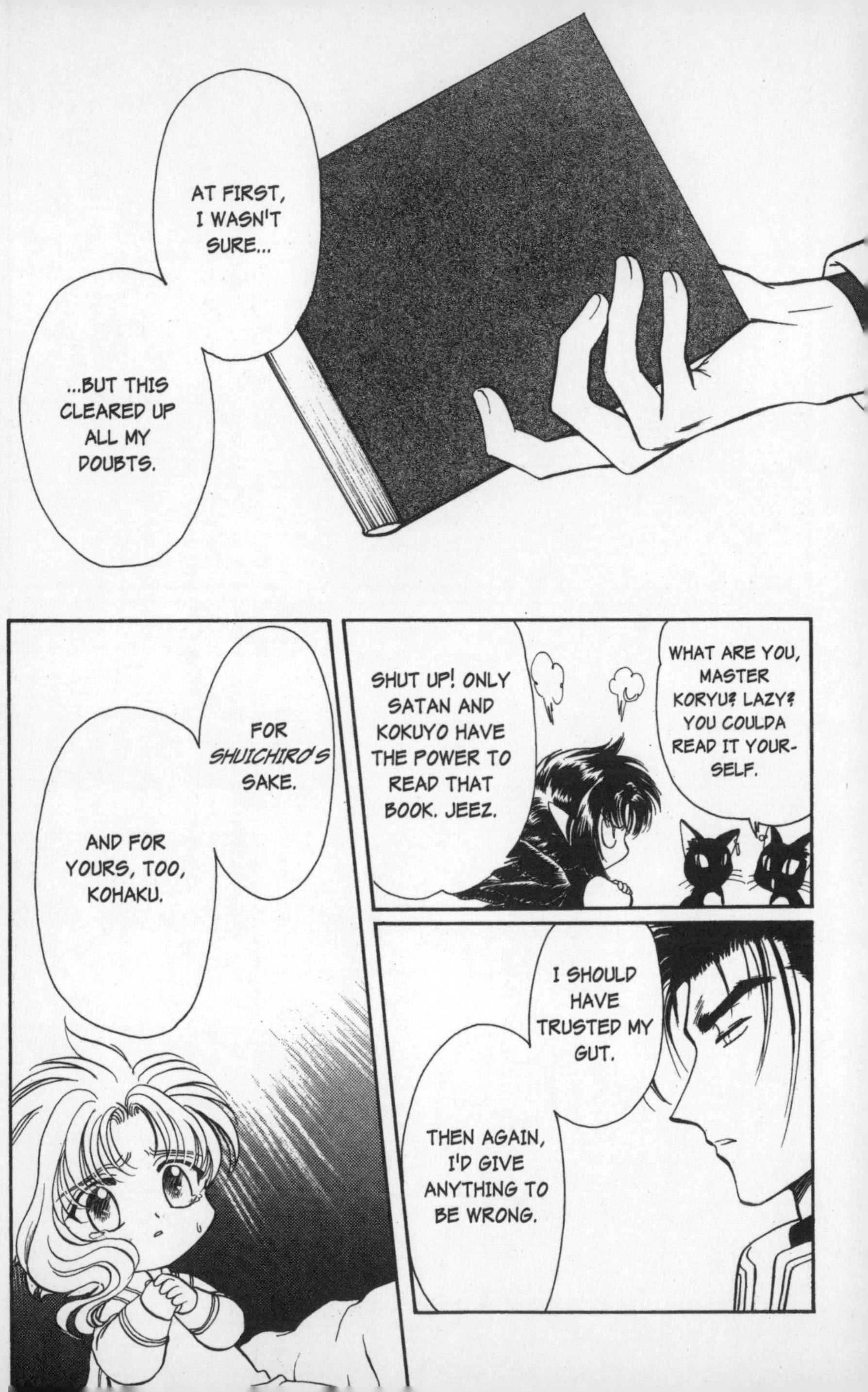
AT FIRST, I WASN'T SURE...
...BUT THIS CLEARED UP ALL MY DOUBTS.
WHAT ARE YOU, MASTER KORYU? LAZY? YOU COULDA READ IT YOUR-SELF.
SHUT UP! ONLY SATAN AND KOKUYO HAVE THE POWER TO READ THAT BOOK. JEEZ.
I SHOULD HAVE TRUSTED MY GUT.
THEN AGAIN, I'D GIVE ANYTHING TO BE WRONG.
FOR *SHUICHIRO'S* SAKE.
AND FOR YOURS, TOO, KOHAKU.

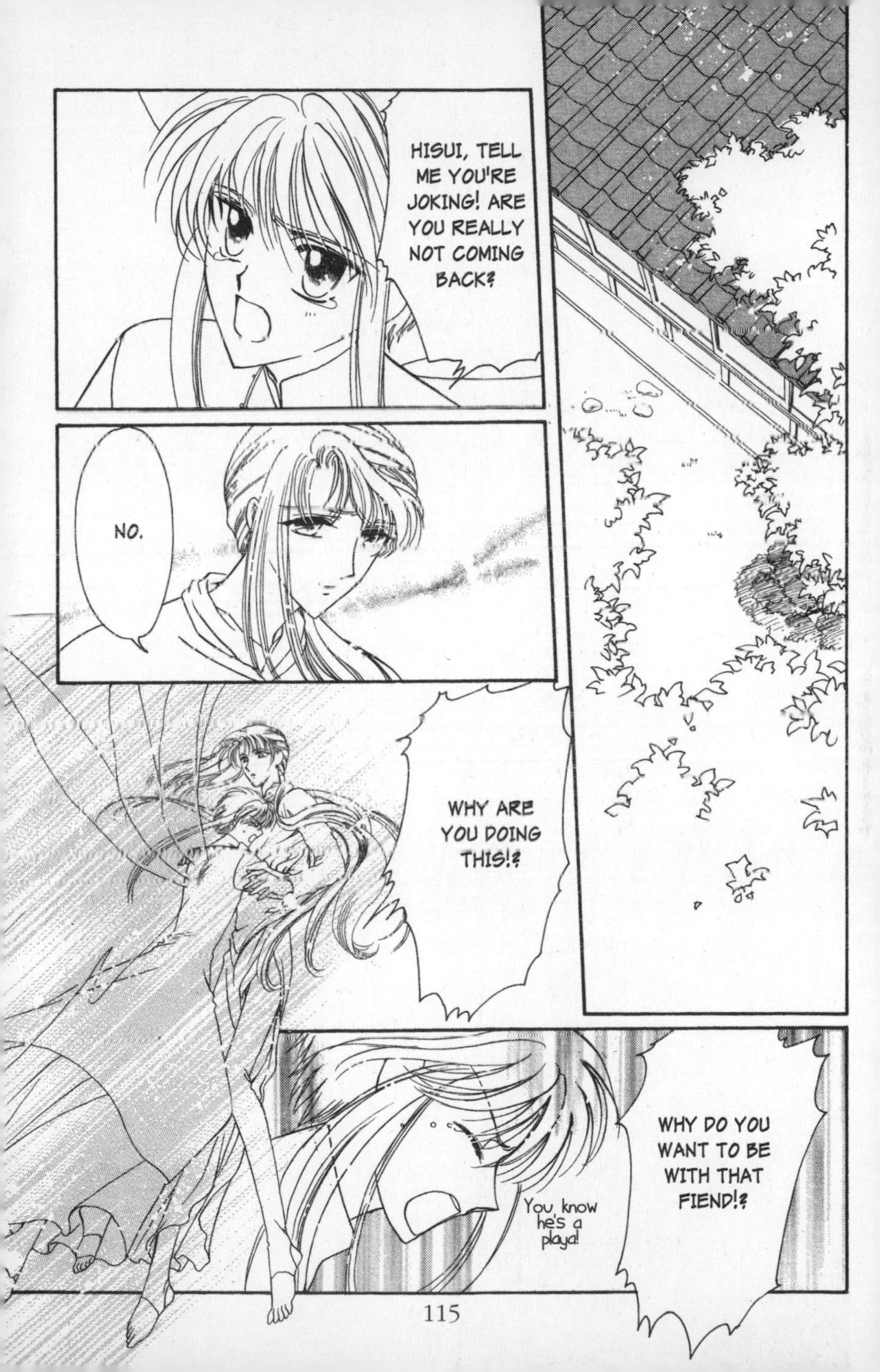
HISUI, TELL ME YOU'RE JOKING! ARE YOU REALLY NOT COMING BACK?
NO.
WHY ARE YOU DOING THIS!?
WHY DO YOU WANT TO BE WITH THAT FIEND!?
You know he's a playa!

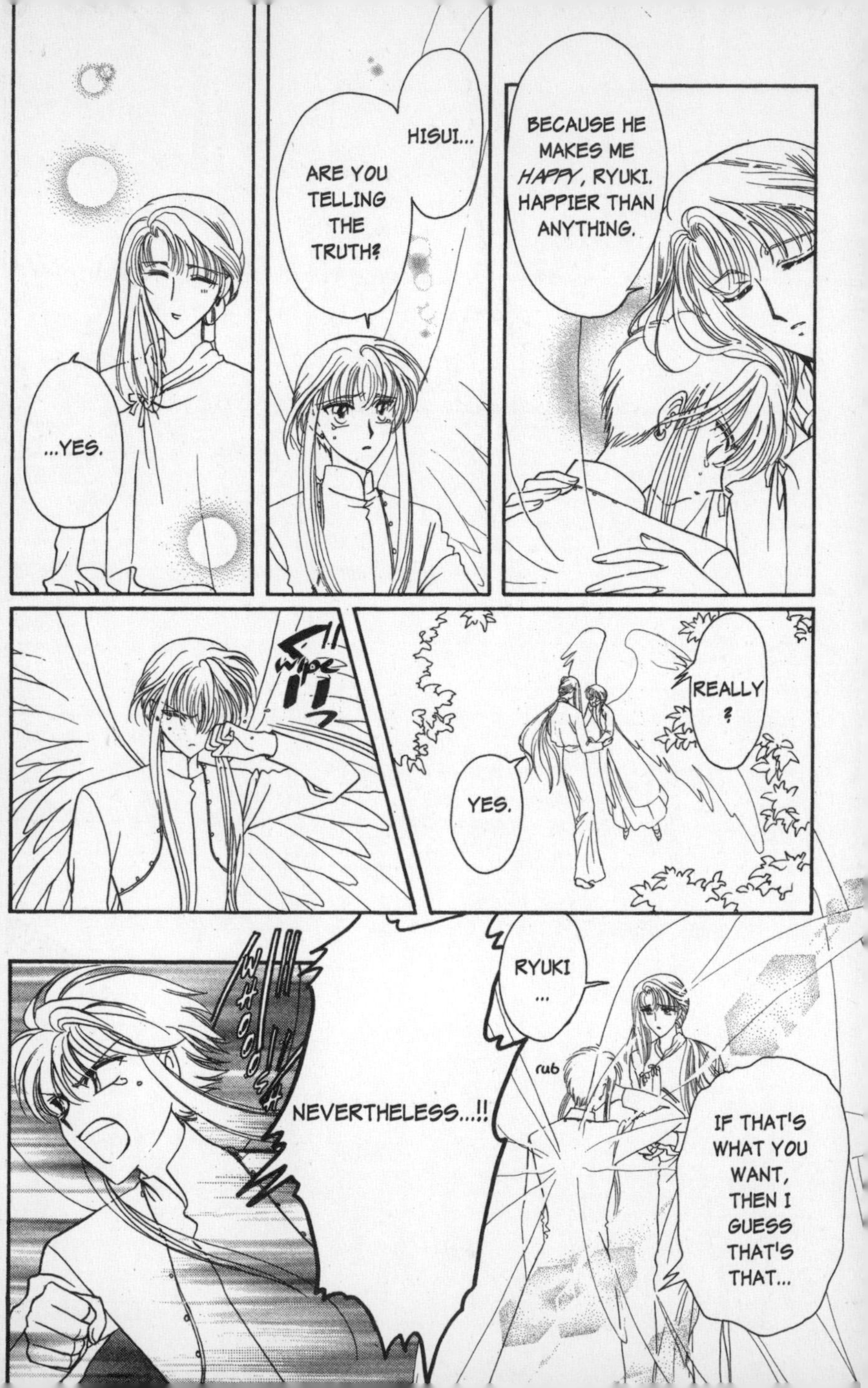
BECAUSE HE MAKES ME *HAPPY*, RYUKI. HAPPIER THAN ANYTHING.
HISUI...
ARE YOU TELLING THE TRUTH?
...YES.
REALLY?
YES.
wipe
RYUKI ...
rub
IF THAT'S WHAT YOU WANT, THEN I GUESS THAT'S THAT...
NEVERTHELESS...!!

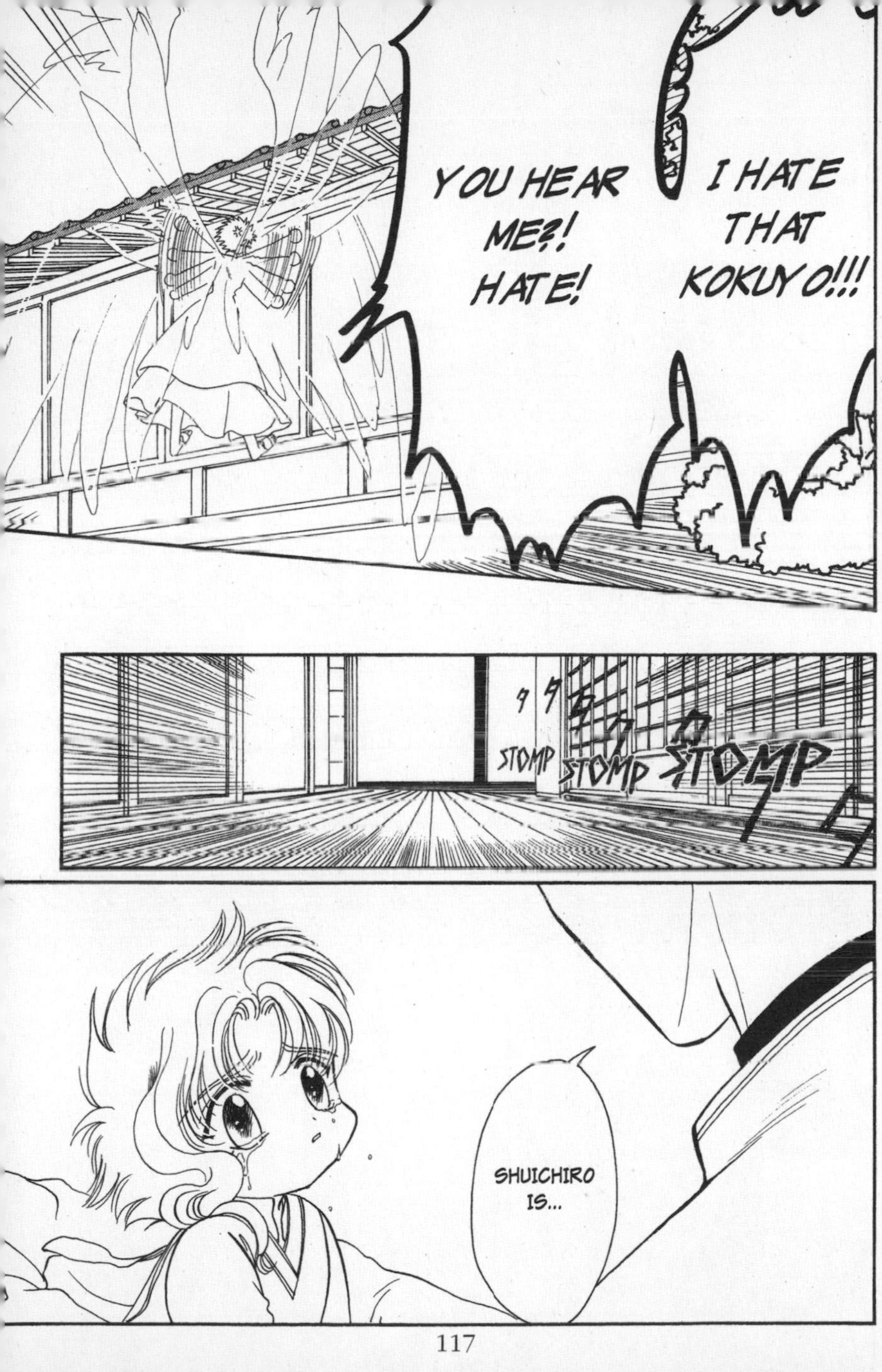
I HATE THAT KOKUYO!!!
YOU HEAR ME?! HATE!
STOMP
STOMP
STOMP
SHUICHIRO IS...

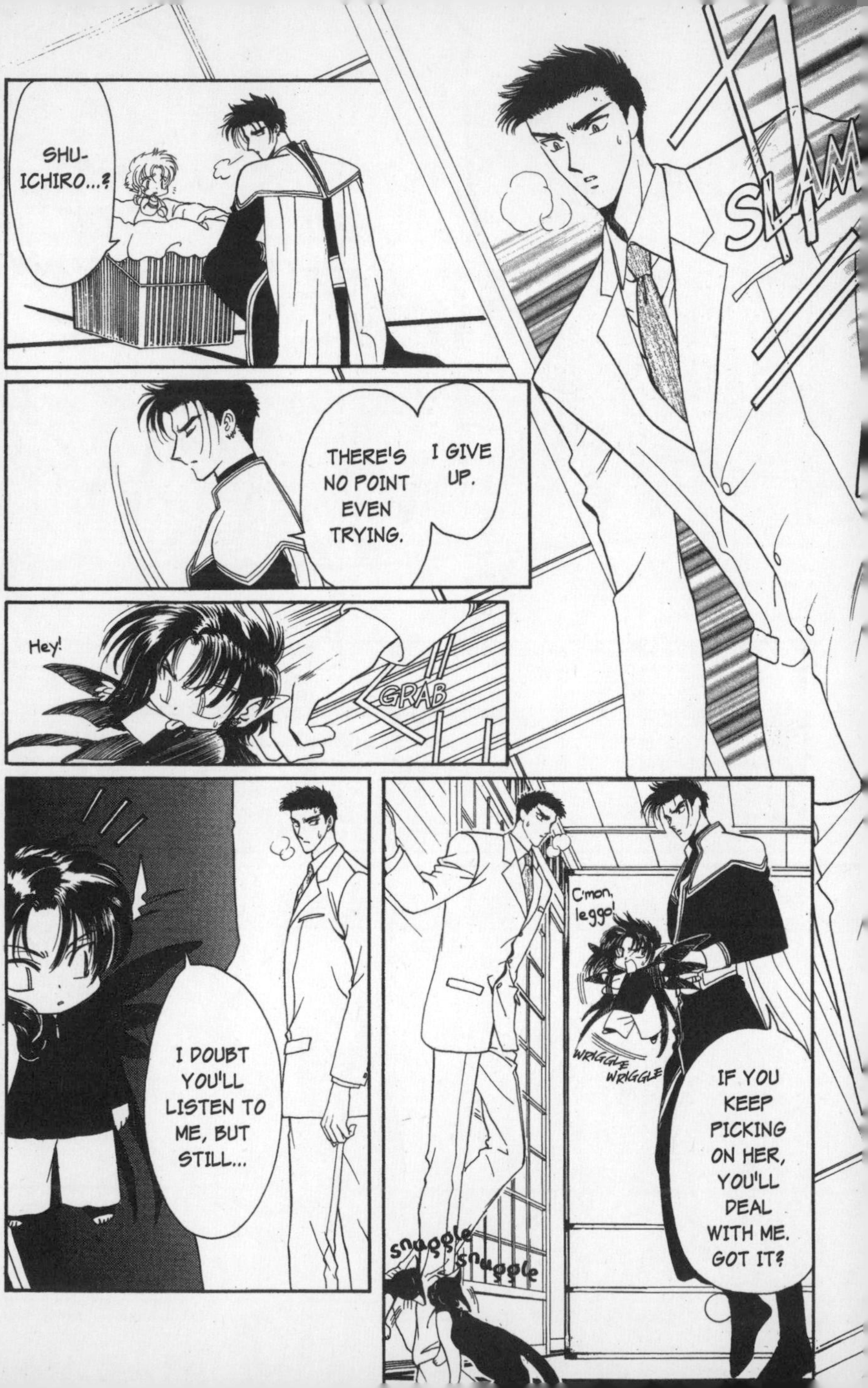
SLAM
SHU-ICHIRO...?
I GIVE UP.
THERE'S NO POINT EVEN TRYING.
Hey!
GRAB
IF YOU KEEP PICKING ON HER, YOU'LL DEAL WITH ME. GOT IT?
C'mon, leggo!
WRIGGLE WRIGGLE
snuggle snuggle
I DOUBT YOU'LL LISTEN TO ME, BUT STILL...

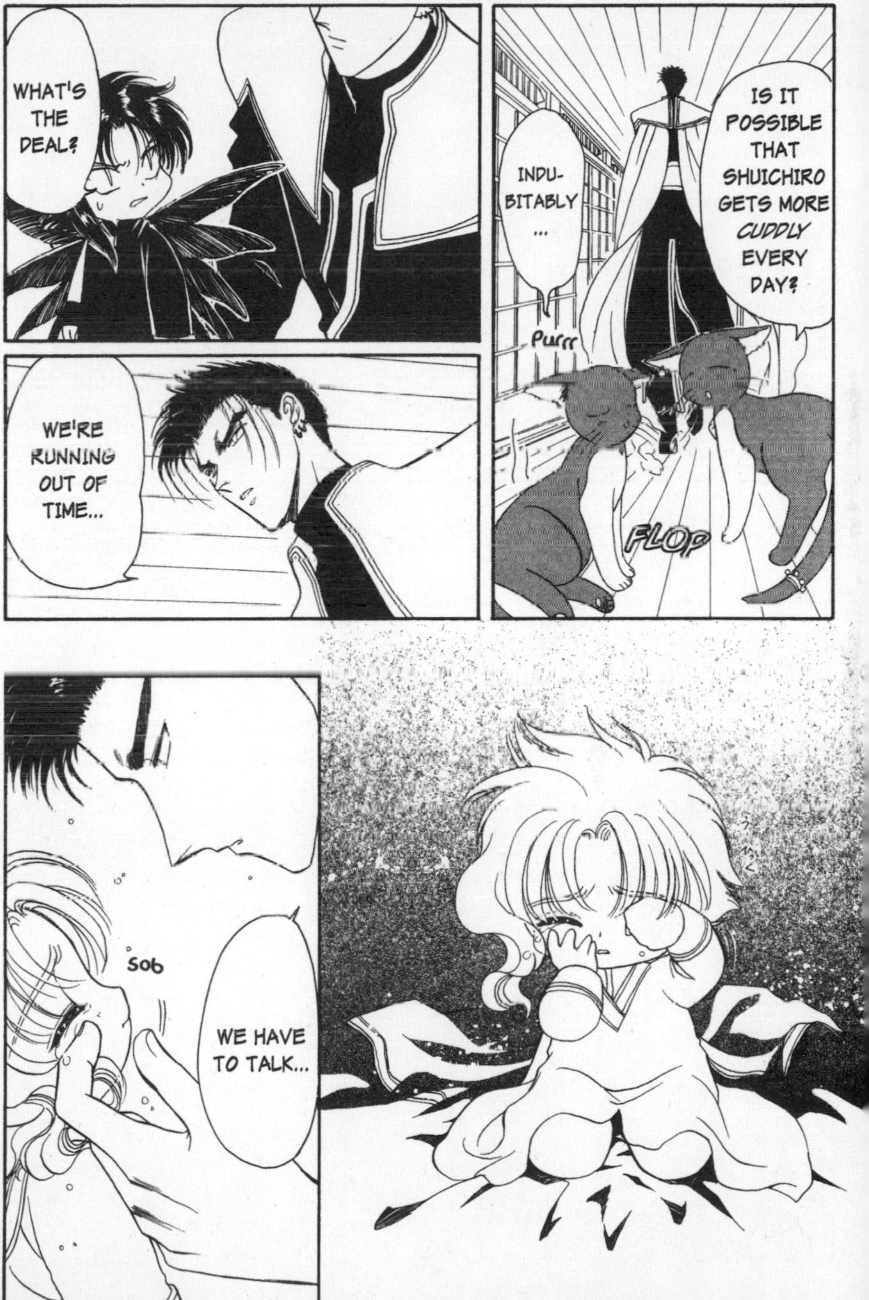
IS IT POSSIBLE THAT SHUICHIRO GETS MORE *CUDDLY* EVERY DAY?
INDU-BITABLY ...
Purrr
FLOP
WHAT'S THE DEAL?
WE'RE RUNNING OUT OF TIME...
sob
WE HAVE TO TALK...

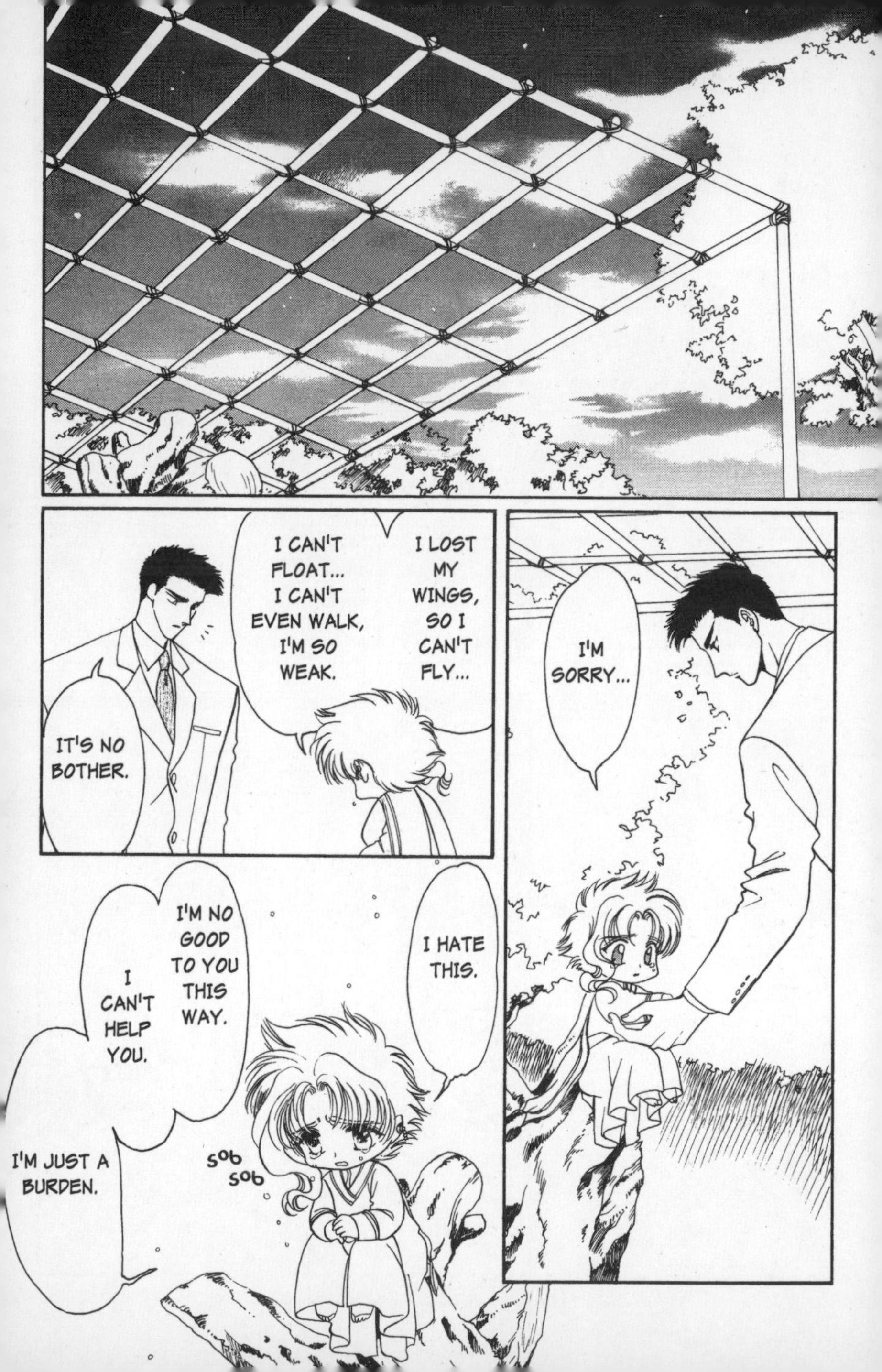
I'M SORRY...
I LOST MY WINGS, SO I CAN'T FLY...
I CAN'T FLOAT... I CAN'T EVEN WALK, I'M SO WEAK.
IT'S NO BOTHER.
I HATE THIS.
I'M NO GOOD TO YOU THIS WAY.
I CAN'T HELP YOU.
I'M JUST A BURDEN.
SOB SOB

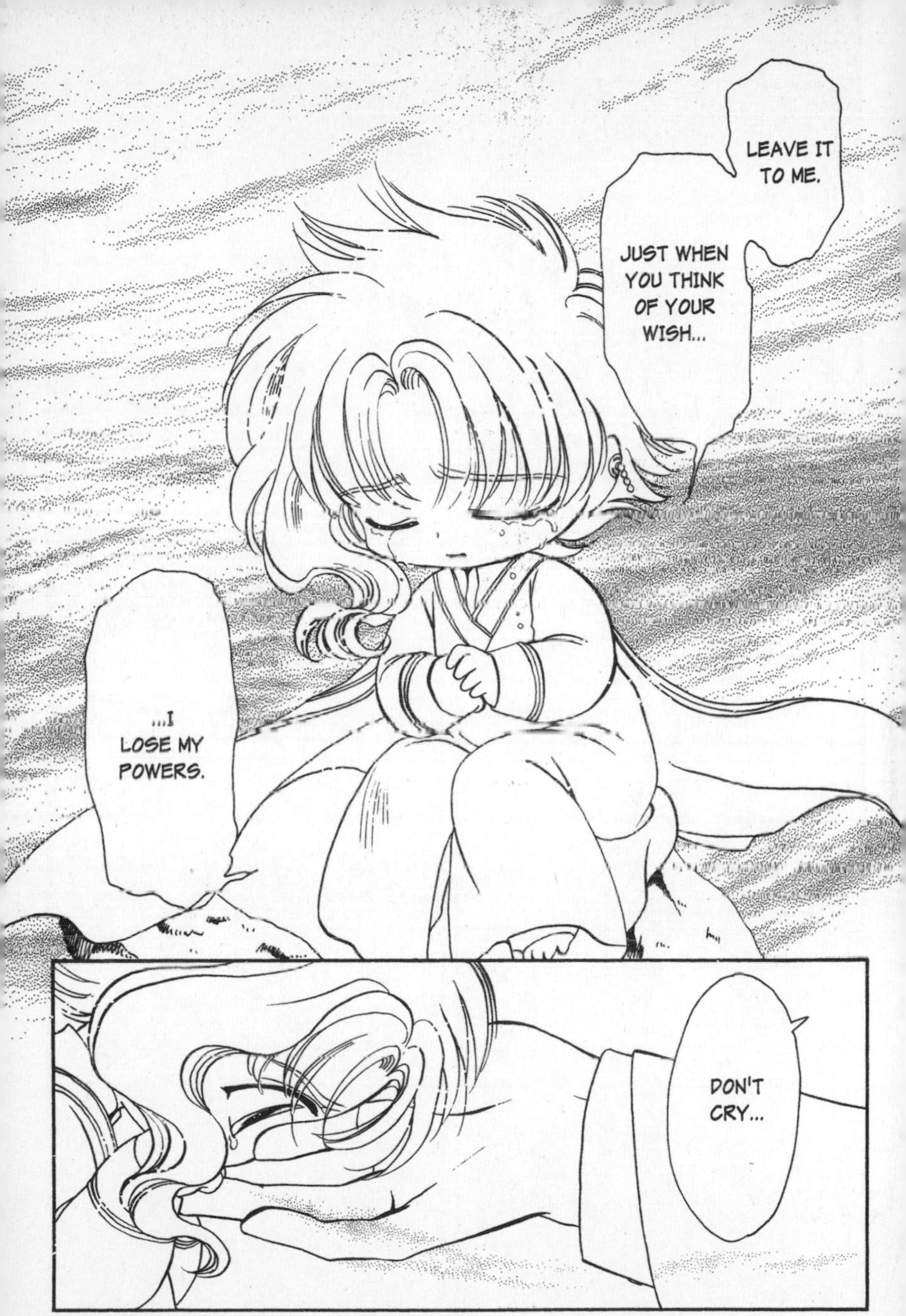
LEAVE IT TO ME.
JUST WHEN YOU THINK OF YOUR WISH...
...I LOSE MY POWERS.
DON'T CRY...

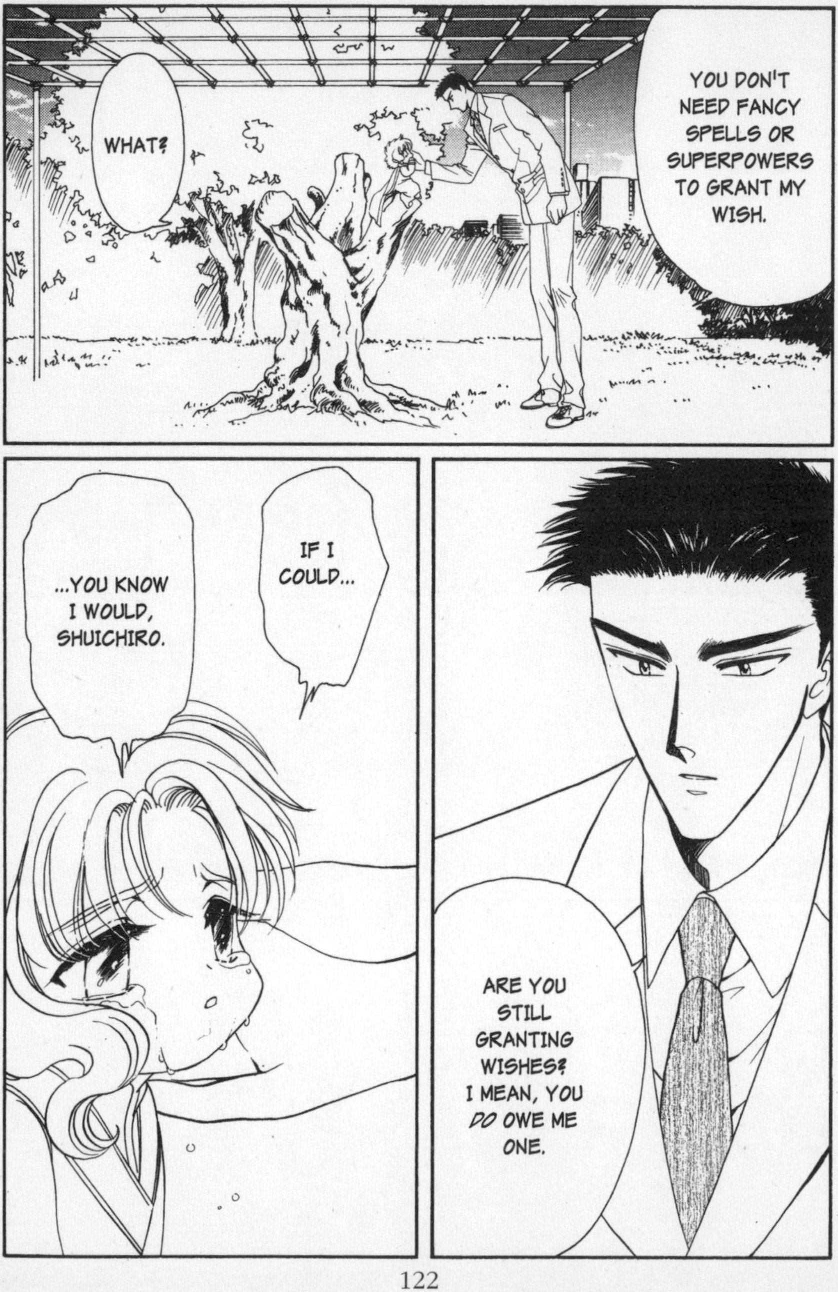
YOU DON'T NEED FANCY SPELLS OR SUPERPOWERS TO GRANT MY WISH.
WHAT?
ARE YOU STILL GRANTING WISHES? I MEAN, YOU *DO* OWE ME ONE.
IF I COULD...
...YOU KNOW I WOULD, SHUICHIRO.

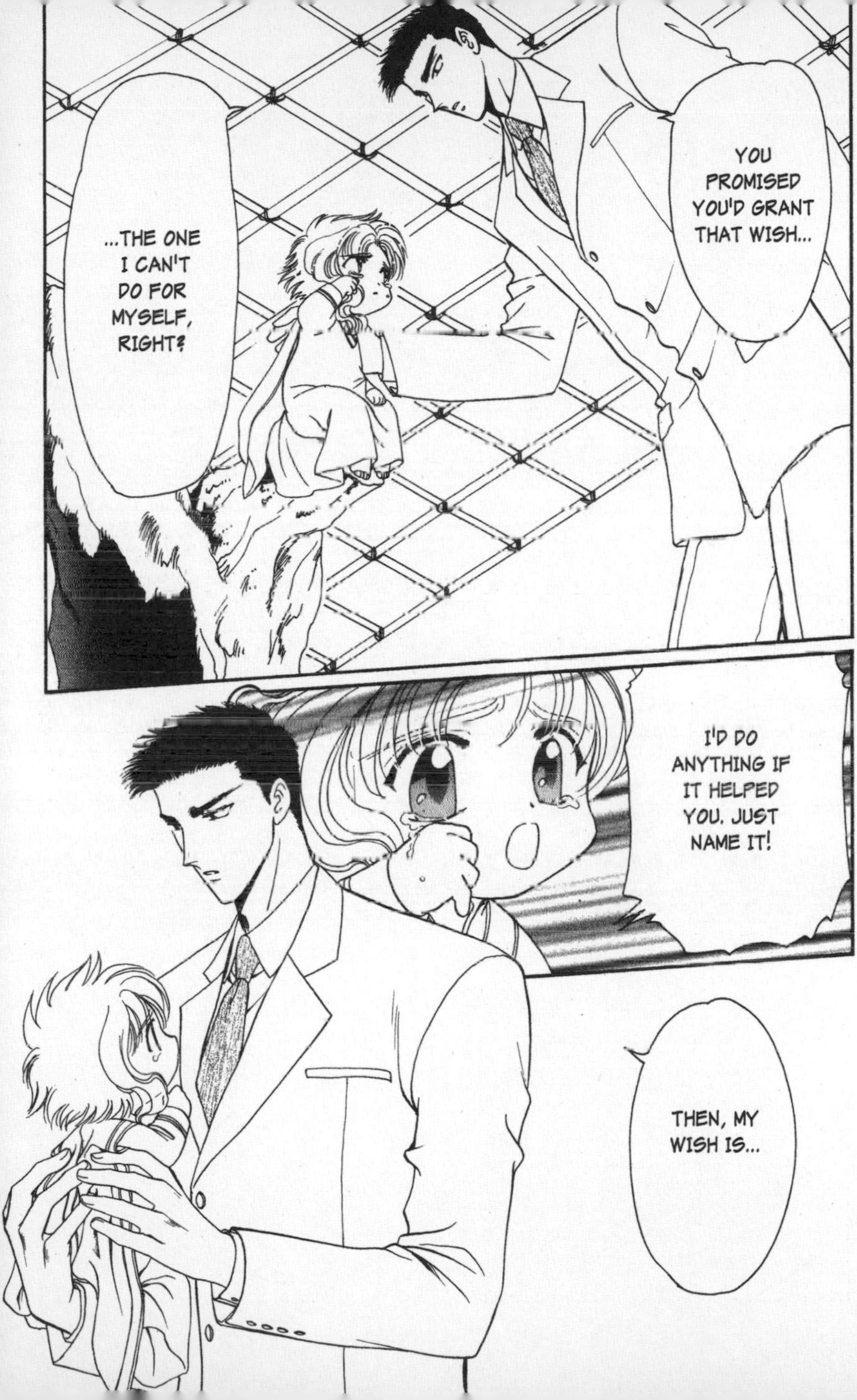
YOU PROMISED YOU'D GRANT THAT WISH...
...THE ONE I CAN'T DO FOR MYSELF, RIGHT?
I'D DO ANYTHING IF IT HELPED YOU. JUST NAME IT!
THEN, MY WISH IS...

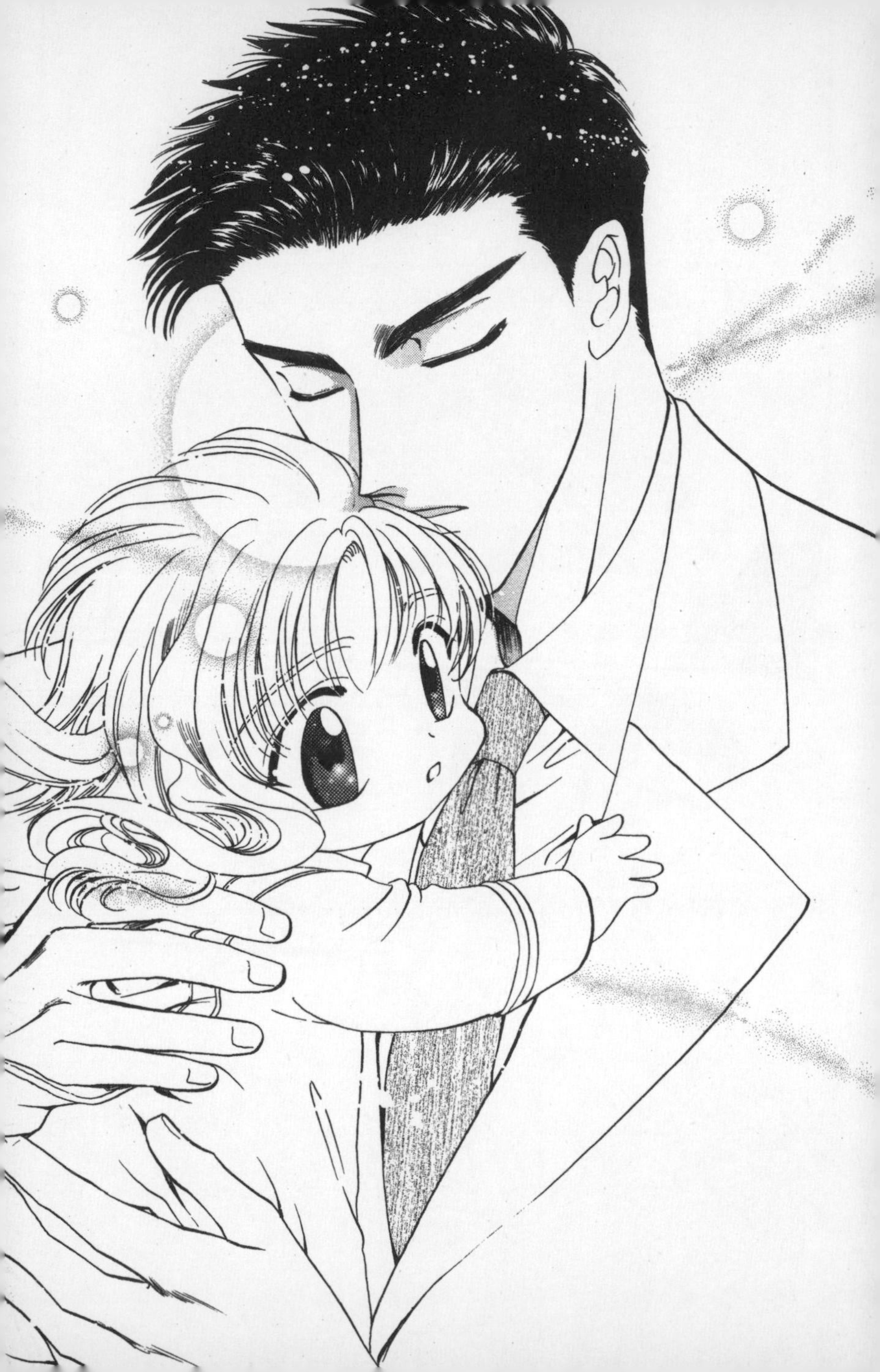

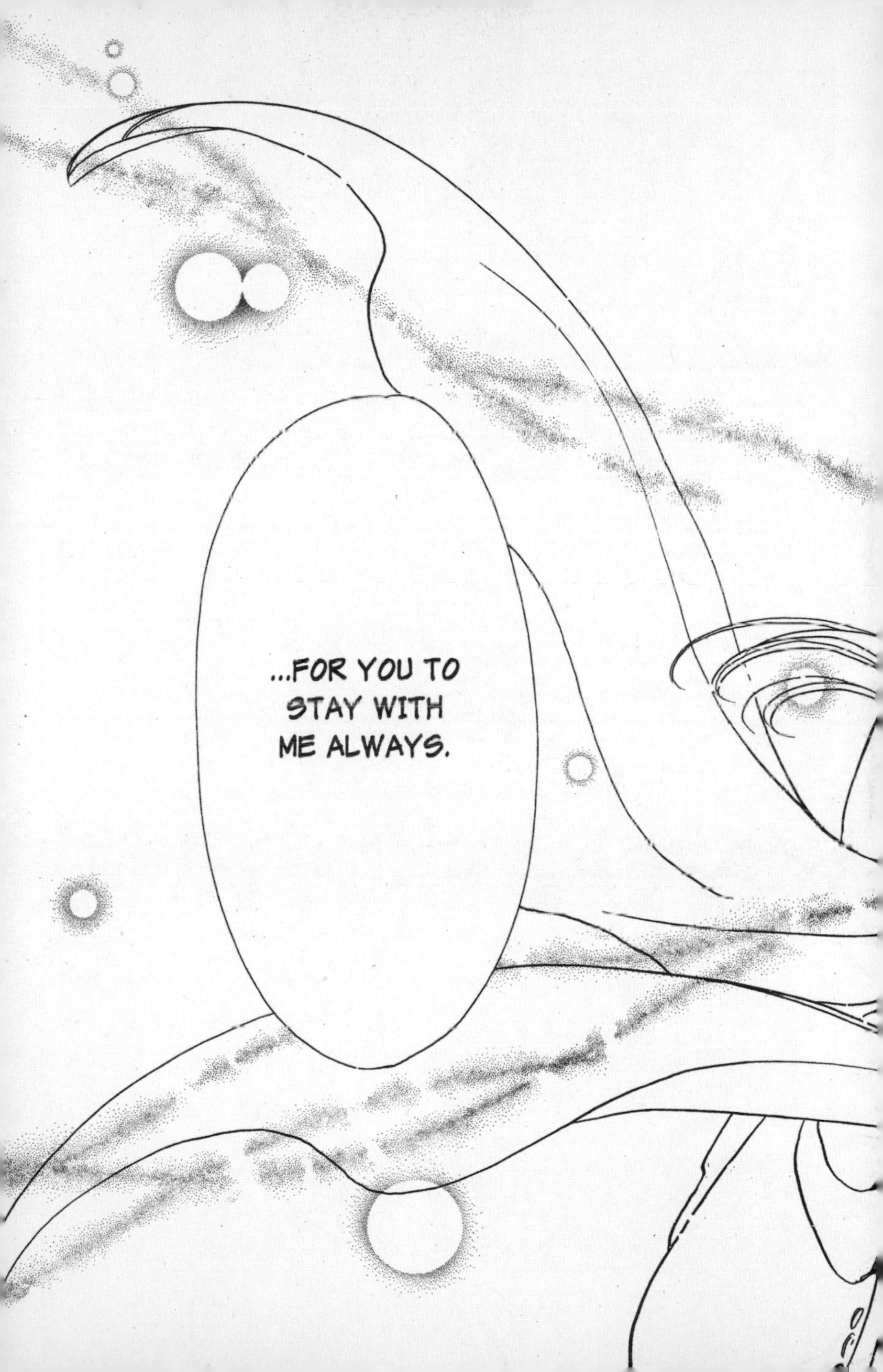
...FOR YOU TO STAY WITH ME ALWAYS.

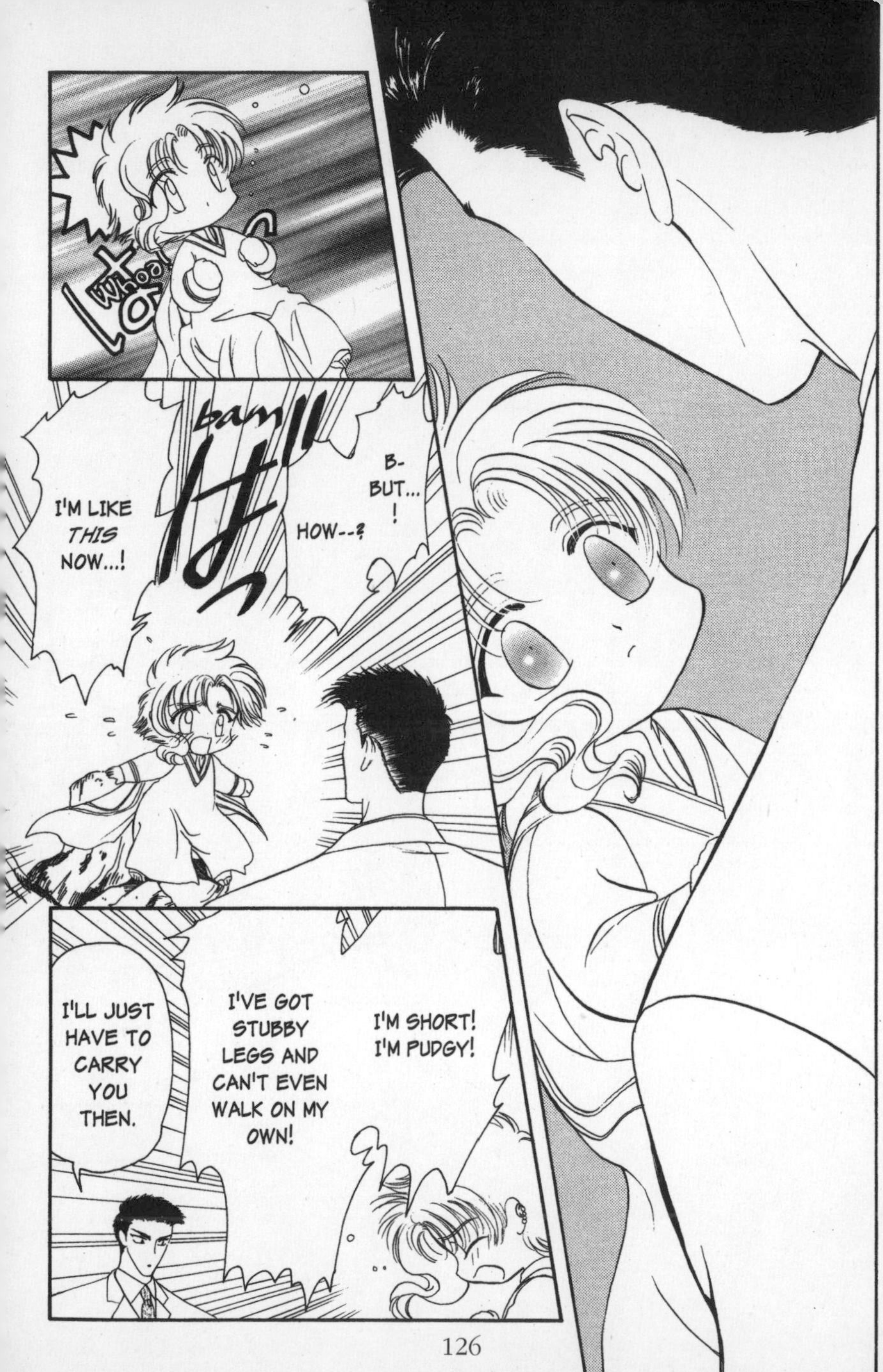
Whoa!
B- BUT... !
HOW--?
bam!!
I'M LIKE THIS NOW...!
I'M SHORT! I'M PUDGY!
I'VE GOT STUBBY LEGS AND CAN'T EVEN WALK ON MY OWN!
I'LL JUST HAVE TO CARRY YOU THEN.

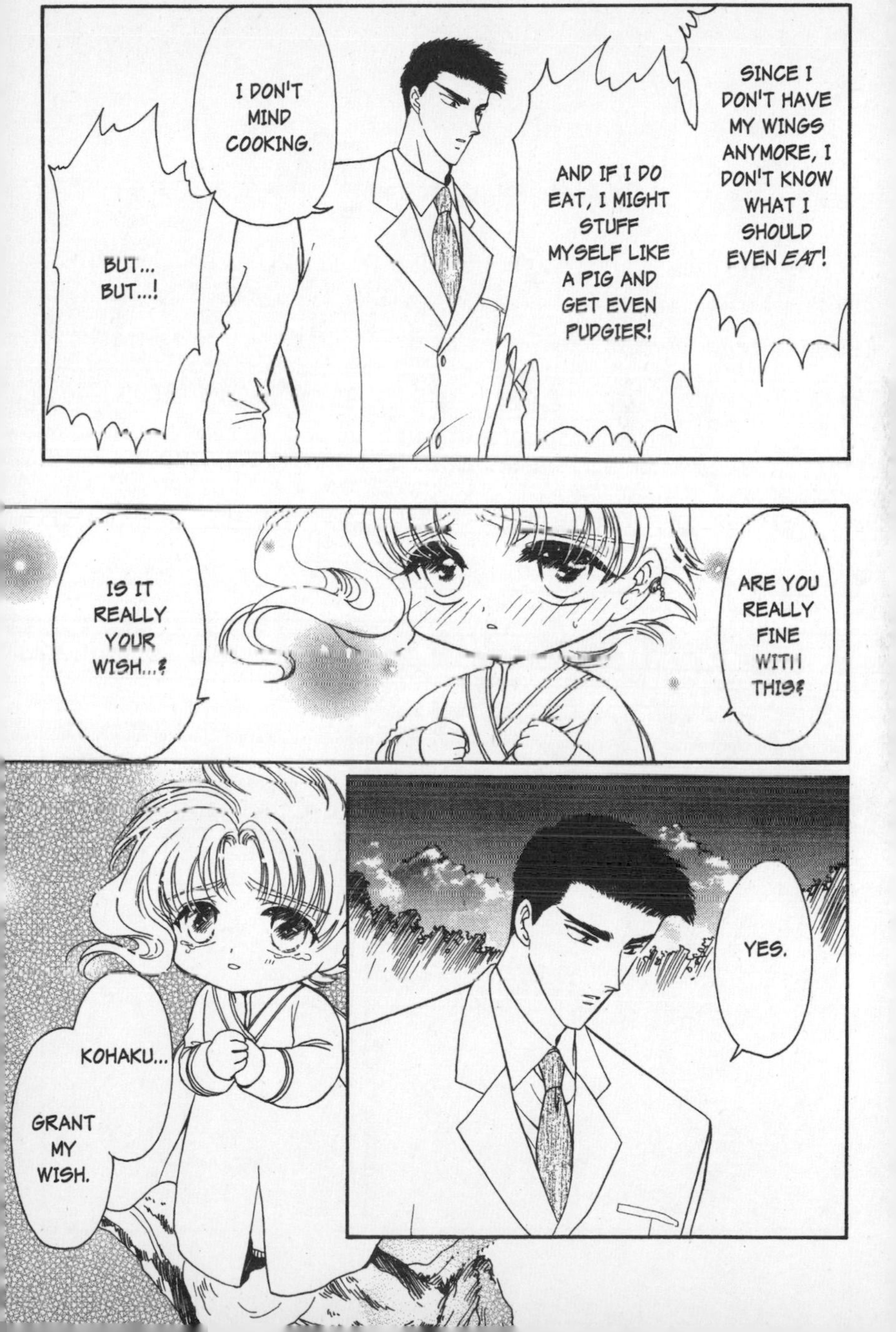
SINCE I DON'T HAVE MY WINGS ANYMORE, I DON'T KNOW WHAT I SHOULD EVEN *EAT*!
AND IF I DO EAT, I MIGHT STUFF MYSELF LIKE A PIG AND GET EVEN PUDGIER!
I DON'T MIND COOKING.
BUT... BUT...!
ARE YOU REALLY FINE WITH THIS?
IS IT REALLY YOUR WISH...?
YES.
KOHAKU...
GRANT MY WISH.

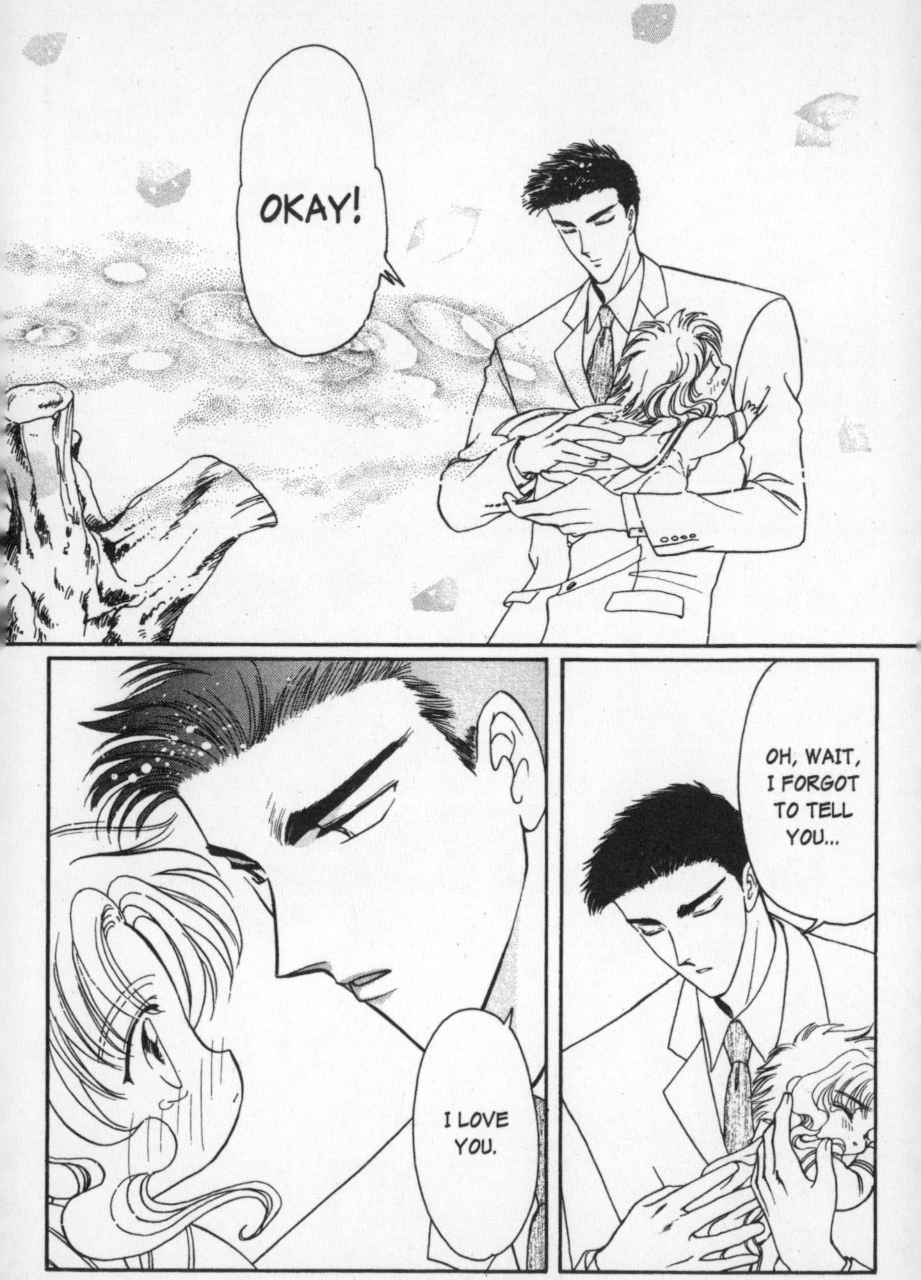
OKAY!
OH, WAIT, I FORGOT TO TELL YOU...
I LOVE YOU.

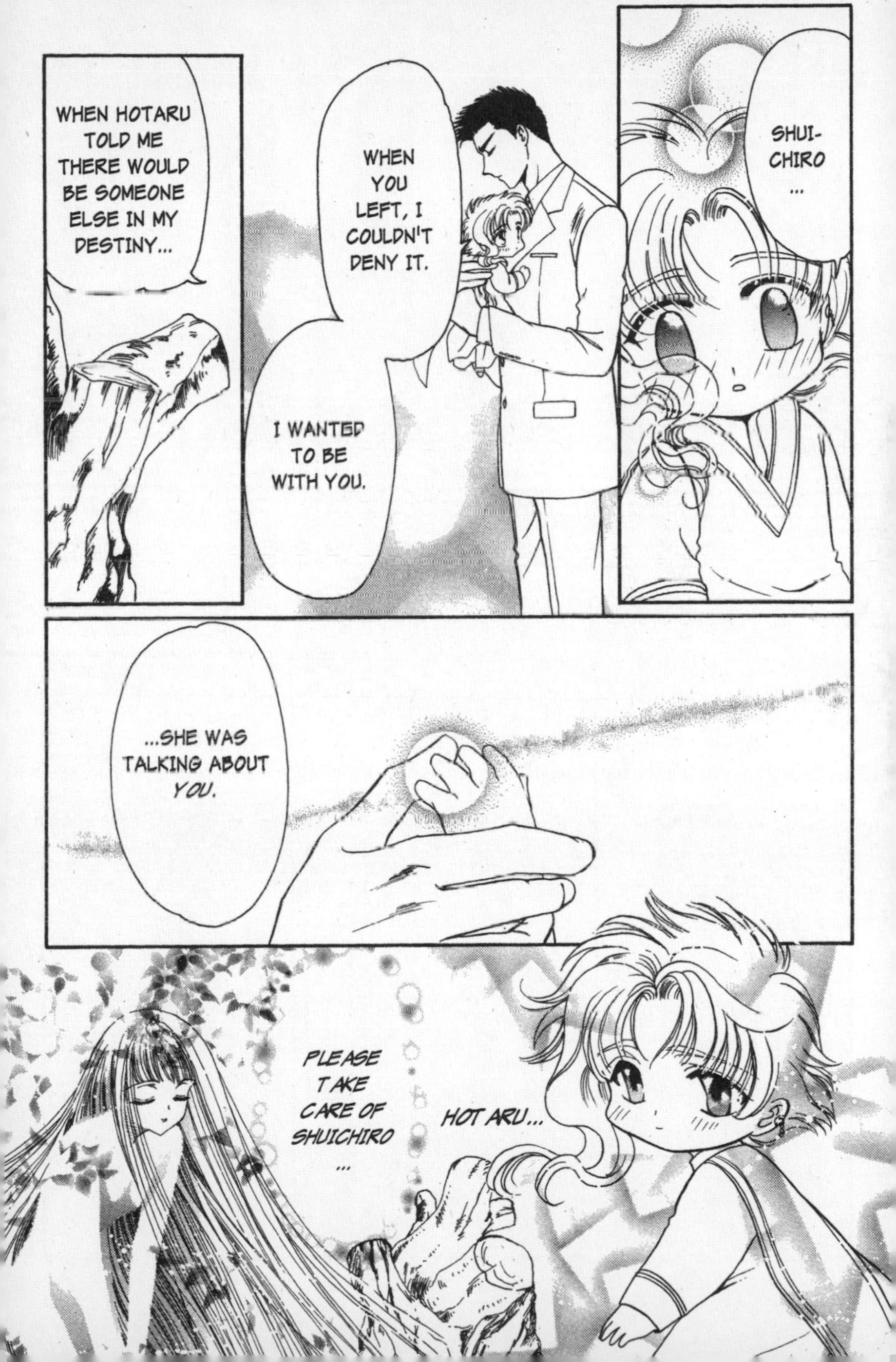

SHUI-CHIRO ...
WHEN YOU LEFT, I COULDN'T DENY IT.
I WANTED TO BE WITH YOU.
WHEN HOTARU TOLD ME THERE WOULD BE SOMEONE ELSE IN MY DESTINY...
...SHE WAS TALKING ABOUT *YOU*.
HOTARU...
PLEASE TAKE CARE OF SHUICHIRO ...

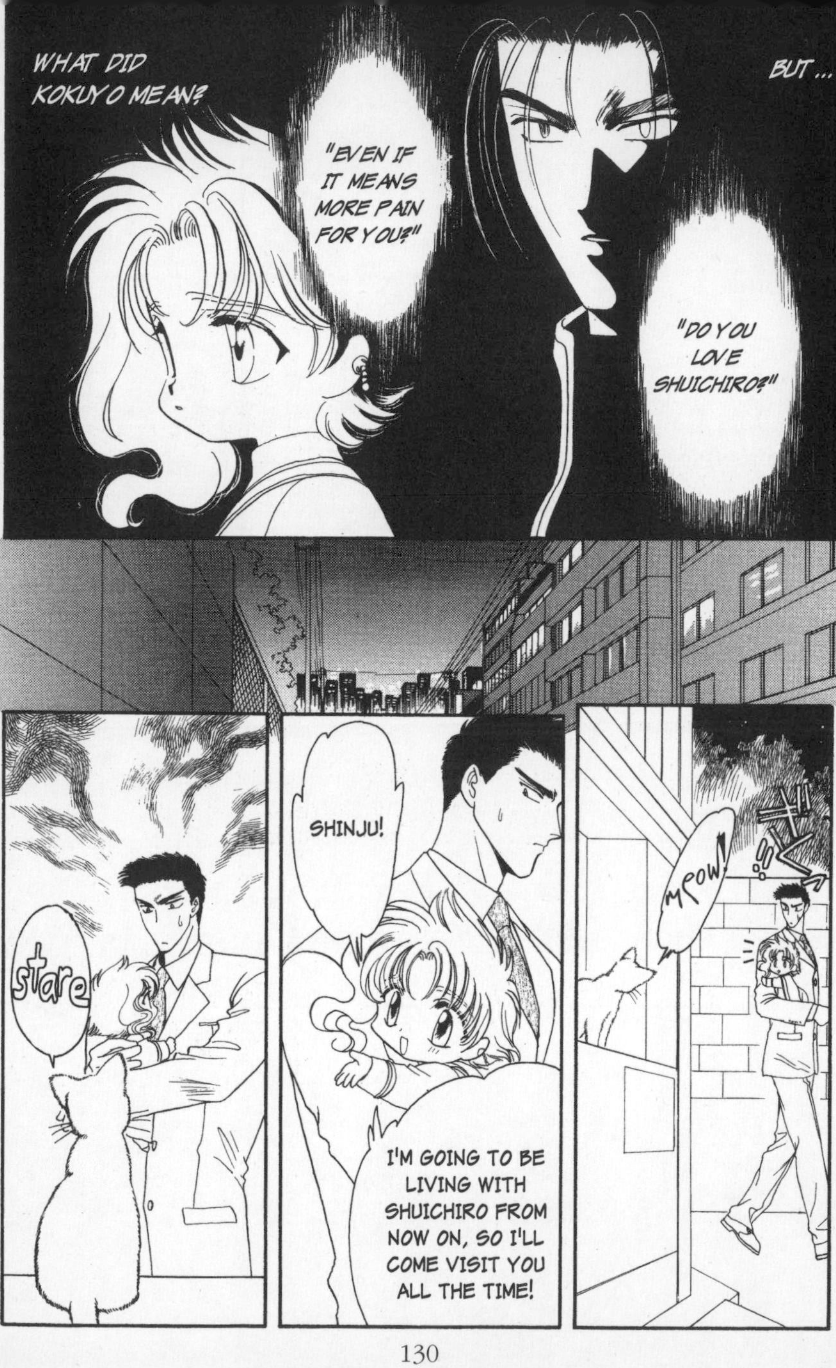
BUT ...
"DO YOU LOVE SHUICHIRO?"
"EVEN IF IT MEANS MORE PAIN FOR YOU?"
WHAT DID KOKUYO MEAN?
MEOW!
SHINJU!
I'M GOING TO BE LIVING WITH SHUICHIRO FROM NOW ON, SO I'LL COME VISIT YOU ALL THE TIME!
stare

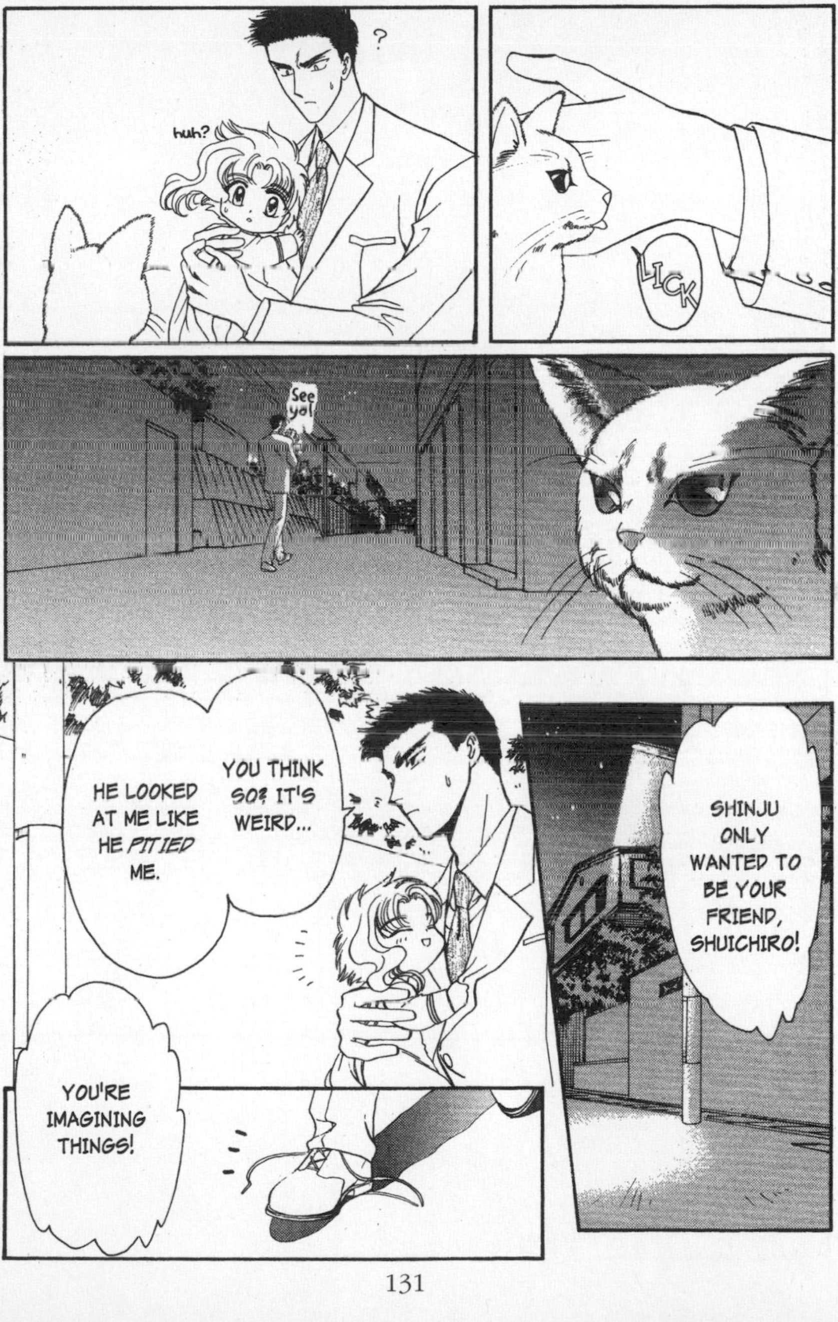
LICK
?
huh?
See ya!
SHINJU ONLY WANTED TO BE YOUR FRIEND, SHUICHIRO!
YOU THINK SO? IT'S WEIRD...
HE LOOKED AT ME LIKE HE *PITIED* ME.
YOU'RE IMAGINING THINGS!

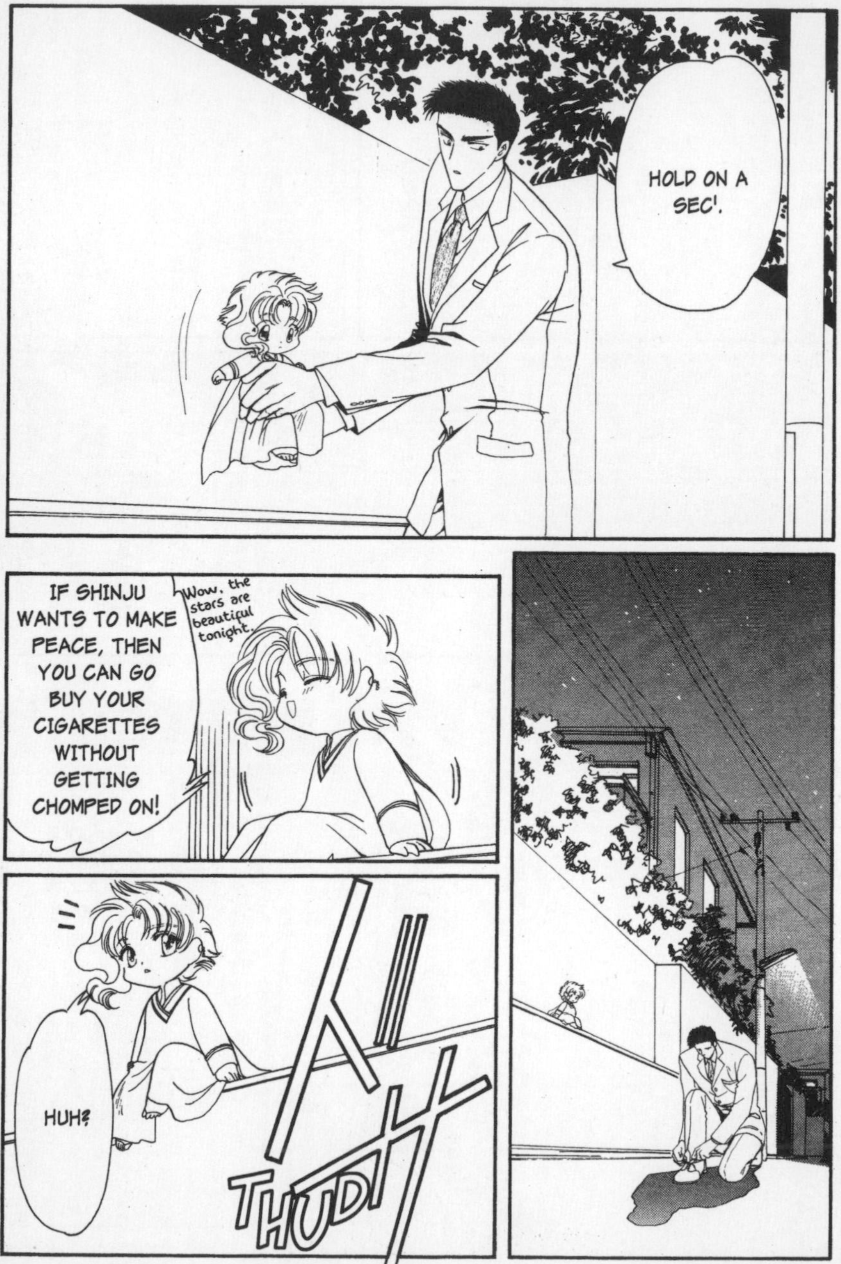
HOLD ON A SEC'.
Wow, the stars are beautiful tonight.
IF SHINJU WANTS TO MAKE PEACE, THEN YOU CAN GO BUY YOUR CIGARETTES WITHOUT GETTING CHOMPED ON!
THUD
HUH?

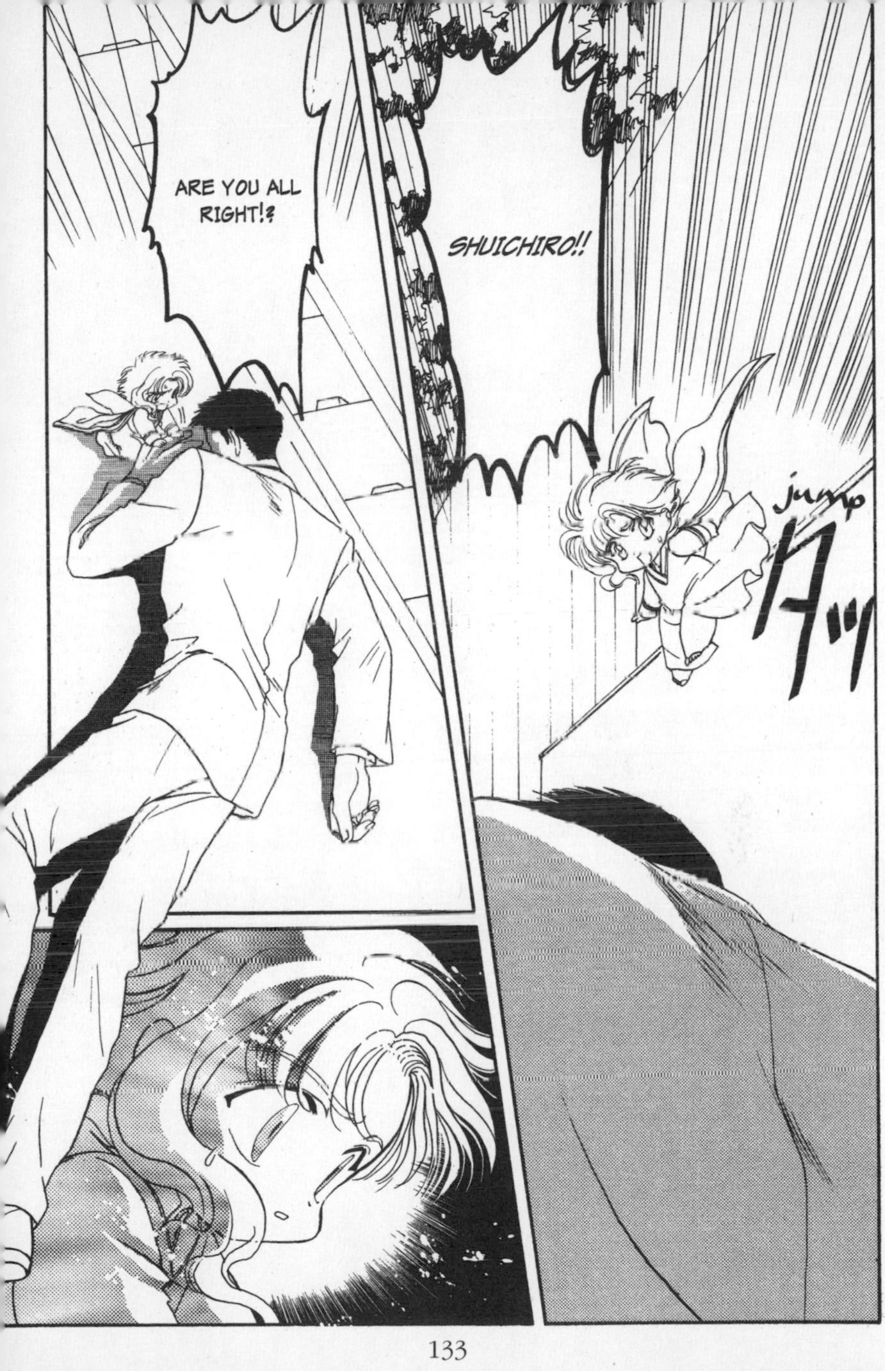
SHUICHIRO!!
jump
ARE YOU ALL RIGHT!?

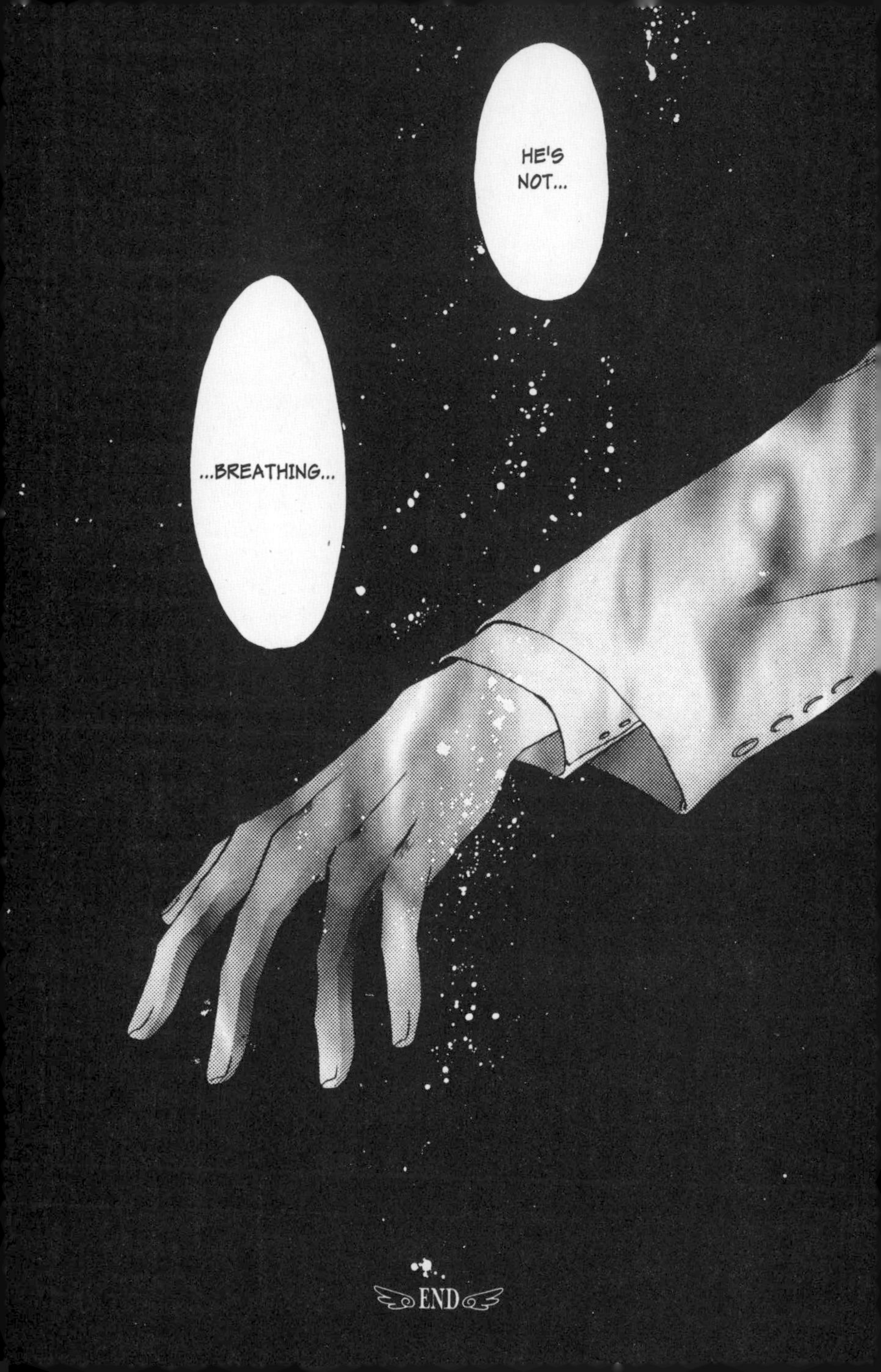
HE'S NOT...
...BREATHING...
END

ずっと一緒に

Contact.23 Together Forever

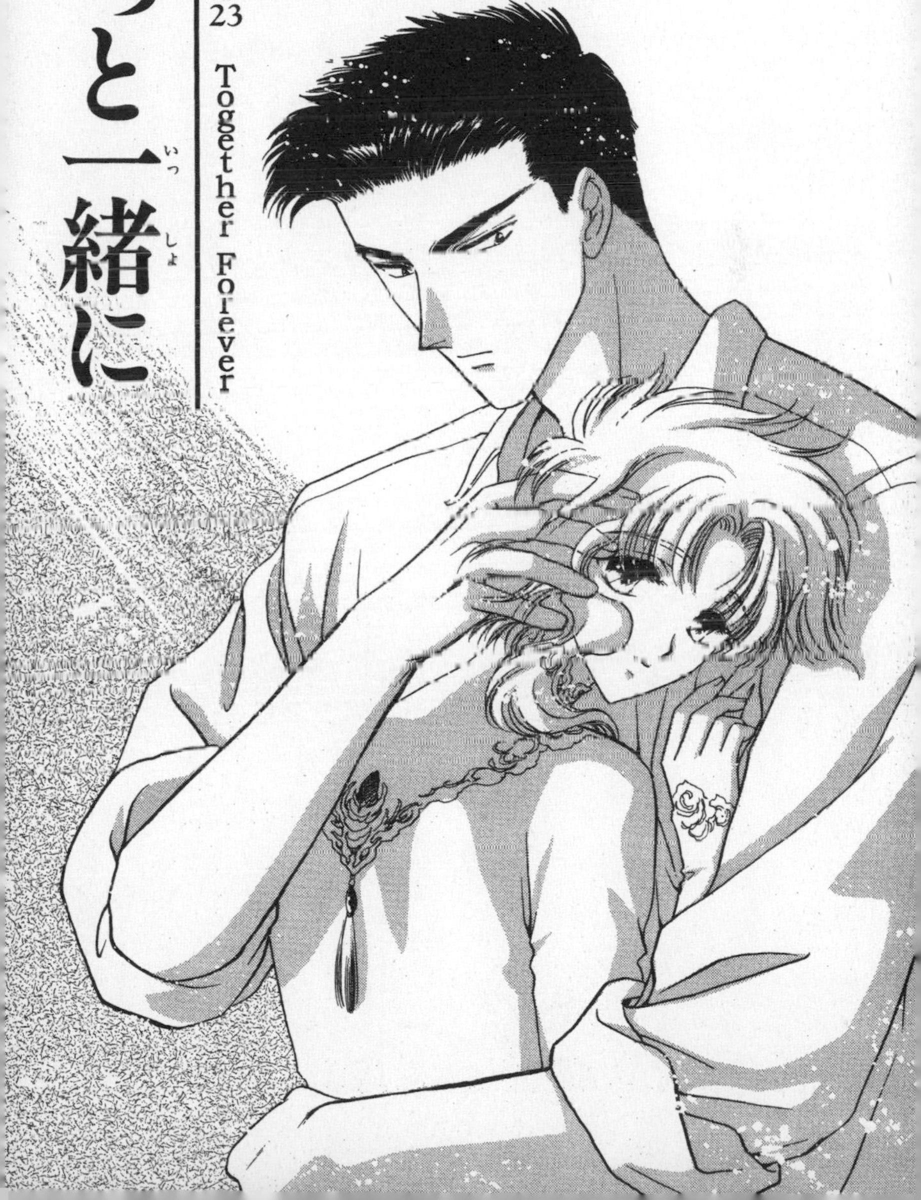

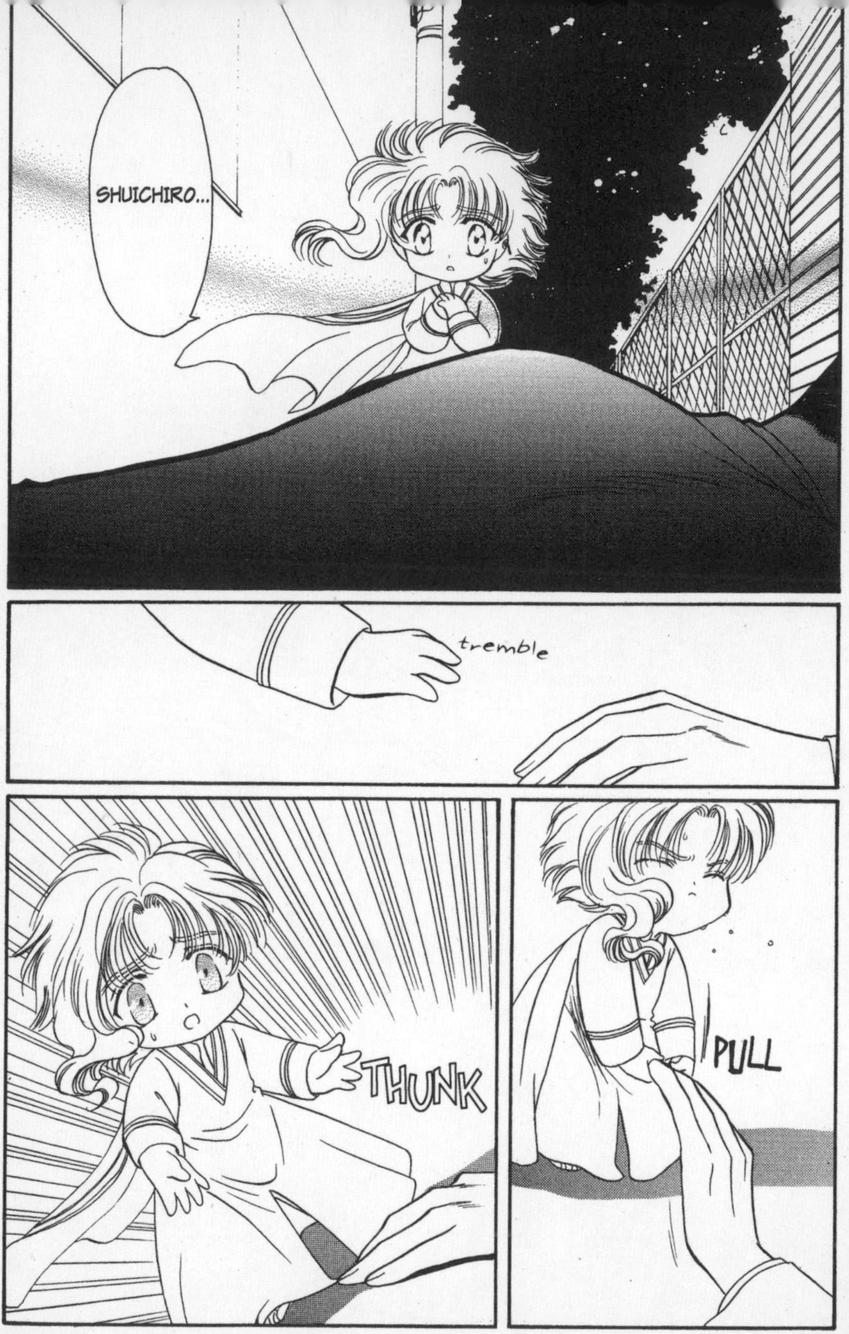
SHUICHIRO...
tremble
PULL
THUNK

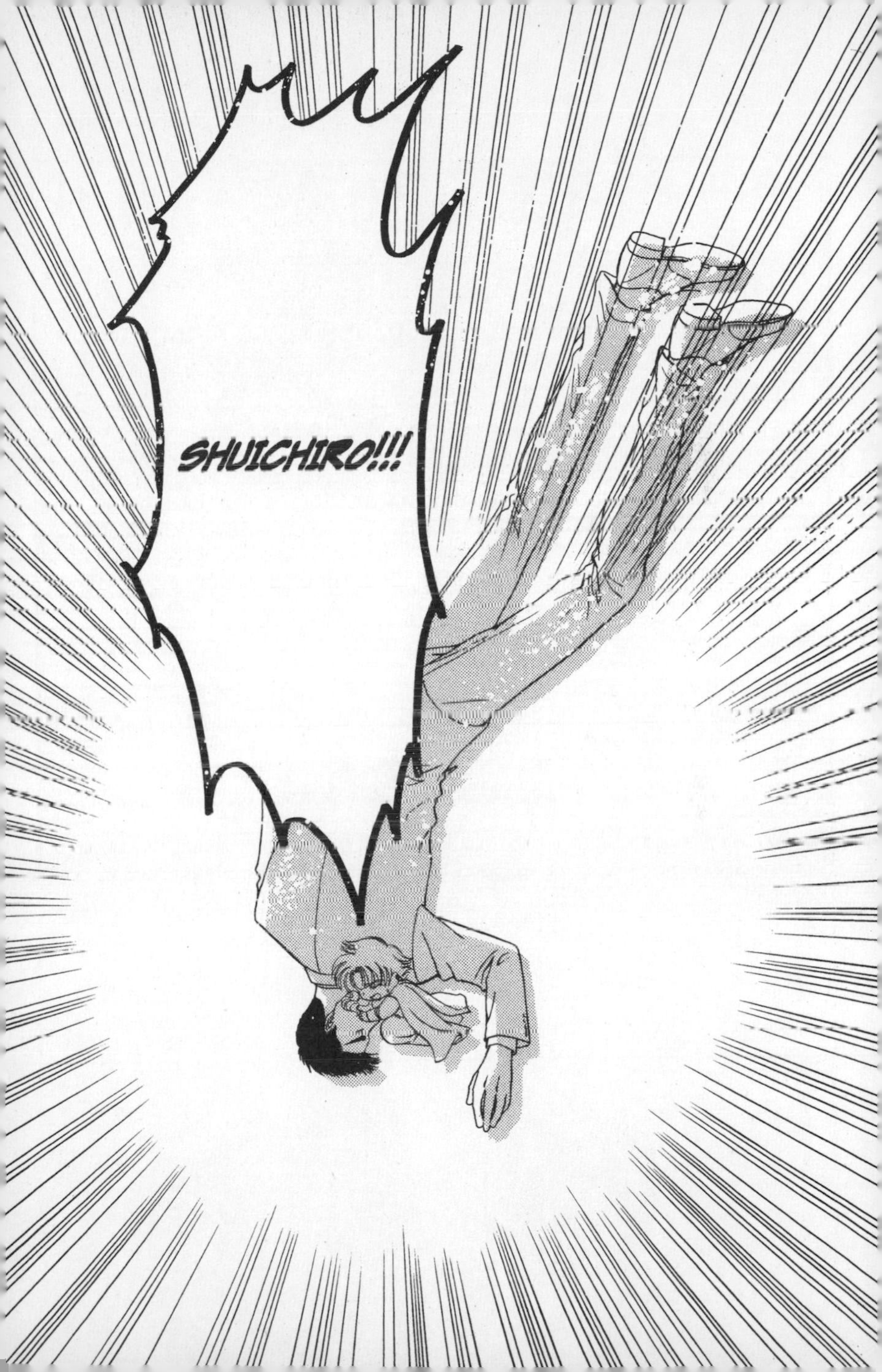
SHUICHIRO!!!

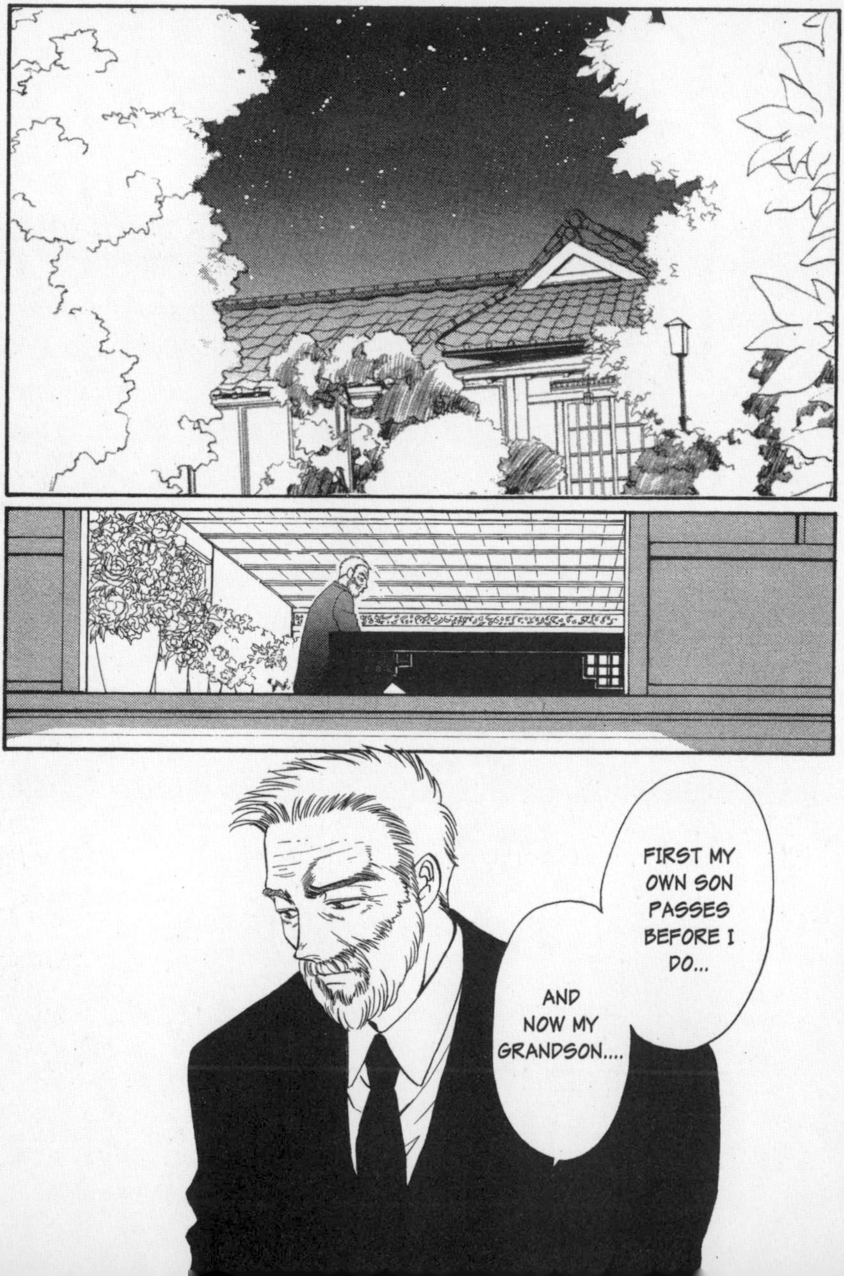
FIRST MY OWN SON PASSES BEFORE I DO...
AND NOW MY GRANDSON....

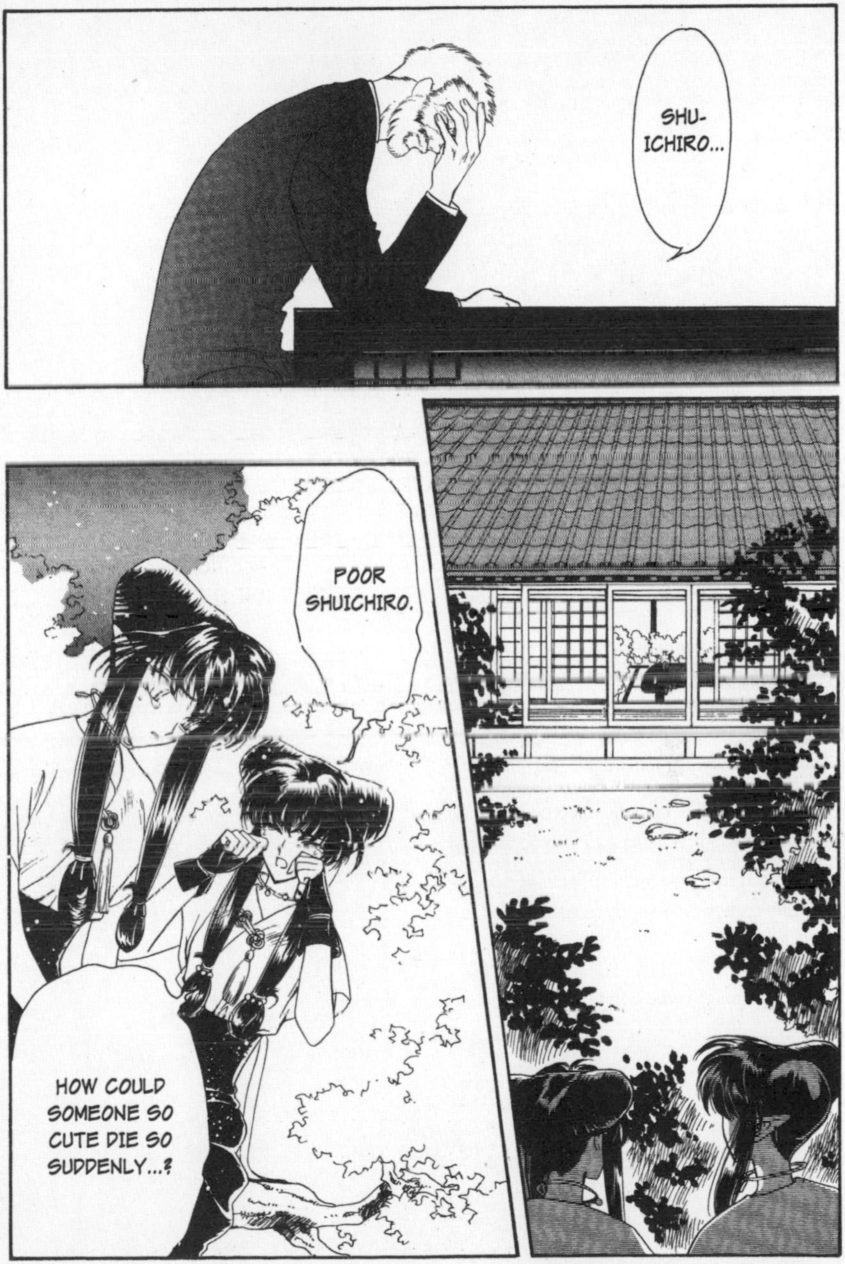
SHU-ICHIRO...
POOR SHUICHIRO.
HOW COULD SOMEONE SO CUTE DIE SO SUDDENLY...?

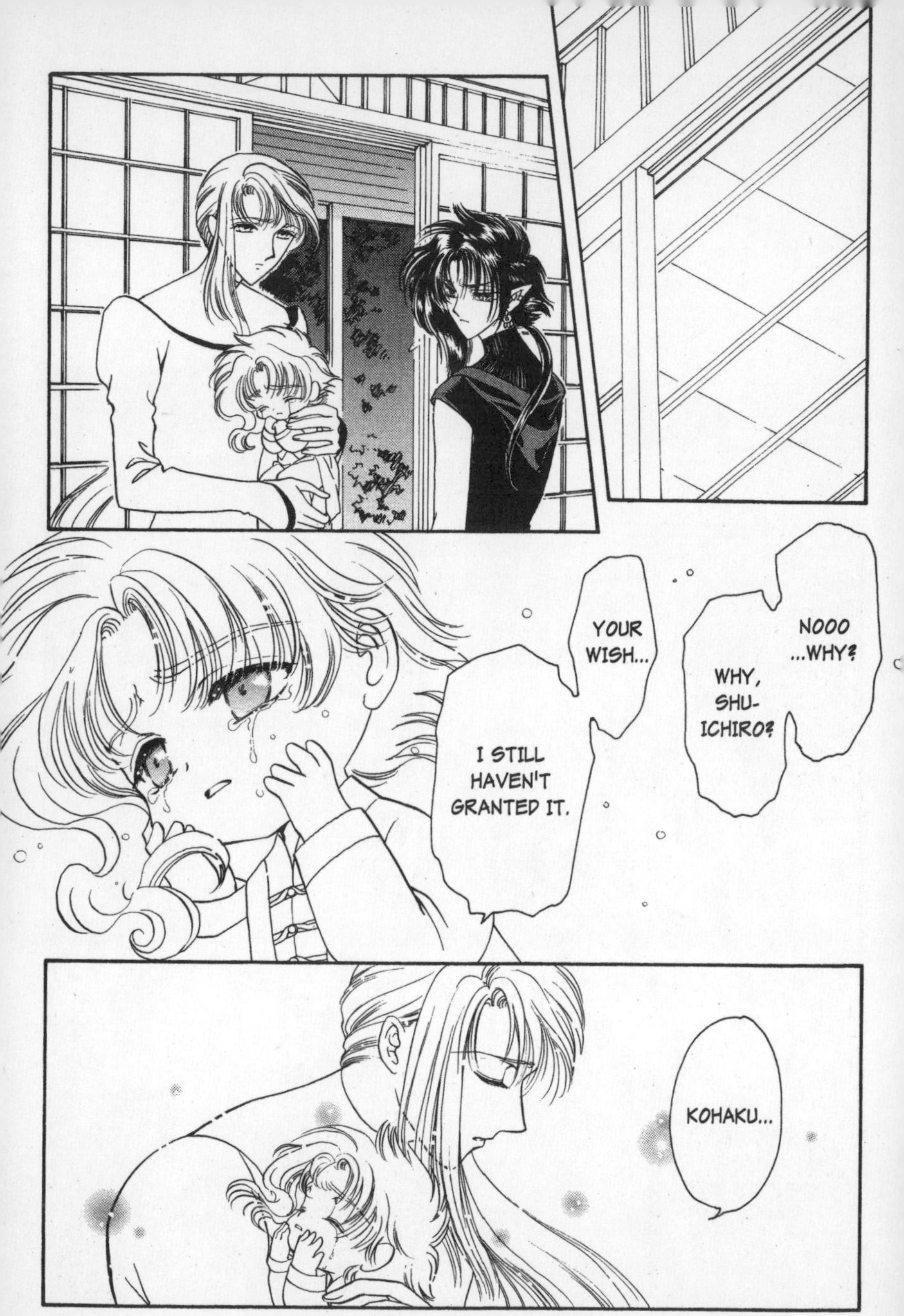
NOOO ...WHY? WHY, SHU-ICHIRO?
YOUR WISH...
I STILL HAVEN'T GRANTED IT.
KOHAKU...

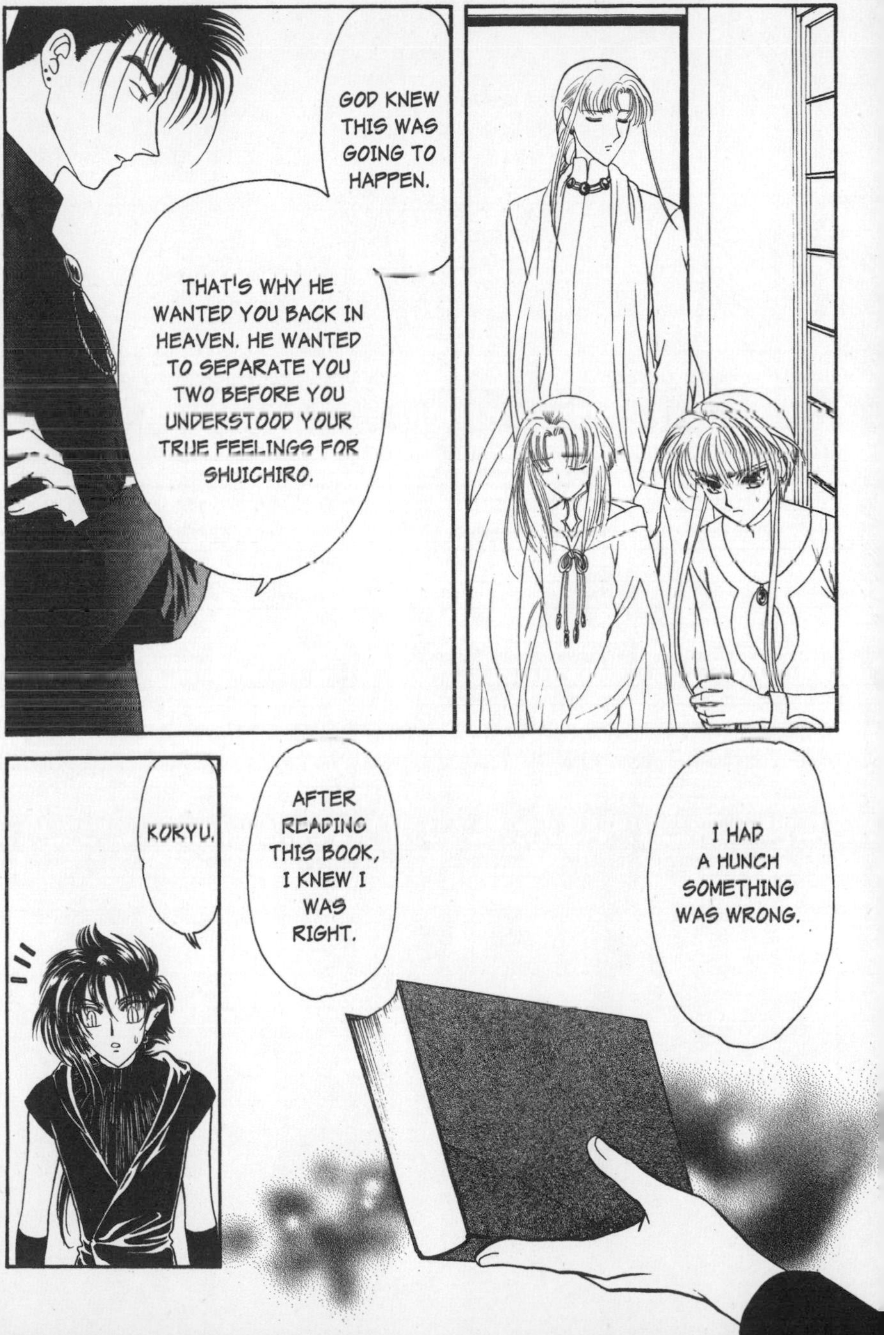
GOD KNEW THIS WAS GOING TO HAPPEN.
THAT'S WHY HE WANTED YOU BACK IN HEAVEN. HE WANTED TO SEPARATE YOU TWO BEFORE YOU UNDERSTOOD YOUR TRUE FEELINGS FOR SHUICHIRO.
I HAD A HUNCH SOMETHING WAS WRONG.
AFTER READING THIS BOOK, I KNEW I WAS RIGHT.
KOKYU.

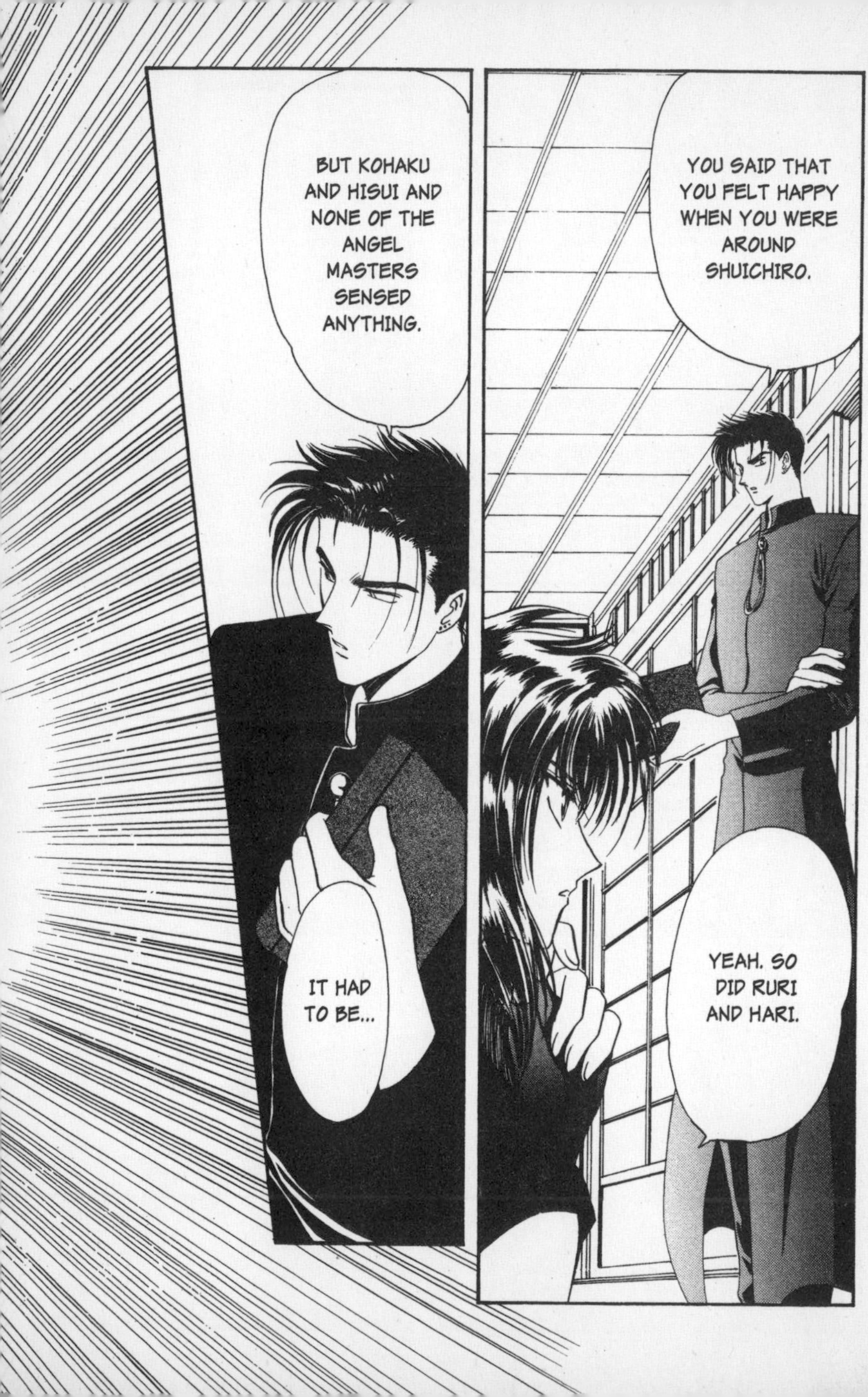
YOU SAID THAT YOU FELT HAPPY WHEN YOU WERE AROUND SHUICHIRO.
YEAH. SO DID RURI AND HARI.
BUT KOHAKU AND HISUI AND NONE OF THE ANGEL MASTERS SENSED ANYTHING.
IT HAD TO BE...

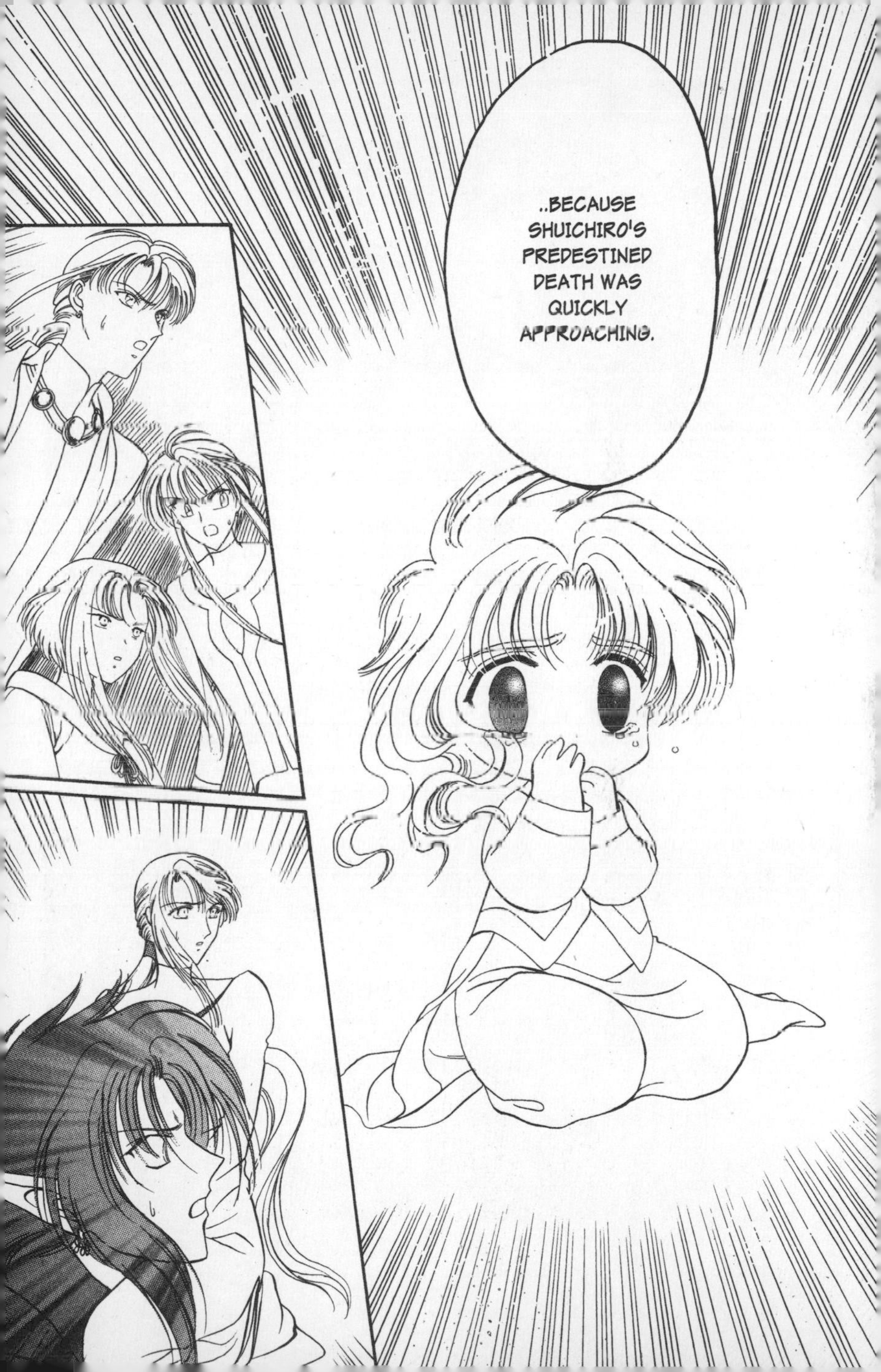
..BECAUSE SHUICHIRO'S PREDESTINED DEATH WAS QUICKLY APPROACHING.

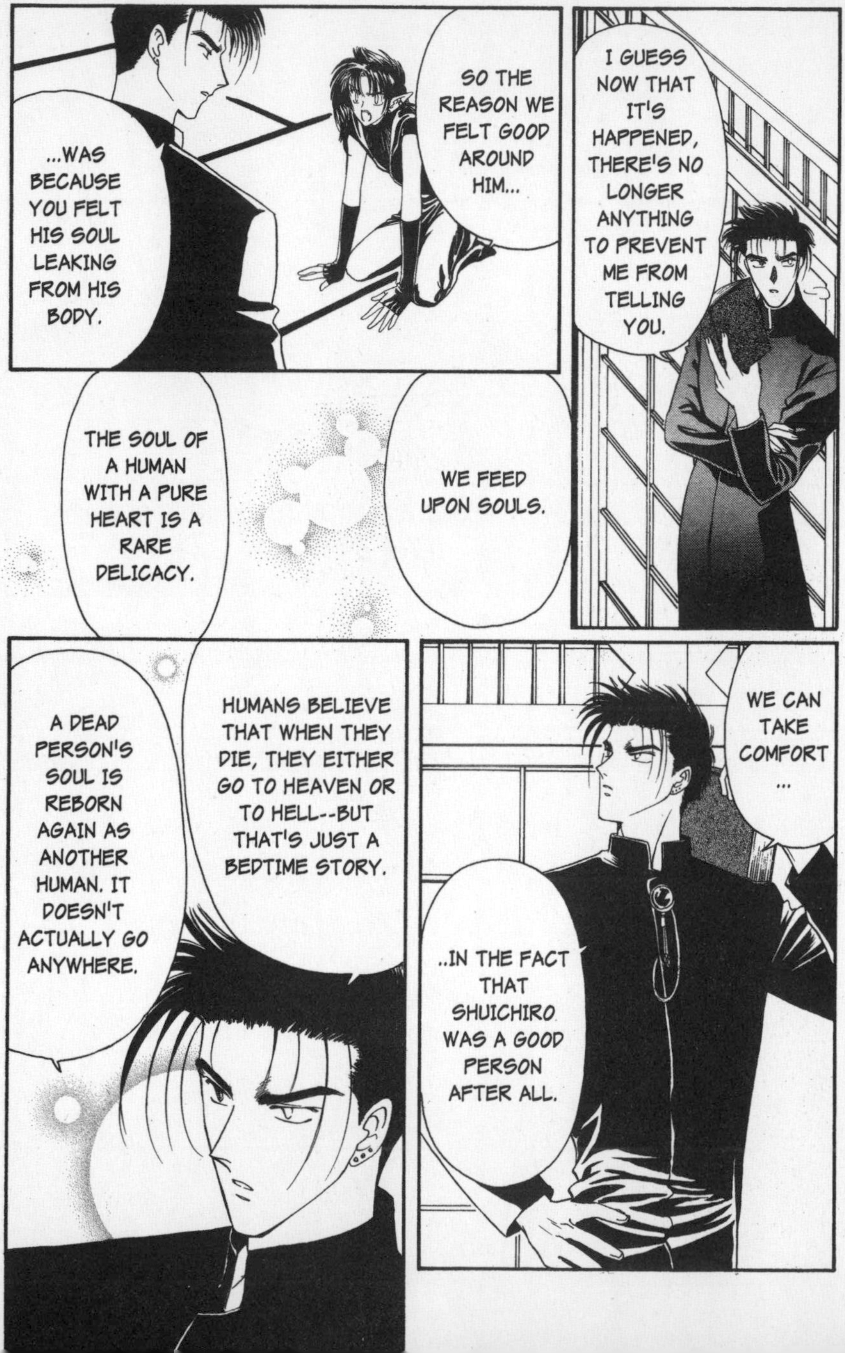
I GUESS NOW THAT IT'S HAPPENED, THERE'S NO LONGER ANYTHING TO PREVENT ME FROM TELLING YOU.
SO THE REASON WE FELT GOOD AROUND HIM...
...WAS BECAUSE YOU FELT HIS SOUL LEAKING FROM HIS BODY.
WE CAN TAKE COMFORT ...
..IN THE FACT THAT SHUICHIRO WAS A GOOD PERSON AFTER ALL.
WE FEED UPON SOULS.
THE SOUL OF A HUMAN WITH A PURE HEART IS A RARE DELICACY.
HUMANS BELIEVE THAT WHEN THEY DIE, THEY EITHER GO TO HEAVEN OR TO HELL--BUT THAT'S JUST A BEDTIME STORY.
A DEAD PERSON'S SOUL IS REBORN AGAIN AS ANOTHER HUMAN. IT DOESN'T ACTUALLY GO ANYWHERE.

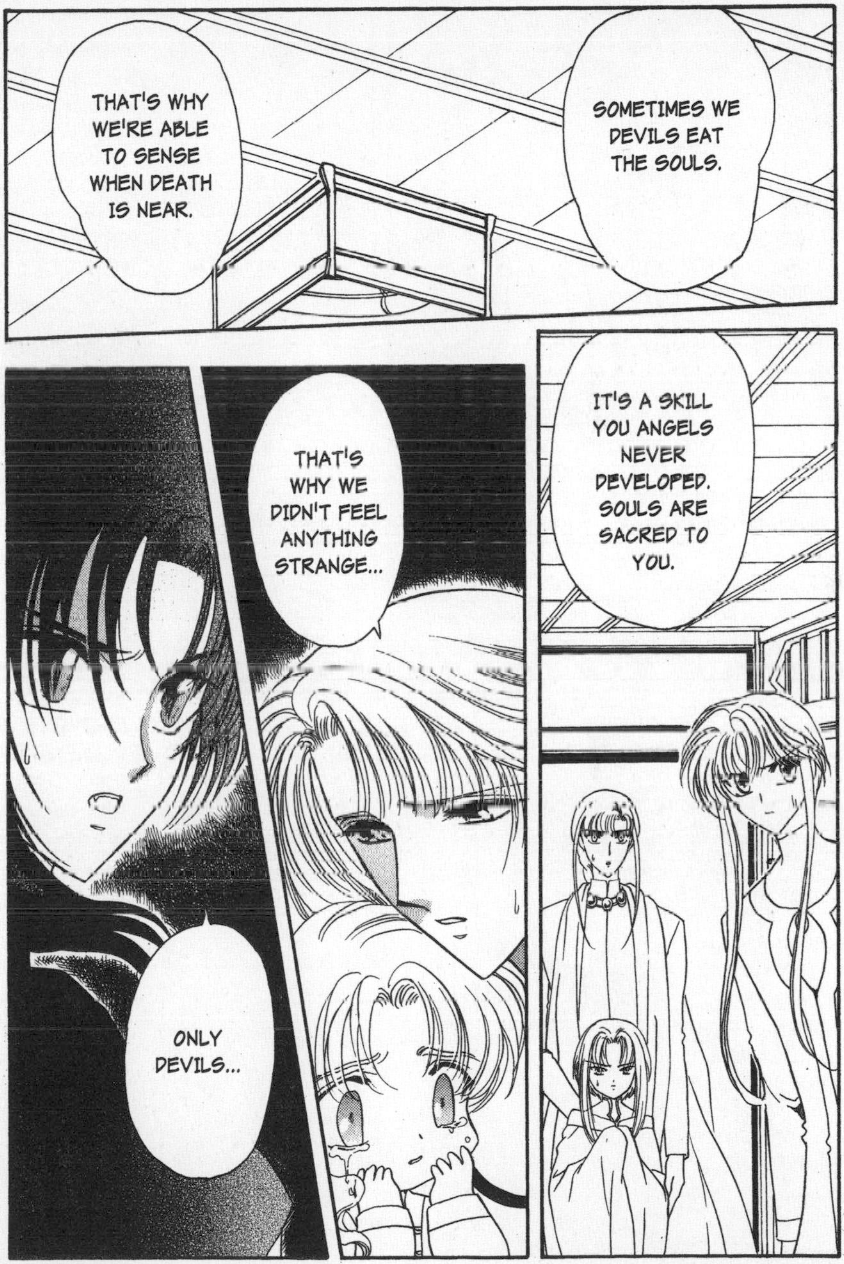
SOMETIMES WE DEVILS EAT THE SOULS.
THAT'S WHY WE'RE ABLE TO SENSE WHEN DEATH IS NEAR.
IT'S A SKILL YOU ANGELS NEVER DEVELOPED. SOULS ARE SACRED TO YOU.
THAT'S WHY WE DIDN'T FEEL ANYTHING STRANGE...
ONLY DEVILS...

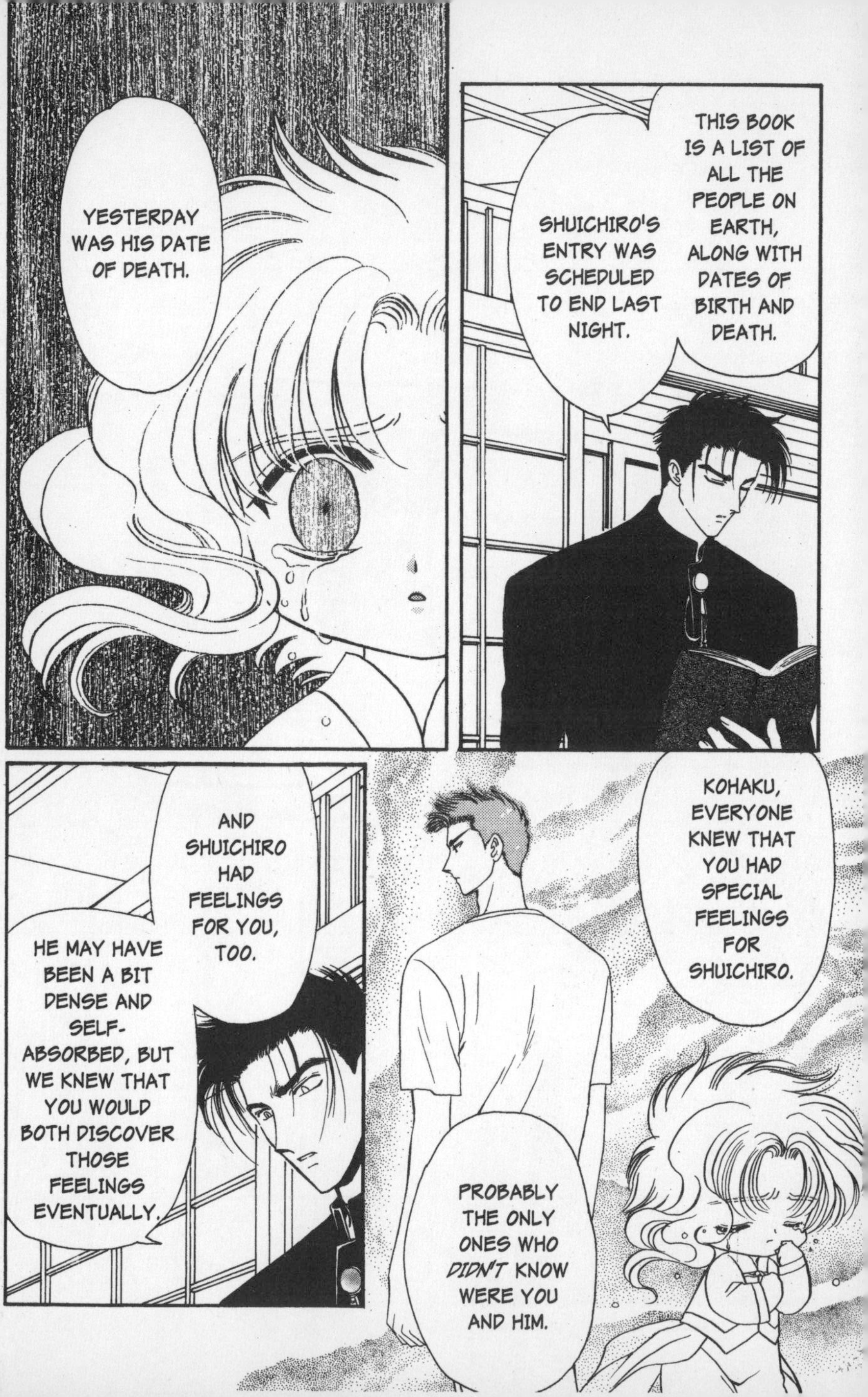
THIS BOOK IS A LIST OF ALL THE PEOPLE ON EARTH, ALONG WITH DATES OF BIRTH AND DEATH.
SHUICHIRO'S ENTRY WAS SCHEDULED TO END LAST NIGHT.
YESTERDAY WAS HIS DATE OF DEATH.
KOHAKU, EVERYONE KNEW THAT YOU HAD SPECIAL FEELINGS FOR SHUICHIRO.
PROBABLY THE ONLY ONES WHO *DIDN'T* KNOW WERE YOU AND HIM.
AND SHUICHIRO HAD FEELINGS FOR YOU, TOO.
HE MAY HAVE BEEN A BIT DENSE AND SELF-ABSORBED, BUT WE KNEW THAT YOU WOULD BOTH DISCOVER THOSE FEELINGS EVENTUALLY.

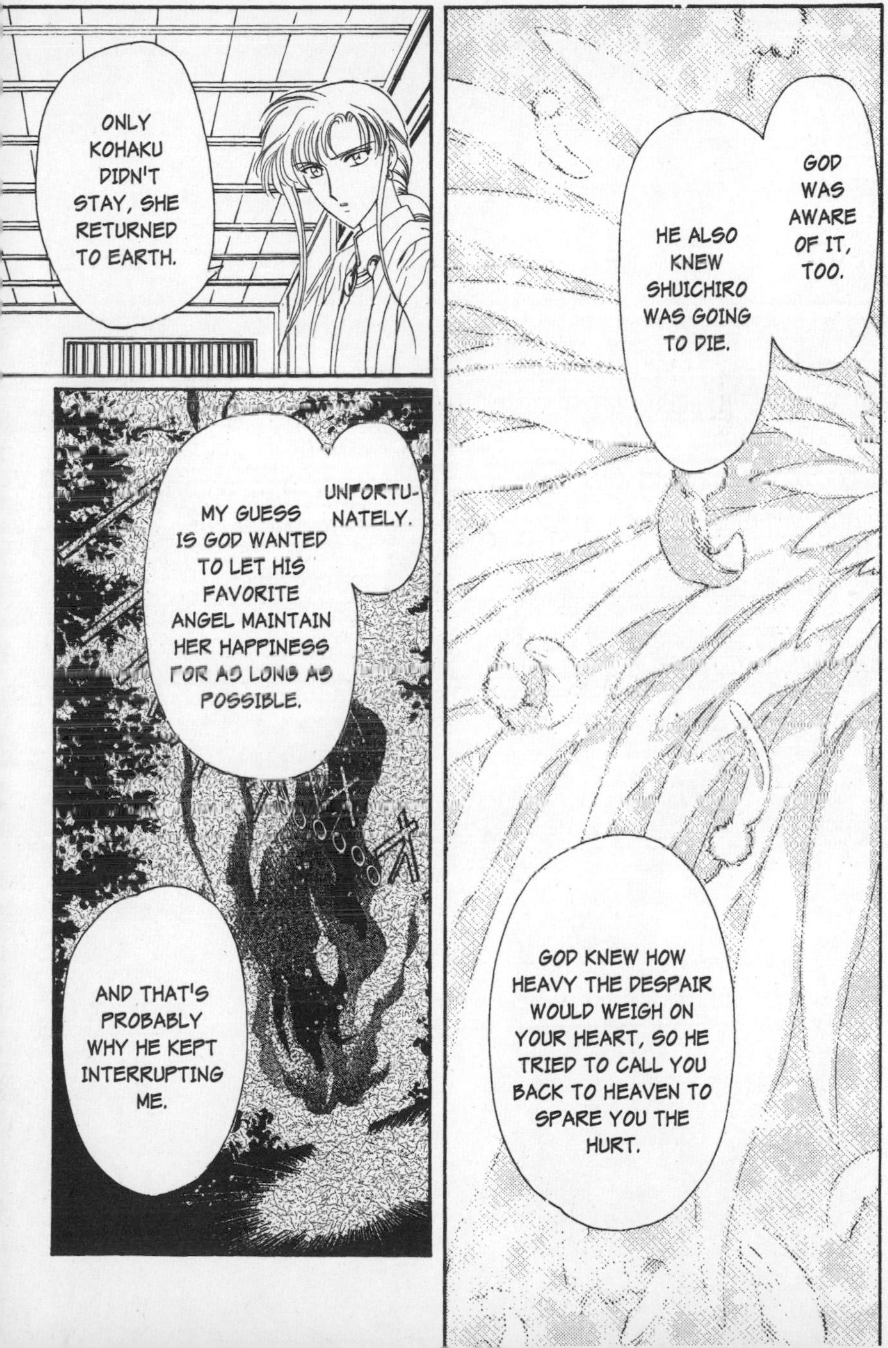
GOD WAS AWARE OF IT, TOO.
HE ALSO KNEW SHUICHIRO WAS GOING TO DIE.
GOD KNEW HOW HEAVY THE DESPAIR WOULD WEIGH ON YOUR HEART, SO HE TRIED TO CALL YOU BACK TO HEAVEN TO SPARE YOU THE HURT.
ONLY KOHAKU DIDN'T STAY, SHE RETURNED TO EARTH.
UNFORTU-NATELY.
MY GUESS IS GOD WANTED TO LET HIS FAVORITE ANGEL MAINTAIN HER HAPPINESS FOR AS LONG AS POSSIBLE.
AND THAT'S PROBABLY WHY HE KEPT INTERRUPTING ME.

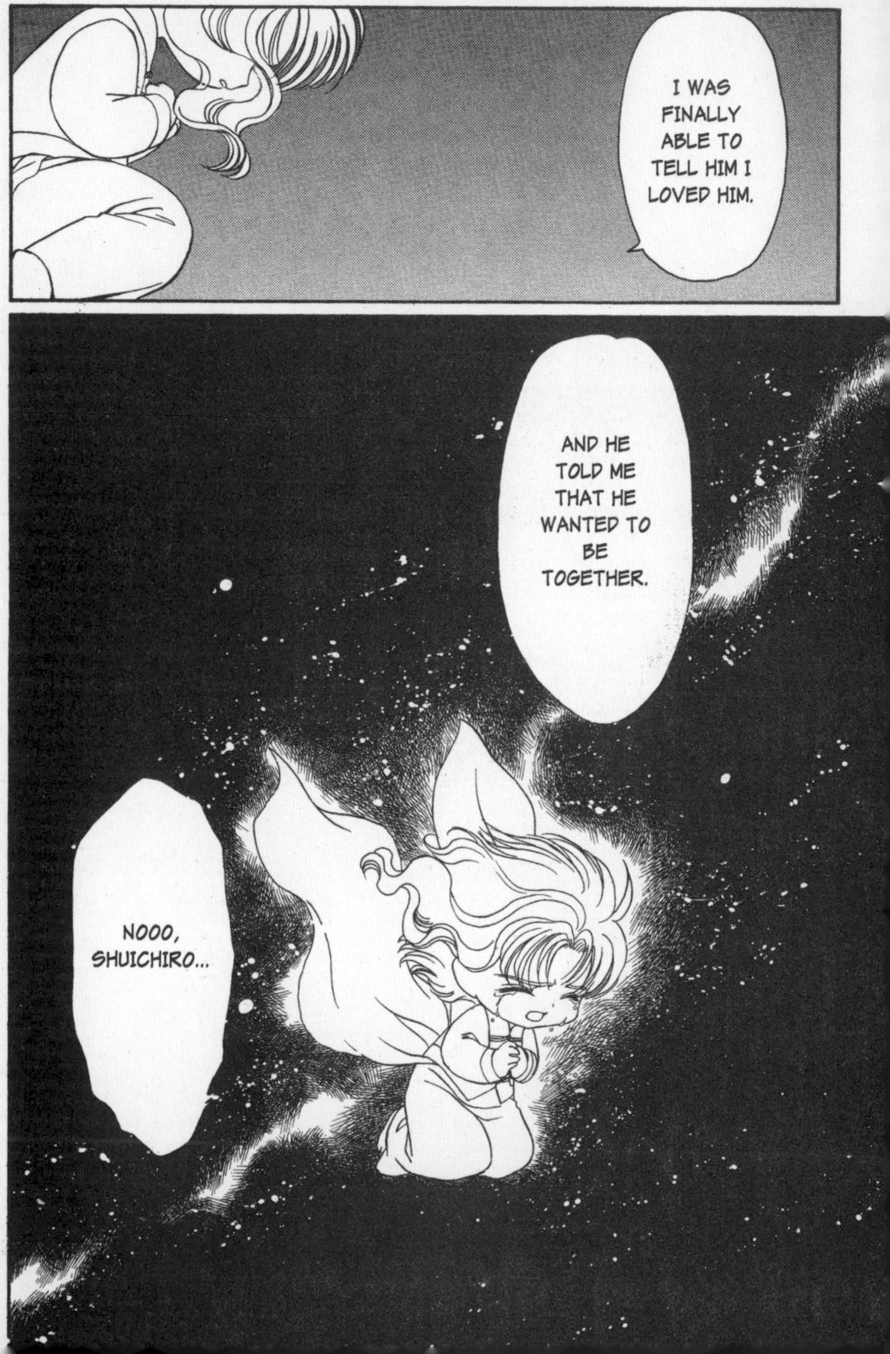
I WAS FINALLY ABLE TO TELL HIM I LOVED HIM.
AND HE TOLD ME THAT HE WANTED TO BE TOGETHER.
NOOO, SHUICHIRO...

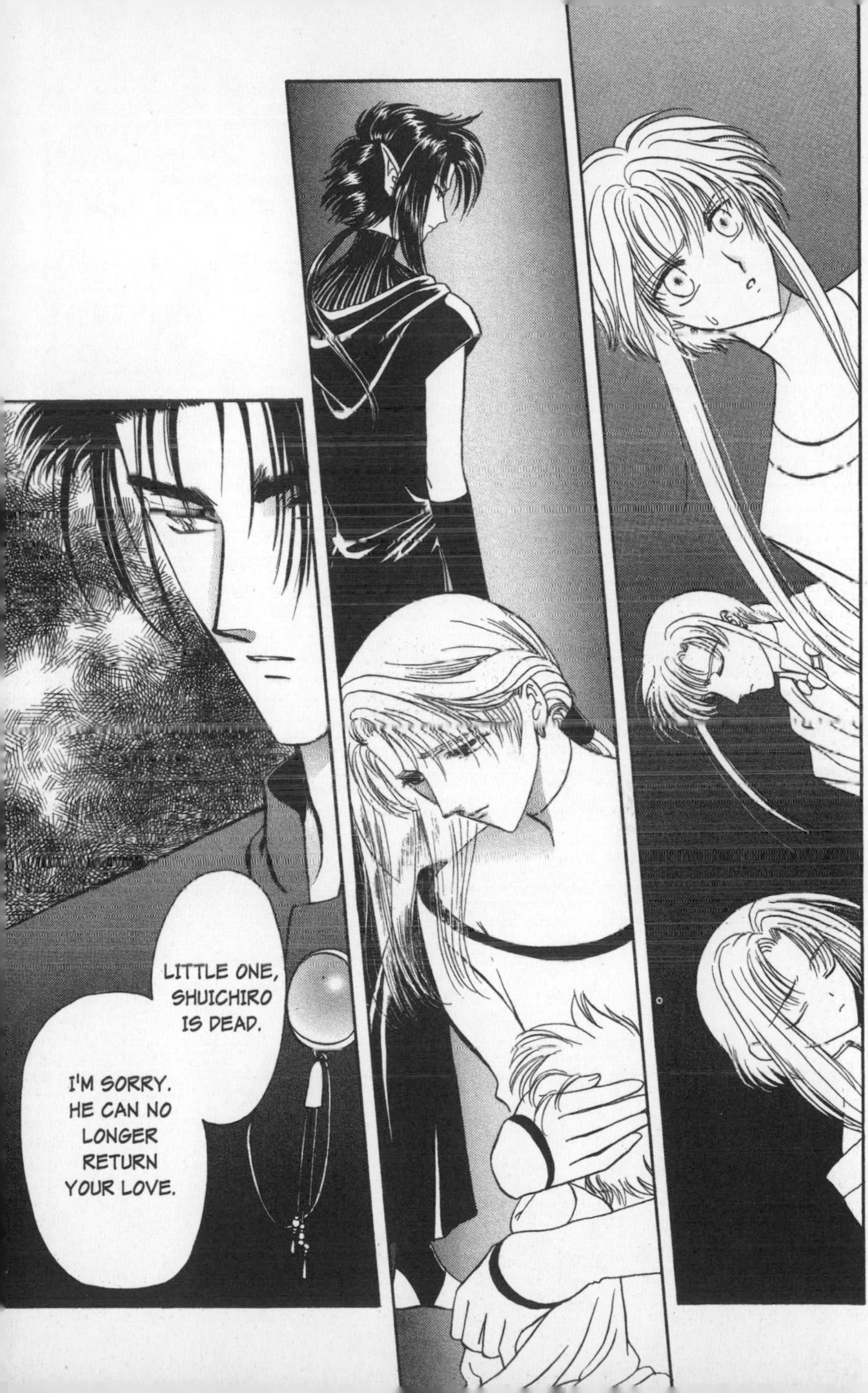
LITTLE ONE, SHUICHIRO IS DEAD.
I'M SORRY. HE CAN NO LONGER RETURN YOUR LOVE.

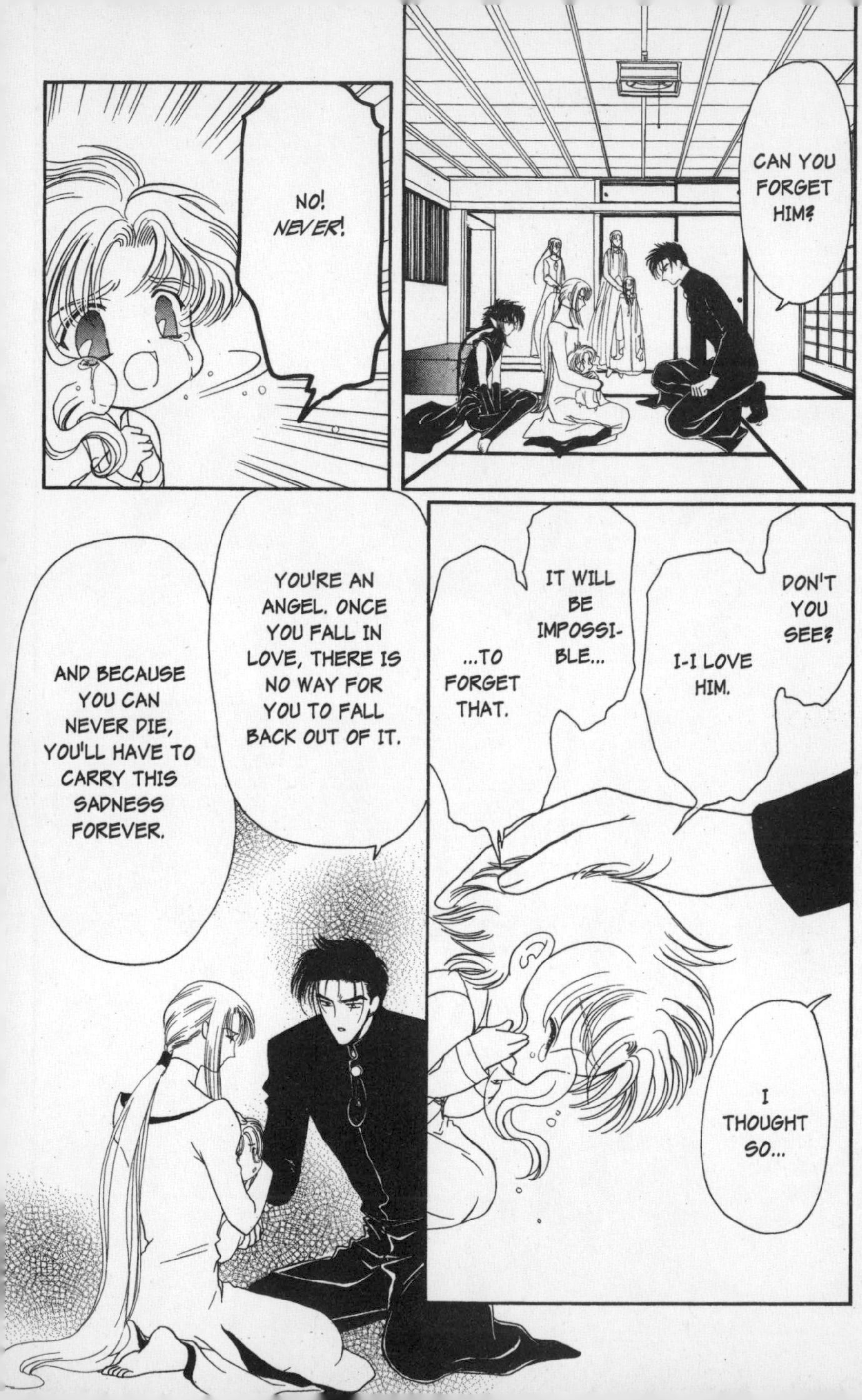
CAN YOU FORGET HIM?
NO! *NEVER!*
DON'T YOU SEE?
I-I LOVE HIM.
IT WILL BE IMPOSSI-BLE...
...TO FORGET THAT.
I THOUGHT SO...
YOU'RE AN ANGEL. ONCE YOU FALL IN LOVE, THERE IS NO WAY FOR YOU TO FALL BACK OUT OF IT.
AND BECAUSE YOU CAN NEVER DIE, YOU'LL HAVE TO CARRY THIS SADNESS FOREVER.

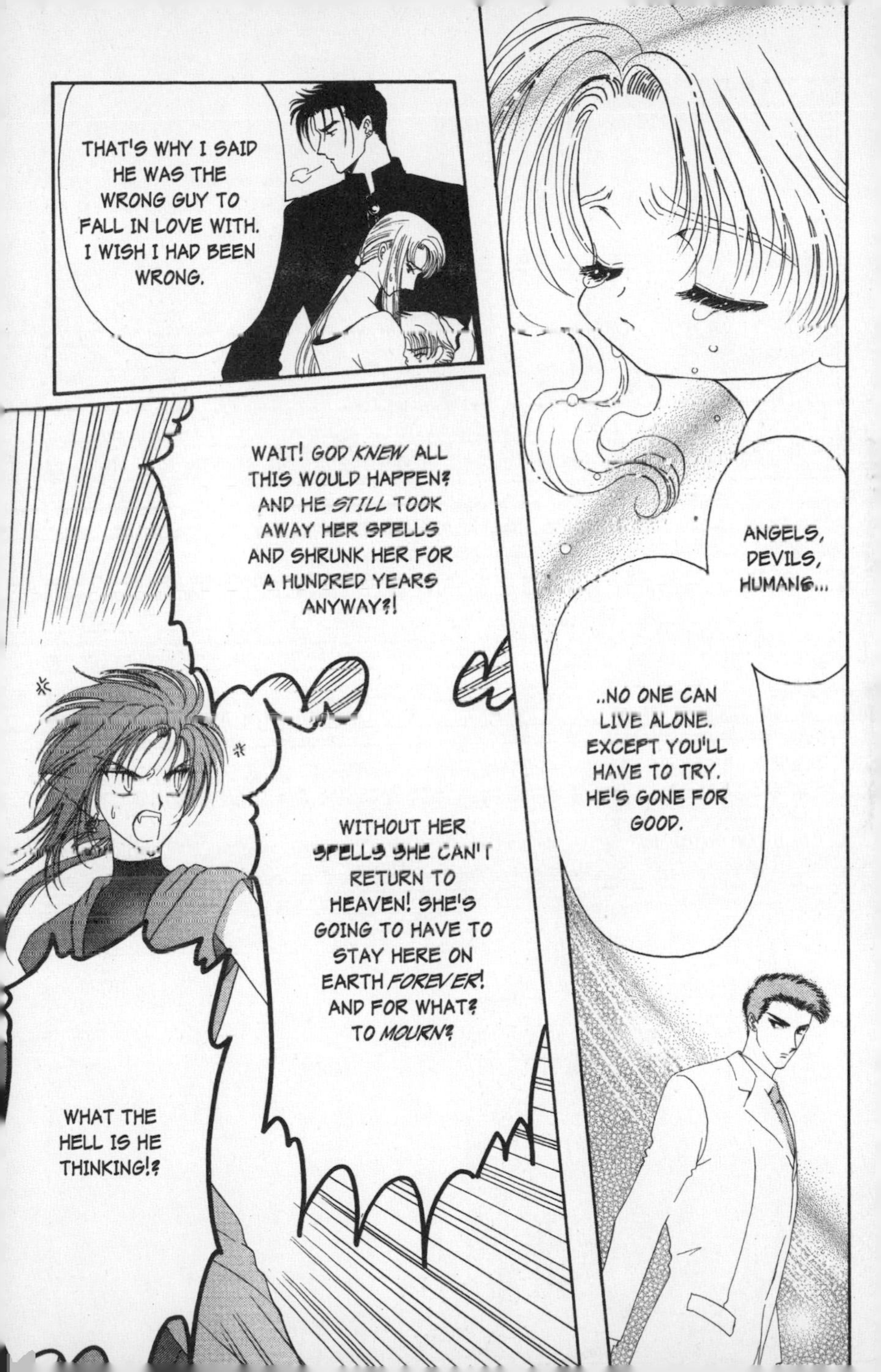
ANGELS, DEVILS, HUMANS...
..NO ONE CAN LIVE ALONE. EXCEPT YOU'LL HAVE TO TRY. HE'S GONE FOR GOOD.
THAT'S WHY I SAID HE WAS THE WRONG GUY TO FALL IN LOVE WITH. I WISH I HAD BEEN WRONG.
WAIT! GOD *KNEW* ALL THIS WOULD HAPPEN? AND HE *STILL* TOOK AWAY HER SPELLS AND SHRUNK HER FOR A HUNDRED YEARS ANYWAY?!
WITHOUT HER SPELLS SHE CAN'T RETURN TO HEAVEN! SHE'S GOING TO HAVE TO STAY HERE ON EARTH *FOREVER*! AND FOR WHAT? TO *MOURN*?
WHAT THE HELL IS HE THINKING!?

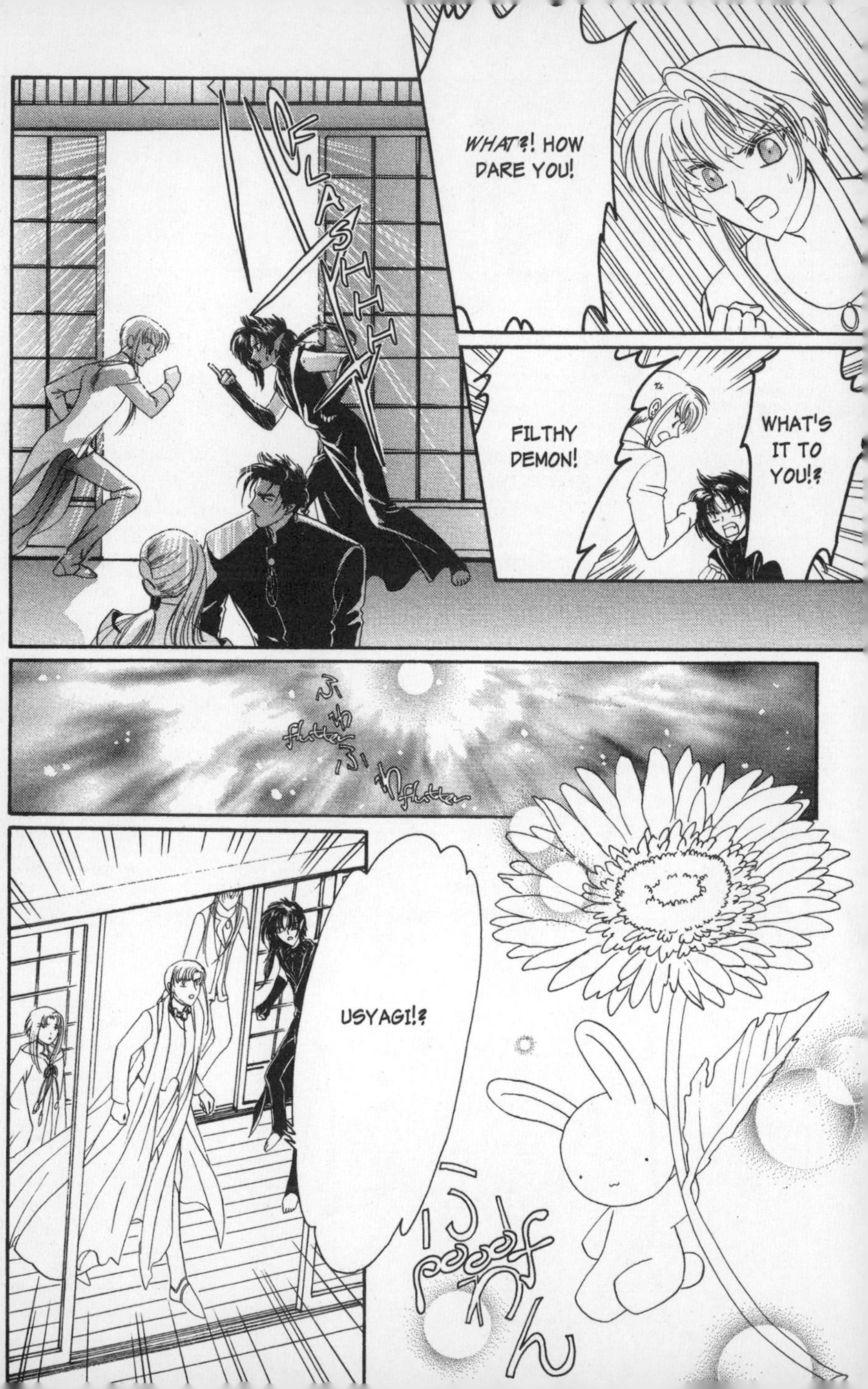
WHAT?! HOW DARE YOU!
WHAT'S IT TO YOU!?
FILTHY DEMON!
FLASHHH
flutter
flutter
poof
USYAGI!?

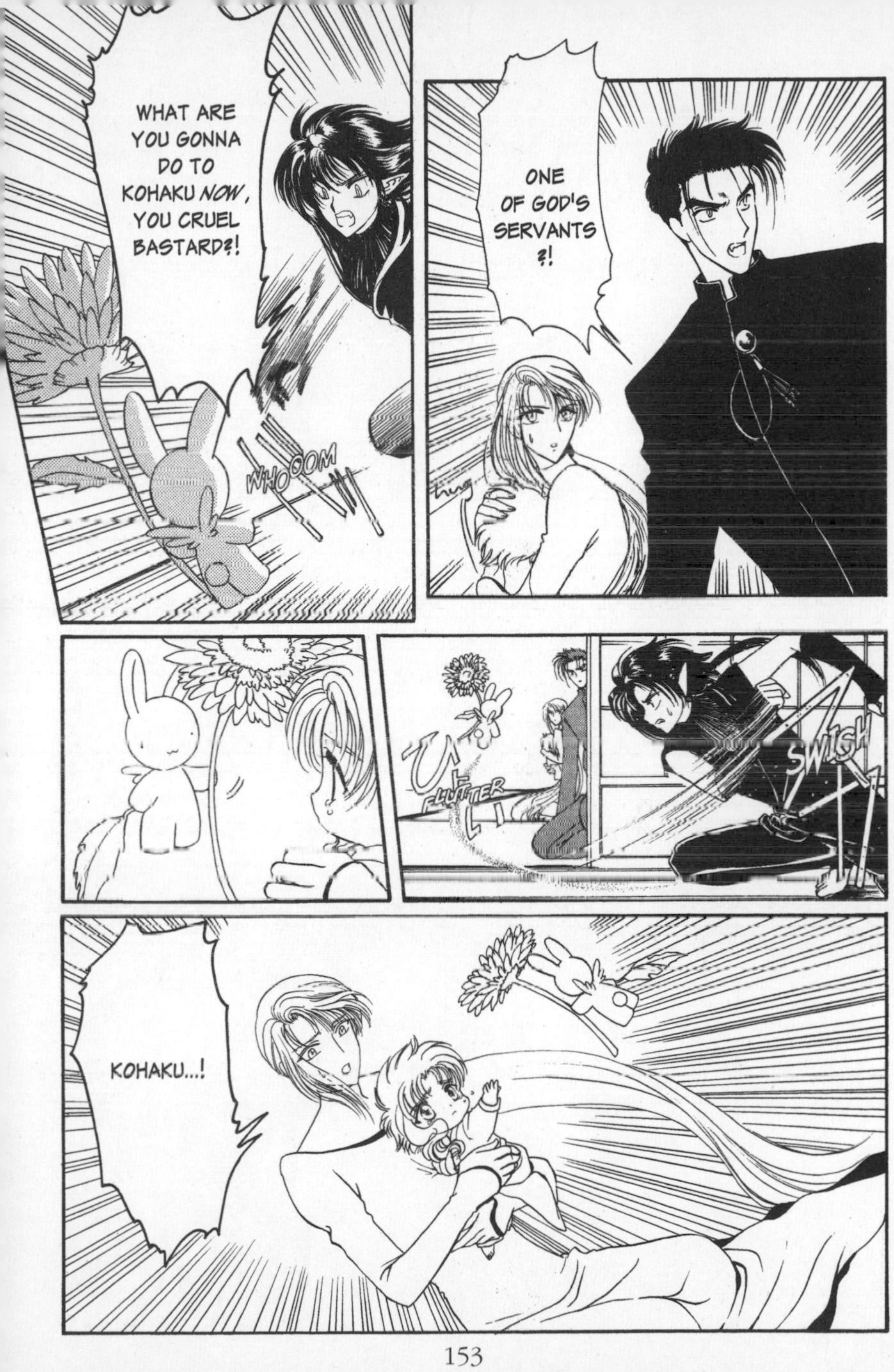
ONE OF GOD'S SERVANTS?!
thug
WHAT ARE YOU GONNA DO TO KOHAKU *NOW*, YOU CRUEL BASTARD?!
WHOOOM
SWISH
FLUTTER
KOHAKU...!

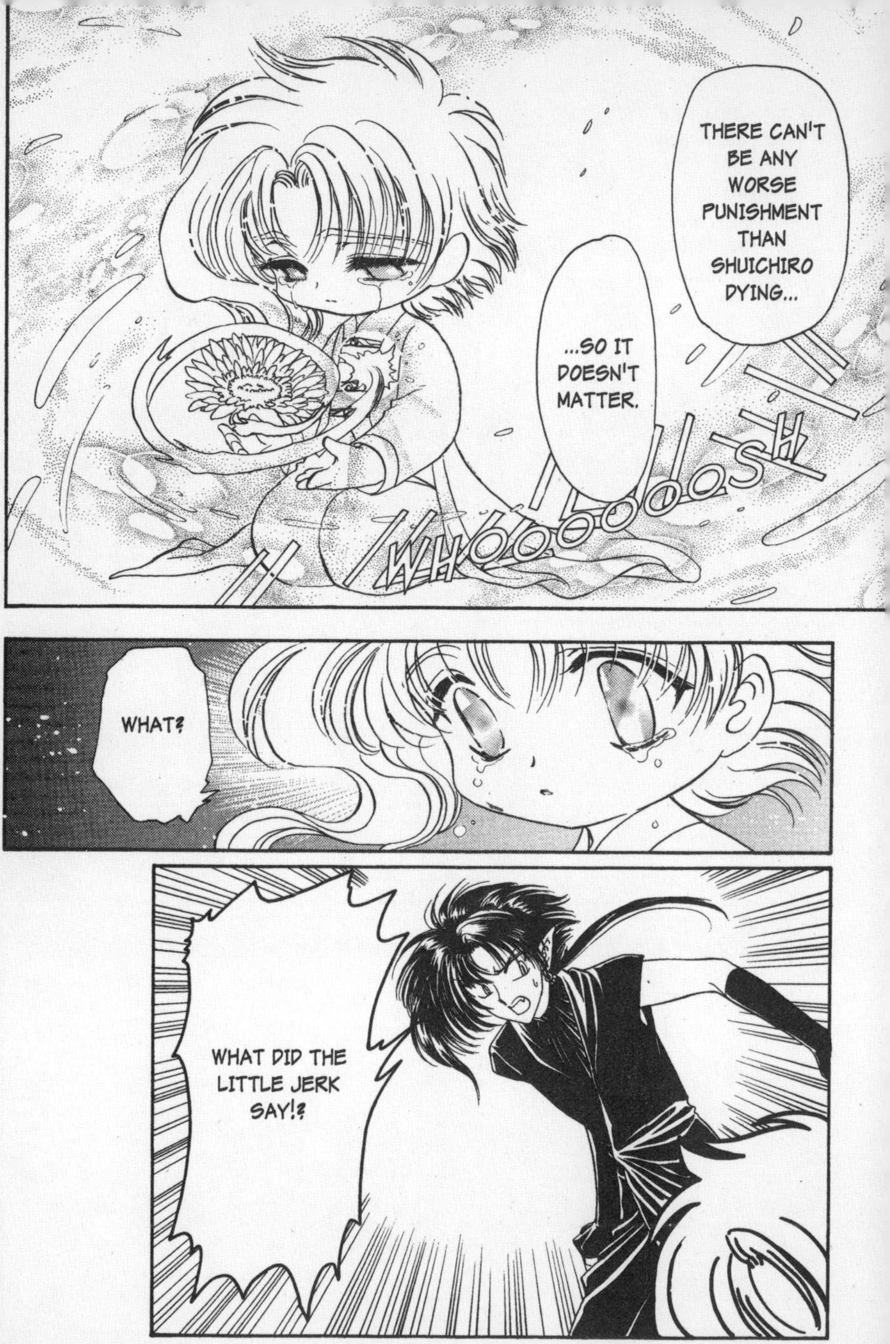
THERE CAN'T BE ANY WORSE PUNISHMENT THAN SHUICHIRO DYING...
...SO IT DOESN'T MATTER.
WHOOOOOOOOSH
WHAT?
WHAT DID THE LITTLE JERK SAY!?

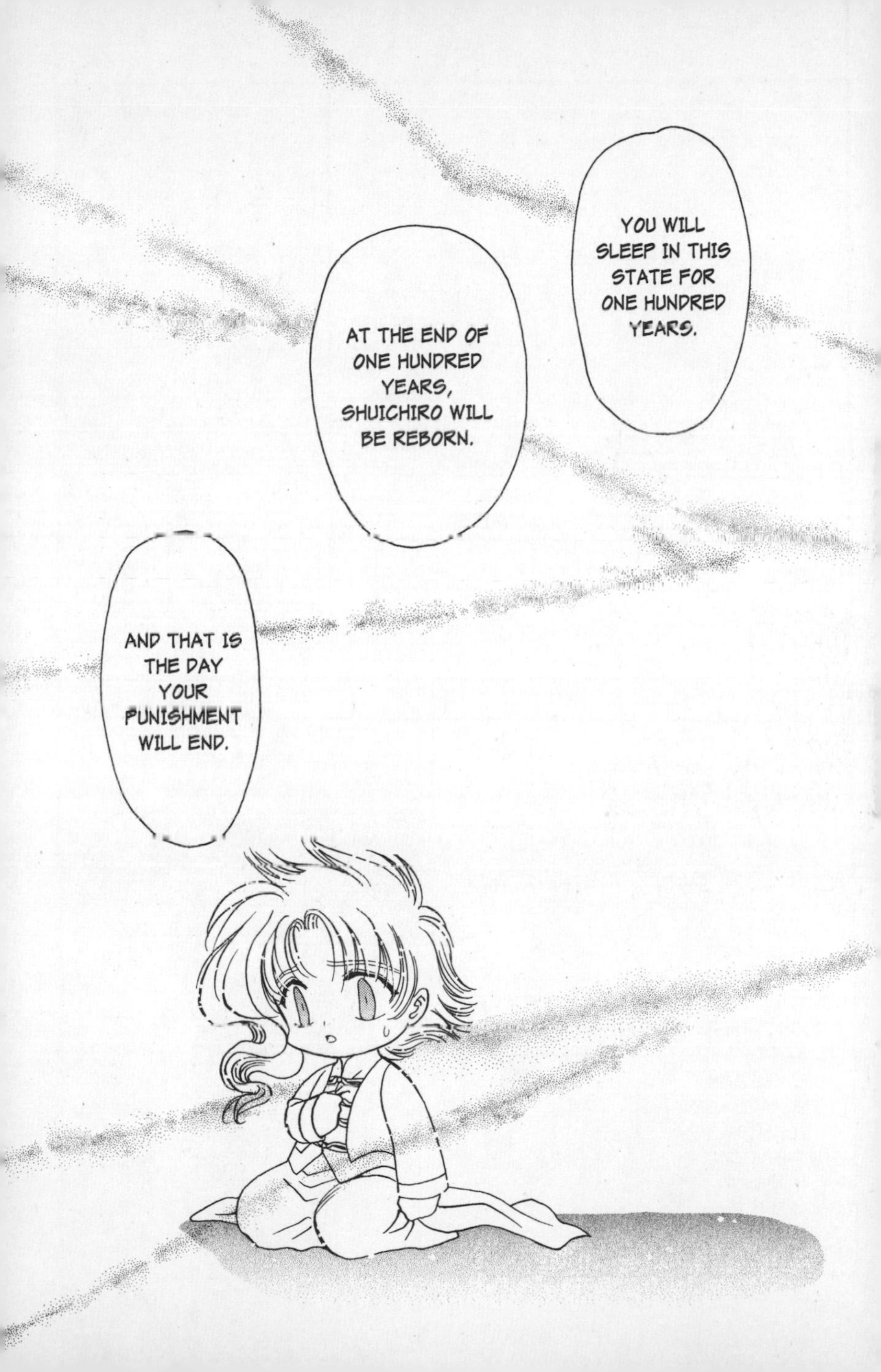
YOU WILL SLEEP IN THIS STATE FOR ONE HUNDRED YEARS.
AT THE END OF ONE HUNDRED YEARS, SHUICHIRO WILL BE REBORN.
AND THAT IS THE DAY YOUR PUNISHMENT WILL END.

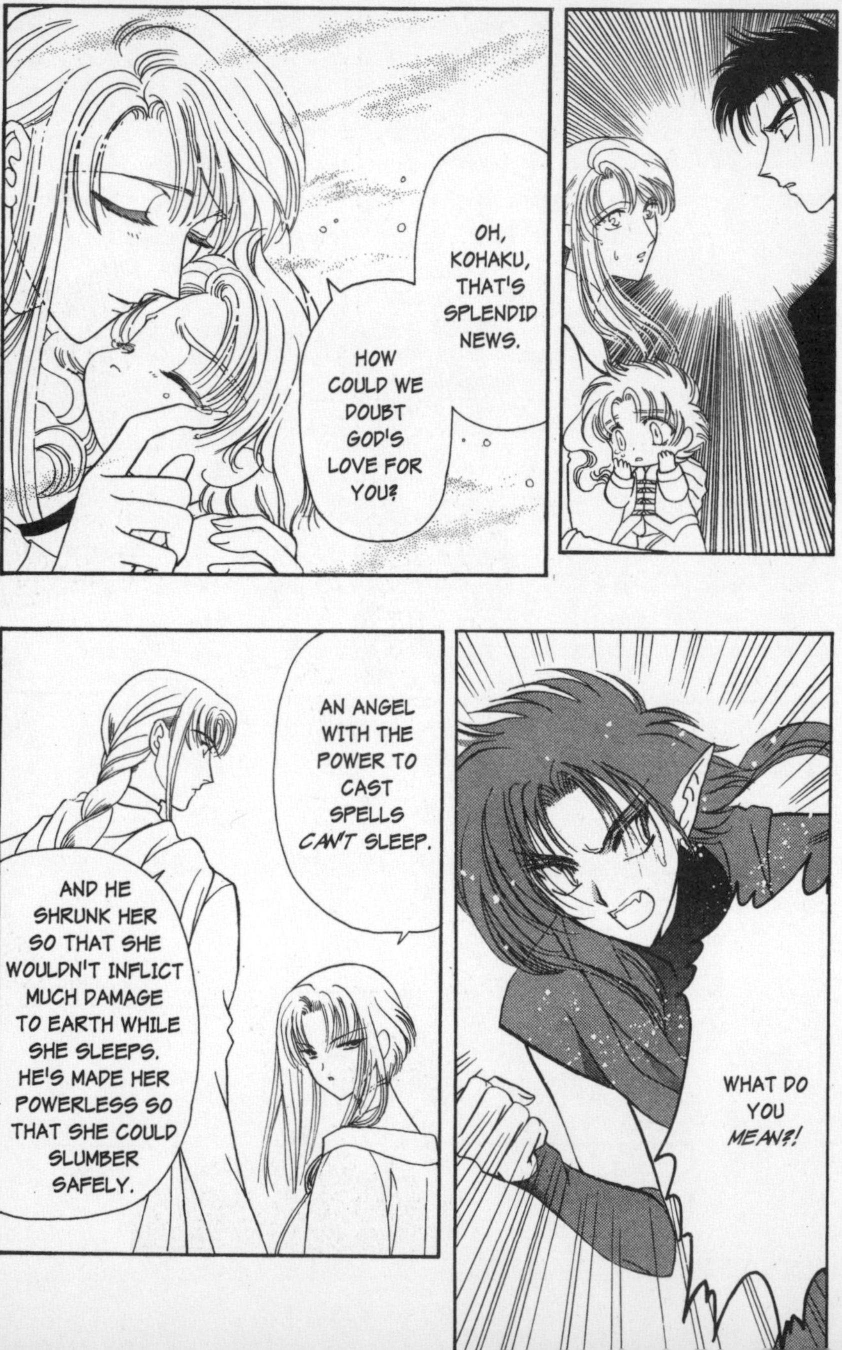
OH, KOHAKU, THAT'S SPLENDID NEWS.
HOW COULD WE DOUBT GOD'S LOVE FOR YOU?
WHAT DO YOU *MEAN?!*
AN ANGEL WITH THE POWER TO CAST SPELLS *CAN'T* SLEEP.
AND HE SHRUNK HER SO THAT SHE WOULDN'T INFLICT MUCH DAMAGE TO EARTH WHILE SHE SLEEPS. HE'S MADE HER POWERLESS SO THAT SHE COULD SLUMBER SAFELY.

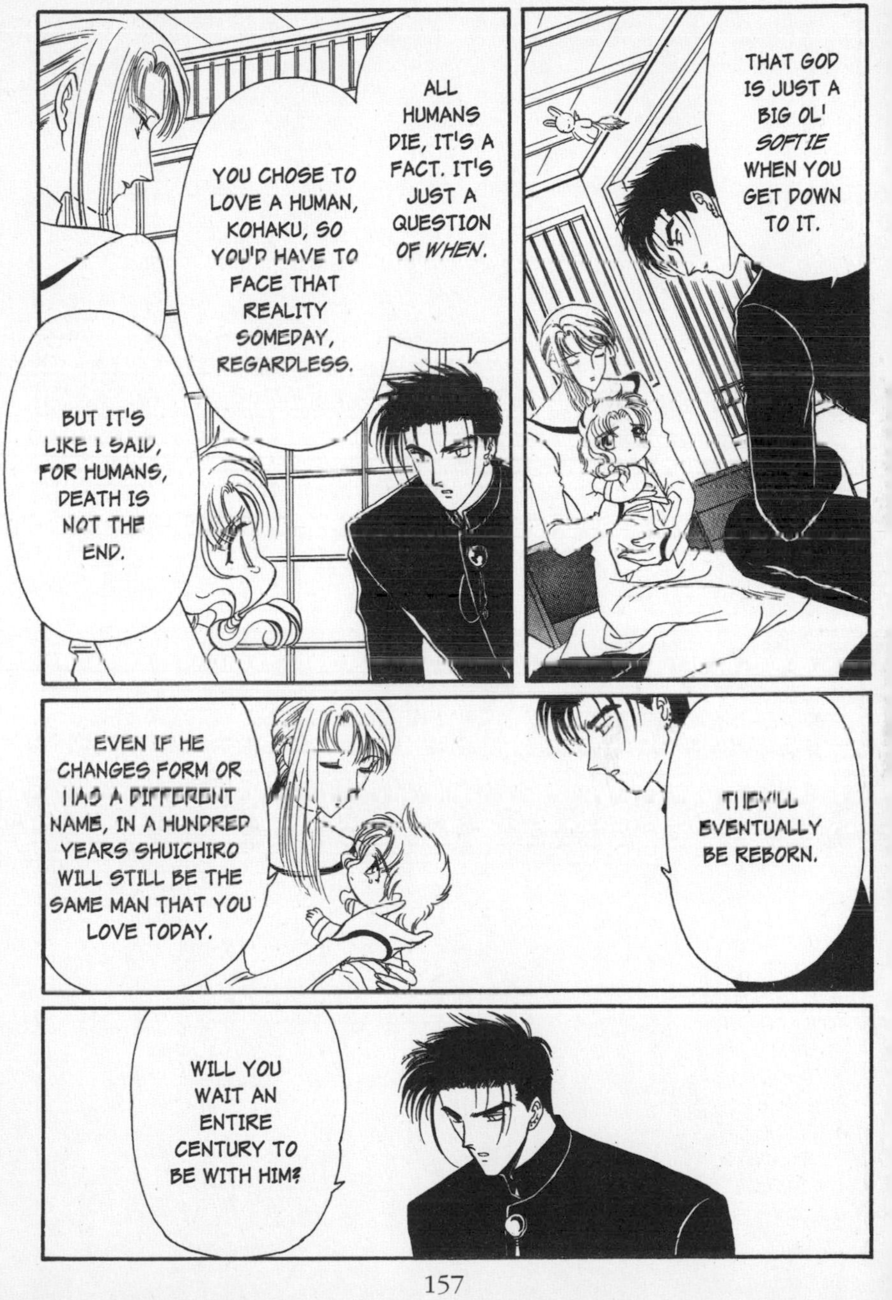
THAT GOD IS JUST A BIG OL' *SOFTIE* WHEN YOU GET DOWN TO IT.
ALL HUMANS DIE, IT'S A FACT. IT'S JUST A QUESTION OF *WHEN*.
YOU CHOSE TO LOVE A HUMAN, KOHAKU, SO YOU'D HAVE TO FACE THAT REALITY SOMEDAY, REGARDLESS.
BUT IT'S LIKE I SAID, FOR HUMANS, DEATH IS NOT THE END.
THEY'LL EVENTUALLY BE REBORN.
EVEN IF HE CHANGES FORM OR HAS A DIFFERENT NAME, IN A HUNDRED YEARS SHUICHIRO WILL STILL BE THE SAME MAN THAT YOU LOVE TODAY.
WILL YOU WAIT AN ENTIRE CENTURY TO BE WITH HIM?

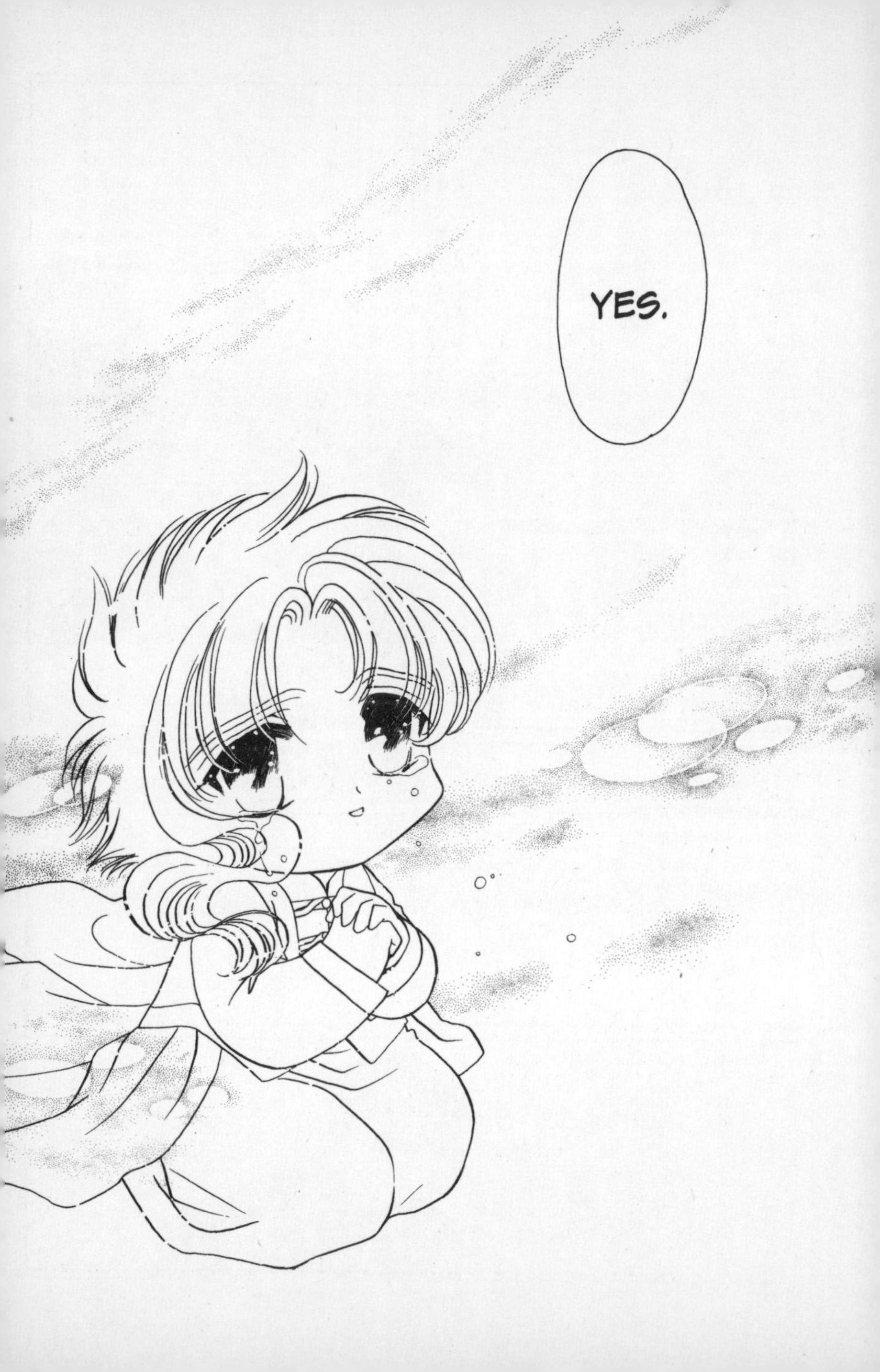
YES.

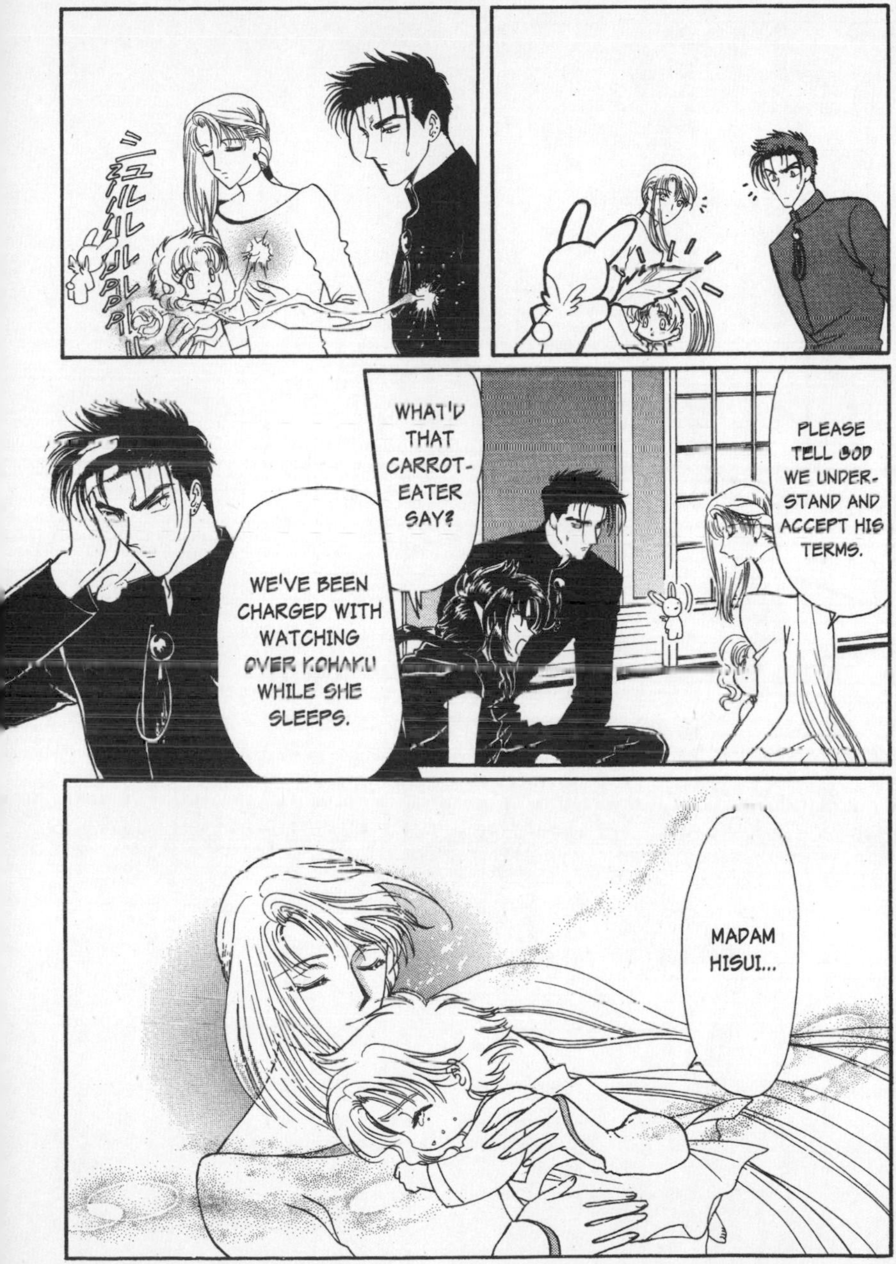
PLEASE TELL GOD WE UNDERSTAND AND ACCEPT HIS TERMS.
WHAT'D THAT CARROT-EATER SAY?
WE'VE BEEN CHARGED WITH WATCHING OVER KOHAKU WHILE SHE SLEEPS.
MADAM HISUI...

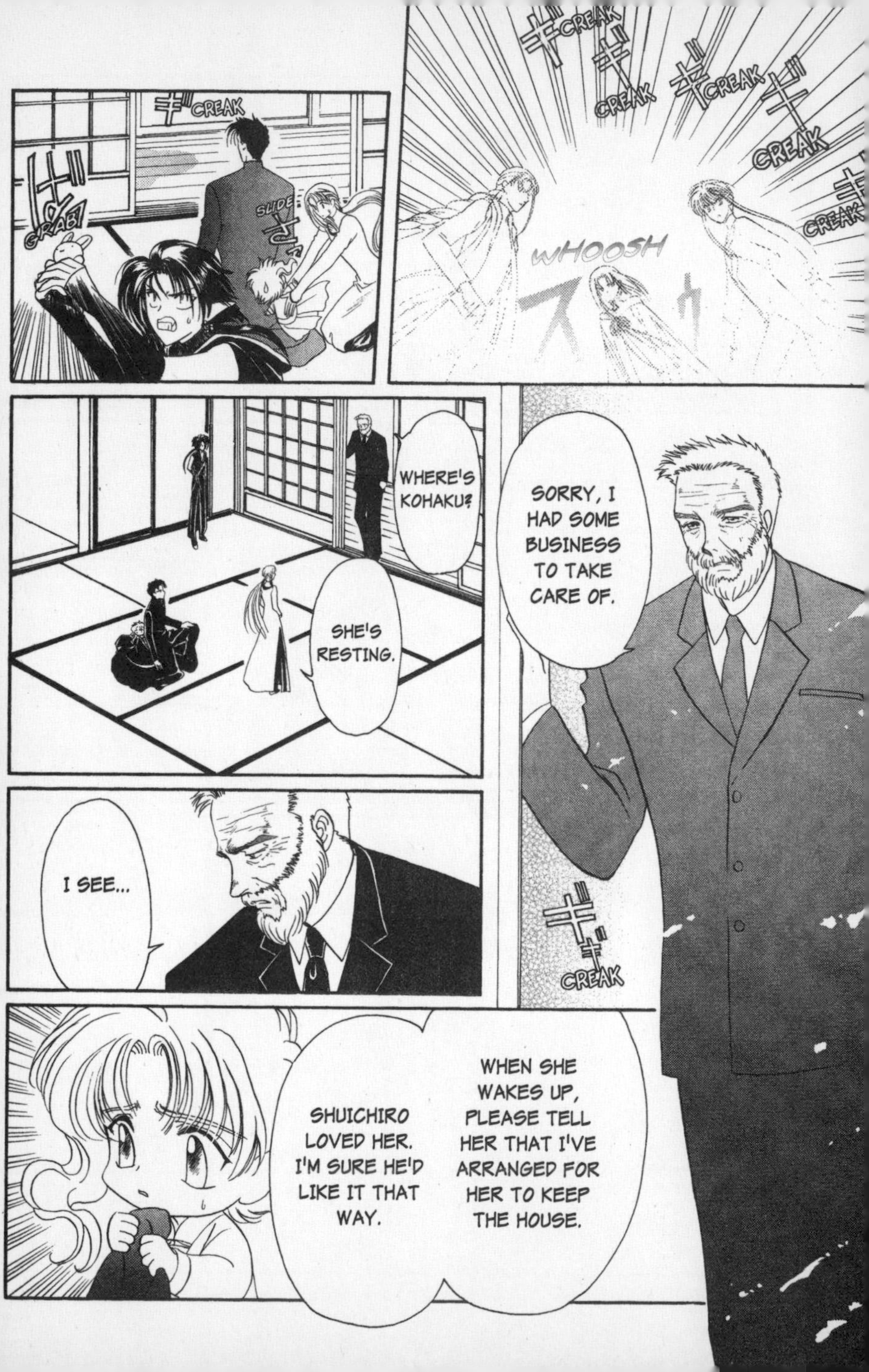
CREAK
CREAK
CREAK
CREAK
CREAK
WHOOSH
CREAK
GRAB!
SLIDE
SORRY, I HAD SOME BUSINESS TO TAKE CARE OF.
CREAK
WHERE'S KOHAKU?
SHE'S RESTING.
I SEE...
WHEN SHE WAKES UP, PLEASE TELL HER THAT I'VE ARRANGED FOR HER TO KEEP THE HOUSE.
SHUICHIRO LOVED HER. I'M SURE HE'D LIKE IT THAT WAY.

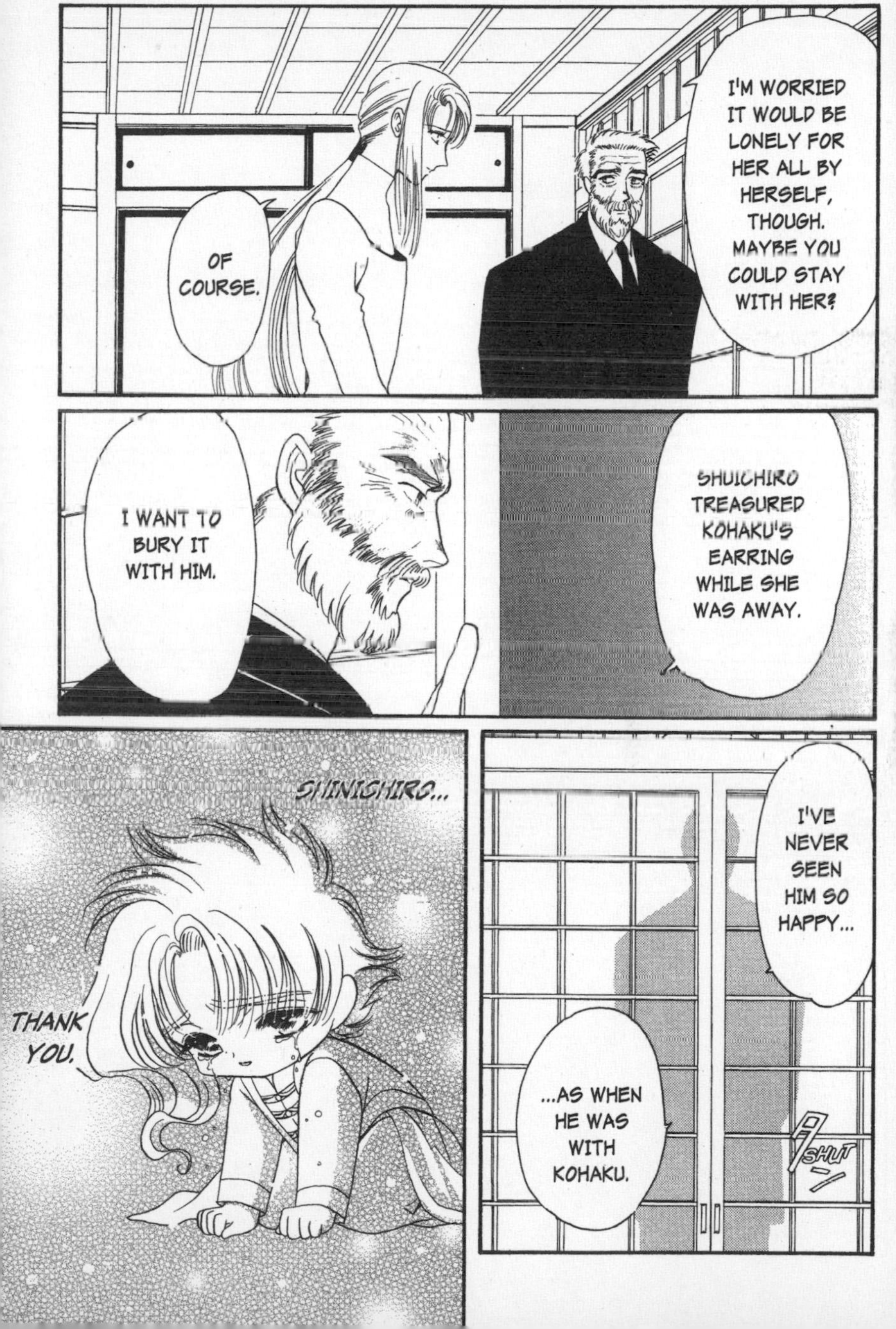
I'M WORRIED IT WOULD BE LONELY FOR HER ALL BY HERSELF, THOUGH. MAYBE YOU COULD STAY WITH HER?
OF COURSE.
SHUICHIRO TREASURED KOHAKU'S EARRING WHILE SHE WAS AWAY.
I WANT TO BURY IT WITH HIM.
I'VE NEVER SEEN HIM SO HAPPY...
...AS WHEN HE WAS WITH KOHAKU.
SHUT
SHUICHIRO...
THANK YOU.

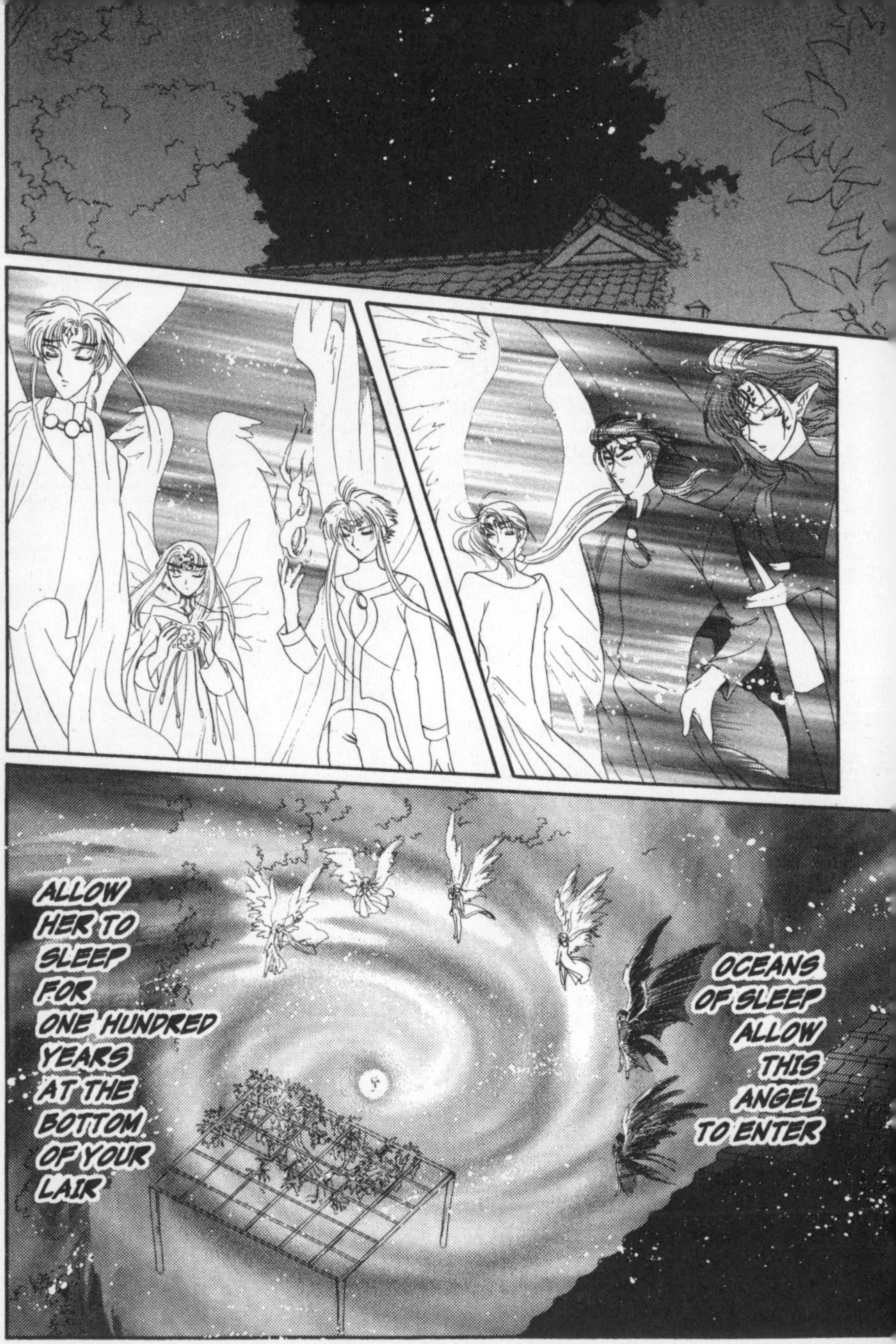
OCEANS OF SLEEP ALLOW THIS ANGEL TO ENTER
ALLOW HER TO SLEEP FOR ONE HUNDRED YEARS AT THE BOTTOM OF YOUR LAIR

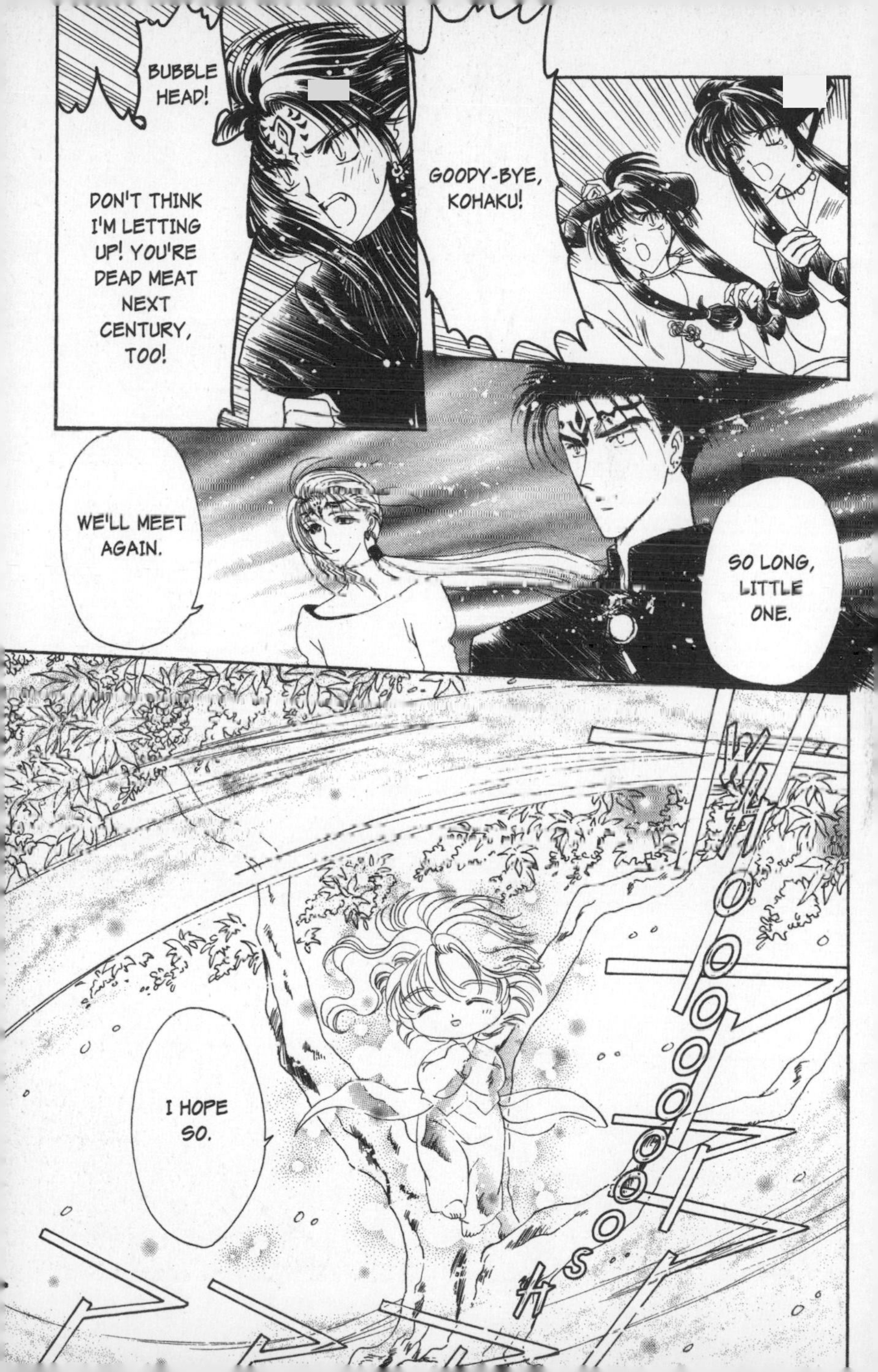
GOODY-BYE, KOHAKU!
BUBBLE HEAD!
DON'T THINK I'M LETTING UP! YOU'RE DEAD MEAT NEXT CENTURY, TOO!
SO LONG, LITTLE ONE.
WE'LL MEET AGAIN.
WHOOOOOOOOSH
I HOPE SO.

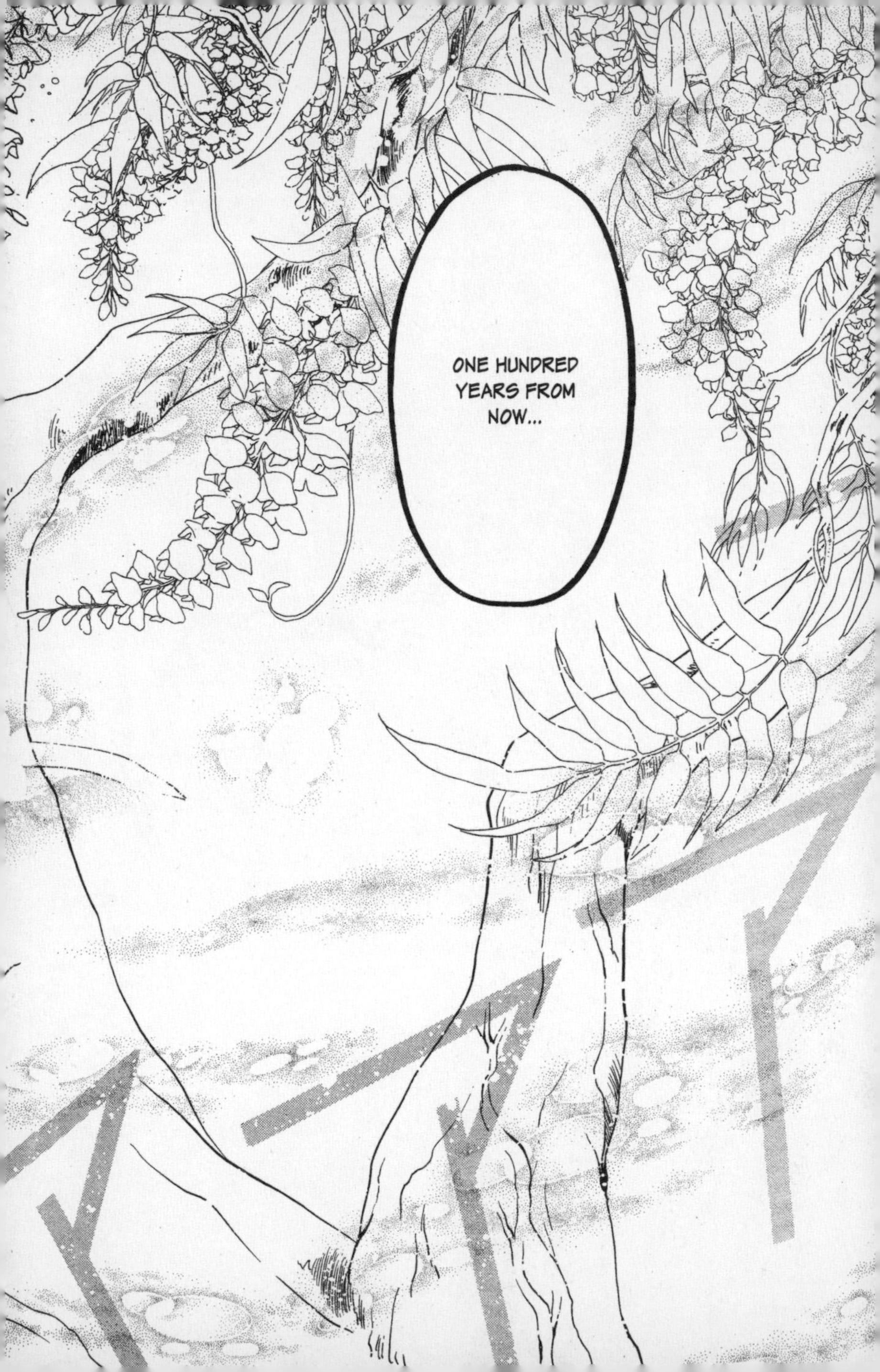
ONE HUNDRED YEARS FROM NOW...

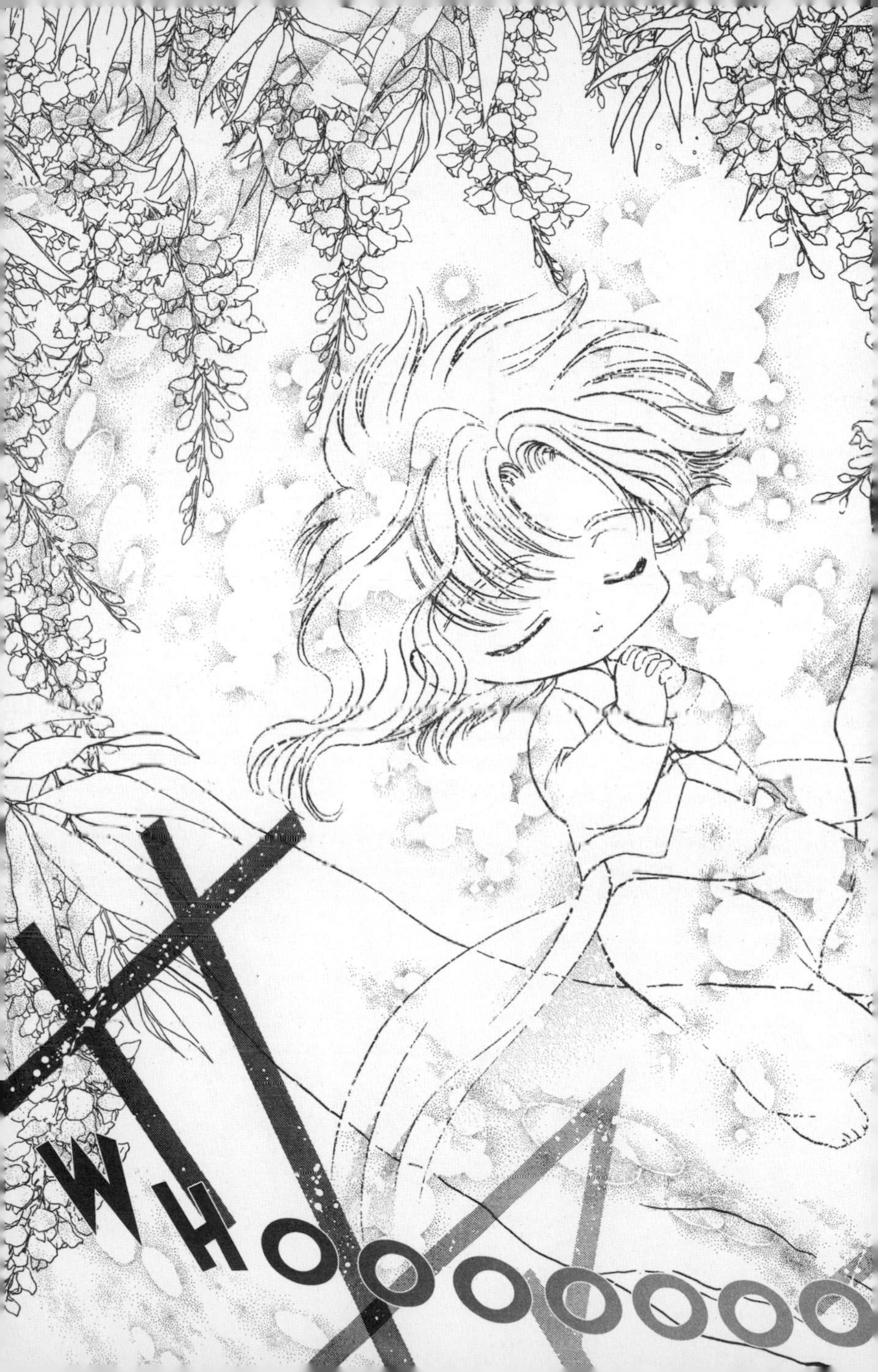
WHOOOOOOO

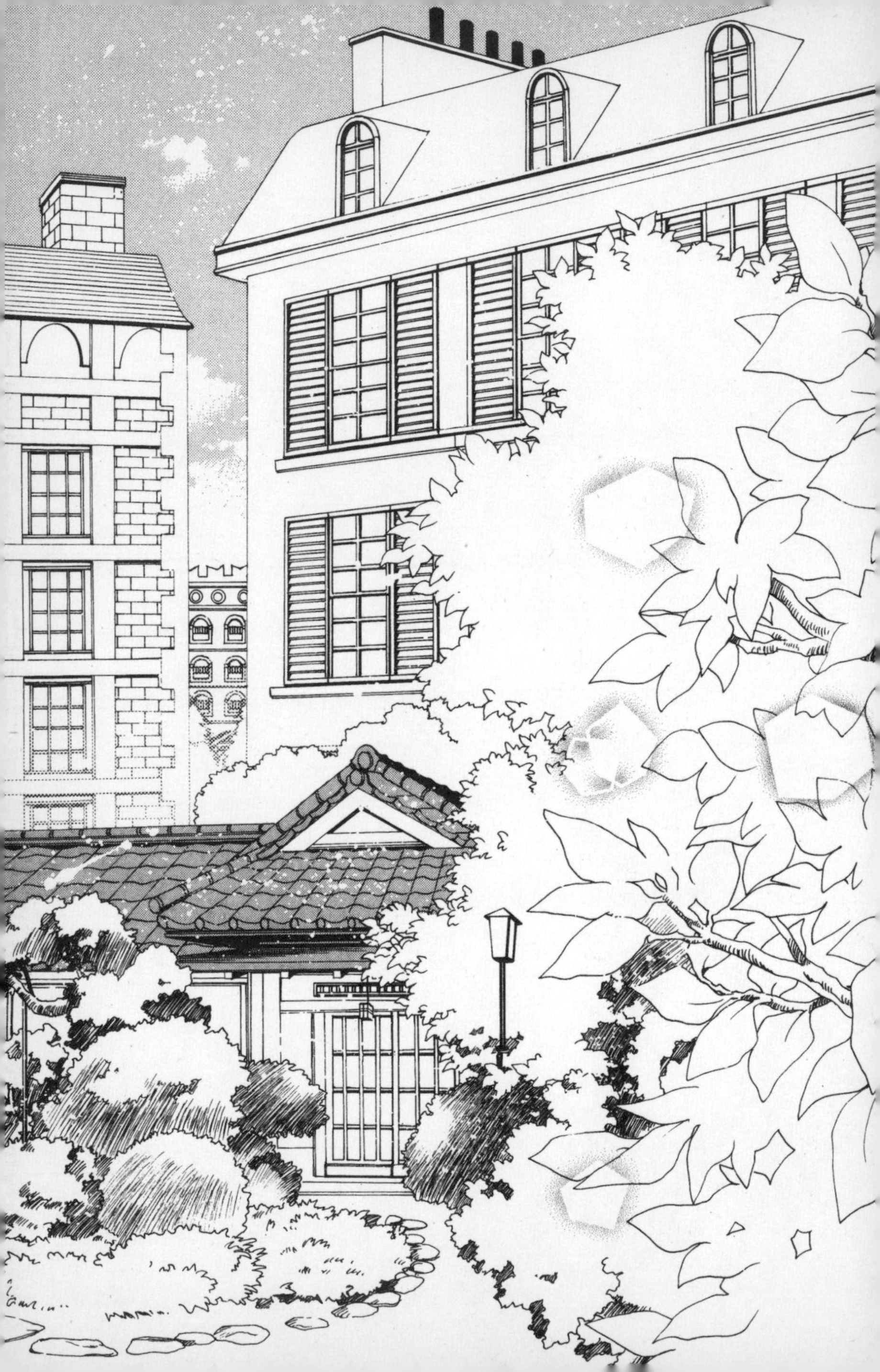

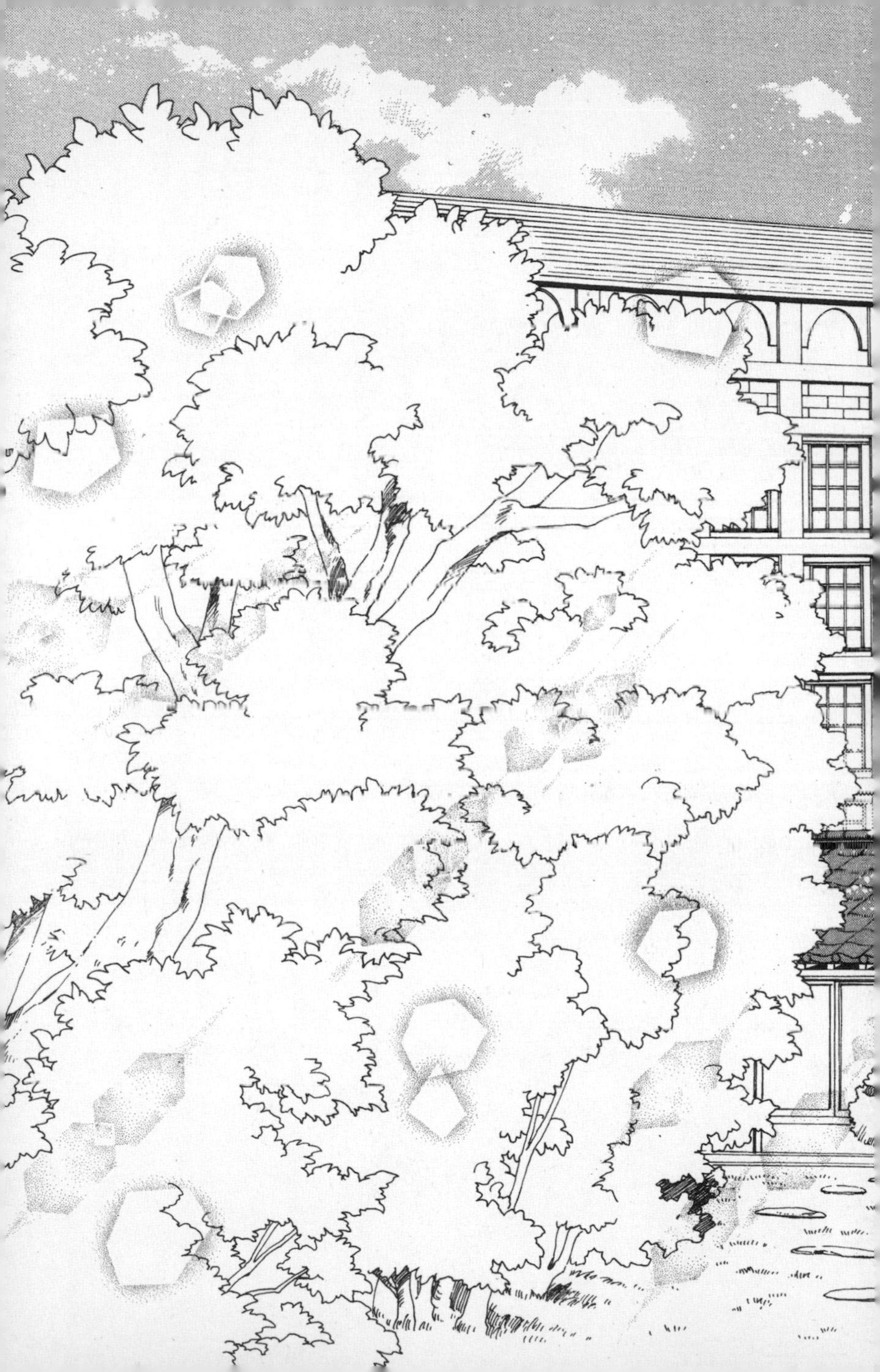

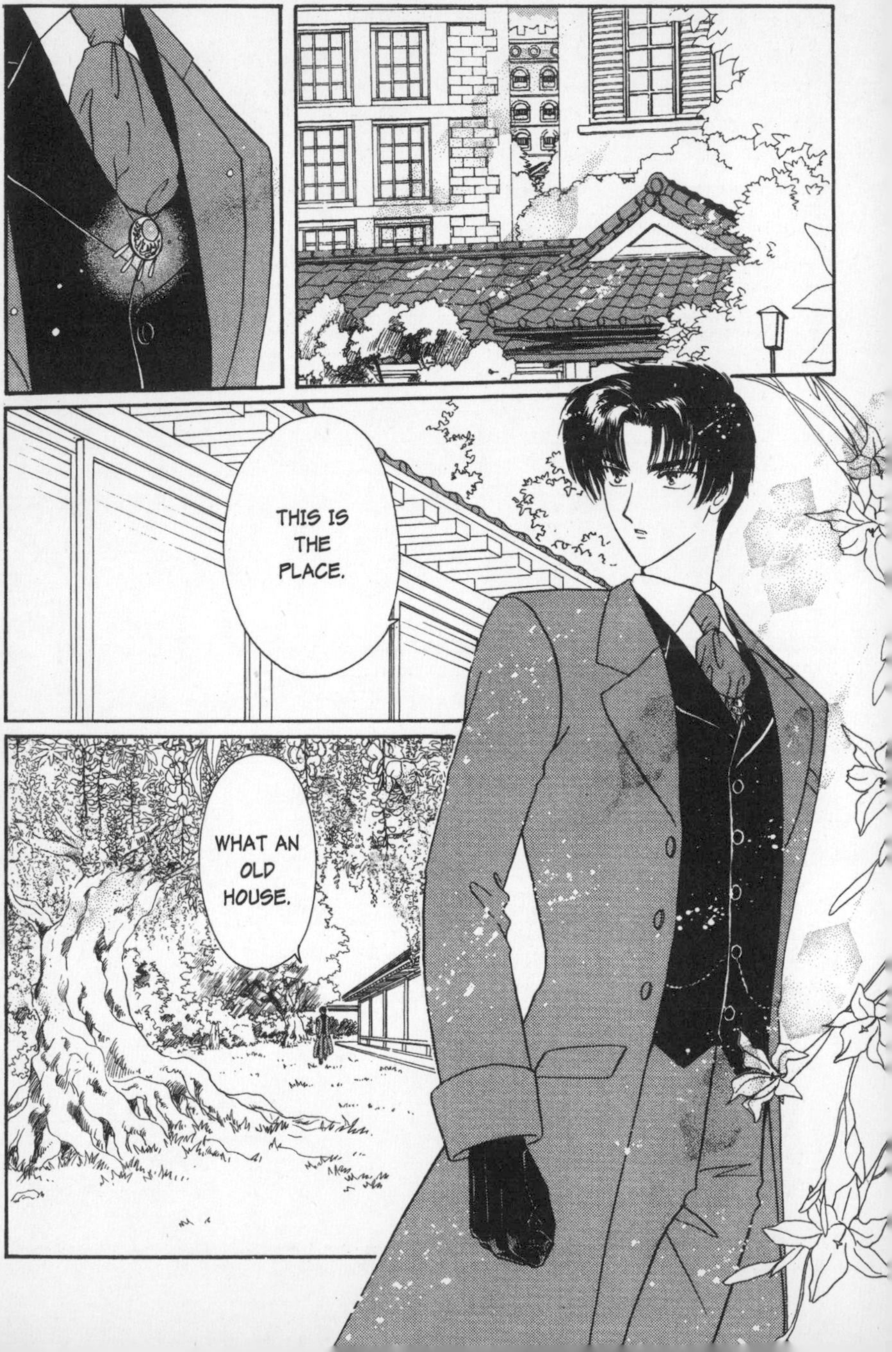
THIS IS THE PLACE.
WHAT AN OLD HOUSE.

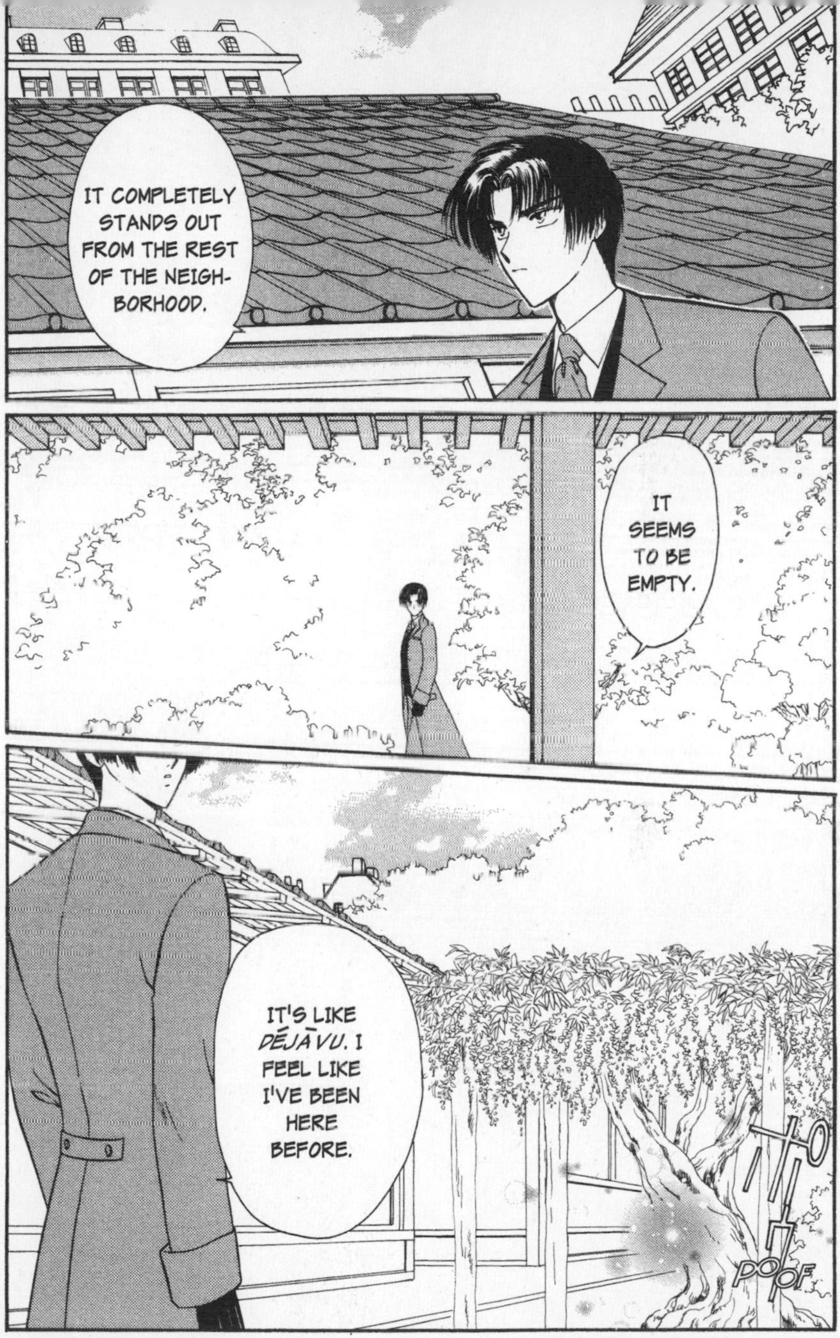
IT COMPLETELY STANDS OUT FROM THE REST OF THE NEIGH-BORHOOD.
IT SEEMS TO BE EMPTY.
POOF
IT'S LIKE DÉJÀ VU. I FEEL LIKE I'VE BEEN HERE BEFORE.

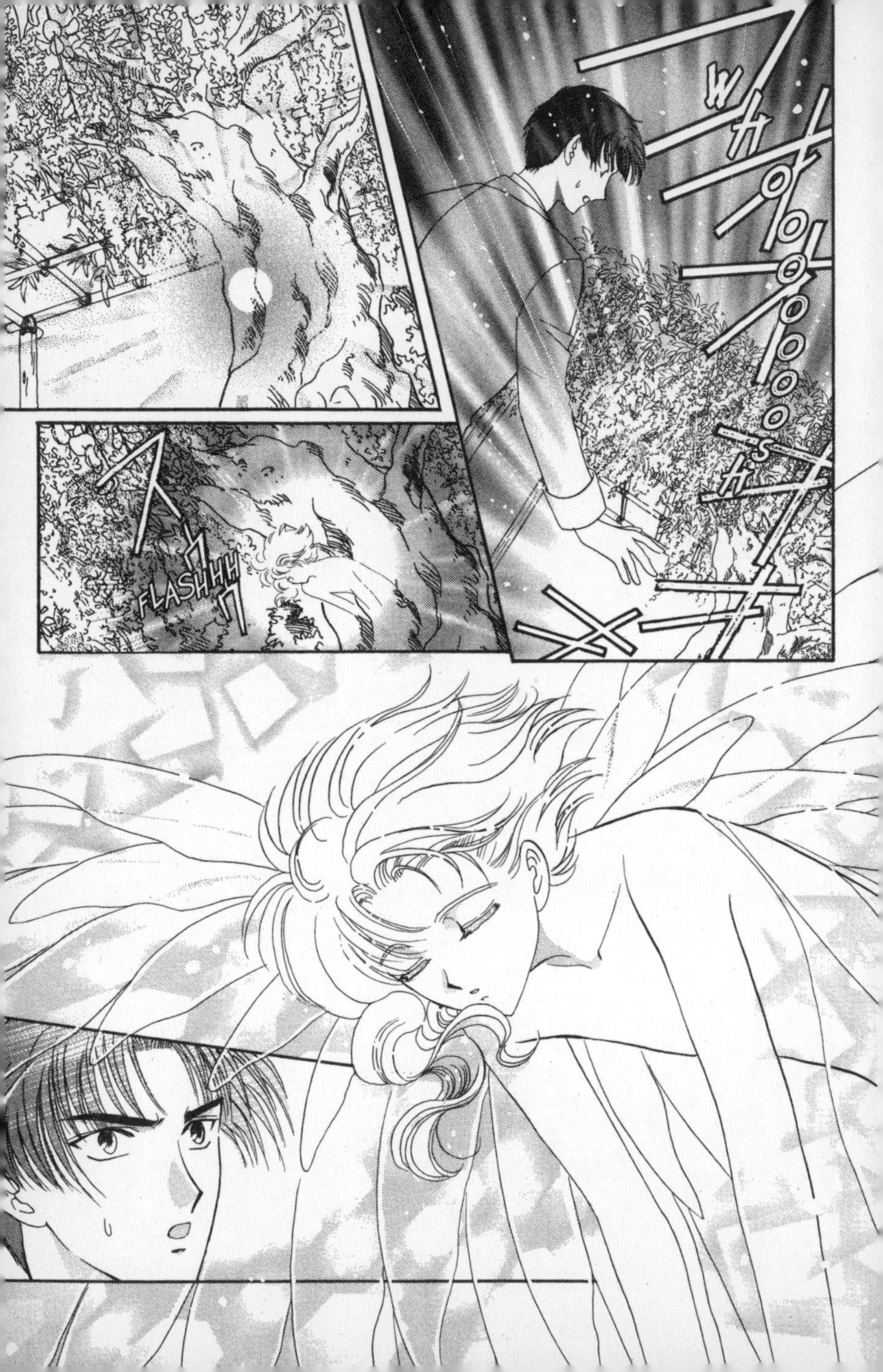
WHOOOOOOOOSH
FLASHHH

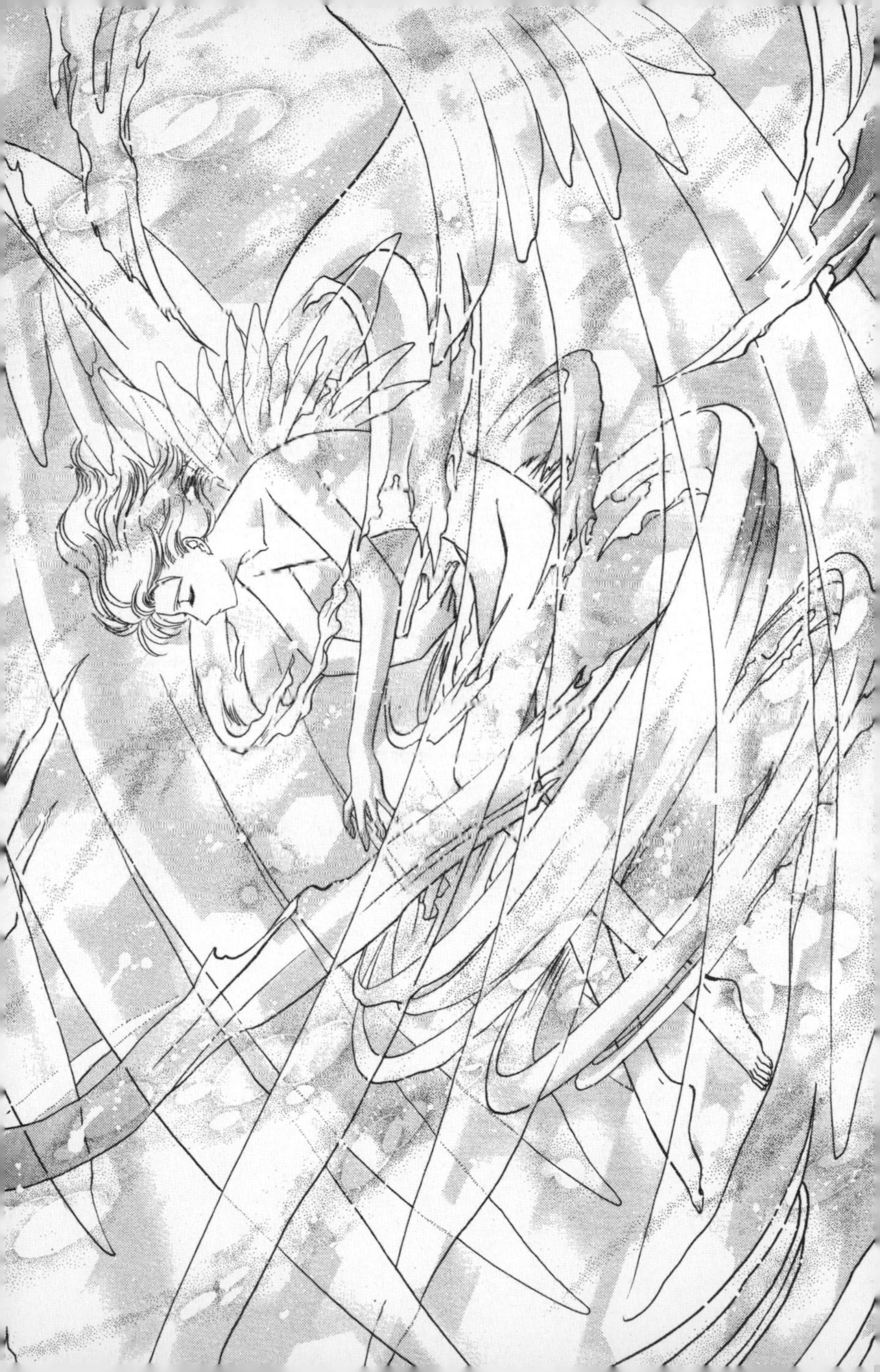

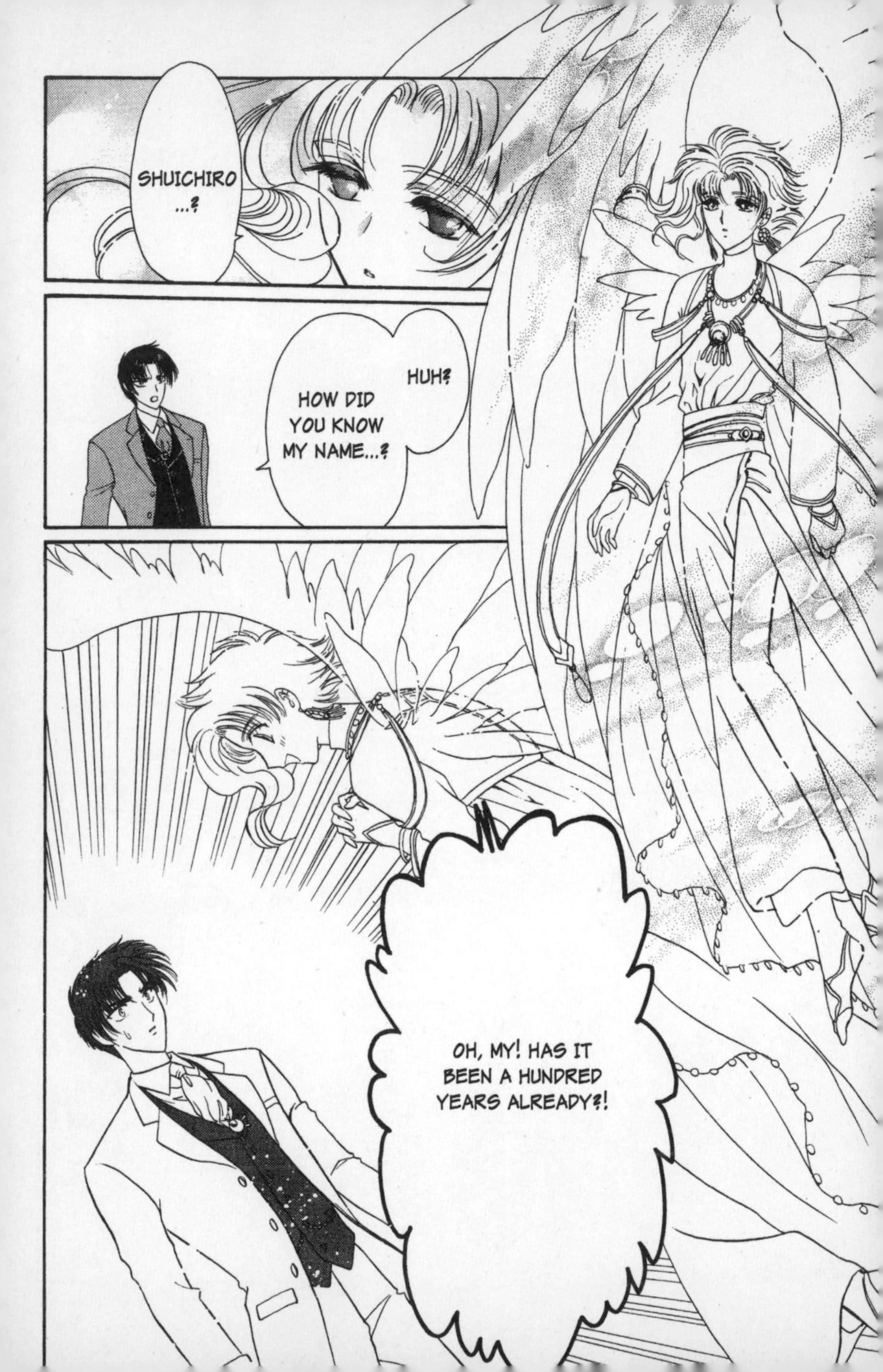
SHUICHIRO ...?
HUH?
HOW DID YOU KNOW MY NAME...?
OH, MY! HAS IT BEEN A HUNDRED YEARS ALREADY?!

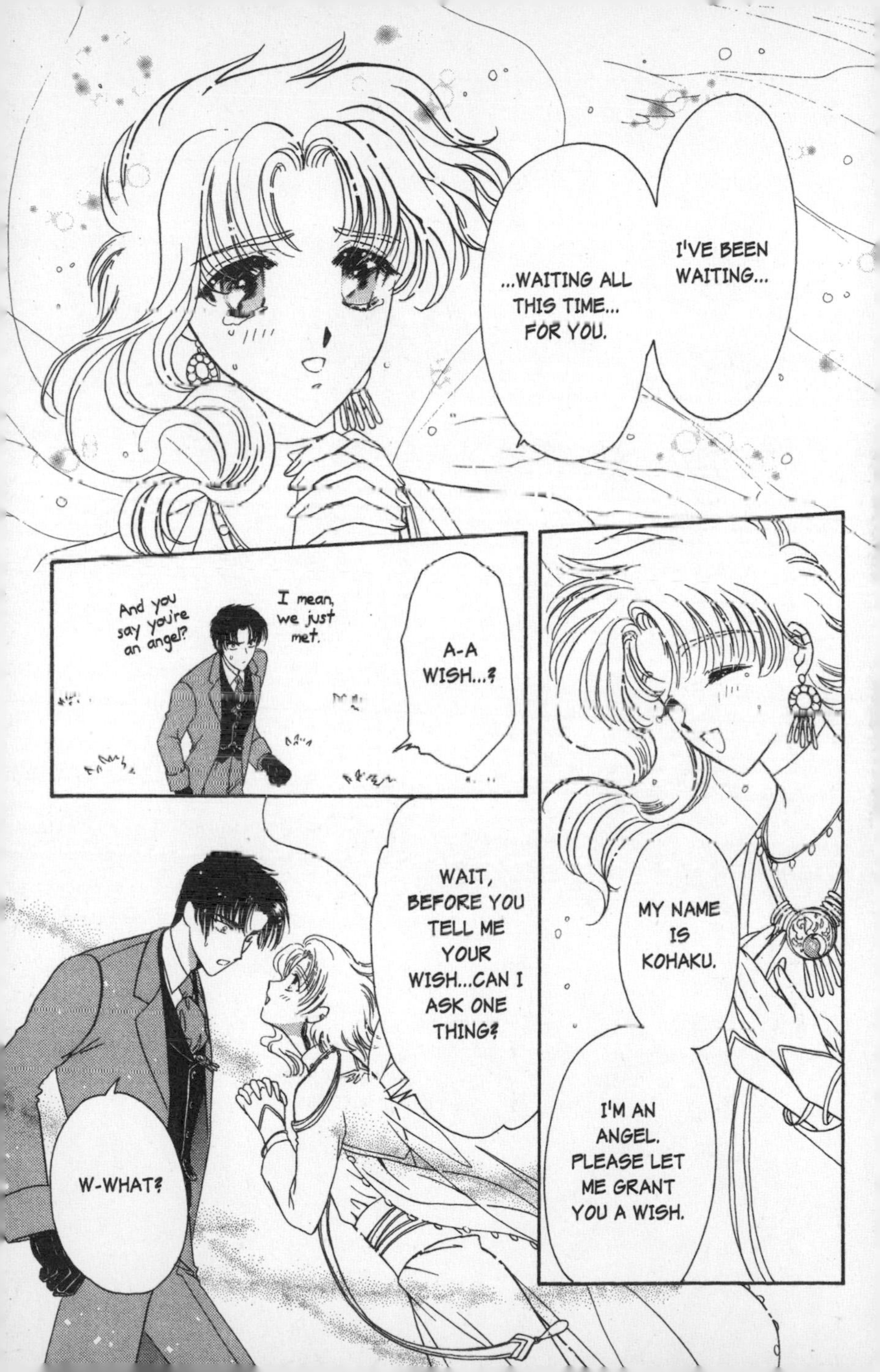
I'VE BEEN WAITING...
...WAITING ALL THIS TIME... FOR YOU.
MY NAME IS KOHAKU.
I'M AN ANGEL. PLEASE LET ME GRANT YOU A WISH.
A-A WISH...?
I mean, we just met.
And you say you're an angel?
WAIT, BEFORE YOU TELL ME YOUR WISH...CAN I ASK ONE THING?
W-WHAT?

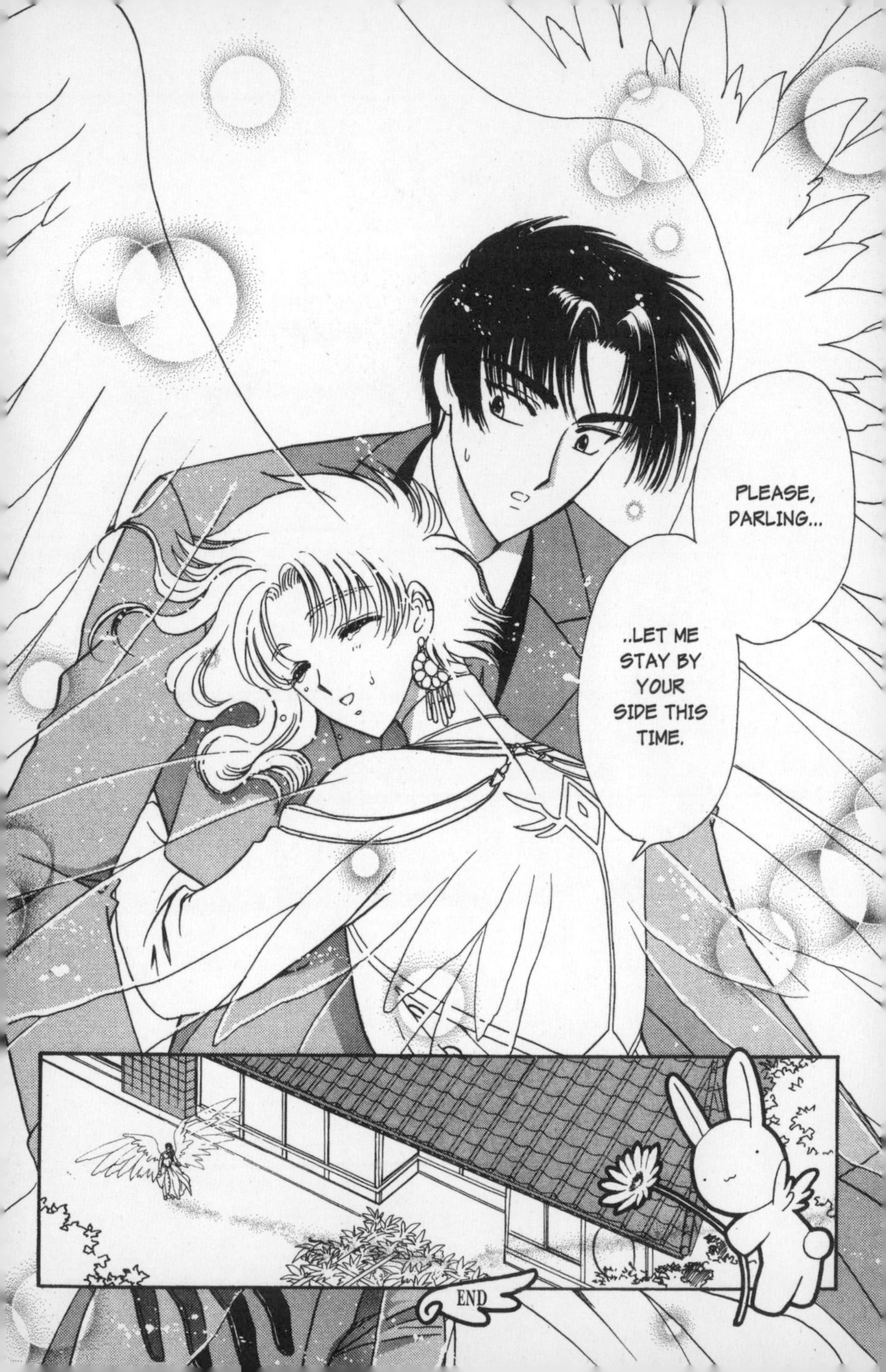
PLEASE, DARLING...
..LET ME STAY BY YOUR SIDE THIS TIME.
END

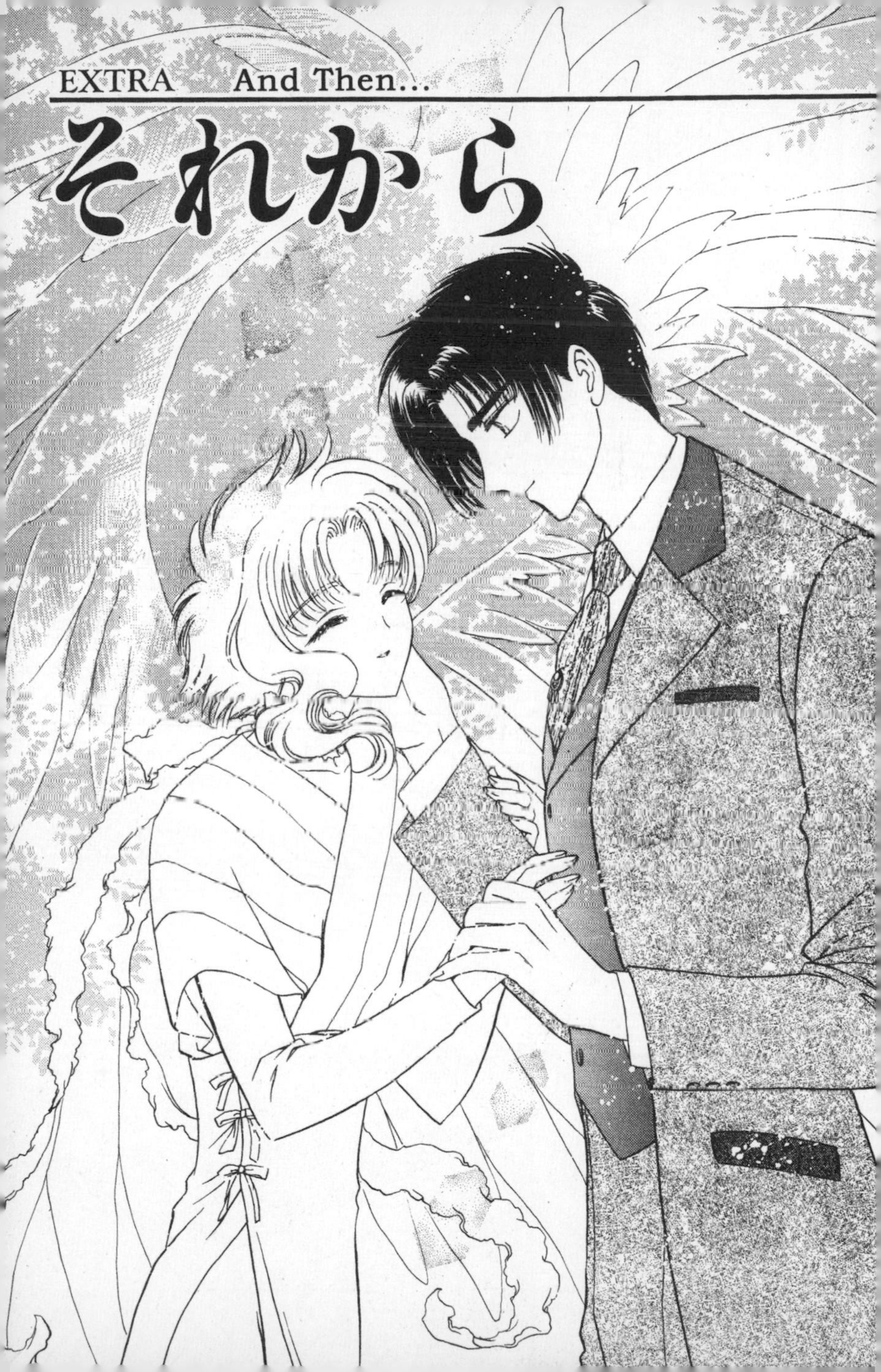
EXTRA And Then...
それから

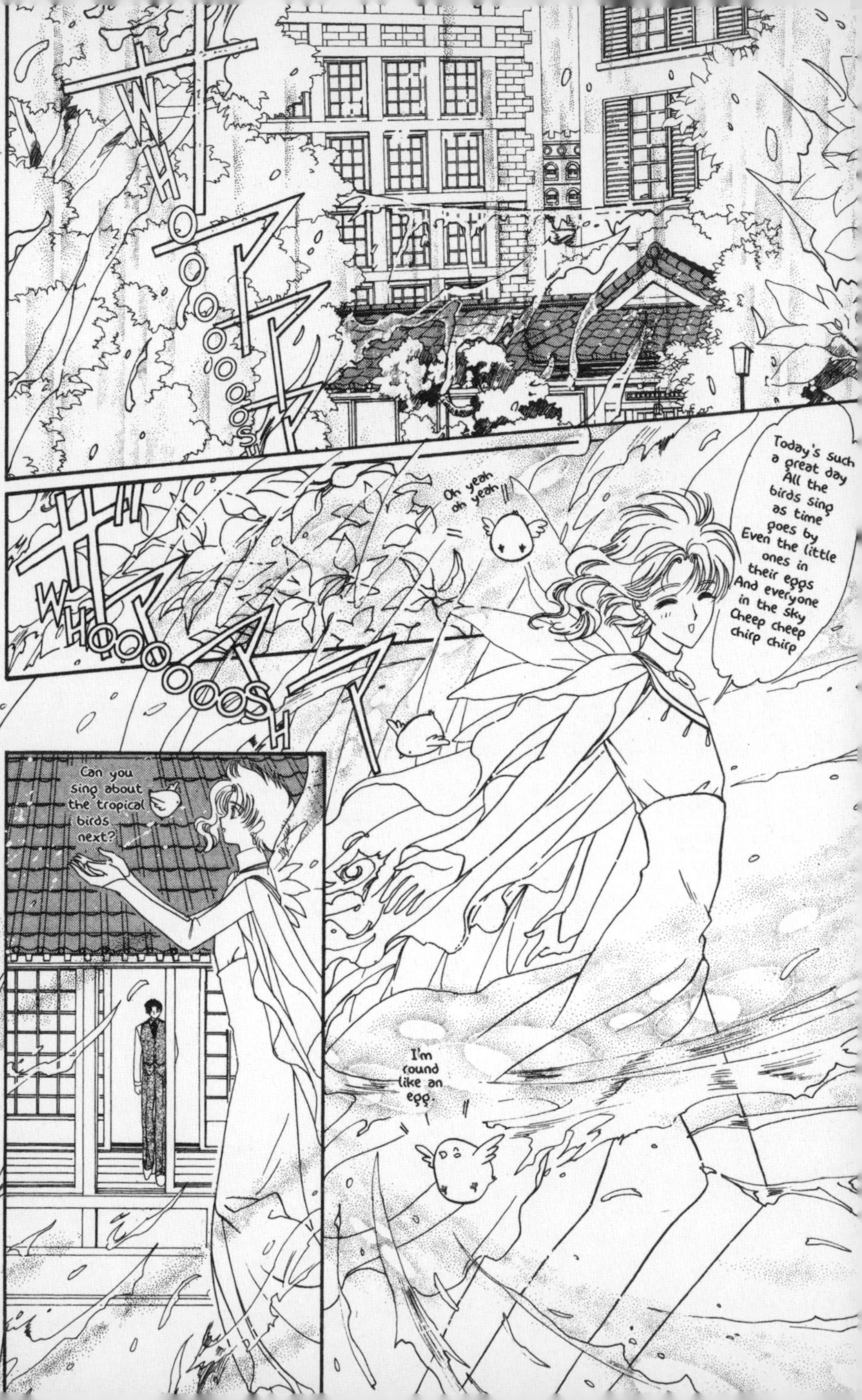
WHOOOOOOSH
Today's such a great day All the birds sing as time goes by Even the little ones in their eggs And everyone in the sky Cheep cheep chirp chirp
Oh yeah oh yeah
WHOOOOOOSH
I'm round like an egg.
Can you sing about the tropical birds next?

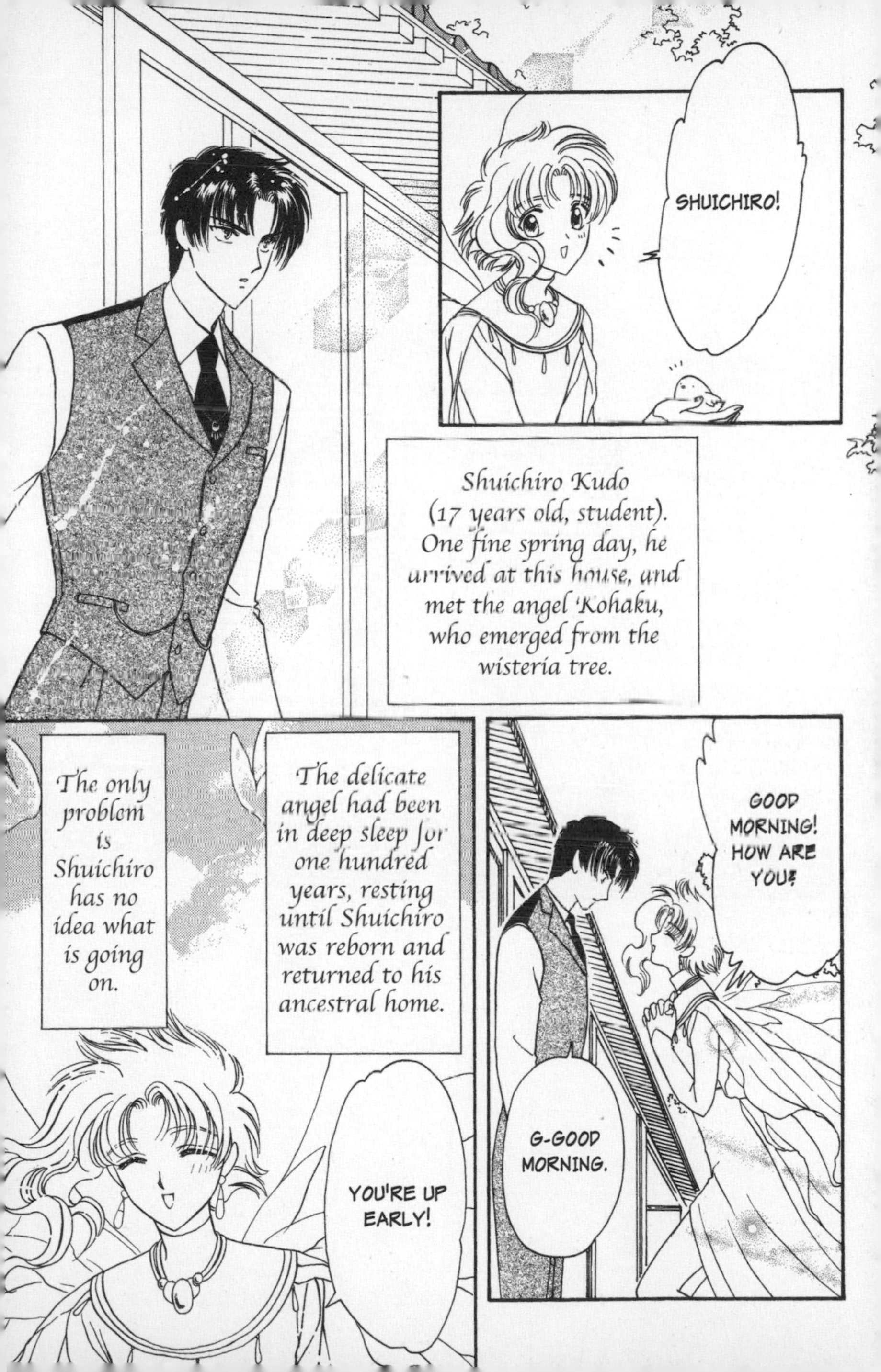
SHUICHIRO!
Shuichiro Kudo (17 years old, student). One fine spring day, he arrived at this house, and met the angel Kohaku, who emerged from the wisteria tree.
GOOD MORNING! HOW ARE YOU?
G-GOOD MORNING.
The delicate angel had been in deep sleep for one hundred years, resting until Shuichiro was reborn and returned to his ancestral home.
The only problem is Shuichiro has no idea what is going on.
YOU'RE UP EARLY!

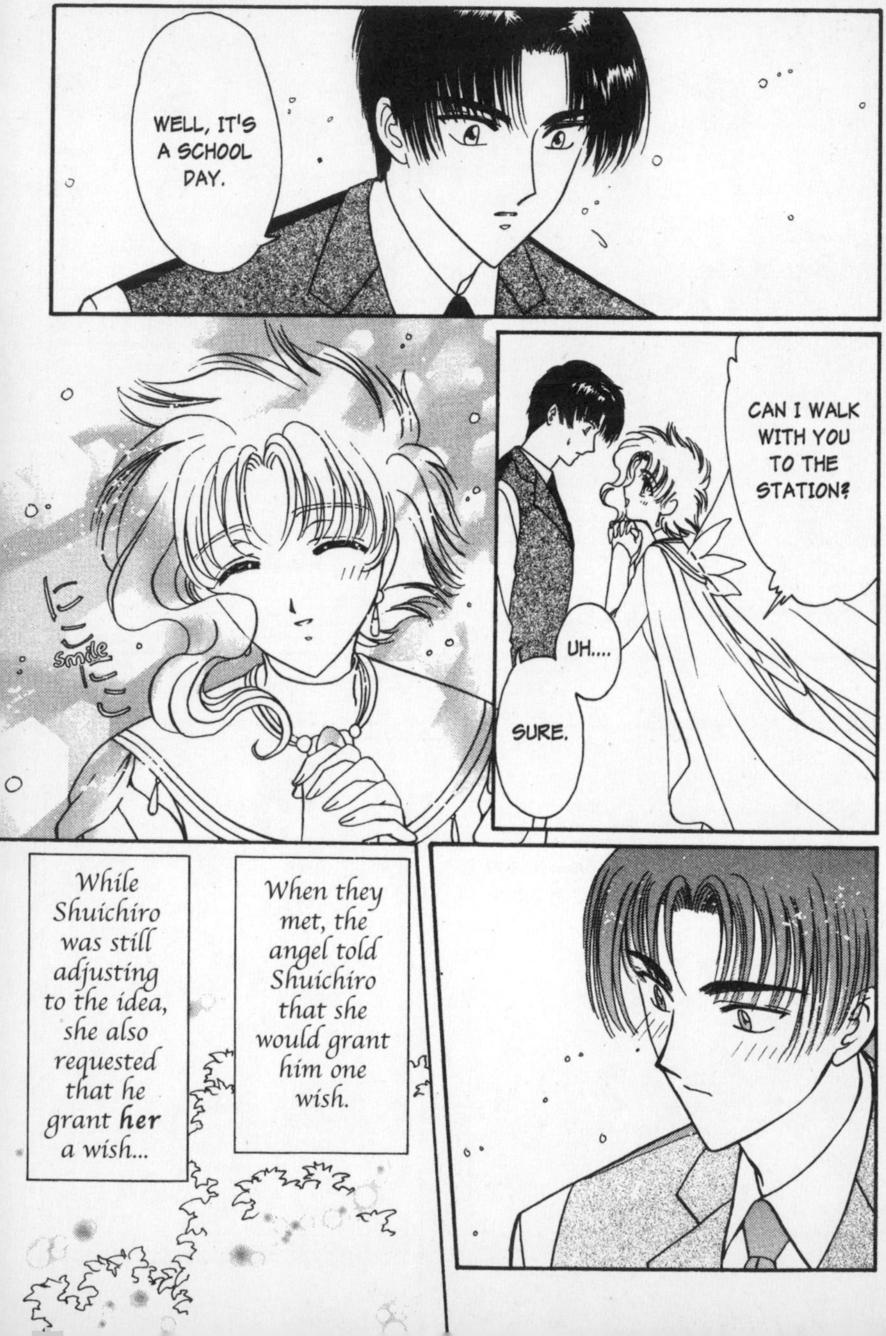
WELL, IT'S A SCHOOL DAY.
CAN I WALK WITH YOU TO THE STATION?
UH.... SURE.
smile
When they met, the angel told Shuichiro that she would grant him one wish.
While Shuichiro was still adjusting to the idea, she also requested that he grant **her** a wish...

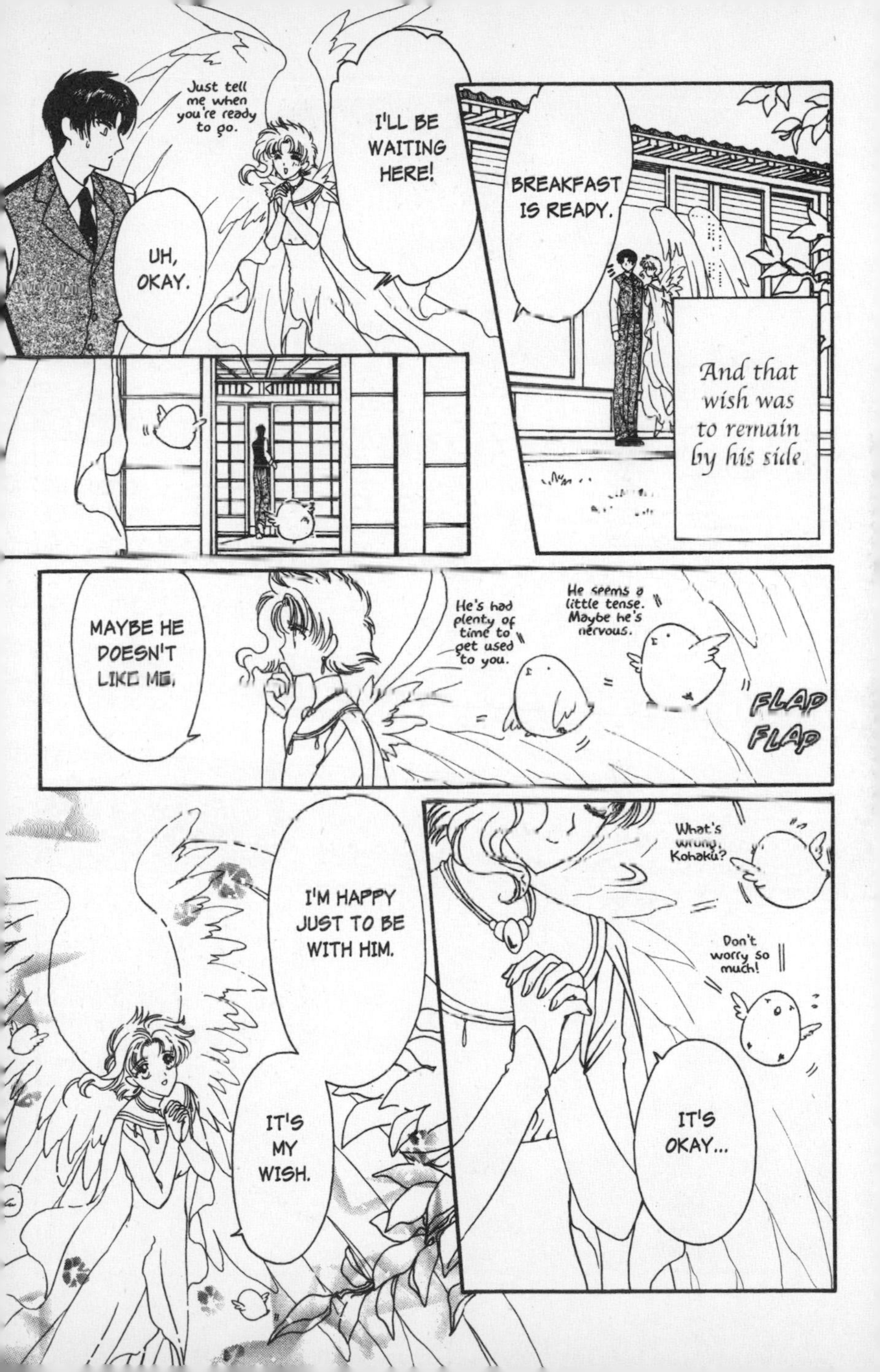
BREAKFAST IS READY.
And that wish was to remain by his side.
I'LL BE WAITING HERE!
Just tell me when you're ready to go.
UH, OKAY.
FLAP FLAP
He seems a little tense. Maybe he's nervous.
He's had plenty of time to get used to you.
MAYBE HE DOESN'T LIKE ME.
What's wrong, Kohaku?
Don't worry so much!
IT'S OKAY...
I'M HAPPY JUST TO BE WITH HIM.
IT'S MY WISH.

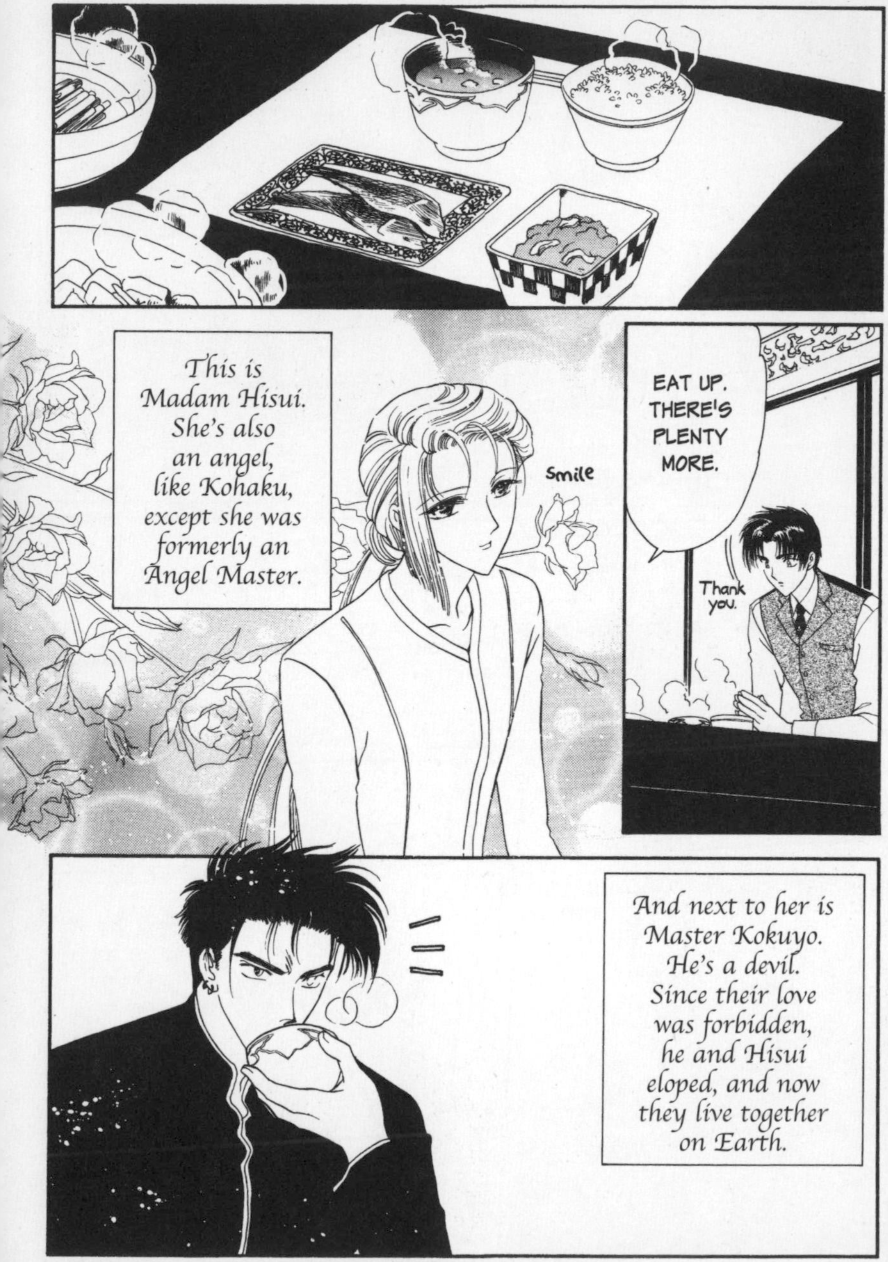
EAT UP. THERE'S PLENTY MORE.
Thank you.
This is Madam Hisui. She's also an angel, like Kohaku, except she was formerly an Angel Master.
Smile
And next to her is Master Kokuyo. He's a devil. Since their love was forbidden, he and Hisui eloped, and now they live together on Earth.

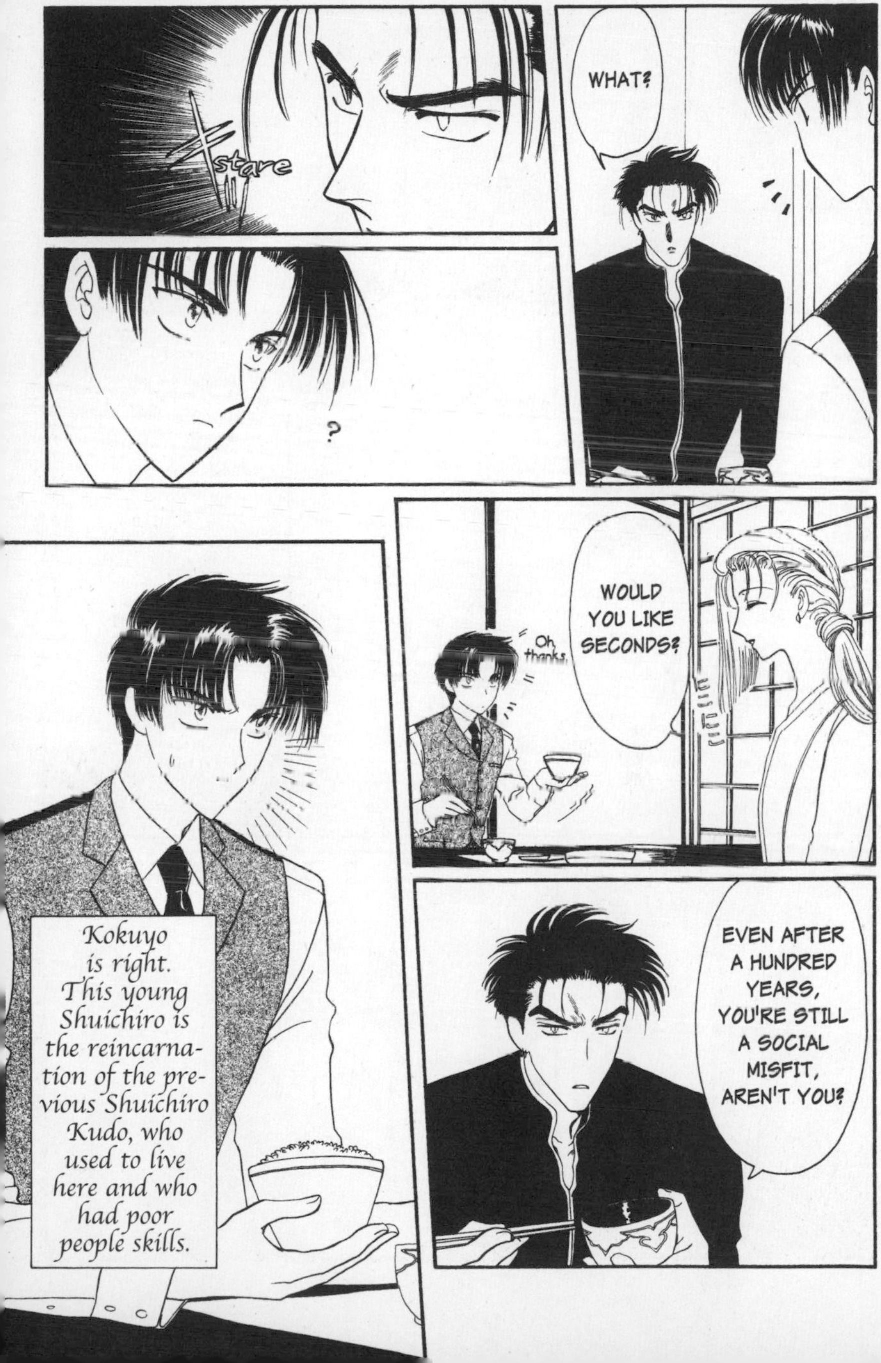
WHAT?
stare
?
WOULD YOU LIKE SECONDS?
Oh, thanks.
EVEN AFTER A HUNDRED YEARS, YOU'RE STILL A SOCIAL MISFIT, AREN'T YOU?
Kokuyo is right. This young Shuichiro is the reincarnation of the previous Shuichiro Kudo, who used to live here and who had poor people skills.

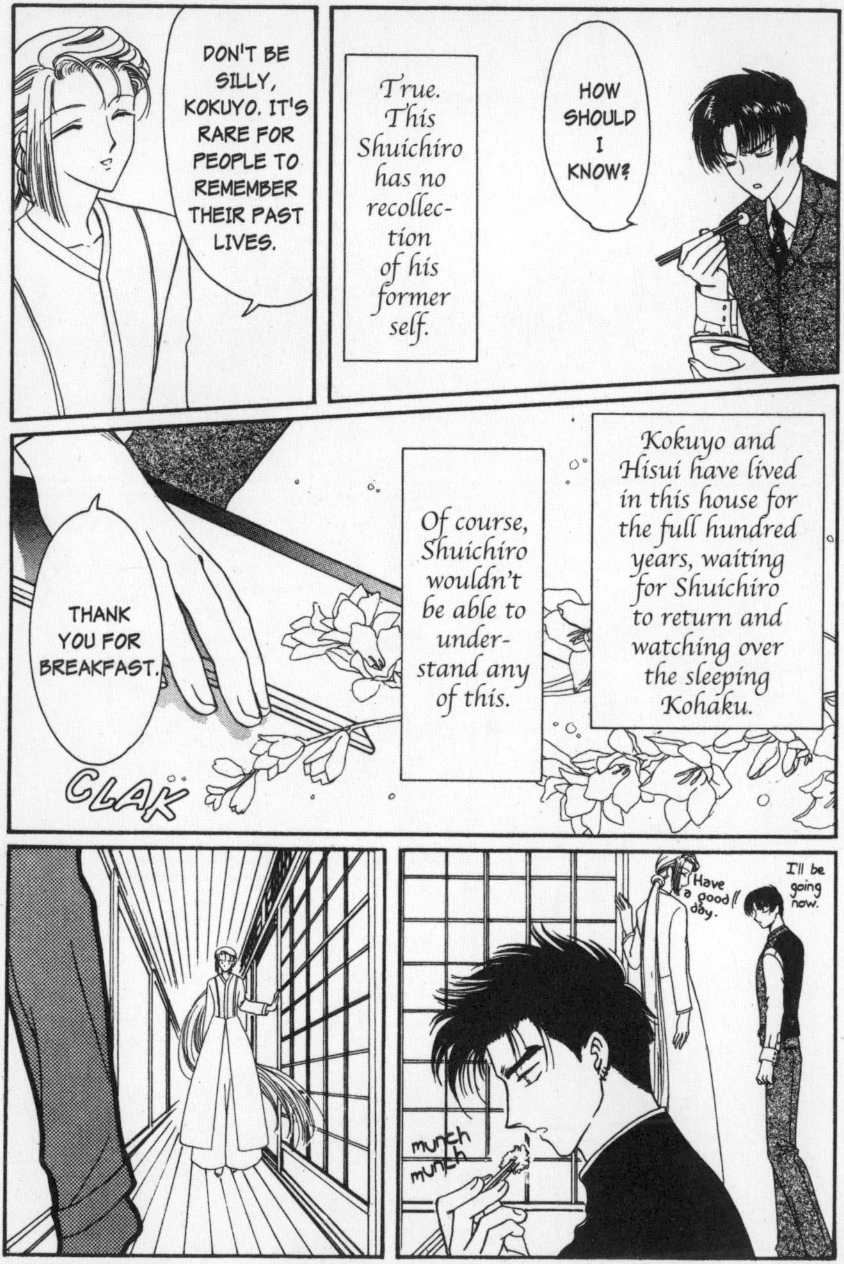
HOW SHOULD I KNOW?
True. This Shuichiro has no recollection of his former self.
DON'T BE SILLY, KOKUYO. IT'S RARE FOR PEOPLE TO REMEMBER THEIR PAST LIVES.
Kokuyo and Hisui have lived in this house for the full hundred years, waiting for Shuichiro to return and watching over the sleeping Kohaku.
Of course, Shuichiro wouldn't be able to understand any of this.
THANK YOU FOR BREAKFAST.
CLAK
I'll be going now.
Have a good day!!
munch munch

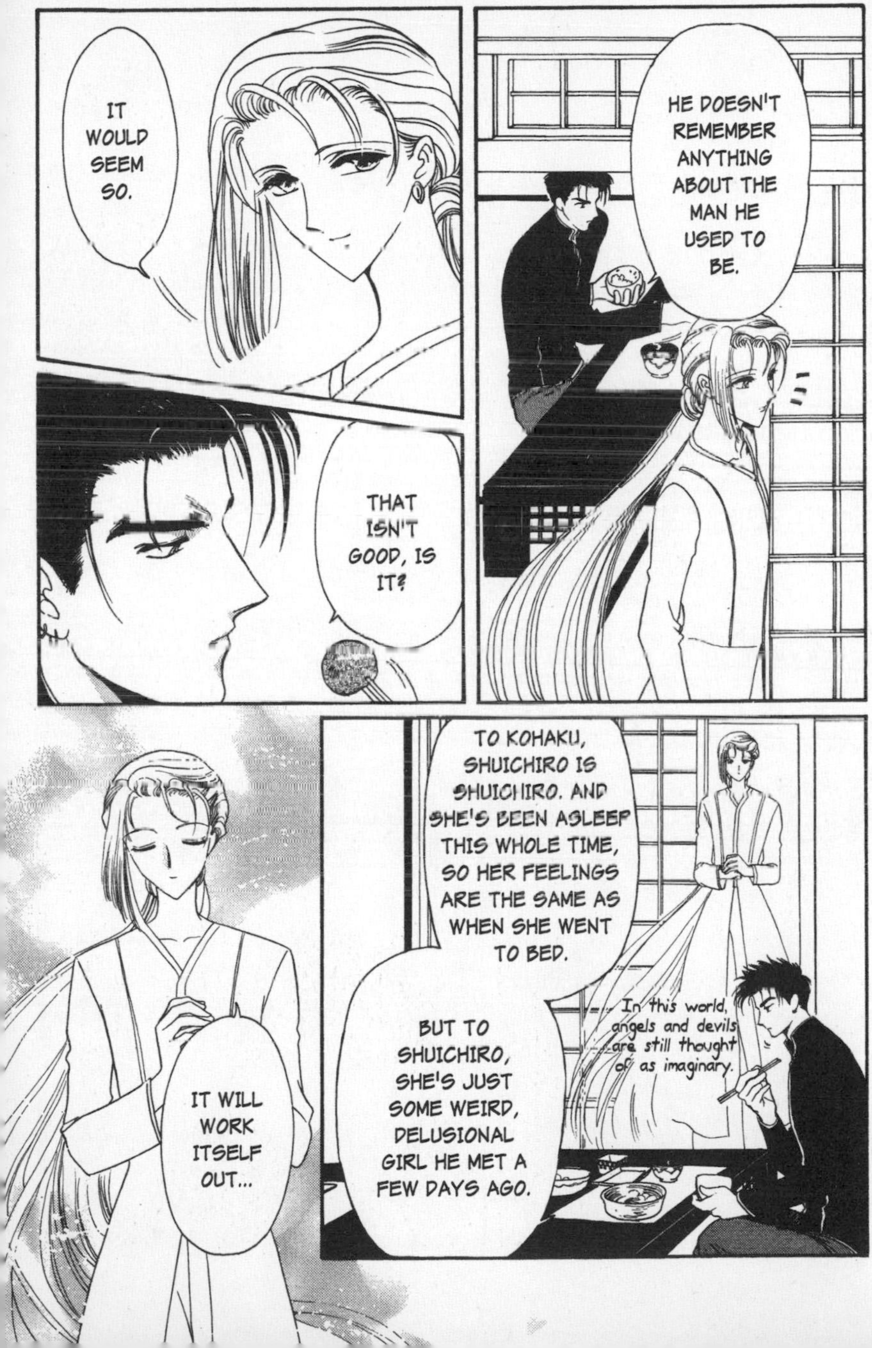
HE DOESN'T REMEMBER ANYTHING ABOUT THE MAN HE USED TO BE.
IT WOULD SEEM SO.
THAT ISN'T GOOD, IS IT?
TO KOHAKU, SHUICHIRO IS SHUICHIRO. AND SHE'S BEEN ASLEEP THIS WHOLE TIME, SO HER FEELINGS ARE THE SAME AS WHEN SHE WENT TO BED.
In this world, angels and devils are still thought of as imaginary.
BUT TO SHUICHIRO, SHE'S JUST SOME WEIRD, DELUSIONAL GIRL HE MET A FEW DAYS AGO.
IT WILL WORK ITSELF OUT...

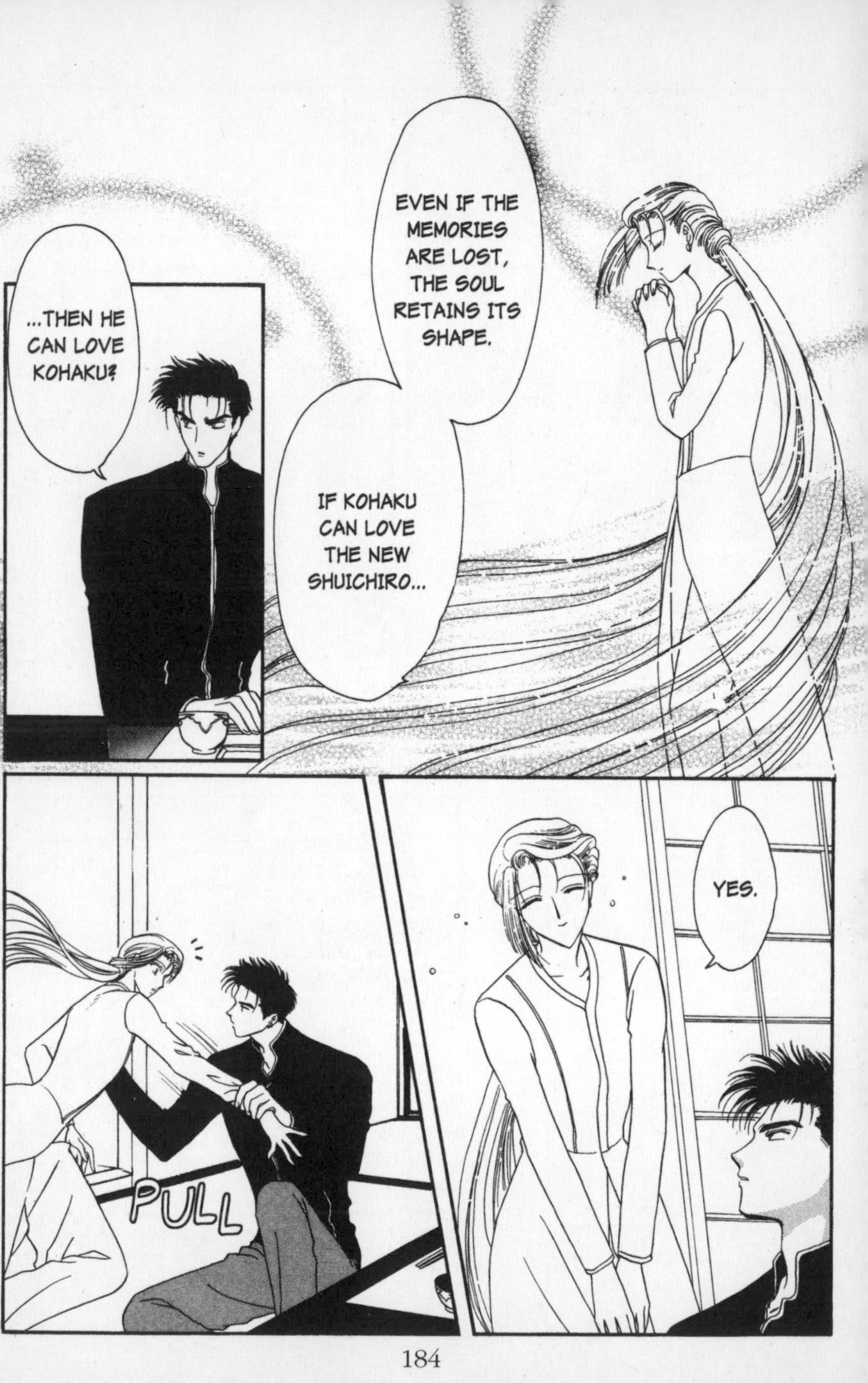
EVEN IF THE MEMORIES ARE LOST, THE SOUL RETAINS ITS SHAPE.
IF KOHAKU CAN LOVE THE NEW SHUICHIRO...
...THEN HE CAN LOVE KOHAKU?
YES.
PULL

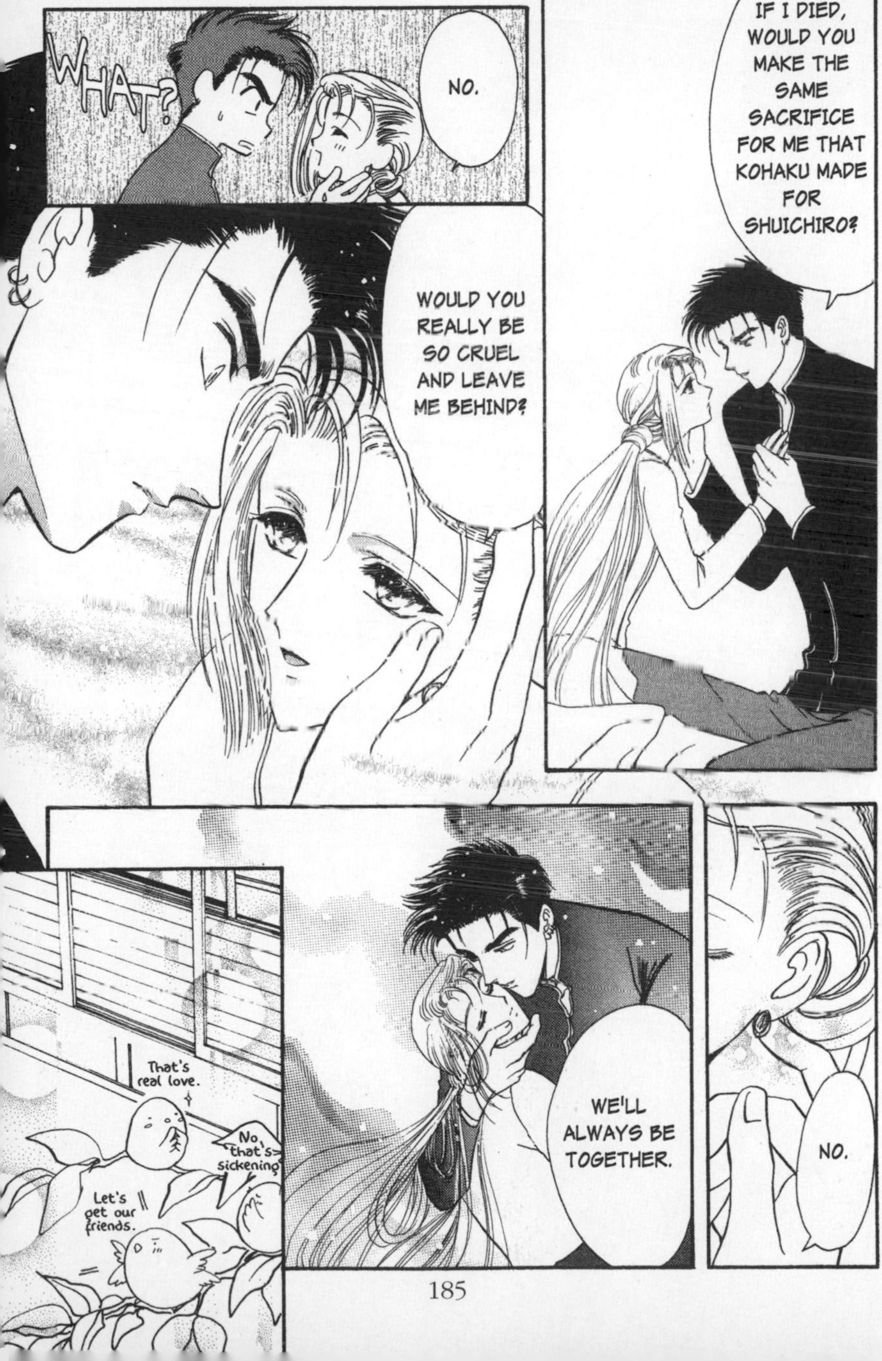
IF I DIED, WOULD YOU MAKE THE SAME SACRIFICE FOR ME THAT KOHAKU MADE FOR SHUICHIRO?
NO.
WHAT?
WOULD YOU REALLY BE SO CRUEL AND LEAVE ME BEHIND?
NO.
WE'LL ALWAYS BE TOGETHER.
That's real love.
No, that's sickening
Let's get our friends.

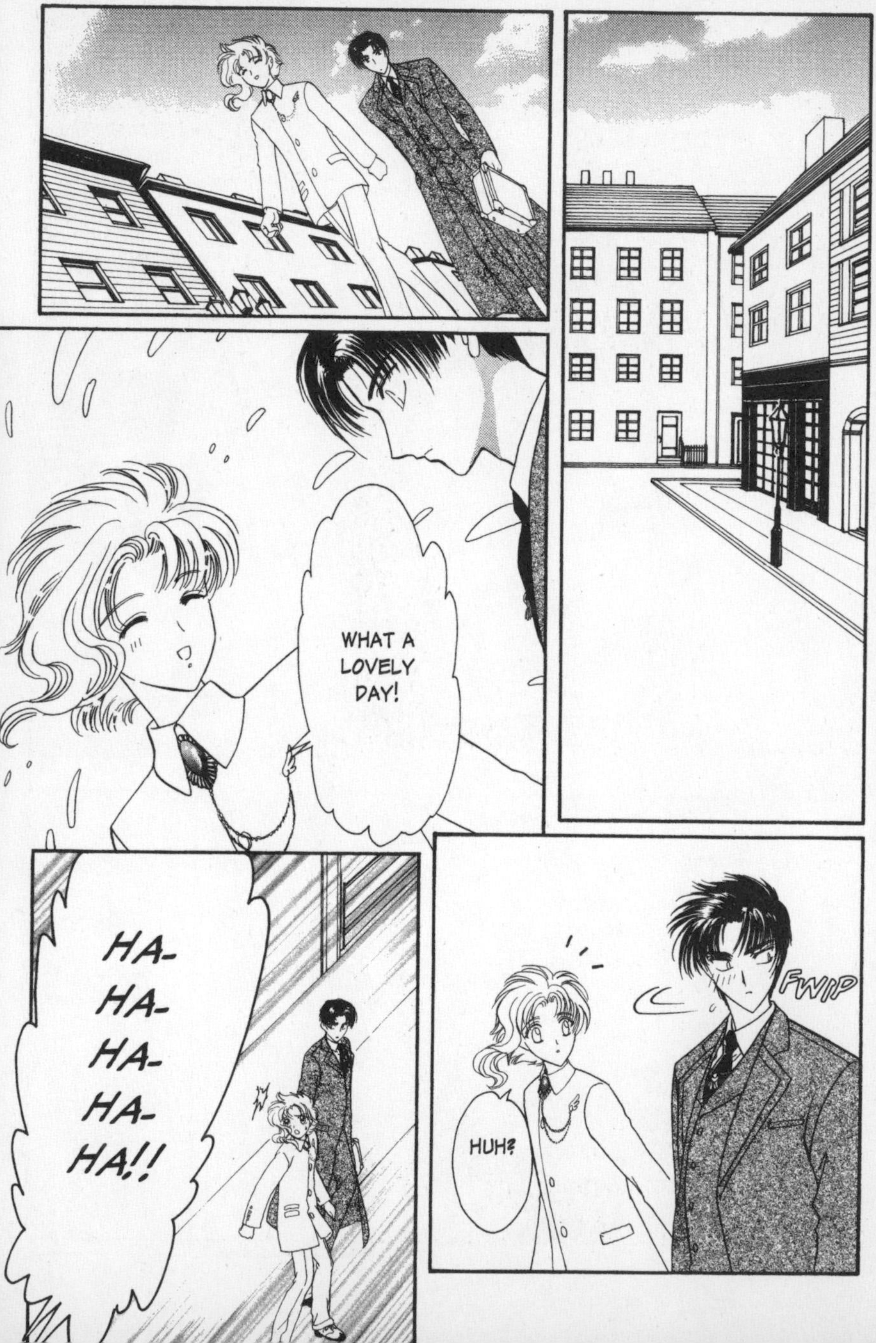
WHAT A LOVELY DAY!
FWIP
HUH?
HA-HA-HA-HA-HA!!

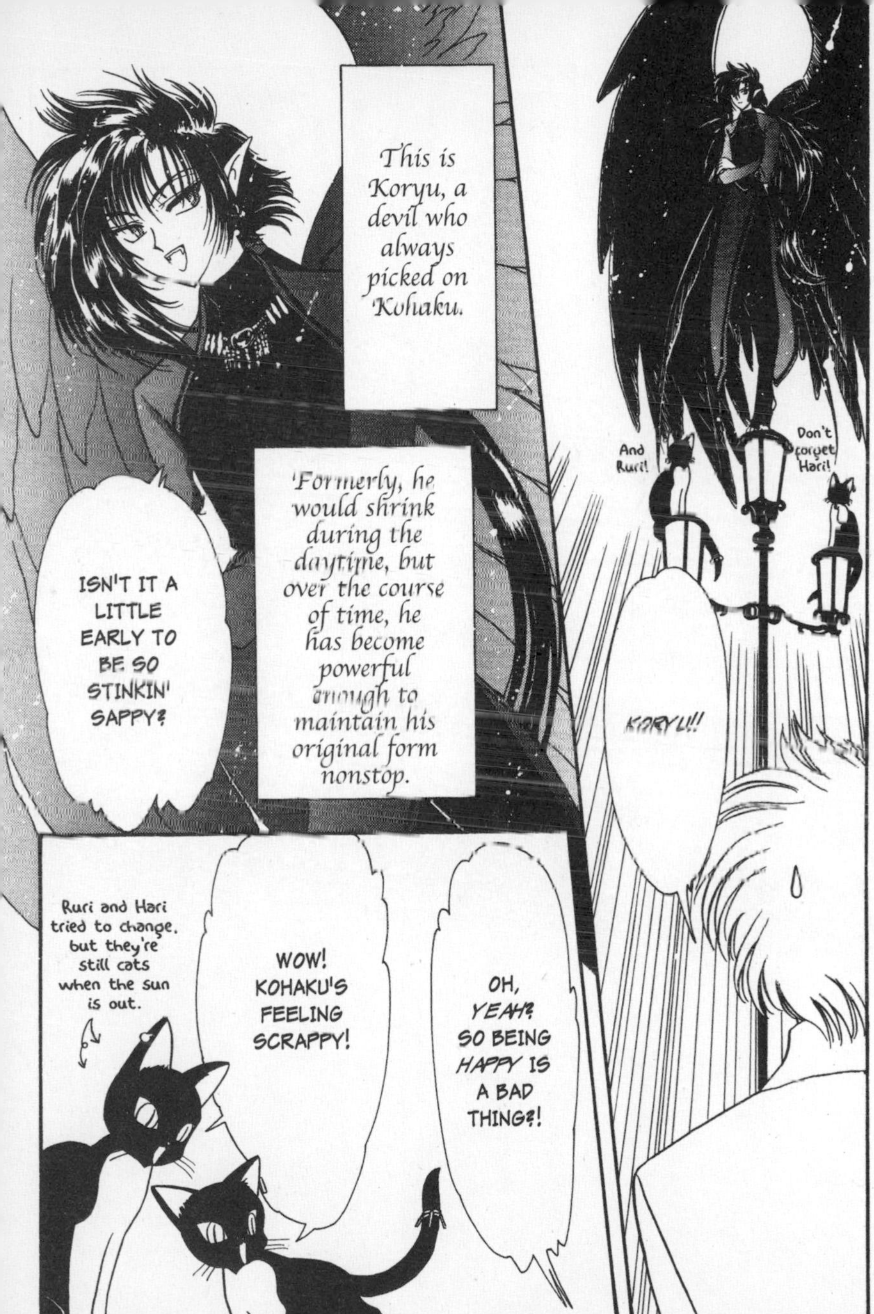
Don't forget Hari!
And Ruri!
KORYU!!
This is Koryu, a devil who always picked on Kohaku.
Formerly, he would shrink during the daytime, but over the course of time, he has become powerful enough to maintain his original form nonstop.
ISN'T IT A LITTLE EARLY TO BE SO STINKIN' SAPPY?
OH, YEAH? SO BEING HAPPY IS A BAD THING?!
WOW! KOHAKU'S FEELING SCRAPPY!
Ruri and Hari tried to change, but they're still cats when the sun is out.

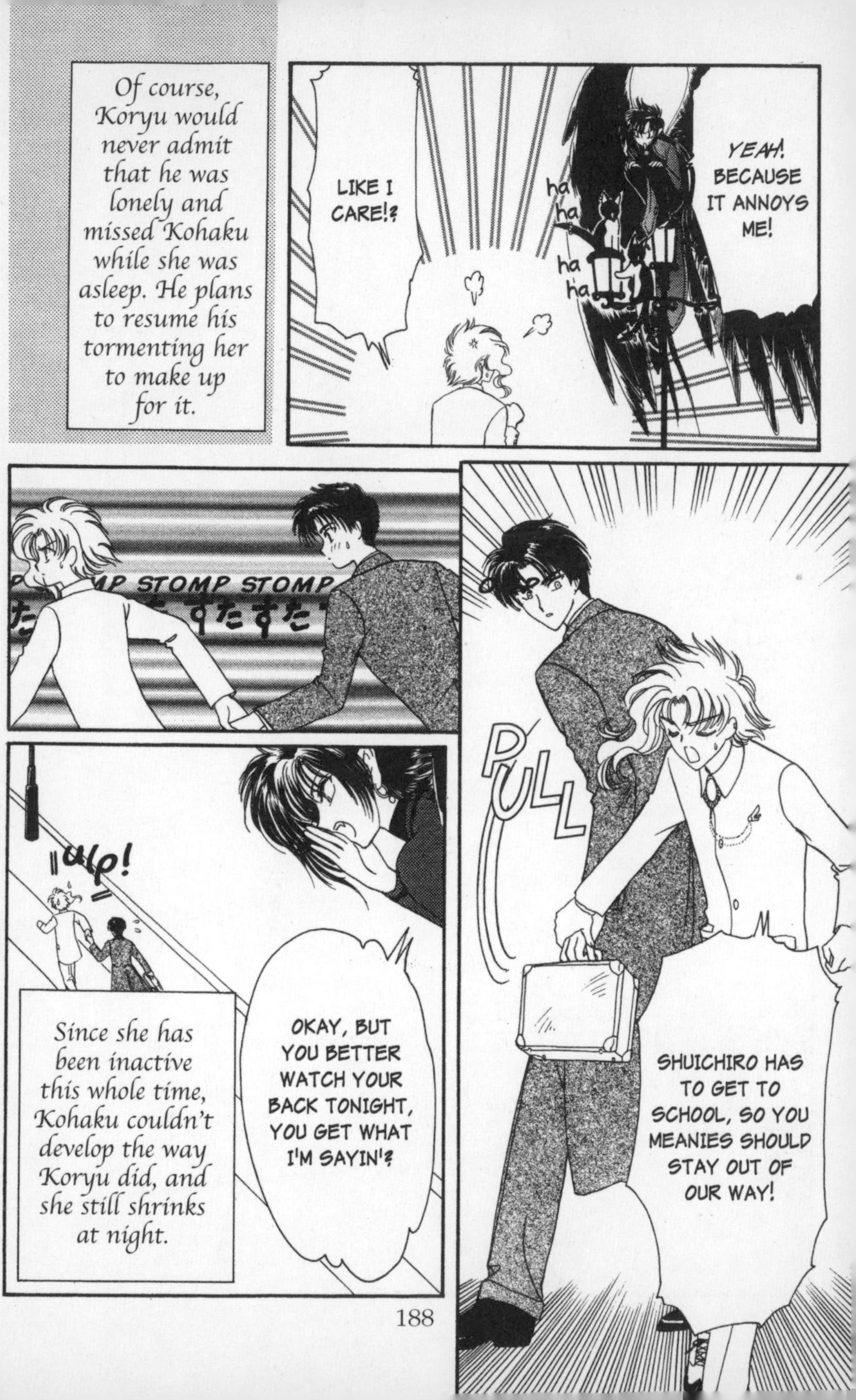
YEAH! BECAUSE IT ANNOYS ME!
ha ha ha ha
LIKE I CARE!?
Of course, Koryu would never admit that he was lonely and missed Kohaku while she was asleep. He plans to resume his tormenting her to make up for it.
PULL
SHUICHIRO HAS TO GET TO SCHOOL, SO YOU MEANIES SHOULD STAY OUT OF OUR WAY!
STOMP STOMP
すたすた
GULP!
OKAY, BUT YOU BETTER WATCH YOUR BACK TONIGHT, YOU GET WHAT I'M SAYIN'!?
Since she has been inactive this whole time, Kohaku couldn't develop the way Koryu did, and she still shrinks at night.

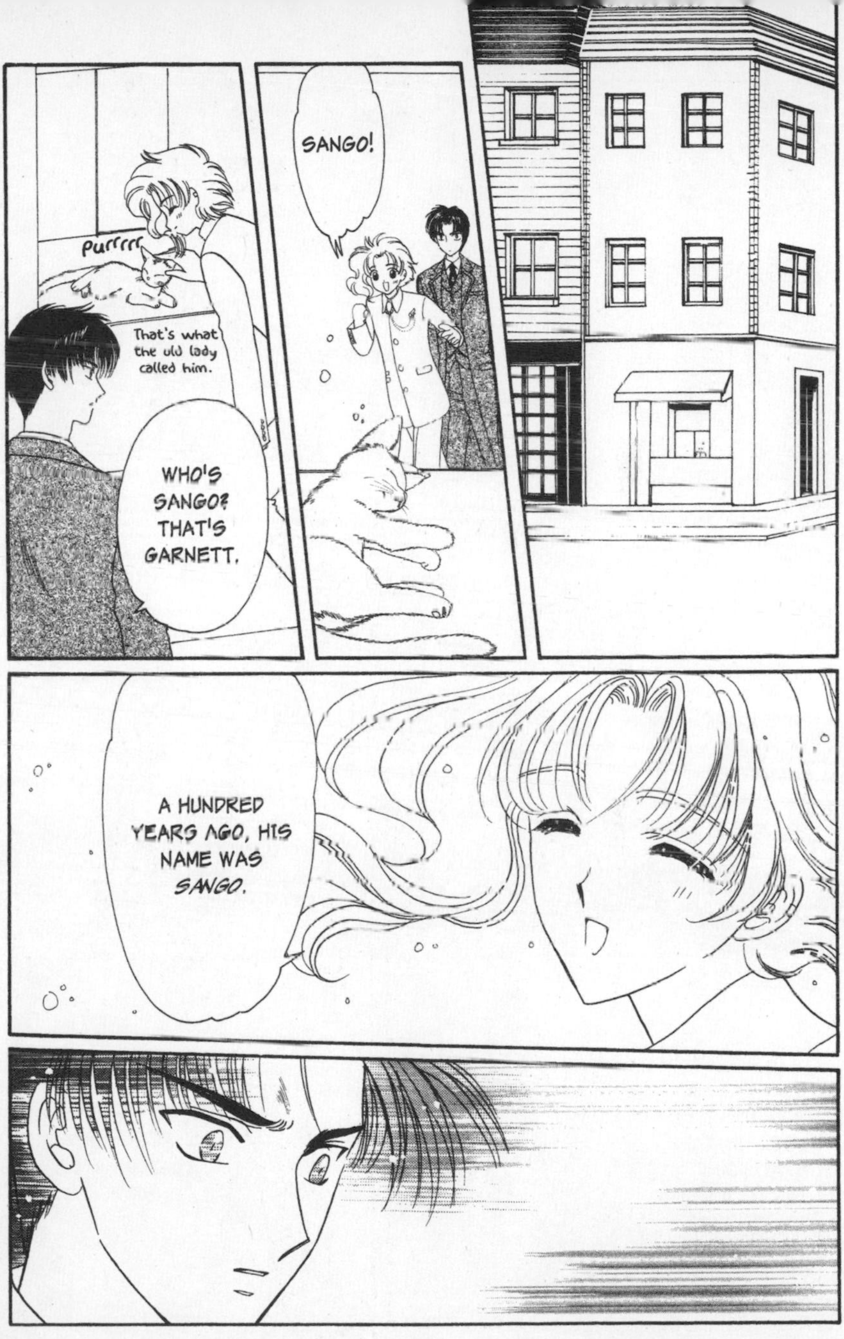
SANGO!
Purrrrr
That's what the old lady called him.
WHO'S SANGO? THAT'S GARNETT.
A HUNDRED YEARS AGO, HIS NAME WAS SANGO.

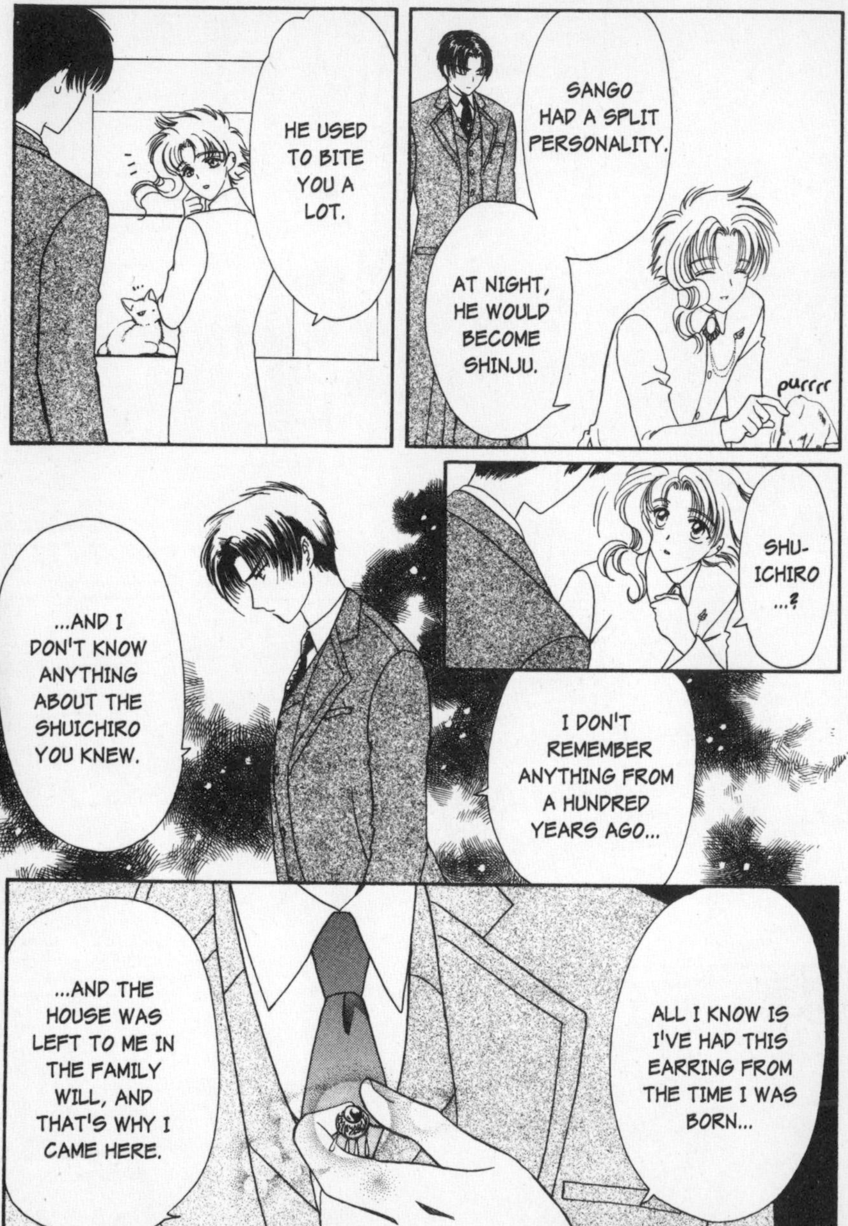
SANGO HAD A SPLIT PERSONALITY.
AT NIGHT, HE WOULD BECOME SHINJU.
purrrr
HE USED TO BITE YOU A LOT.
SHU-ICHIRO ...?
I DON'T REMEMBER ANYTHING FROM A HUNDRED YEARS AGO...
...AND I DON'T KNOW ANYTHING ABOUT THE SHUICHIRO YOU KNEW.
ALL I KNOW IS I'VE HAD THIS EARRING FROM THE TIME I WAS BORN...
...AND THE HOUSE WAS LEFT TO ME IN THE FAMILY WILL, AND THAT'S WHY I CAME HERE.

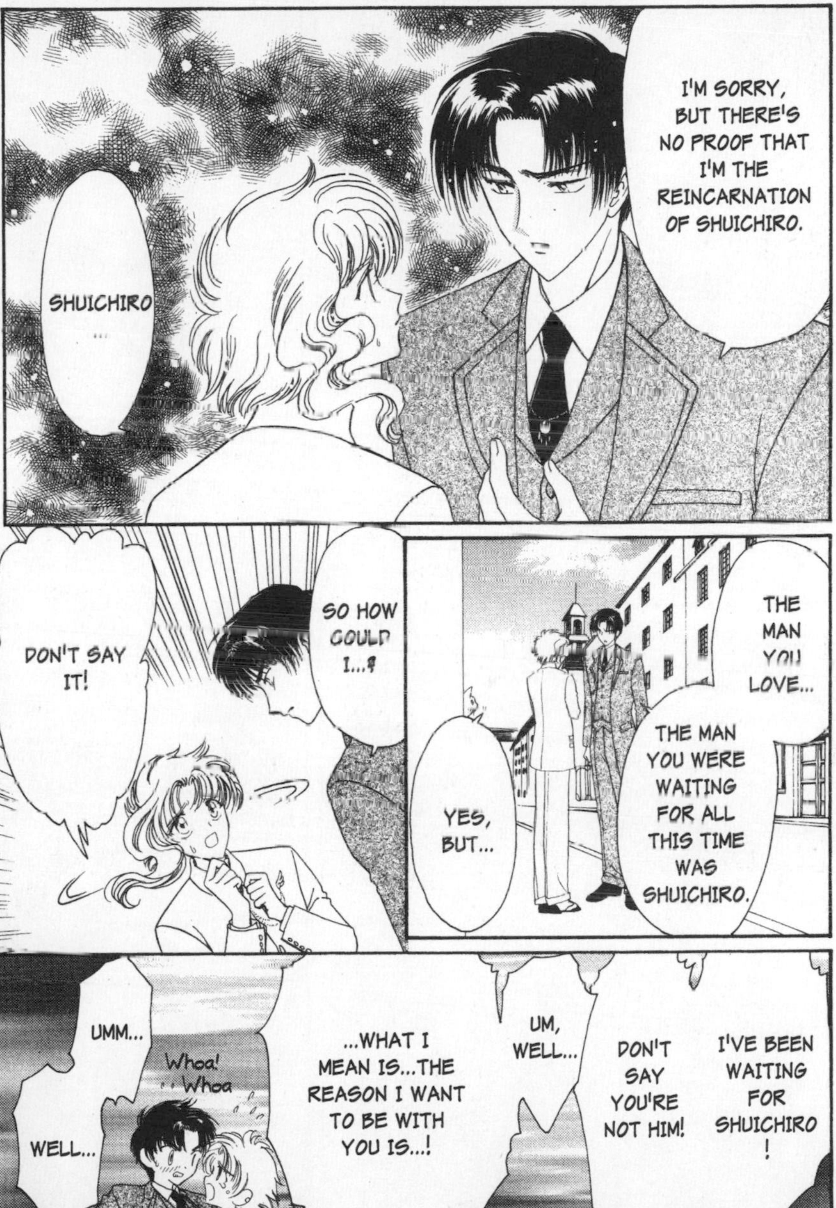

I'M SORRY, BUT THERE'S NO PROOF THAT I'M THE REINCARNATION OF SHUICHIRO.
SHUICHIRO ...
THE MAN YOU LOVE...
THE MAN YOU WERE WAITING FOR ALL THIS TIME WAS SHUICHIRO.
YES, BUT...
SO HOW COULD I...?
DON'T SAY IT!
I'VE BEEN WAITING FOR SHUICHIRO !
DON'T SAY YOU'RE NOT HIM!
UM, WELL...
...WHAT I MEAN IS...THE REASON I WANT TO BE WITH YOU IS...!
UMM...
Whoa! Whoa
WELL...

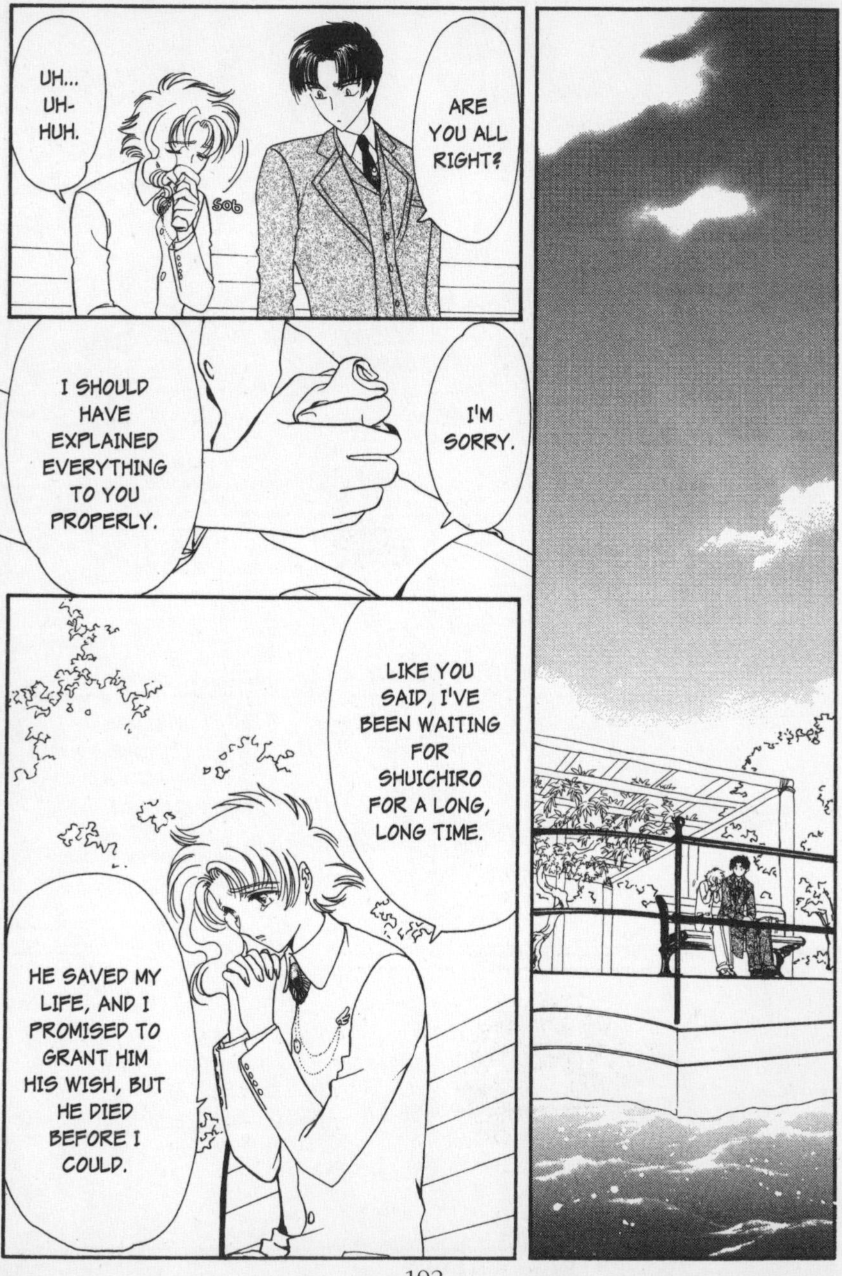
ARE YOU ALL RIGHT?
UH... UH-HUH.
SOB
I'M SORRY.
I SHOULD HAVE EXPLAINED EVERYTHING TO YOU PROPERLY.
LIKE YOU SAID, I'VE BEEN WAITING FOR SHUICHIRO FOR A LONG, LONG TIME.
HE SAVED MY LIFE, AND I PROMISED TO GRANT HIM HIS WISH, BUT HE DIED BEFORE I COULD.

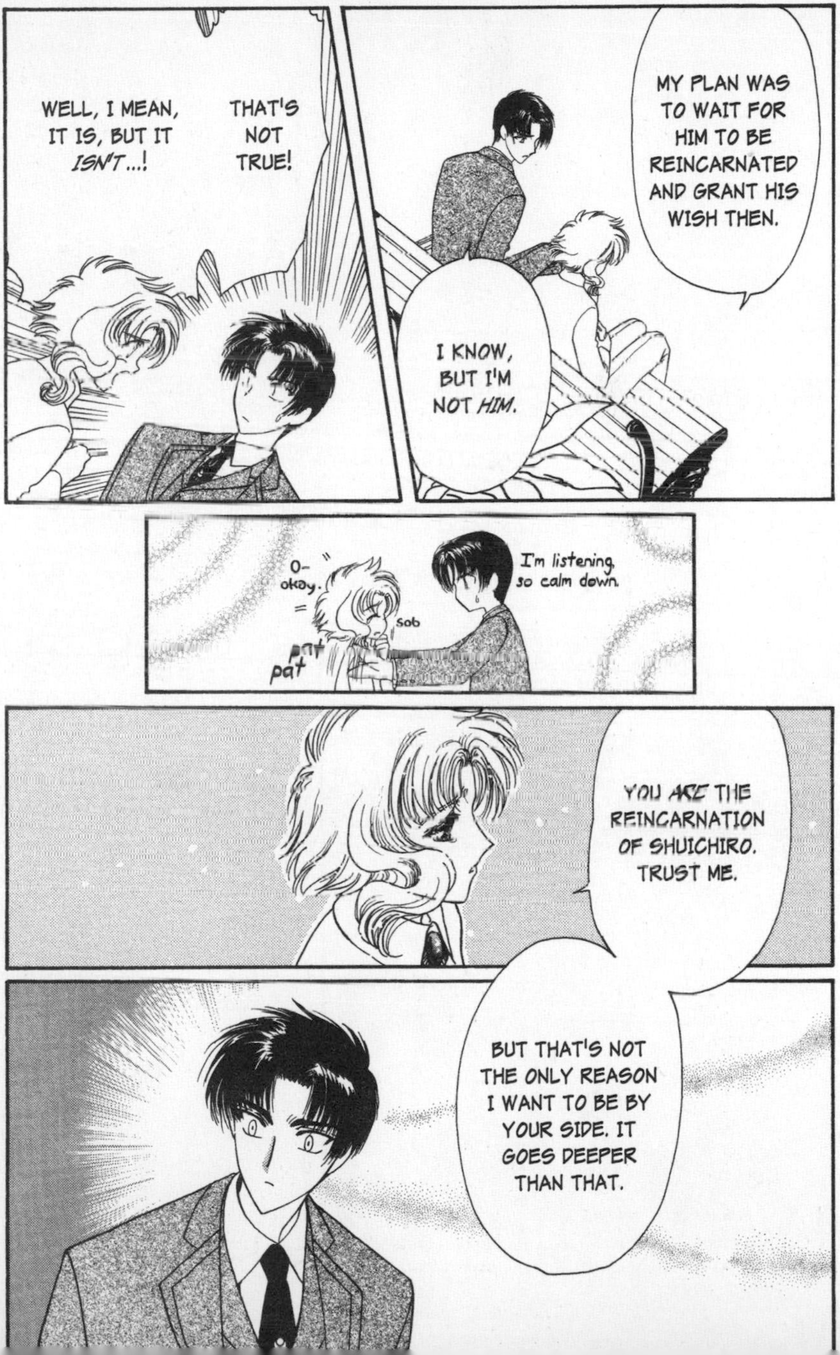
MY PLAN WAS TO WAIT FOR HIM TO BE REINCARNATED AND GRANT HIS WISH THEN.
I KNOW, BUT I'M NOT *HIM*.
THAT'S NOT TRUE!
WELL, I MEAN, IT IS, BUT IT *ISN'T*...!
I'm listening, so calm down.
sob
O-okay.
pat pat
YOU *ARE* THE REINCARNATION OF SHUICHIRO. TRUST ME.
BUT THAT'S NOT THE ONLY REASON I WANT TO BE BY YOUR SIDE. IT GOES DEEPER THAN THAT.

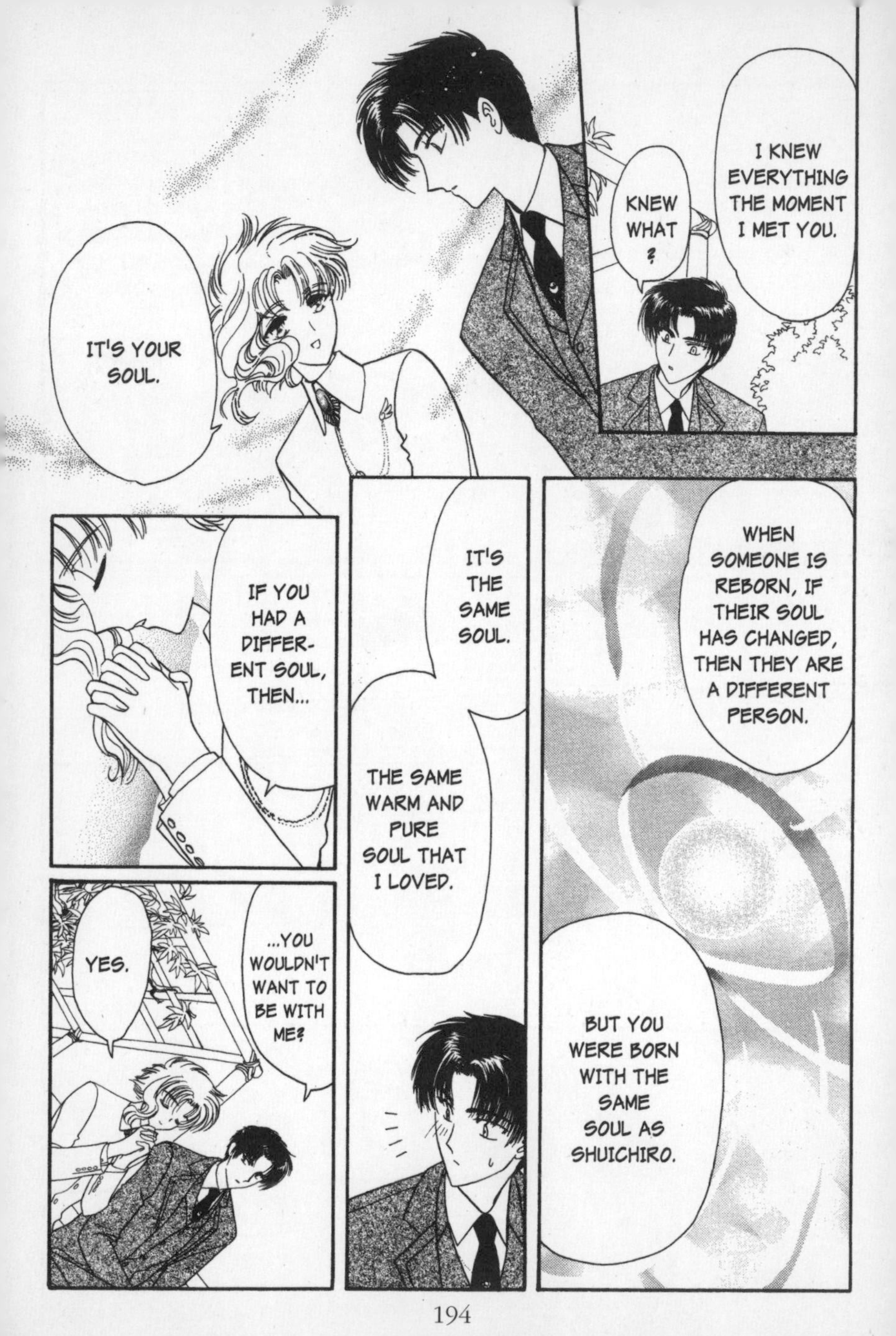
I KNEW EVERYTHING THE MOMENT I MET YOU.
KNEW WHAT?
IT'S YOUR SOUL.
WHEN SOMEONE IS REBORN, IF THEIR SOUL HAS CHANGED, THEN THEY ARE A DIFFERENT PERSON.
BUT YOU WERE BORN WITH THE SAME SOUL AS SHUICHIRO.
IT'S THE SAME SOUL.
THE SAME WARM AND PURE SOUL THAT I LOVED.
IF YOU HAD A DIFFERENT SOUL, THEN...
...YOU WOULDN'T WANT TO BE WITH ME?
YES.

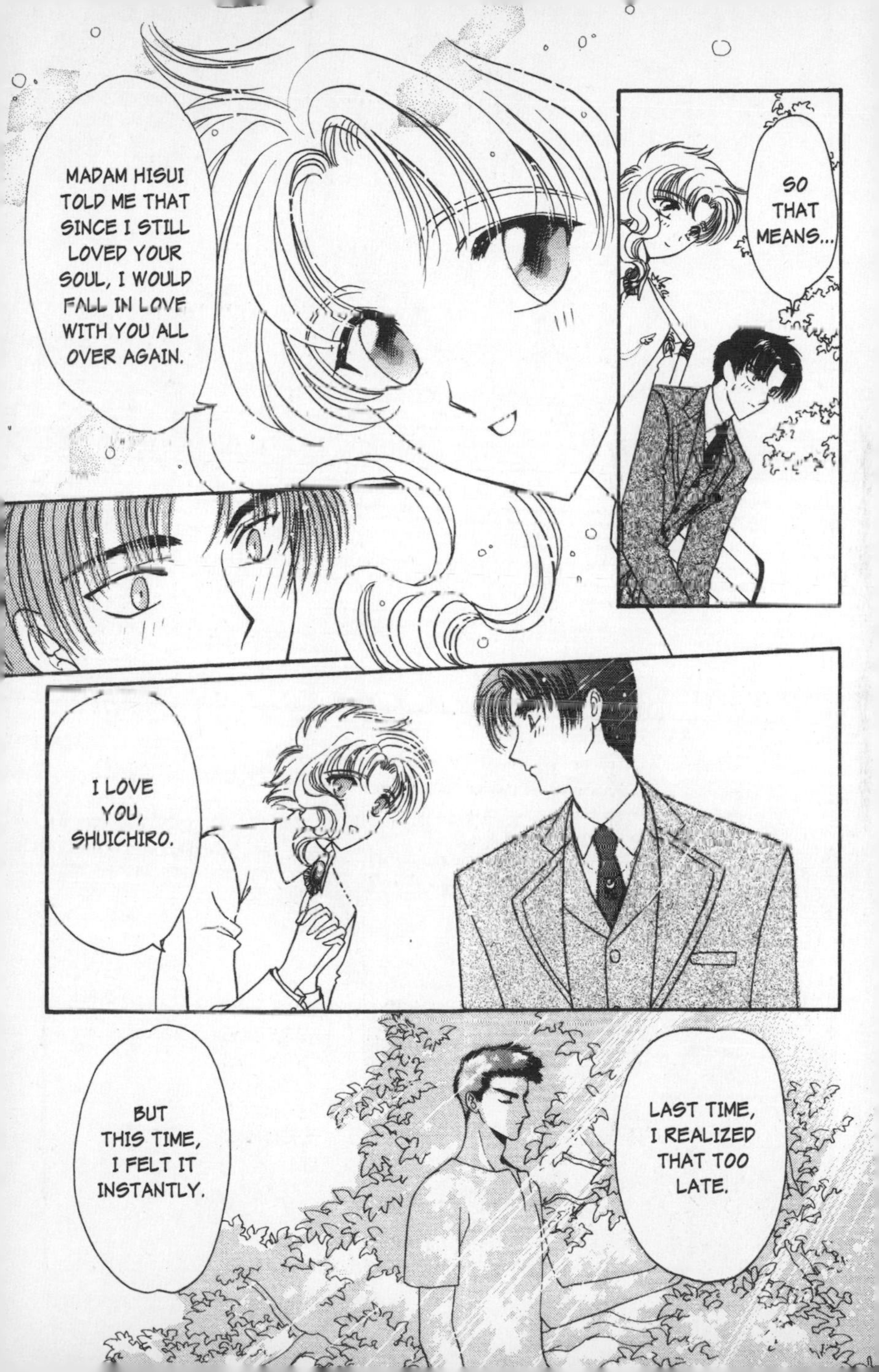
SO THAT MEANS...
MADAM HISUI TOLD ME THAT SINCE I STILL LOVED YOUR SOUL, I WOULD FALL IN LOVE WITH YOU ALL OVER AGAIN.
I LOVE YOU, SHUICHIRO.
LAST TIME, I REALIZED THAT TOO LATE.
BUT THIS TIME, I FELT IT INSTANTLY.

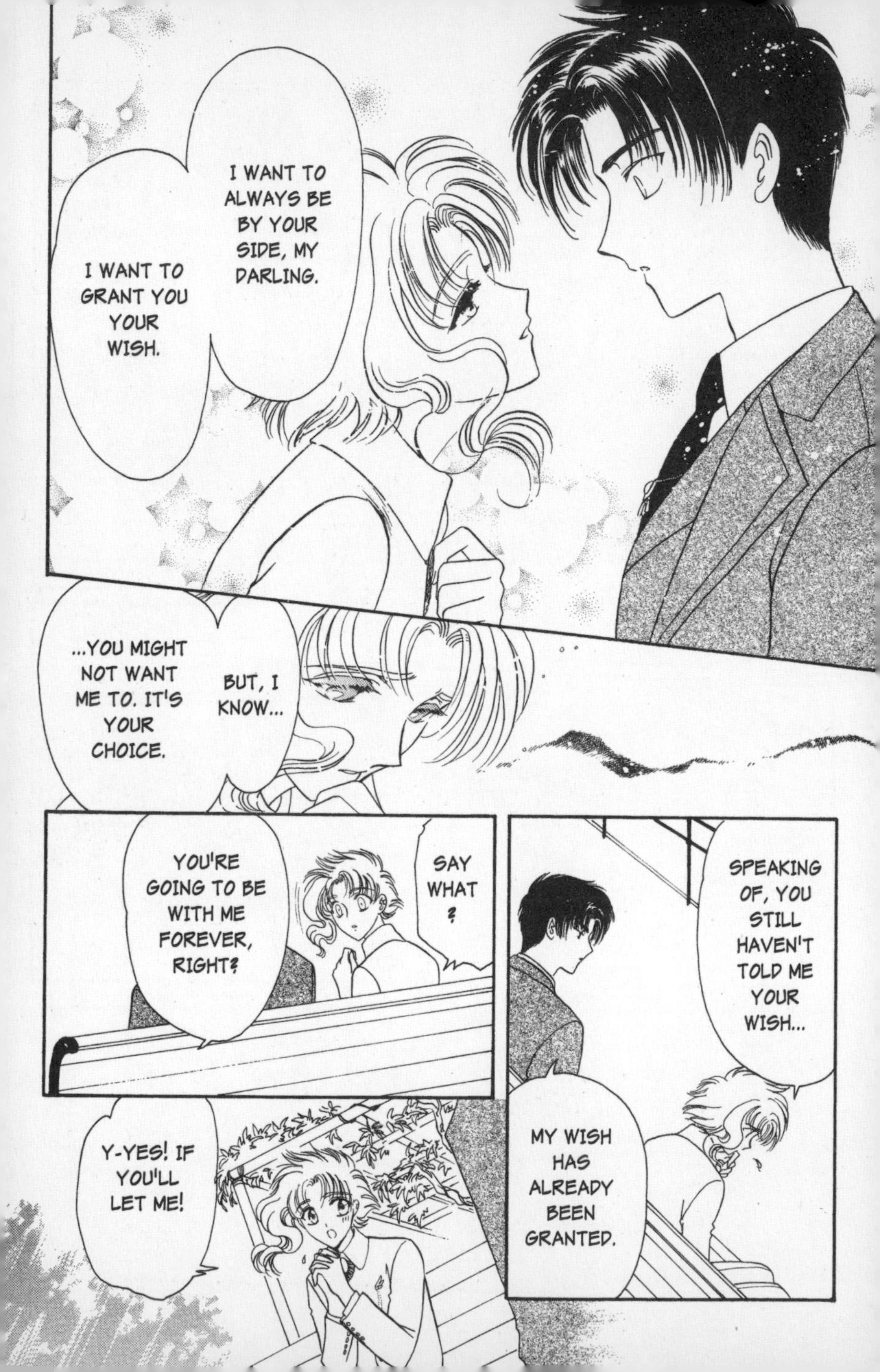
I WANT TO ALWAYS BE BY YOUR SIDE, MY DARLING.
I WANT TO GRANT YOU YOUR WISH.
BUT, I KNOW...
...YOU MIGHT NOT WANT ME TO. IT'S YOUR CHOICE.
SPEAKING OF, YOU STILL HAVEN'T TOLD ME YOUR WISH...
MY WISH HAS ALREADY BEEN GRANTED.
SAY WHAT?
YOU'RE GOING TO BE WITH ME FOREVER, RIGHT?
Y-YES! IF YOU'LL LET ME!

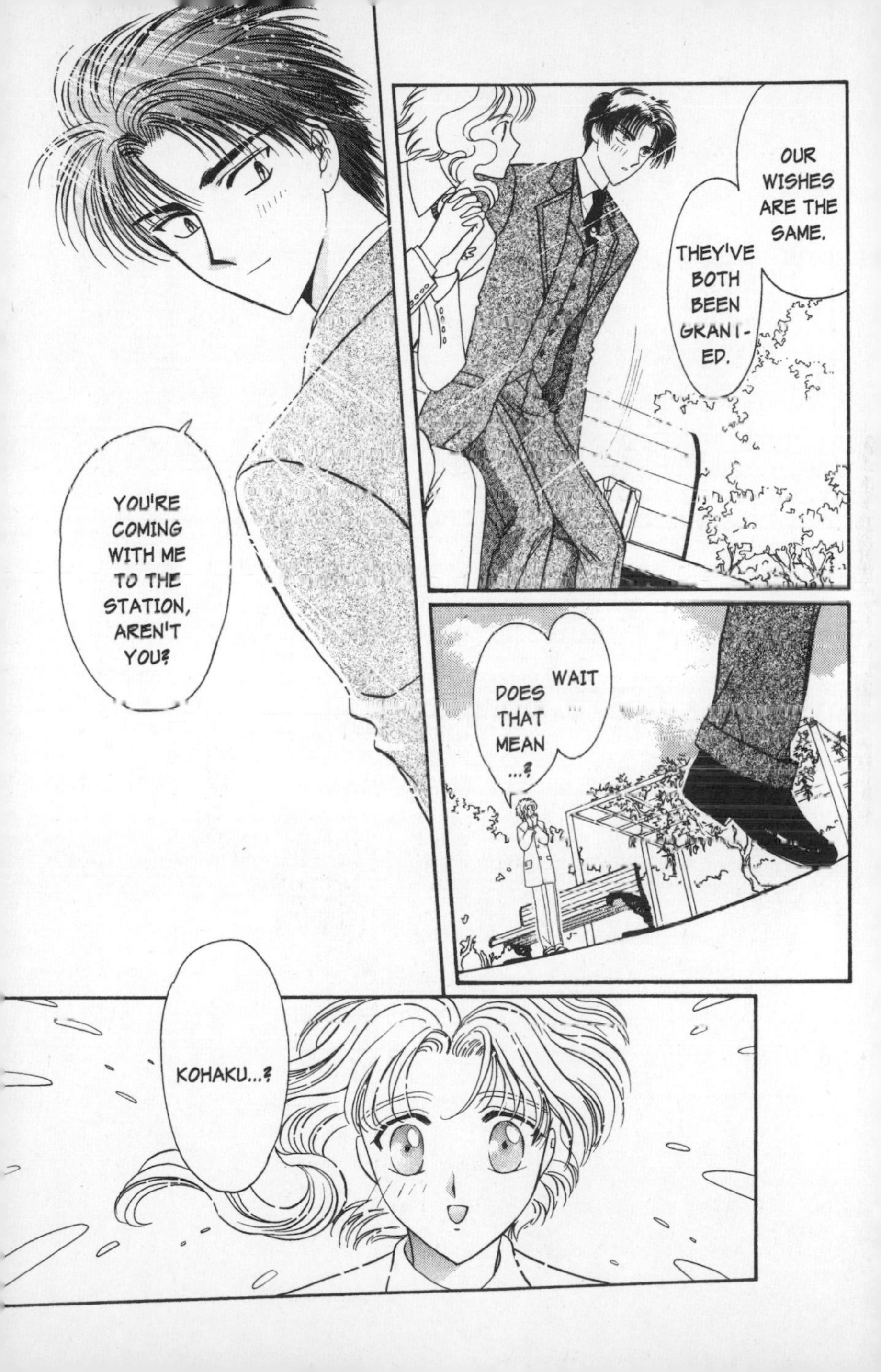
OUR WISHES ARE THE SAME.
THEY'VE BOTH BEEN GRANT-ED.
WAIT ... DOES THAT MEAN ...?
YOU'RE COMING WITH ME TO THE STATION, AREN'T YOU?
KOHAKU...?

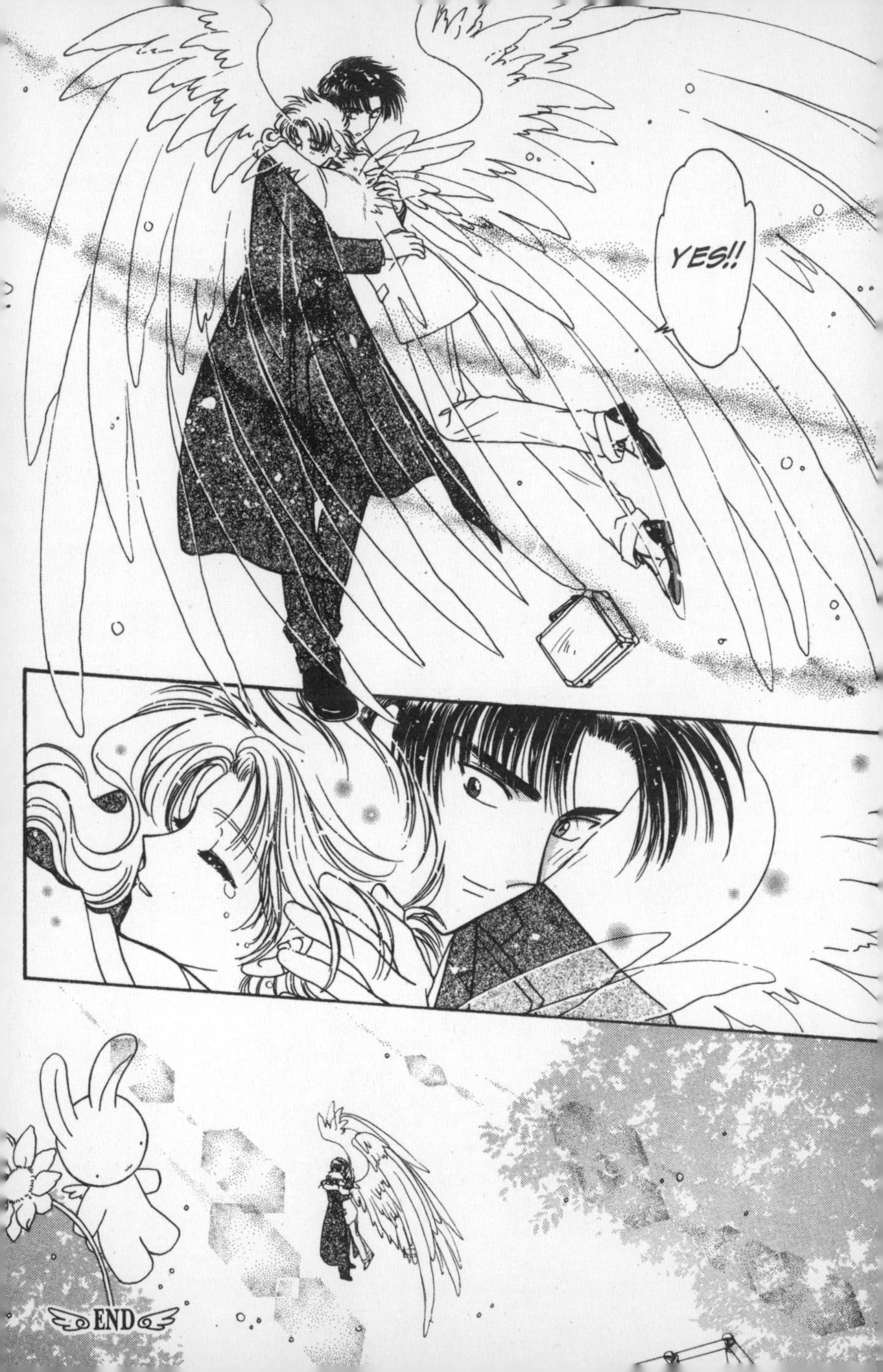
YES!!
END

Wish

The end.

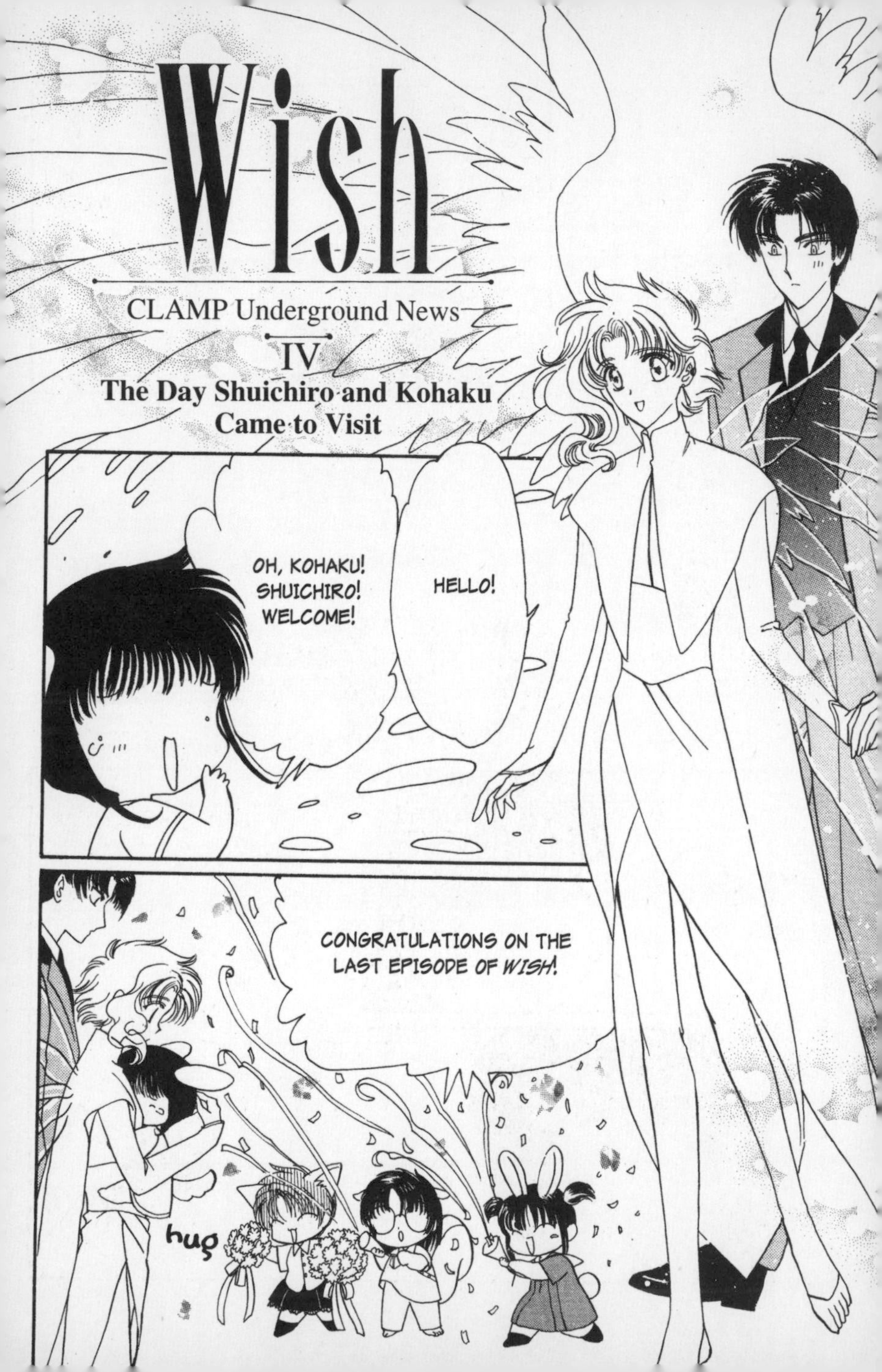
Wish
CLAMP Underground News
IV
The Day Shuichiro and Kohaku Came to Visit
HELLO!
OH, KOHAKU! SHUICHIRO! WELCOME!
CONGRATULATIONS ON THE LAST EPISODE OF *WISH*!
hug

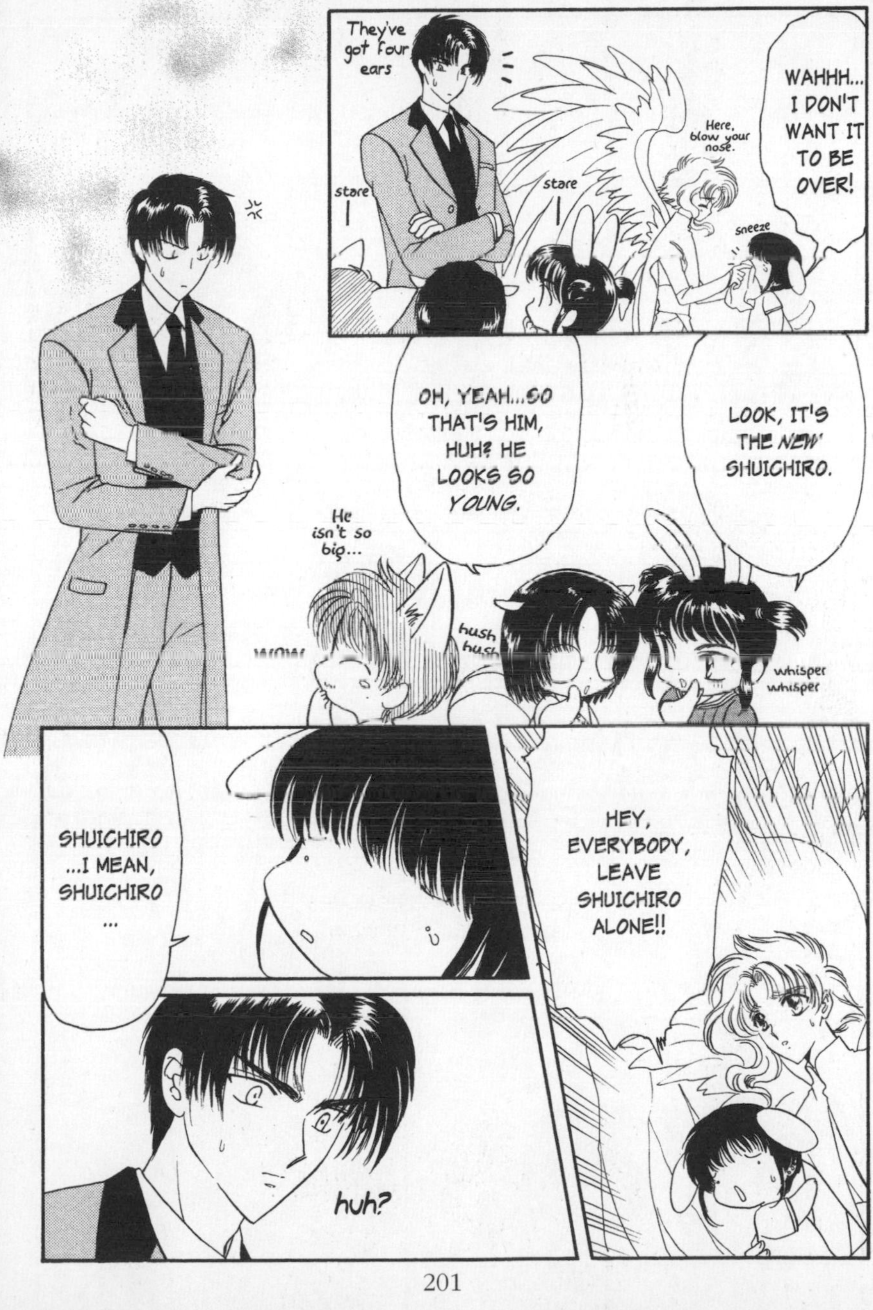
WAHHH... I DON'T WANT IT TO BE OVER!
Here, blow your nose.
sneeze
stare
They've got four ears
stare
LOOK, IT'S THE *NEW* SHUICHIRO.
OH, YEAH...SO THAT'S HIM, HUH? HE LOOKS SO *YOUNG*.
whisper whisper
hush hush
He isn't so big...
WOW
HEY, EVERYBODY, LEAVE SHUICHIRO ALONE!!
SHUICHIRO ...I MEAN, SHUICHIRO ...
huh?

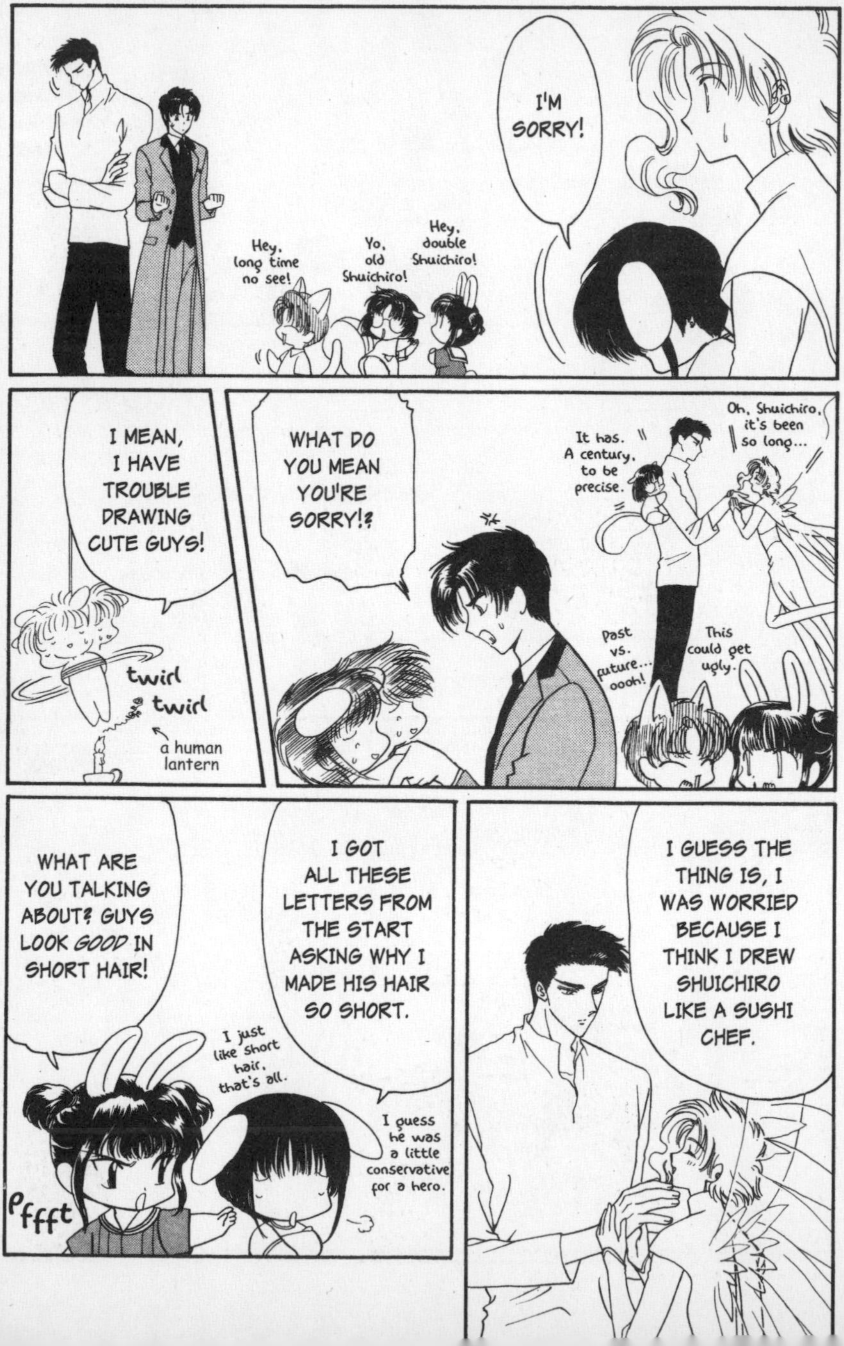
I'M SORRY!
Hey, double Shuichiro!
Yo, old Shuichiro!
Hey, long time no see!
Oh, Shuichiro, it's been so long...
It has. A century, to be precise.
WHAT DO YOU MEAN YOU'RE SORRY!?
This could get ugly.
Past vs. future... oooh!
I MEAN, I HAVE TROUBLE DRAWING CUTE GUYS!
twirl twirl
a human lantern
I GUESS THE THING IS, I WAS WORRIED BECAUSE I THINK I DREW SHUICHIRO LIKE A SUSHI CHEF.
I GOT ALL THESE LETTERS FROM THE START ASKING WHY I MADE HIS HAIR SO SHORT.
WHAT ARE YOU TALKING ABOUT? GUYS LOOK *GOOD* IN SHORT HAIR!
I just like short hair, that's all.
I guess he was a little conservative for a hero.
pffft

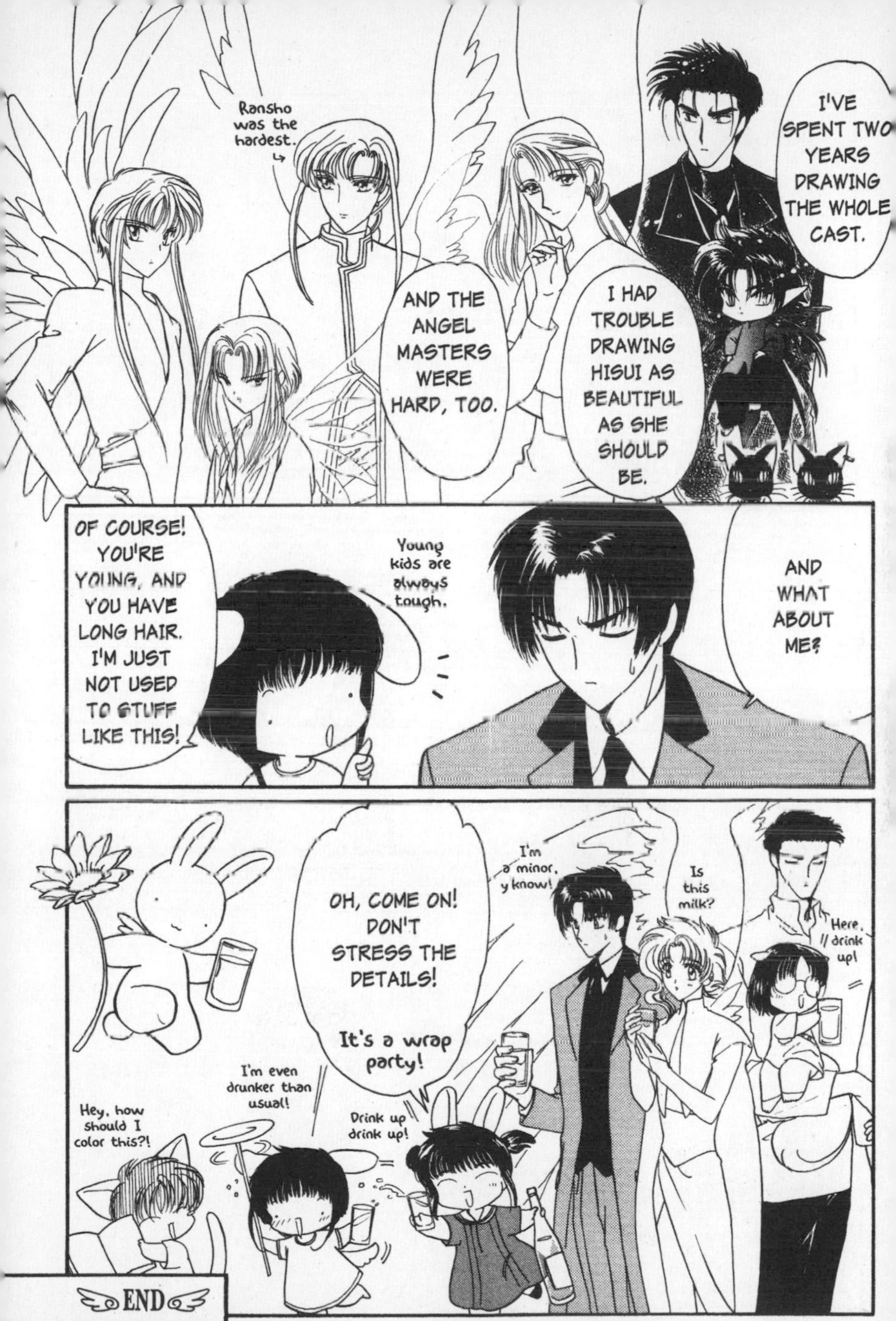
I'VE SPENT TWO YEARS DRAWING THE WHOLE CAST.
I HAD TROUBLE DRAWING HISUI AS BEAUTIFUL AS SHE SHOULD BE.
AND THE ANGEL MASTERS WERE HARD, TOO.
Ransho was the hardest.
AND WHAT ABOUT ME?
Young kids are always tough.
OF COURSE! YOU'RE YOUNG, AND YOU HAVE LONG HAIR. I'M JUST NOT USED TO STUFF LIKE THIS!
Here, drink up!
Is this milk?
I'm a minor, y know!
OH, COME ON! DON'T STRESS THE DETAILS!
It's a wrap party!
Drink up drink up!
I'm even drunker than usual!
Hey, how should I color this?!
END

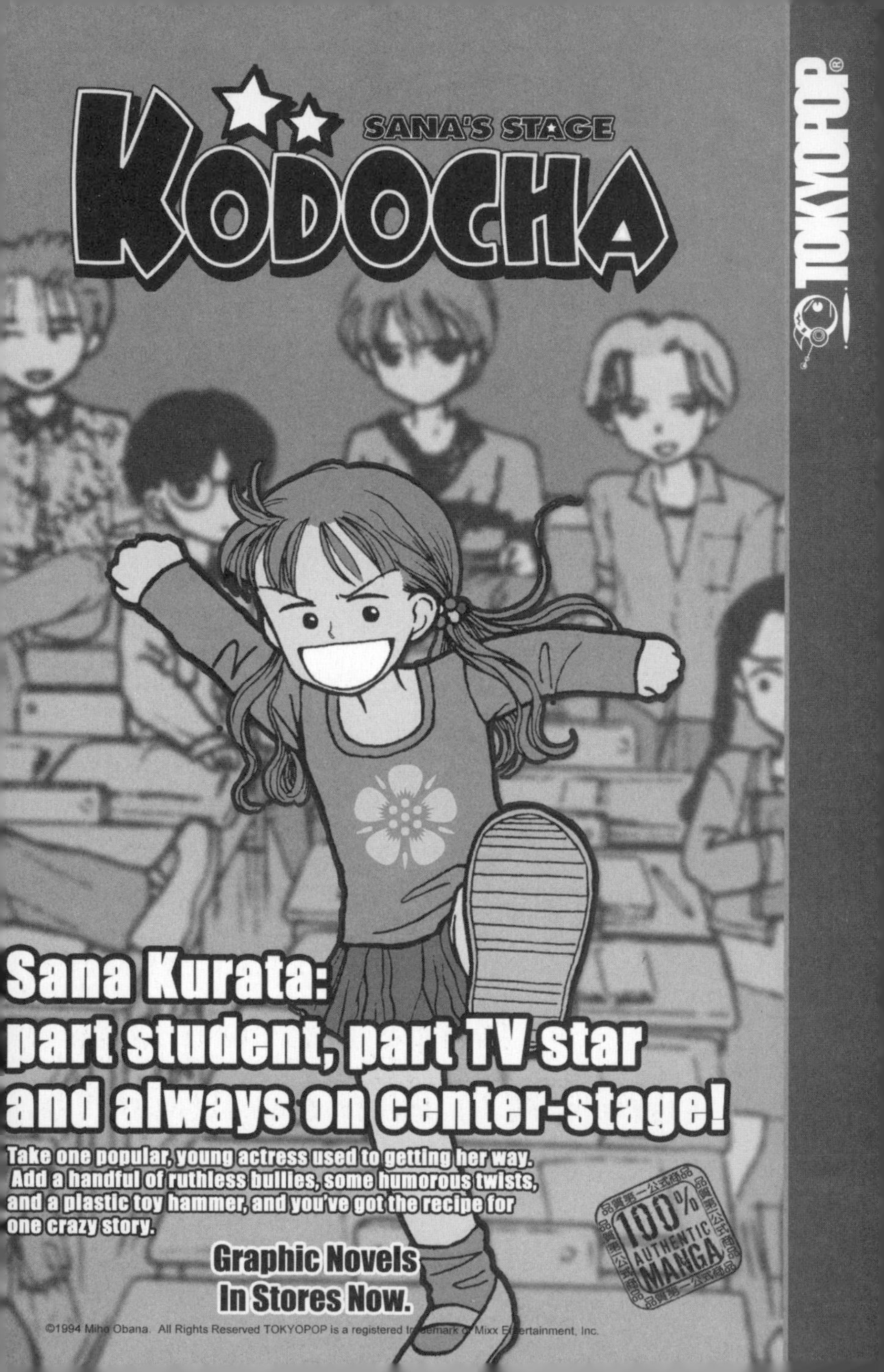
KODOCHA
SANA'S STAGE
TOKYOPOP
Sana Kurata:
part student, part TV star
and always on center-stage!
Take one popular, young actress used to getting her way.
Add a handful of ruthless bullies, some humorous twists,
and a plastic toy hammer, and you've got the recipe for
one crazy story.
100% AUTHENTIC MANGA
Graphic Novels
In Stores Now.
©1994 Miho Obana. All Rights Reserved TOKYOPOP is a registered trademark of Mixx Entertainment, Inc.

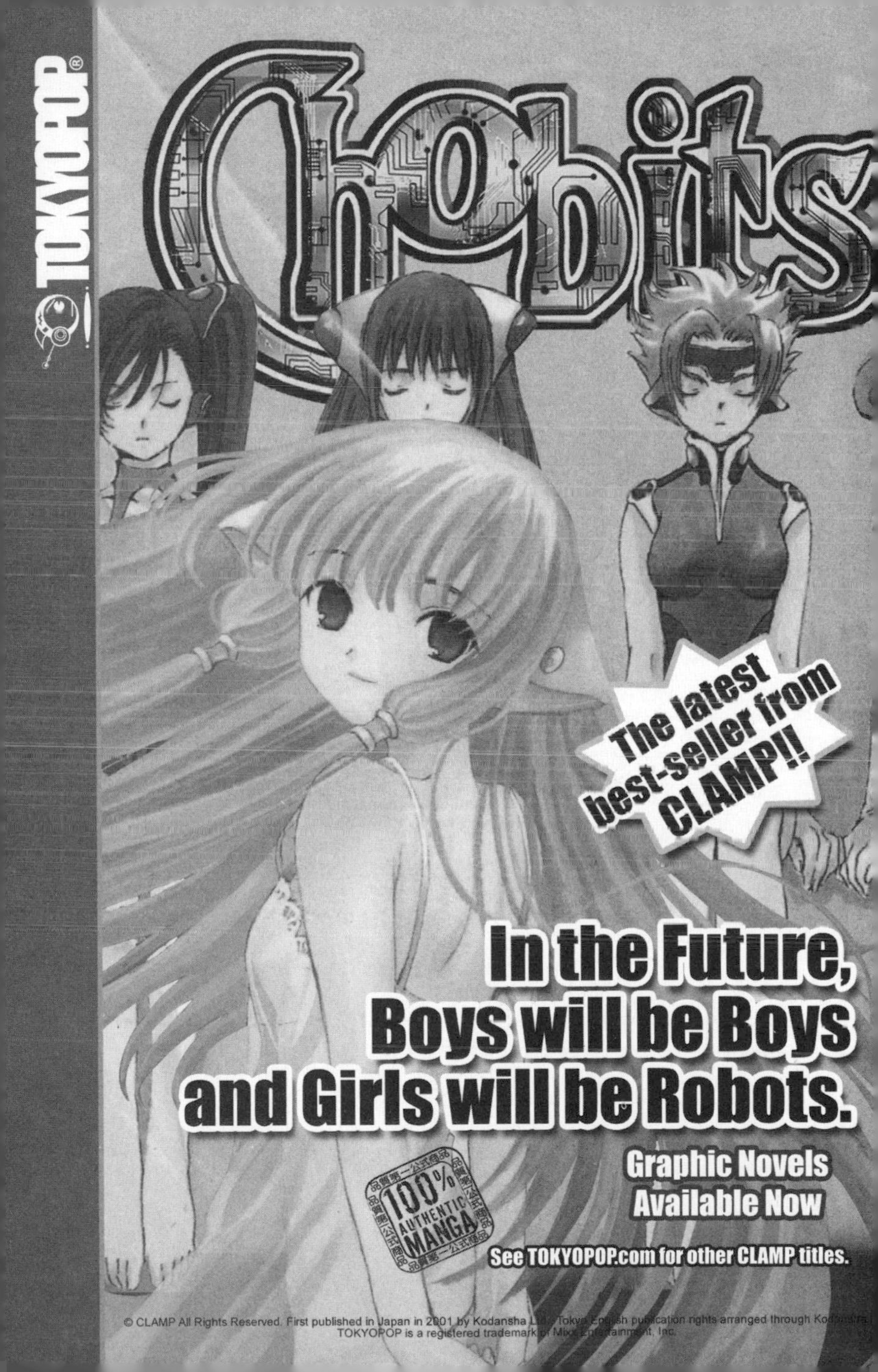
TOKYOPOP
Chobits
The latest best-seller from CLAMP!!
In the Future, Boys will be Boys and Girls will be Robots.
Graphic Novels Available Now
100% AUTHENTIC MANGA
See TOKYOPOP.com for other CLAMP titles.
© CLAMP All Rights Reserved. First published in Japan in 2001 by Kodansha Ltd., Tokyo English publication rights arranged through Kodansha Ltd.
TOKYOPOP is a registered trademark of Mixx Entertainment, Inc.

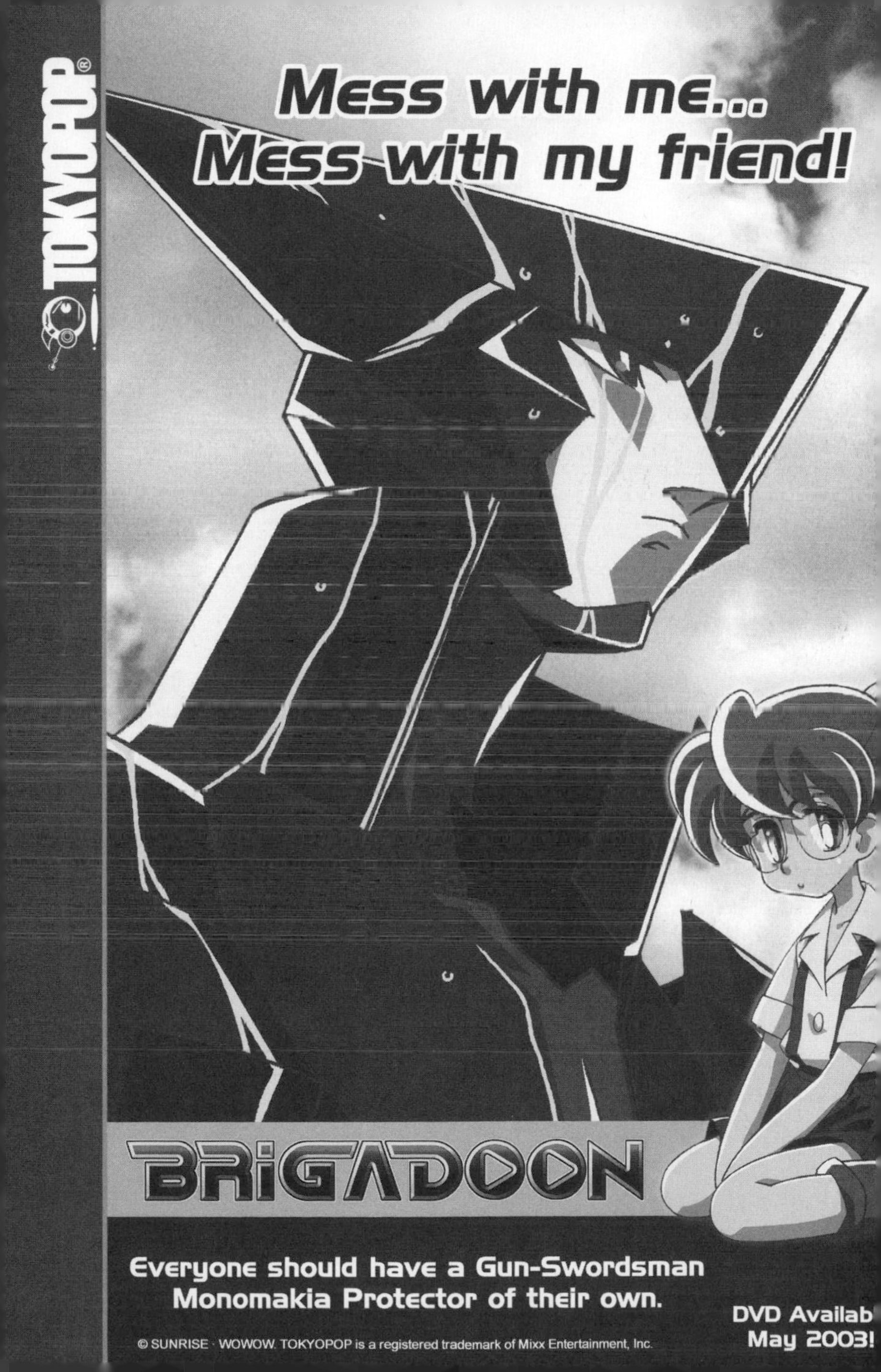
TOKYOPOP®
Mess with me...
Mess with my friend!
BRIGADOON
Everyone should have a Gun-Swordsman
Monomakia Protector of their own.
DVD Availab
May 2003!
© SUNRISE · WOWOW. TOKYOPOP is a registered trademark of Mixx Entertainment, Inc.

STOP!

This is the back of the book.
You wouldn't want to spoil a great ending!

This book is printed "manga-style," in the authentic Japanese right-to-left format. Since none of the artwork has been flipped or altered, readers get to experience the story just as the creator intended. You've been asking for it, so TOKYOPOP® delivered: authentic, hot-off-the-press, and far more fun!

DIRECTIONS

If this is your first time reading manga-style, here's a quick guide to help you understand how it works.

It's easy... just start in the top right panel and follow the numbers. Have fun, and look for more 100% authentic manga from TOKYOPOP®!